VIGIL

LETTERS FROM ASIA

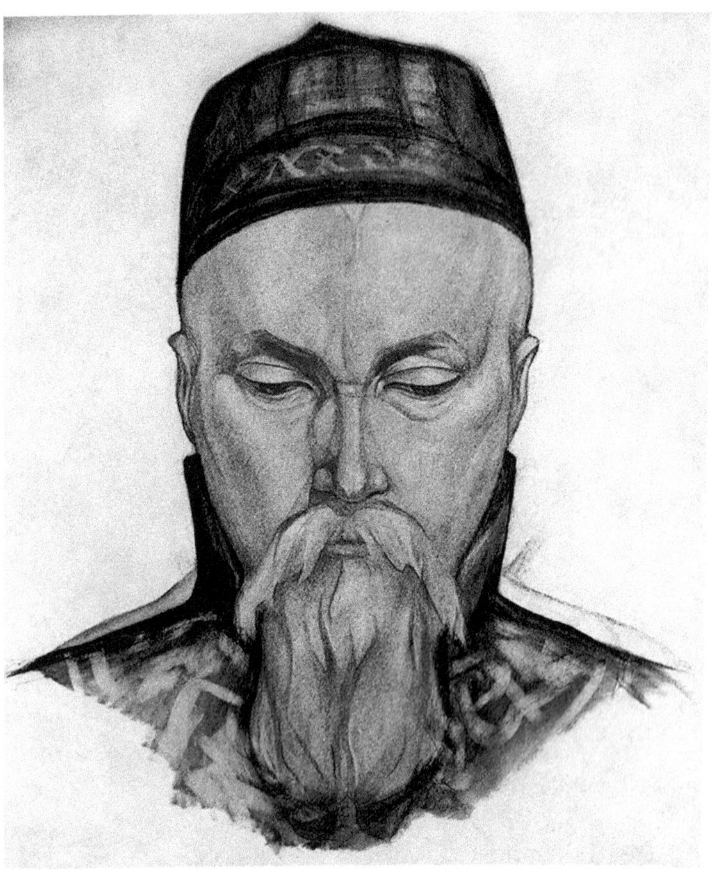

Portrait of Nicholas Roerich by Svetoslav Roerich

VIGIL

NICHOLAS ROERICH

LETTERS FROM ASIA

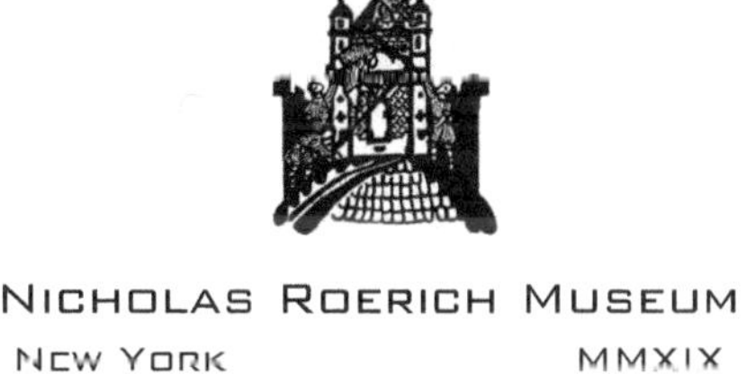

NICHOLAS ROERICH MUSEUM
NEW YORK   MMXIX

Nicholas Roerich Museum
319 West 107th Street
New York NY 10025
www.roerich.org

Cover illustration:
Nicholas Roerich. *Pearl of Searching.* 1924.

PUBLISHER'S NOTE

*V*IGIL: *Letters from Asia* is the thirteenth book in the *Nicholas Roerich: Collected Writings* series. The book presents a collection of one hundred articles and essays, most of which were published in different Indian magazines between 1934 and 1938. Nicholas Roerich sent the manuscript of the book to New York in 1939, but World War II and the author's death in 1947 prevented the book from being published at that time.

You may wonder whether observations and thoughts about various countries and people, about the world's problems, penned more than eighty years ago, arc still rcl evant today. As we observed in our note to an earlier volume in this series, Roerich's perspective focus on the universal and his insightful messages resonate today just as powerfully as they did when he first wrote them. His most fundamental message, one that weaves its way throughout all of his work, both on the page and on the canvas, is this: that culture— its celebration and preservation—is the basis for creating a better future for all mankind.

Among the many ideas Roerich discusses in this book are the power of beauty and wisdom, the importance of respecting all living beings, and the need for creating art with limitless potential. Roerich remains ever hopeful, which speaks to the strength of his convictions despite the uncertainty and conflict of his time. Here, he proves himself to be a thought leader in the philosophy of culture and its place in our society.

As his work continues to resonate with people from all over the world, we hope that this book will find its way on to the shelves and into the libraries of readers who care about art, culture and their fate in future generations.

We would like to thank all those who helped in the preparation of this book, and without whom its publication would not have been possible. Our special thanks go to White Mountain Education Association, particularly to Joleen Dianne DuBois and Kathryn Agrell, who worked so assiduously on editing the texts.

CONTENTS

I
EXPEDITION LEAVES
India, China, Mongolia, Tibet

GIFTS OF THE EAST

THERE is before us an ancient Mongol coin. On it are reproduced the sun, the moon, and the seven stars of the Great Bear or the Seven Elders. This is a broad dream of the heavens. A dream of miracles and wonders of the Great Blue Sky of Chengiz Khan.

Verily a broad concept.

Is it not striking that the Mongols bathed their horses in the Adriatic? The Mongols were in Paris, Lyons, and Valencia. The Mongols supplied helmets to the army of Philip the Beautiful. Alançon comes from the Alans. The Alans are esteemed in the Mongolian camps.

All this is boundless, as is also the whole advance of the East to the West, under the sign of the Crusades and following the trails of great travelers. The West often forgets how many heritages of the East it has accepted during many ages in the time of Marco Polo, Plano Karpini, Rubruquvist, Lonjumo, d'Anselico, and other daring spirits.

"The Mongol invasions have left such a hatred behind them that their artistic elements are always neglected. It is forgotten that the mysterious cradle of Asia has produced these quaint people and has enwrapped them in the gorgeous veils of China, Tibet, and Hindustan. Russia has not only suffered from the Tartar swords, but has also heard through their jingling the wonder tales known to the clever Greeks and the intelligent Arabians, who wandered along the Great Road from the Normans to the East.

The Mongol manuscripts and the annals of the foreign envoys of these days tell us of an unaccountable mixture of cruelty and refinement with the great nomads. The best artists and masters were to be found at the headquarters of the Tartar Khans."

Thus I emphasized in my lecture "Joy of Art."

In 1202, the Italian, Leonardo da Pisa, writes the mathematical treatise *Liber abacci* already with Arabic figures. He also uses for the first time the Arabic cipher—zero, voidness—vacuum. Arabic figures! But the Arabs themselves in full justice call them Indian figures. Often we come across the Indian cradle. The gifts of the East are unlimited. And even now the Khozars, this old tribe, lives in Afghanistan.

Algebra, Alidad, Zenith, Nadir, Azimuth, and finally Aldebaran, Algol, Altair—they all come from the Arabs, from the East.

From the same source there come many conceptions in medicine and the natural science. Alcohol, alembic, alkal, amalgam, and many others—are from the East. In Spain we see an Arabian university at Kordova, and the same in the south of Italy at Salerno. The physician of the Sultan of Egypt cures Louis IX. The words sirop, julep, elixir, camphor, and many others were already recorded in the medicine of the East.

Even in agriculture the East gave useful advices to the West. Maize is from Asia, the sugarcane, rice, indigo, saffron, tea, and a whole series of fruit trees and vegetables have their home in the East. Many pilgrims carried in their travelling bags various seeds, and saturated with them their home country. The apricot was called the pear of Damask. The eschalot is from Askalon. Artichokes, spinach, estragon—are all from the Arabs. The wines of Cyprus, Ghaza, Askalon, the raisins of Greece and Palestine are all the gifts of the East. Arabian horses, karabahs, karashars, donkeys, mules, and finally the hunting leopards, so beautifully depicted on the canvasses of Gozzolo—all this is from the vastnesses of Asia. It is stated that even the windmills are from Asia.

The industry of the East has since long tempted

Europe—the sugar of Antiochia and Tripoli; the cotton from Beyreuth, Aleppo, Akra; the silk from Tyre, Tortosa, Tiveriada; the muslin cloth from Mossul, Muar; the taft and saffron from the Arabs; the carpets from Iran; the Eastern compositions of color; the leather from Kordova, the celebrated Spanish-Mauritian faiences.

In the terminology of seafaring—bussol, admiral, arsenal, musson, feluka, corvet, shalanda, tartana—all from the East.

On the battlefields the Eastern armies were mighty enemies. More than once, the West, during encounters with the East, learned new military strategies, discipline, watchfulness, and alertness. Powerful orders of knights were inaugurated after coming in contact with the East. Western warriors imitated from the East excellent armors. Swords of Damask up to now have the reputation of the highest quality.

Torches, small shields, came from the East. Saracinian (armor) *bakhteret*, the Eastern helmets (*misurka*), and a quantity of manifold armor and saddlery has its origin in the East. Let us not forget that the word *ulan*, which is applied in many armies, is a purely Mongolian word. In the Russian, Polish, and Lithuanian vocabulary there are many Mongolian and other Eastern words that have become deeply enrooted: *essual* (an officer's rank), *kuyack* (a helmet), *meren* (a horse), *tamga* (a seal), *yam* (a postal station), *yarlyck* (a label), *yar* (a steep river bank), *karaul* (a watchman), *dokha* (a fur coat), *chumbur* (bridle), *argamack* (a steed), and many other similar and widely applied words.

In the East the crusaders, in order to be distinguished during battle, began to depict on their shields the first symbolic signs, which remained afterward as coats of arms. Many heraldic animals have their origin in the East: the unicorn, elephant, lion, griffin, dragon. On our shield the stars are Eastern. The very coloring of the shield, even in terminology, brings to mind Iran and other countries of the East.

Innumerable scents, perfumes, pomades, and all sorts

of cosmetics came from the East. Many terms in the households, and of furniture came from the same source—divan, baldachin, alcove, sunduck, carafe, jar—all are from there, as also the name of many precious stones. Even the word *galeta* reminds us of Galata.

Often the Eastern nations were pictured by prejudiced chroniclers as intolerant, cruel, even treacherous and immoral. Yet at the same time we have irrefutable historical data about their tolerance, humaneness, honor, and charity. We admire the valor and daring of Chengiz Khan, and of many warriors of the East. The Saracinians were called by some historians ignorant barbarians, yet at the same time in their universities and from their cultures in science, in art, one could see how they excelled the conceited Westerners of those days. Contact with Eastern nations was one of the main impulses of the Middle Ages. It called forth in several domains of life a kind of awakening. This was a precursor of the Renaissance.

The first impressions of a foreigner crossing Mongolia will be unfavorable as regards the military strength of this country, but in reality the military force of Mongolia is not so small as a casual observer may think. Every Mongol is an excellent rider and marksman. The whole population loves hunting as a sport. The Mongols shoot from their saddle and, from childhood, are accustomed to archery and lassoing from galloping horses.

The bow and arrow, even quite recently, were the main weapons of the Mongols. Archery competitions are up to now the main entertainment during the Annual Festival. A sure eye and a steady hand are required to mark the target when turning back from a horse at full gallop. In this way the Mongols also have become masters of the rifle, with which they acquaint themselves with surprising ease. Almost no shot in a battle misses its aim.

The Mongols love their country more than many other people. They have many advantages in the defense of their country. They quickly judge distances, are used to the air of the heights; they are clever in maneuvering across their hilly country.

The Mongols can endure great hardships without food and water, and can stand the terrific local hurricanes. Besides an active resistance, the Mongols also have great patience and persistence. The Mongol population living in *yurtas* can leave their whole settlement overnight. The cattle will be driven away, the well will be destroyed, and the intruder will find himself in an empty desert without food and water, left to the mercy of the harshness of nature.

The Mongols can stand a great deal, and the heroic deeds described in annals since the time of Chengiz Khan are not fairy tales.

The same may be stated of many peoples in the East. And the West in the past has acquired many gifts from the East. Religion, philosophy, and many other most precious treasures of spirit and culture in full justice should be ascribed to the East, to Asia. Why this is so is not for us to judge. The historian can but base himself on reality. And no one can diminish the great value of the gifts of the East.

I was glad to receive the book of Dr. Hara Davan about Chengiz Khan. The author belongs to the East, and therefore his enlightened judgment is the more convincing. He knows of what he speaks. He understands the deep culture at the foundation of many great movements, which may be incomprehensible to outsiders. Also the recently deceased Vadimirtzeff correctly evaluated the treasures of Asia.

Gratitude is the quality of Arhats. Following with great ordainment, let us be grateful for all great gifts, in all their multifacetedness and significance.

Let us remember all the great gifts of India. Let us remember how unexpectedly appreciation was often expressed there, where in medieval distances one might have expected insufficient knowledge. Dante in his *Paradise* inspiringly mentions the Orient, the Ganges, and the Blessed One!

"Di questa costa, là dov'ella frange Piu sua rattezza, nacque al mondo un sole, come fa questo talvolta di Gange.
"Però chi dèsso loco fa parole non dica Ascesi, chè direbbe corto, ma Oriente, se proprio dir vuole."

Dante. *Paradiso.*

SACRED ASHRAMS

KAILASA, Manasarowar, Badrinath, Kedarnath, Trilokinath, Ravalsar—these glorious gems of the Highest always fill the heart with special blissful tremor. When we were within a day's journey from Manasarowar, the entire caravan already became uplifted—thus far around does the aura of a holy ashram act.

Another vivid recollection arises from the path to Trilokinath. A long line of Sadhus and Lamas stretches along this road—the old sanctuary, the site of pilgrimage and prayer. These pilgrims have met here from many different roads. Some already completing their spiritual journeyings, are walking along with a trident; some carry bamboo staves; others are without anything, even without clothing. And the snow of the Rotang Pass is no impediment to them.

The pilgrims proceed, knowing that the Rishis and the Pandavas dwelt here. Here is the Beas of Vyasa; here is Vyasakund—the place of the fulfillment of all wishes. Here Vyasa Rishi compiled the Mahabharata.

Not in legend alone, but in reality, did the great Rishis live here. Their presence breathes life into the cliffs that are crowned with glaciers, into the emerald pastures where the yaks graze, and into the caves and the roaring torrents. From here were sent forth those spiritual calls of which humanity has heard through all ages. These calls are taught in schools; they have been translated into many languages—and this crystal of acquisitions has been stratified on the cliffs of the Himalayas.

"Where can one find words with which to praise

the Creator after seeing the incomparable beauty of the Himalayas?" sings the Hindu. Along the paths of the Guru, along the peaks of the Rishi, along the mountain paths of the pilgrims of the spirit, lies that treasure, which no torrent of rain can wear away, nor any lightning turn to ashes. He who walks toward the Good is blessed on all paths. How touching are all the narratives which tell of the meeting of the righteous ones of various nations! The tops of the deodars in the forest touch each other in the wind. Thus, everything that is of the highest meets without injury and harm. Time was when quarrels were settled by single combat, and decisions were reached by a conference of chiefs. So do the deodars discuss matters between themselves. What a meaningful word: deodar—the gift of God. And this significant name is not without reason: for the resin of the deodar has healing powers. Deodar, musk, valerian, roses, and other similar substances comprise the beneficent medicines of the Rishis. Some have wanted to do away with these medicines by substituting an invasion of new discoveries; however, humanity again reverts to the foundations.

Here is a photograph of a man who walks through fire without harming himself. This is not a fiction. Witnesses will tell you of the same trials by fire in Madras, Lucknow, Benares. And not only does the Sadhu walk harmlessly on the flaming coals, but he leads behind him those who desire to follow him and hold on to him.

In Benares a Sadhu sits in sacred posture upon the water of the Ganges. His crossed legs are covered by the brim of the water. The people flock to the banks, amazed at the holy man.

Still another Sadhu has been buried alive for many days; another swallows various poisons without any harm. Here is a Lama who can levitate himself; another Lama by means of *tumo* can generate his own heat, thus protecting himself against snow and mountain glaciers; there a Lama can give the death stroke with his "deadly eye" to a mad dog. A venerated Lama from Bhutan relates, how during his stay in the Tzang district in Tibet, a Lama asked the ferryman to take him across from Tzampo free of charge, but the cunning man replied: "I will gladly take you over, if you can prove that you are a great Lama. A mad dog is running about here, doing great harm—kill it." The Lama said nothing; but looking at the dog, he raised his hand and said a few words, and the dog fell dead! The Bhutanese Lama saw this himself. One hears frequently in Tibet and in India of the same "deadly eye" and the "eye of Kapila." And on a map of the seventeenth century printed in Antwerp, by authority of the Catholic clergy, is mentioned the name of the country, Shambhala.

If one can walk through fire, and another can sit on water, and a third remain suspended in the air, and a fourth repose on nails, and a fifth swallow poison, and a sixth kill with a glance, and a seventh lie buried without harm, then one may collect all those grains of knowledge in himself. And thus the obstacles of lower matter can be transmuted! Not in a remote age, but now, right here, where Millikan's cosmic rays, Rhine's thought-transference, and the reality of finest psychic energy are also being studied and affirmed.

Every Rishi pronounced in his own language the sacred pledge for the construction of a revived, refined, and beautiful world!

For the sake of a single righteous being, a whole city was saved. As beacons, lightning rods, and citadels of God stood the Rishis of various nations, of various creeds, of various ages, yet one in the spirit of salvation and ascension for all!

Whether the Rishi came upon fire, whether he arrived home upon a stone, whether he came upon the whirlwind, he always hastened for the general good. Whether he prayed on mountain summits, or on a steep riverbank, or in a hidden cave, he always sent out his prayers for the unknown, for the stranger, for the laborers, for the sick and the crippled.

Whether the Rishi sent out white horses to save the

unknown pilgrims, or whether he blessed unknown seafarers, or guarded a city by night, he always stood as a pillar of light for all, without condemnation and without extinguishing the flame.

Without condemnation, without mutual suspicion, without weakening each other, ever upwards, the Rishis ascended the eternal Mount Meru.

Before us is the road to Kailas. There rises one of the fifteen wonders described in Tibetan books: The Mount of the Bell! Along sharp ridges one climbs to its summit. It stands higher than the last junipers, higher than the last yellow and white mountain ranges. There Padma Sambhava once walked—this is recorded in the ancient monastery Gandola. It is exactly here that the caves of Milarepa are situated. And not one but many have been sanctified with the name of the hermit who hearkened before dawn to the voices of the Devas. Not far away are also legends which surround Pahari Baba. Here also are the spiritual strongholds of Gautama Rishi. Many Rishis walked here. And he who gave the mountain its enticing name, "Mount of the Bell," also thought of the call of the Bell for all, of helping all, of the Universal Good!

Here Rishis lived for Universal Good!

When Rishis meet on the mountain paths, they do not ask each other: "From where do you come? Is it from the East, or West, or South, or North?" This is quite apparent: that they come from the Good and go to the Good. An exalted, refined flaming heart knows where is the Good and, in it, what can be found.

Some of the travelers in our caravan were once discussing the qualities of the various Rishis, but a gray-haired pilgrim, pointing to snowy peaks, effulgent in their complete beauty, said:

"Are we to judge the qualities of these summits? We can but bow in admiration before their unattainable splendor!

Satyam, Shivam, Sundaram.

CHANDOGYA UPANISHADS

"THE breath is saturated; the eye is saturated; the sun is saturated; the heavens are saturated. Everything under the sky and under the sun is saturated.

"Whence then is all that takes place saturated: herds, nourishment, strength, splendor, solemnity of Service?"

"Viyana is saturated; the earth is saturated; the moon is saturated; the heavenly dominions are saturated. Everything beneath them and beneath the moon is saturated.

"Whence then is all that takes place saturated: herds, nourishment, strength, splendor, solemnity of service?"

"Anana is saturated; the world is saturated; fire is saturated; earth is saturated. Everything under fire and earth is saturated.

"Whence then is all that takes place saturated: herds, nourishment, strength, splendor, solemnity of Service?"

"Samana is saturated; spirit is saturated; vortices are saturated; the hurricane is saturated. Everything beneath the vortices in the hurricane is saturated.

"Whence then is all that takes place saturated: herds, nourishment, strength, splendor, solemnity of Service?"

"Udana is saturated; air is saturated; space is saturated. Everything aerial and spatial is saturated.

"Whence then is all that takes place saturated: herds, nourishment, strength, splendor, solemnity of Service?"

"Whoever, knowing this, serves Agnihotra, serves in all worlds, in all that exists, in everything."

"As children huddle together around the mother, so do beings cluster around Agnihotra —around Agnihotra."

* * *

"All has been spiritualized from the Subtlest Entity. This is the sole Reality. This is Atman."

"Verily, dead is the body, abandoned by the spirit. The spirit then does not die. All has been spiritualized by the Subtlest Entity. This is the sole Reality, this is Atman."

"Cast this salt in the water and return to me tomorrow morning."

"Taste now this water, what do you find?" "It is salty." "Draw from this water more deeply, what do you find?" "It is salty." "Taste it from the bottom. What do you find?" "It is salty." "Taste again and come here to me." "It is all the same." "Thus, verily, my friend, you still do not notice the essence, yet it is everywhere."

* * *

"Tell me all that you know, and I will tell you what follows."

"I know the Rig-Veda, the Yajur-Veda, the Sama-Veda, the Atharva-Veda, the ancient sayings, the Veda of Vedas; I know the ceremonials; I know calculations, the science of predictions, weather forecasting, logic, the rules of behavior, etymology, the science of sacred texts, the science of arms, astronomy, the facts about the serpent and the djinn. That is what I know."

"All that you have enumerated are only words."

"Words—Rig-Veda and Yajur-Veda, and Sama-Veda, and Atharva-Veda and ancient sayings, and the science of predictions, and the perception of time, and logic, and the rules of behavior, and etymology, and the science of sacred texts, and the science of arms, and astronomy, and the science of the serpent and the djinn; all these are only words. Apprehend the proper understanding of words."

"When one understands in the words of Brahman, he can do all that he wishes within the power of these words." — "Teacher, tell this to me."

"It, the Word, is verily greater than all words. This

Word enables one to understand the Rig-Veda, and the Yajur-Veda, and the Sama-Veda, and the Atharva-Veda and the ancient sayings, and grammar, and the rules of calculation, and the science of predictions, and knowledge of time, and logic, and the rules of behavior, and etymology, and the science of sacred texts, and the science of arms, and astronomy, and the knowledge of the serpents and the djinn, heaven and earth, air, ether, waters, the light-bearing quality of higher entities, people, animals, birds, plants, and trees—all creations even to the smallest, and the insect, and to the ants, the righteous and the iniquitous, the true and the false, the good and the evil, the pleasant and the unpleasant. If the Word did not exist, neither the just nor the unjust would be cognized, neither true nor false, good nor evil, pleasant nor unpleasant; this Word enables one to distinguish all. Apprehend the proper understanding of the Word."

* * *

"Only when service takes place justly; without sacrifice there will be no justice.

This alone makes service just, but it is needful to wish to cognize service."

"Only when you feel an inner joy at service. He serves not who is in suffering.

Only when one has been filled with joy does service result, but it is needful to cognize joy."

"There is no joy without infiniteness. There is no joy in the finite. Joy is infinity, but it is needful to wish to cognize infinity."

* * *

"Whoever strives to the peace world of fathers, with them will he also dwell. Surrounded by the peace world of fathers, he may be happy. Whoever strives to the peace world of mothers, only to think, will also dwell with them. Surrounded by the peace world of mothers, he will be happy."

* * *

"The truly clear-sighted sees neither deaths nor diseases nor sufferings. The truly clear-sighted sees, and everywhere he attains all."

* * *

"Atman, the sole true reality, is in the heart. This it is that explains the expression: It is in the heart. Day by Day, he who knows this attains the heavenly peace world."

* * *

The lofty spiritual mood in which a Hindu recites the words of the sacred tradition is something not easily forgotten. The poet Tagore, whose sensitive heart is a storehouse of these great rhythms, knows how to evoke all their beauties.

In India, when the verses of the Mahabharata, the Upanishads, and the Puranas are being recited, then there is joy, despite all troubles; and even if the modernization of India is inevitable, the beauty of such sacred poetry will live on forever.

One is, of course, struck by the endless repetitions in the translation of such texts, and yet if one listens to the rhythmic periods of the original, one recognizes that they are an integral part of the melody. Such repetitions are often a way of laying stress on the most important passages. For centuries the Rig-Veda and the other sacred books were transmitted orally, and in this, rhythmic repetition was a great aid to the memory.

If one considers the large number of philosophical and religious periodicals and books now published in India, one is forced to admire a people who care so much for thought and culture. Such a virtue covers many defects, and from the towering Himalayas to the burning South, there are plenty of signs that point in this direction.

From the poorest coolie to the most learned Hindu, you will always meet with someone ready to converse with you on the most lofty subjects; and after a short time, you will come to realize that every Hindu, whatever be his personal way of life or that of the society to which he belongs, will always prefer to discuss lofty subjects, for these alone to him seem real.

Despite the confusion of today, India still maintains her lofty tradition of Teacher and disciple. The Guru still lives on and the relationship of Guru and disciple is always an edifying one. This noble and conscious cult of the Teacher can hardly be found in other countries. There is nothing servile or belittling in it, no narrowing of outlook or loss of personality, for it is a noble recognition of the Law of Hierarchy.

Even in the details of daily life, the disciples will always respect the Teachers' dignity, a quality that can only be developed by mutual respect.

The Teacher is a father and adviser and a guide in all the events of life.

It is characteristic of the Guru to be concerned about the inner and outer program of his disciple, and the disciples, on their part, have many beautiful expressions that show their deep respect for the Guru. Belittlement, on their part, is inadmissible even in the smallest details, and they will make every endeavor to preserve in their own minds the essential character of the Teacher.

From this mutual understanding, the art of thinking is born, and joy arises around the comprehension of higher things—a joy not confined to palaces and temples, but one that enters the poorest dwelling and transforms the burden of life into something easy.

He who knows India—not as the tourist or sightseer but as one who has come in contact with the people and with the life of the great country—will never forget its charm.

And the heart of India will respond to all genuine sympathy. No words or assurances can compare with the judgment of the heart, which is something steadfast, something that can dive beneath the surface and recognize the essential.

In India, moreover, there is a remarkable psychic awareness; so if you glance at anyone in a distant crowd, he will respond to your attention at once. This we have remarked upon not once or twice but on many occasions.

Such a delicate sense of awareness is not to be acquired by any voluntary training.

It is the heritage of centuries of lofty thought and a natural characteristic of the race. In order to acquire the habit of lofty thought, one must come to prefer it to other ways of thought; in fact, one must rejoice in it, for, as we are told in the Upanishads, it is only through joy that our efforts can become effective.

This inner joy of the heart is something that we have to cultivate and learn how to retain so that it takes up its abode in the heart so that this beneficent joy of the heart becomes a lasting power to disperse all the forces of darkness.

Whether we think of those sublime temples of Southern India, of the grandeur of Chittur and Gwalior and the great strongholds of Rajputana, or the solemn spirit of the Himalayas, everywhere we will find the joy of great thoughts.

On the moonlit Ganges, in the mystery of Benares seen at night, and in the great cadences of the Himalayan waterfalls, we will find the same lofty sense of joy.

In the repetition of such ancient names as Manu, Arjuna, Krishna of the Pandavas—Rishis, heroes, creators and great constructors—we recognize a loving respect for the past.

From the Mother of the World, from the Queen of Peace, we receive this delicate flowerlike joy of the heart.

Marvelous India! Splendid in outer beauty, most beautiful in its secret inner life.

Beautiful, beloved India!

SCRIPTURES OF ASIA

IN the torn and yellow manuscripts of Turfan, we find hymns to "The God of Light," "To the Sun," "To the Eternal Living Soul." We find prayers of peace and quiet and ascension, where the word peace is often repeated.

Besides an immense collection of Buddhist texts, discoveries were also made of many Chinese, Manichean, Nestorian, Tibetan, Iranian, and other Central Asian manuscripts.

The deserted temples are now in ruins, and the vestiges of towers and ramparts buried beneath the sands, indicate the sites of flourishing cities. The frescoes have gone, the libraries have been scattered, and all their treasures ransacked. The traveler today, who goes by another route, no longer sees those brilliant colors, that shining metalware, but only darkness.

These manuscripts have suffered as much from the hands of vandals as from dampness and decay, and yet their mildewed pages still remind us that these dark and deserted ruins were at one time the abode of clean and luminous thought. The soul of many an ancient scribe is still enshrined in lofty messages.

A recent translation from one of the Turfan hymns reads thus: (Omissions shown by .... or ...)

"A hymn to the Living Soul . . . all the sins, all the hesitations, internal and external, all the thoughts, all that has been thought and said mixture of good and evil thoughts, unconsciousness. 'Know Thyself,' the pure word that leads to the soul. Through the soul understand all the wicked words of the Master of Evil, which are likely to lead you toward the eternal Darkness.

"As a judge, weigh every word that is said and manifested. Understand the transmigration of the soul and behold the depths of hell where the souls suffer torments.

"Preserve the purity of your soul and the treasures of the Word. . . .

"O devouring fire of Man! And you luminous-winged Free Soul.

"Predestination and transmigration defend your heart and thought from all wicked impulses.

"Go to the land of Light by the road of Peace. . . .

"I sing Thee O God omnipotent, O Living Soul, O gift of the Father.

"By the saintly path return to thy home. O Power so generously dispensing happiness.

"Wisdom . . . all . . . Herself . . . Trembling . . . hearing . . . peace . . . you the Son of the Almighty.

"All the persecutions, all the torments and poverty and need which you have assumed, who could endure them? Thou art the Luminous One, the Gracious One, the Blessed One, the Powerful and Noble Master. . . .

"Proceeding from the Light, from God, I have lost my native land, I have been exiled.

"Be blessed he who will deliver my soul from torments

"You will receive Eternal Life.

"Purify your luminous soul, and she will liberate you.

"Sing beautifully and rejoice in the thought: 'O Luminous Guide of the Soul'!

"Sing that beautiful hymn, the hymn of Good for peace, for confidence.

"With the trumpet declare with joy: 'Guide our souls in unity toward salvation.'

"To the call of the trumpet the sons of God will joyfully respond.

"Say Holy! Holy! Holy! Say Amen, Amen!

"Sing O Luminous Wisdom: Repeat the pure saying,

'The Living word of Truth will liberate the prisoners from their chains.' Glorify the Truth.

"Sing 'Be ardent in the fear of God; unite in the commandments. . . . Light . . . call . . . the herald . . . the great peace, treasures, which the souls, the eyes, the ears . . . Invite the Son of God to the Divine Banquet, decorate the beloved groves, show the way to the Light.'

"Group your members in numbers of five, seven, twelve. There they are the seven glittering noble stones on which the world is based. Through their power the worlds and all beings live. It is like a lamp in the house shining in darkness. . . .

"Do not strike him who has struck you. Do not be revenged on him who takes revenge. Do not seduce those who try to seduce you.

"Receive in a friendly way those who come to you in anger. Do not do unto others what you would not they do to you. Suffer offenses from those higher than yourself, from your equals, and from those inferior.

"Do not let the elephant be bound by the flowers that are thrown at him. Let not the stone be dissolved by drops of water. Offences and calumnies will not shake the long-suffering ones. The long-suffering One will stand like Mount Sumeru.

"The long-suffering will know how to appear at times as a disciple, at times as a master, at others as a slave, or as a lord. . . .

"There is the path, there is the mystery, there is the great commandment and the gates of liberation!

"Let Thy will be done. Let Thy magnificence protect me, and let my patience, righteousness, and fear of God be increased. Thy voice and my ear . . .

"Happy is he who in your purity and justice O God knows the variety, the multiformity, the charitableness, the miracle. . . .

"Here is a disciple of righteous heart and one who loves his master. He follows his master, he honors his name and cherishes him

"Receive those brothers who come to you. If they would draw from thy wisdom then teach them as if they were your own children. . . .

"I like the Lord who takes off his armor and lays aside his weapons to put on his royal robes. Thus the envoy of light sets aside his militant character, and sits in light and in his divine aspect, with a shining crown, with a beautiful crown. And in great joy the luminous Ones hurry to him from right and left singing a hymn of joy. They all gather around the divine miracle like flashes of lightning. . . .

"The noble Lord has kept his promise. I shall sit on high, at the predestined hour, I shall send you help."

So say these moldy manuscripts. In these Pehlevi and Uigur scriptures have been kept the voices from distant lands.

In the frescoes the characteristics of various nations combine harmoniously, and both in imagery and technique you will find the outlines of the Chinese, Iranian, and Hindu genius. Luminous great-eyed figures surrounded by various symbols send up their prayers for peace.

"And from beyond the Himalayas resound the prayers of the ancient Vedas.

"Let all the pain of the world bring us peace. Let God be witness to it.

"Let peace be one and let it reign everywhere.

"Let peace come unto us."

In the midst of the whirlwinds of the West, Dante in his immortal way tells us:

"O Man, what tempests must strike thee, what losses thou must suffer, what shipwreck and loss must ensue, while you strive like a many-headed monster toward evil. You are sick in your consciousness, you are sick in sentiment. Insoluble reasoning will not help your consciousness. The clearest proofs will not convince your low understanding.

"Even sweet and divine clearness does not attract you, though it breathes through the harmonies of the Holy

Spirit. Remember brother how well and agreeable it is to live in unity."

Asia prayed for peace, and the great souls of the West called for the same.

In all the prayers that were inscribed to last, there has been a desire for peace, for the peace of the world.

SRI RAMAKRISHNA

WE are in the desert of Mongolia. It was hot and dusty yesterday. From far away thunder was approaching. Some of our friends became tired from climbing up the stony hills of Shiret Obo. While already returning to the camp, we noticed in the distance a huge elm tree, *karagatch,* lonely, towering amid the surrounding endless desert. The size of the tree, its somewhat familiar outlines, attracted us into its shadow. Botanical considerations lead to believe that in the wide shade of the giant, there may be some interesting herbs for us. Soon all coworkers gathered around the two mighty stems of the karagatch. The deep shadow of the tree covered over fifty feet across. The powerful tree stems were covered with fantastic burr growths. In the rich foliage, birds were singing, and the beautiful branches were stretched out in all directions as if wishing to give shelter to all pilgrims.

On the sands, around the roots, innumerable trails made by animals were visible. Next to the broad imprints of a wolf were small hooves of the *dzeren,* the local antelope. A horse had also passed here, and next to it was the heavy footstep of a bull. All sorts of birds had been here. Apparently the entire local population visited the welcoming shelter of the giant. The elm karagatch especially reminded us of the huge banyan trees of India. Such trees were the meeting place of blessed gatherings. Many travelers found there both bodily and spiritual rest. Sacred narratives were chanted under the inviting branches of the banyan tree. And thus the lonely, giant karagatch in the Mongolian desert vividly turned our memory to the shadow of the banyan. The mighty branches of the karagatch reminded us also of other great achievements of India. What a joy to think of India!

Thoughts turned to the radiant giant of India—Sri Ramakrishna. Around this glorious name there are so many respectful definitions. *Sri Bhagavan Paramahansa*—all the best offerings through which the people wish to express their esteem and reverence. The consciousness of a nation knows how to bestow names of honor. And after all, above all most venerable titles, there remains over the whole world the one great name—Ramakrishna. The personal name has already changed into a great all-nations, universal concept. Who has not heard the Blessed Name! The conception of goodness and benevolence truly befits him. Except for petrified hearts, who would oppose the Good?

We recollect how in various countries has grown the understanding of the radiant Teaching of Ramakrishna. Beyond shameful words of hatred, beyond evil mutual destruction—the word of Bliss, which is close to every human heart, spreads widely like the mighty branches of the sacred banyan tree. On the paths of human searching, these calls of goodwill were shining like beacons. We ourselves witnessed, and have often heard how books of Ramakrishna's Teaching were as if unexpectedly found by sincere seekers. We ourselves came across the book in a most unusual way.

Hundreds of thousands, even as many as a million pilgrims gather on the memorable day in the name of the Blessed *Bhagavan.* They gather, being called by an inner impulse of the heart, in goodwill, and they become rejuvenated by blissful remembrances and strivings. Is this not a most remarkable expression of the voice of the people! This is the nation's judgment, the reverence of the people, which cannot be compelled nor forcefully commanded. As wonderful lights, they spread from one to another forming an inexhaustible flame; hence, such national reverence is not dimmed but radiates throughout the times of contemporary world commotions.

Too many crises grip the people at present. It could happen that the spirit of the people could become confused and distracted from the spiritual fundamentals. The wail about the shattering of the foundations is so often heard nowadays. But are not the millions of pilgrims, who assembled by their own free will, the best living proof that above the confusions of today, there lives in the hearts an inexhaustible spirituality and striving toward the Good? We are optimists and conquer all obstacles through goodwill.

Behold, on an unbearably hot day, not being frightened of distances, pilgrims are hastening in order to venerate the memory of Ramakrishna. Is this not a remarkable event? For it is not an official duty that brings together all the multifarious travelers. A pure heart and a sincere striving imperatively lead them to the places consecrated by the name of Ramakrishna. Such a spiritual gathering is the most precious evidence in our days. It is wonderful that amidst the heavy labor, amid doubts, amid depression, people yet can be lit by the flame of gratitude and veneration. Their hearts call them together. They are gathering not for destruction, nor for quarrels, nor for insults, but in order to unite their thoughts upon the Good.

Great power is contained in a united benevolent thought. Humanity should value such sublime manifestations, which are the cause of all these unifying and constructive thoughts. Creative is the thought of Good! The good never destroys; it untiringly elevates and builds. By commands of good are affirmed those eternal foundations, which have been ordained to humanity on all the best tablets. The call of the Blessed *Bhagavan* for creative Good will forever remain the great spiritual heritage of humanity.

Light is especially precious during the hours of darkness. May the Light be eternally preserved! In his parables about the Good, Ramakrishna never belittled anyone. And not only in the Teaching, in parables, but in his own deeds, he never tolerated bemoaning. Let us remember his reverent attitude toward all religions. Such broad understanding will move even a stony heart. In his broad outlook, the Blessed *Bhagavan*, of course, possessed a real straight-knowledge. His power of healing he in turn gave out freely. He never hid anything useful. He exhausted his strength in innumerable blessed givings. And even his illness, of course, was due to such a constant, self-sacrificing outpouring of his spiritual energy for the healing of others. And in these generous gifts, Ramakrishna manifested his greatness.

In all parts of the world, the name of Ramakrishna is venerated. Also is revered Swami Vivekananda, who symbolizes true discipleship. The names of Ramakrishna, Vivekananda, and the glorious host of their followers remain on the most remarkable pages of the history of the spiritual culture of India. The astounding depth of thought, which is characteristic for India, the beautiful manifestation of *Guru* and *Chela*—remind the whole world of basic ideals. Ages pass, whole civilizations change, but the *Guru* and the *Chela* remain in the same wise relationship, which since antiquity was established in India. Many millenniums ago the words of wisdom were already recorded in India. And how many more millenniums were they reserved even before, in verbal transmission. And in this sacred mouth to ear transmission, they were kept perhaps even safer than on written records. The ability to keep up the correct meaning depends on a developed, wise consciousness, and in this is contained the application of precious stones of the past for the radiant future.

Not only the everlasting value of the Teaching of Good affirmed by Ramakrishna, but precisely the necessity of these words especially for our times is unquestionable. When spirituality, as such, is being so often refuted through wrongly interpreted formulae, then the radiant constructive affirmation as a beacon becomes especially precious. One has but to know the colossal number of editions of the Ramakrishna Mission. One has but to remember the large number of cities in which these Missions have their branches. These figures require no exaggeration. There is no unnatural nervousness, and no premeditatedness in these quiet thought-creating gatherings. Everything is deeply realized not in tumult and rush but grows in highest co-measurement.

The thoughts about the Good, which Ramakrishna so generously taught, should awaken the best sides of human hearts. Ramakrishna always preached against deniers and destroyers. He was in all respects a builder for the Good, and his admirers should unfold, on the examples of his Teaching, the best hidden treasures of their hearts. Such beneficial creativeness is very active. And it naturally is also transmuted into the best achievements on all paths of life. Gathering on the memorable day of Ramakrishna's anniversary, the pilgrims do not fear the dust of the road; they are not frightened by the fatiguing heat, but they are filled with a striving toward the Good, toward the great service to humanity. Service to Humanity—great is this ordainment of Ramakrishna!

Reverence to the Teacher!

"I recall a small Hindu who found his Teacher. We asked him: 'Is it possible that the sun would glow to you if you would see it without the Teacher?'

The boy smiled. 'The sun would remain as the sun. But in the presence of the Teacher, twelve suns would shine to me!'

The sun of the wisdom of India shall shine because upon the shores of a river there sits a boy who knows the Teacher."

UNFADING FLOWERS

VERILY, the flowers of Great Truths never fade.
On the eve of the memorable day, let us take from the shelves our good friends—our beloved Books. What do they say?

"These two extremes, monks, are not to be practiced by one who has gone forth from the world. What are the two? That conjoined with the passions and luxury, low, vulgar, common, ignoble, and useless, and that conjoined with self-torture, painful, ignoble and useless. Avoiding these two extremes, the Tathagata has gained the enlightenment of the Middle Path, which produces insight and knowledge, and tends to calm, to higher knowledge, enlightenment, Nirvana." (*Samyutta*, v, 420).

"With his mind thus concentrated, purified, and cleansed, without lust, free from the depravities, subtle, ready to act, firm, and impassible, he turns and directs his mind to the knowledge of the destruction of the asavas. He duly understands, 'This is pain'; he duly understands, 'This is the cause of pain'; he duly understands, 'This is the cessation of pain'; he duly understands, 'This is the path that leads to the cessation of pain'; he duly understands, 'These are the asavas'; he duly understands, 'This is the cause of the asavas.' As he thus knows and thus perceives, his mind is released from the asava of sensual desire, from the asava of desire for existence, from the asava of ignorance. In the released is the knowledge of his release: ignorance is destroyed, the religious life has been led, done is what was to be done, there is nothing further for this world." (*Samannaphala-s., Digha.*, i, 47).

"But is there any householder, not having cast off the fetters of a householder, who with the dissolution of the body has reached heaven?"—"Not merely one, Vaccha, nor even a hundred or two, three, four, or five hundred, but far more householders who have not cast off the fetters of a householder, with the dissolution of the body have reached heaven." (*Tevijjavacchagotta-s., Majjhima,* i, 482).

"Thus, Chunda, in matters concerning the past, future, and present, the Tathagata speaks at the right time, speaks truthfully, speaks profitably; he speaks of the doctrine and discipline. Therefore, he is called Tathagata."—"Whatever, Chunda, in the world with its gods, Mara, Brahma, among beings with ascetics, brahmins, gods, and men, has been seen, heard, perceived, known, attained, sought after, or pondered over in mind, all that has been comprehended by the Tathagata. Therefore, he is called Tathagata. As the Tathagata speaks, thus he does. As he does, thus he speaks. Hence, as speaking, thus doing; as doing, thus speaking; therefore, he is called Tathagata." (*Pasadika-s., Digha,* iii, 134).

"He rightly knows whither all paths lead. . . . He rightly knows the nature of the universe with its many and various groups and elements. . . . He rightly knows the impurity and growth of the trances, releases, concentrations, and attainments. . . ." (*Mahasihanada-s., Majjhima,* i, 69).

"The wise man endowed with virtue, gentle and skilled in speech, of lowly conduct, not obstinate, such a one wins fame. Energetic, not lazy, he trembles not in misfortunes; of flawless conduct, intelligent, such a one wins fame. Friendly, a maker of friends, kind, free from avarice, guide, instructor, and adviser; such a one wins fame. Liberality, affability, useful conduct toward others, impartiality in affairs toward each according to his worth. Now these elements of sympathy in the world are like the linchpin of a chariot in making it go; without these elements of sympathy, a mother would get no respect or reverence for having a son, nor would a father. In so far as the wise ponder these elements of sympathy, to that extent do they attain greatness and become praised." *(Sigalovada-s., Digha,* iii, 180).

"Dwelling in a fit region, the merit of former good deeds and right resolution about oneself—that is a supreme blessing. Great learning and skill and well-trained moral discipline, and speech that is well-spoken—that is a supreme blessing. Caring for mother and father, cherishing wife and children and undisturbed occupations— that is a supreme blessing. Giving alms, following the teaching, cherishing one's relatives, blameless actions— that is a supreme blessing. Shunning evil and refraining from it, restraint in strong drink, watchfulness over one's thoughts—that is a supreme blessing. He whose mind is not shaken by contact with things of the world is free from sorrow, free from stain, and at peace—that is a supreme blessing. They that do such things are in all ways undefeated; in all ways they go to happiness—that is their supreme blessing." *(Mahamangala-s., Sutta-nipata,* ii, 4).

Thus the Books say.

And whether it was ordained ages ago or today, the Truth stands immutable. Verily these unfading flowers retain their same beautiful fragrance!

HIMALAYA

MANY expeditions are striving to conquer the gorgeous peaks of the Himalayas. Severely the unconquered giants meet the daring intruders. Again Everest refused to welcome the newcomers. And Nanga Parbat does not facilitate matters in the attempted conquest. And the Kinchanjunga peak is not even contested. And yet from all sides, various nations aspire to reach the resplendent Himalayan summits. Such a procession turns into an homage of pilgrims to the highest of the world.

The local Lamas smile mysteriously when they hear that yet another attempt was defeated. If they have confidence in you, they will tell you in whispers some ancient prophecies that assert that certain sacred summits will never be defiled. Not long ago, a well-known Lama, who is now dead, told us: "Curious people are the pelings. Why do they undertake such dangers in the physical body, when we can visit these summits and do so in our subtle body?"

Indeed, in every striving to the summits, in every ascent, is contained an untold joy. An inner impulse irresistibly calls people toward the heights.

If someone would begin to trace historically these aspirations, having the Himalayas as their goal, an unusually significant study would result. Truly, if one could trace back the force of attraction of these heights for a thousand years, one could readily see why the Himalayas have been called "incomparable." Since times immemorial innumerable tokens of divinity have been connected with this country of mountains. Even in the dark middle ages, remote countries dreamed of beautiful India, which was epitomized in the imagination of people by the mysterious sacred snowy giants.

Let us mentally compare all these beautiful legends, which could only be conceived in the Himalayas. First of all, we will be astonished at the amazing diversity of this heritage. It is true that this wealth of legends has originated in the accumulations of many tribes, becoming more bounteous through the grateful contributions of many millenniums, and is crowned by the achievements of great seekers after truth. All this is so. But for such supreme achievements a magnificent environ is necessary, and what could be more majestic than the unconquered mountains with all their inexpressible radiance and all their exquisite variations of forms.

It would be a rather unfortunate and feeble effort to compare the Himalayas with any of the other splendid mountain ranges of the world. The Andes, the Caucasus, the Alps, the Altai—all the most beautiful heights will appear to be but single peaks when compared with the supreme mountain ranges of the Himalayas.

What does it not encompass, this multiform Beauty? Tropical approaches, Alpine slopes and, finally, all the incalculable glaciers, powdered with meteoric dust. No one describes the Himalayas as overwhelming; no one would dare to call them gloomy portals, nor mention the word monotony, in thinking of the Himalayas. Truly, a great part of the human vocabulary must be forgotten when you enter the realm of the Himalayan Snow—the part of one's vocabulary comprising its sinister and effete expressions.

The human spirit, seeking to overcome all obstacles, is filled with a yearning, which irresistibly impels one onward toward the conquest of these summits. And the very difficulties that at times loom so dangerously become only the most necessary and the most desired steps of ascent, overcoming earthly conventionality. All the dangerous bamboo bridges over the thundering mountain torrents; all the slippery steps on the age-old glaciers over perilous precipices; all the unavoidable inclines before each successive ascent; and the storms, thunder and cold and heat are surmounted when the chalice of achievement is full.

Not the feelings of ambition nor boastfulness alone could inspire so many travelers and searchers to go to the Himalayas. Other difficult peaks could be found for competition and contests. But, above all, thoughts of competition and contests is a yearning toward these world magnets, an ineffable holy aspiration of which heroes are born.

The true magnets are not competitive laurels of contests nor the fleeting front pages of books and newspapers, but the attraction to this surpassing grandeur which sustains the spirit; and in such striving there can be no harm.

"Is this another tribute to the Himalayas?" One may ask.

But does the solemn grandeur of the Himalayas need any tributes?

Of course, in this case tributes are out of place; and any of them, even the most excellent, can be but feeble echoes. But then, why does one think of the Himalayas? Why are we seemingly compelled to think of them, remember them, and strive toward them?

Because even mental communion with their solemn grandeur provides one of the best tonics. Everything is impelled toward the beautiful in its own way. Everyone thinks about beauty, and he will feel an impulse to say something or other about it. The thought of Beauty is so powerful and moving, that man cannot contain it silently within himself, but always tries to clothe it in words. Perhaps in song or in some other expression of his being, man must manifest and record his thought of the Beautiful.

From the tiniest flower, from the wing of the butterfly, from the glow of a crystal and on, further and higher, through beautiful human forms, through the mysterious sublime touch, man wants to fortify himself by the immutably Beautiful. Wherever on earth there have been beautiful creations of human hands, the pilgrim will come to them. He will find calm under their created vaults and in the radiance of their frescoes and stained glass. And if the pilgrim is captivated by mirages of nature's far- off horizons, he will set out toward them. And if, at last, he becomes aware of these loftiest peaks shining far off, he will be drawn to them, and in this very striving he will become stronger, purer, and will be inspired to achievements for the good, for beauty, and for ascent.

The pilgrim is always listened to with special attention near the campfire or at a gathering of men. And not only in ancient chronicles does one read of the respect accorded to those who came from afar. Even now, despite all the speedy ways of communication, when the world has already become small, when people strive into higher strata or down toward the center of the planet, even now, the narrative of the pilgrim still remains the highlight of every gathering.

"Are the Himalayas truly so beautiful?"

"Are they really incomparable?"

"Tell us something about the Himalayas and whether anything unusual is to be found there!"

People expect something unusual in every narrative of a pilgrim. Customs, habits, immovability due to attachments depress even the coarsest heart. Even a depressed spirit strives toward movement. After all, no one thinks of movement as directed downward only.

I recall the story that a traveler once related having begun the descent of the Grand Canyon in Arizona: surrounded by most beautiful colors, he was oppressed by the very thought of such endless descent: "We descended lower and lower, and this thought of descending even prevented our admitting the country."

Of course, exaltation and transport is primarily connected with ascent. During ascent there is the urgent desire to look beyond the snow peaks that soar before you. But when you descend, each parting summit pronounces a sad "goodbye." Therefore, it is so joyous not only to ascend a summit, but at least to follow the ways of ascent in thought. When we hear of new travelers to the Himalayas, we are thankful even for that, for they remind us of the summits of the call ever beautiful and ever necessary.

Himalayas, let me send once more my heartfelt admiration!

Likewise, India, all beautiful, let me send thee another greeting for all the greatness and inspiration, which fill thy meadows, thy ancient cities and sacred rivers!

THE NEW LIFE MOVEMENT

LAST year, General Chiang Kai-shek, the "Father of the Movement," defined the essential principles of this new life. In the introduction to his pamphlet, a parallel is drawn between this movement and the movement of the Oxford Group. Of course, there is very little similarity between the foundations of these two movements. The movement headed by Chiang Kai-shek has a great application to modern life, not for China only but in general.

We have already mentioned that, at present, curious combinations of remote antiquity with ultramodern assertions take place. Likewise, into the foundations of this new movement of the leader of China were laid the most ancient and most noble principles of *Li, Yi, Lien,* and *Chih,* that is to say: polite manners; chivalrous, courageous conduct; honesty and decency and thoroughness of action.

It is very significant that into the foundations of new reforms and achievements are being laid principles inherited in far antiquity. Probably for many superficially modern people, all these principles will appear as abstractions, strange from the lips of a statesman. But to us the appeal to the eternal living ethics is very close. For on unshakable eternal foundations of ethics can also be built the present real success and prosperity of nations. Sobriety, discipline, self-consciousness, the understanding of duties, the striving toward constructiveness will be built not upon negative formulae, destroying the entire past, but precisely on the affirmation of immutable foundations.

The hieroglyph *Li* will remind one of good conduct in life, of true discipline, mutual esteem, and those good family customs from which grows healthy statesmanship. The hieroglyph *Yi* points to the immutability of honor, heroism, and valor, without which human relations are impossible. *Lien* denotes honesty and affirms the language of the heart, the just judgment of which is born by purity of thought, and *Chih* stands as the sign of a conscientious mode of action—in other words, the beautiful art of thinking, without which people invariably return to savagery.

These eternal foundations of existence are recalled in a simple manner. Panhuman is the thinking that can understand them in full reciprocity. There is no abstraction in the construction of life with such calling reminders.

Chiang Kai-shek recalls the five thousand years of Chinese culture and also justly points out that in view of the negligence toward the mentioned foundations, contemporary life has retrograded far from those possibilities that once had existed in the world.

China has thirty-five million square *li* of territory and abounds in natural resources, which if developed could easily make this country one of the wealthiest nations of the world. Yet there is widespread poverty and misery in the land. This again is due to the neglect of the traditional virtues of China, namely *Li*, *Yi*, *Lien*, and *Chih*.

China has 400 million people who used to be well organized in all the essentials of life. But what spectacle do our people present to the rest of the world today? They are disorganized, indolent, cowardly, and torn between conflicting perverse teachings, leading a life little better than that of savages. This again is due to the neglect of *Li*, *Yi*, *Lien*, and *Chih*.

To sum up, the New Life Movement aims at the substitution of a rational mode of living for the present irrational mode of living of the people. How can this be effected? My answer is: by making *Li*, *Yi*, *Lien*, and *Chih* the code of our daily conduct.

In advocating the revival of our traditional virtues such as *Li*, *Yi*, *Lien*, and *Chih*, the object in view is an artistic mode of living for all of our people. Many are apt to think that only a few privileged persons can lead an artistic life. This is a mistake. It is within the reach of all. Every Chinese person should have a decent standard of living, which is another term for an artistic mode of living.

In ancient times China used to have the so-called six arts and sciences: rites, music, archery, horsemanship, calligraphy, and mathematics. These things today have made the Western powers great and strong, although for centuries the Chinese people used them as guiding principles of action in life. The reason why there is so much suspicion, jealousy, and animosity in Chinese society today is that we have forgotten the teachings of our ancients. There is no hope of improvement unless we order our lives in accordance with the principles of *Li*, *Yi*, *Lien*, and *Chih*.

The poverty of China is due to the existence of so many people who cannot produce anything of their own and who live off others. The productivity of the people must be increased. We must develop our immense natural resources and avoid waste. Every one should consider it a shame to depend upon others for his support. In other words, every one must work for his own living. There is no way to relieve the poverty of China and remove the source of civil strife other than to practice the principles of *Li*, *Yi*, *Lien*, and *Chih* in our daily lives.

In advocating *Li*, *Yi*, *Lien*, and *Chih* as the code of our daily conduct, we are inspired by the desire to "discipline" the life of our people. When a nation cannot fight for the defense of its soil against foreign invasion, it cannot be considered a nation. We must cultivate stern measures if we are to overcome the present weakness of our country. China today is overrun by Communist bandits. Civil war has not yet been completely banished from the land. Our national territory is growing smaller and smaller every day. Imperialists join with traitors and communists in oppressing our people and undermining our country. If we wish to deliver China from the present crisis and bring peace and order to the land, we must prepare to "discipline" the whole country. Before this is possible, the people must be trained in the habits of orderliness, discipline, cleanliness, simplicity, and accurate thinking. They must be law-abiding, conscious of their responsibility, and ready to die for the country.

A rational mode of living is realized when the principles of *Li, Yi, Lien,* and *Chih* are applied to the daily conduct of the people, especially in matters pertaining to food, shelter, clothing, and deportment. A great revolution will have been effected and the foundations of a new national structure laid when every Chinese person lives in accordance with the principles of the New Life Movement, which are based on the traditional virtues of *Li, Yi, Lien,* and *Chih.*

Thus it was affirmed on March 1 of last year by General Chiang Kai-shek in Nanchang. The appeal of the head of the government found response throughout the country. Social organizations, private enterprises, provincial departments, municipalities and various administrations immediately decided to join this movement. One of the earliest organizations had already been formed at Nanking on the sixteenth of March. At the opening ceremony, a significant speech was delivered by Mr. Wang Jingwei, followed by a series of friendly demonstrations on the part of workers, students, and trade unions. In his speech Mr. Wang declared that the movement of New Life is the vital spark of the regeneration of the Chinese nation, and called for a sincere support of all responsible organizations and also of all social leaders. He insisted that this movement must be systematically spread and organized. And it was accepted by everyone for immediate application.

If the principle of living ethics were applied in many parts of the world, then the movement of the new life would quite naturally rejuvenate the quests of our days. Finally, whatever name we attribute to these searchings, they will invariably lead to the approaches to the same permanent values. No matter how people try to revaluate the immutable, it will make itself known imperatively and undeviatingly.

It is said that revaluations take place thrice every century—or so it is thought. Probably this term is meant to represent the change of generations. Within normal conditions, such a periodicity of waves of life is rather accurate. It is instructive to follow how the history of ethics and culture, under different names and with various hidden and open approaches, mentions the same Immutable, Eternal.

"Know that to be indestructible, by whom all this is pervaded. Nor can any work the destruction of that imperishable One." Whether we will speak in terms of this or another age, whether we use the expression of wisdom of one or another nation, the theme will be one and the same—of the Eternal, Indestructible, and Immeasurable.

"Ever remaining the same, unperturbed by success and failure, perform thy duties in union with the Divine."

And again on that same memorable field of Kurukshetra!

BEYOND THE GREAT WALL

ON the way with his disciples, Confucius saw a woman weeping near some graves, and he asked the cause of her grief. "Woe," replied the woman. "My father-in-law was killed here by a tiger, then my husband, and now my son has also perished from the same death."

"But why do you not migrate from here?"

"The local government is not a cruel one."

"Here, you see," exclaimed the teacher, "Remember that a bad government is worse than a tiger."

"What are the fundamentals of good government? Honor and respect five excellent principles; expel four abominable ones. A wise and good ruler is virtuous without profligacy; he imposes obligations without driving his people to complaint; his wishes are not covetous; he is exalted without pridefulness; he is inspiring and not violent. The abominations are: cruelty, keeping the people in ignorance, and punishing with death. Oppression, requiring immediate fulfillment of matters not previously explained. Absurdity, giving obscure commands but requiring their precise execution. Impeding production by stinginess in properly rewarding deserving people."

"To cognize and to apply in life what has been studied—can this fail to be true enjoyment? The arrival of a friend from a far country—can this be other than true joy?"

"A man without compassion in his heart—what does he have in common with music?"

"He who is noble does not wander from the path of virtue for a single moment. In stormy times and in hours of tension, he hastens along the same path."

"The man of knowledge rejoices at the sea, the man of virtue rejoices at the mountains because restless is the man of knowledge and tranquil is the man of virtue."

"The man who is spiritually virtuous, who wishes to become steadfast, also evokes steadfastness in those around him. Wishing to become enlightened, he is interested in the enlightenment of those near him in order to make others that which he desires for himself."

"Sincerity and truth form a desire for culture."

"A noble man brings out the best qualities of others and does not emphasize the bad ones. A low man acts in opposite fashion."

"In thy private life, exhibit self-respect; in business, be attentive and solicitous; in actions with others, be honest and conscious. Never, even among savages, depart from these principles."

"A noble man is drawn upward, an inferior one rushes downward."

"A noble man knows neither grief nor fear. The absence of grief and fear—in this is the sign of nobility! If in his heart he finds no guilt, for what should he grieve? Of what should he be afraid?"

"Make awareness and truth thy guiding principles, and thus go to produce obligations about thy neighbor. This is lofty virtue."

"The meaning of good-heartedness is in this: do not to others what you do not wish for yourself."

"The noble man is concerned with nine principles: to see clearly; to hear clearly; to have an amicable outlook; to care for inferiors; to be aware in speech; to be honest in dealings; in doubt, to be cautious; in anger, to think about conscquences; in opportunities for success, to think only about obligations."

"Spiritual virtue is contained in five qualities: self-respect, magnanimity, sincerity, honesty, and benevolence. Exhibit self-respect, and others will respect you. Be magnanimous, and you will open all hearts. Be sincere, and people will trust you. Be honest, and you will attain the great. Be benevolent, and thus you will communicate goodwill to others."

The noble man first esteems uprightness, then courage. A brave man without uprightness is a menace to the state."

"Answer injustice with justice and good with good."

"The principle of good-heartedness makes a place attractive for living."

"The nobleman has neither narrow prejudices nor stubborn hostility. He proceeds by the path of Service."

"The noble man is assiduous in perceiving the path of Service, while the inferior one, only in the making of money."

"The wise man speaks slowly but acts quickly."

"All people are born good."

"The meaning of lofty virtue: conducting yourself in life as if about to meet an exalted guest, governing a nation, being guided as upon a solemn sacred service. What you do not wish for yourself, do not cause others. Both toward people and in the home do not express ill will."

"Whoever sins against heaven cannot expect its intercession."

"We can only go out of a house through the door. Why not pass through life through the gates of virtue?"

"Is virtue far distant? Only show a desire for it, and it is already here."

"He whose mind has already been tested against the slowly penetrating poison of slander and the sharp arrows of denunciations can be called clear-seeing and farseeing."

"Leading unprepared people into battle is the same as throwing them away."

"If a man is everywhere hated or everywhere beloved, the closest observation is necessary."

"Your good-natured people are the thieves of virtue."

"At fifteen years, my mind was bent upon teaching. At thirty years, I stood on firm ground. At forty years, I was free from disillusionment. At fifty years, I understood the laws of Providence. At sixty years, my ears hearkened to truth. At seventy years, I could follow the dictates of my heart."

Thus cognition, liberation, understanding of the laws, attention to Truth—all led to following the commands of the heart. This briefest yet fullest biography ends with a heartfelt prayer about the righteous paths. And the great philosopher did not bewail the fact that his carriage was kept harnessed. The bridled horses, ready to drive swiftly to the paths of the heart, were already a blessing. Not to any great houses had to go the carriage, which was not one of exile but of attainment.

The lordly liberation from grief and fear, the power of Tao, paved a firm path. "The throneless prince"—thus was Confucius called. Did he not in his carriage travel along the great wall in unrelieved vigil? Do not his horses follow the tracks of the white steeds of the great wall? Who saw him? Who followed the ascents and descents? His believing heart, behind the white horse, passed over cliffs and mountains. Let us not predetermine the course of the white horse.

To all of his paths, Confucius could add still one more conclusion. All enemies who pursued him were evil people and abominable. Their names have been lost or have remained on a black page in history. This means that in this connection his righteousness was both affirmed and glorified by history.

Recently we have learned that "the work of restoring the Mausoleum in Chufu has been discussed by the Shantung authorities."

"Extensive works for the restoration of the Mausoleum of Confucius in Chufu, Shantung, were decided upon at a session in the presence of representatives of the Nanking government.

The provincial powers, besides cooperating in restoring the Mausoleum of Confucius, which for many years has remained in neglect, have also selected a committee for instituting a Day of Confucius throughout all China. It is learned that the Central Government will render special honors to a descendent of the great sage."

Again a victory of Confucius! The day consecrated to him will be a day of culture.

It is strange to read this news, where so sadly yet casually is spoken about the fact that the Mausoleum of Confucius has been left in neglect over a period of many years. Precisely what agitations and vicissitudes compelled the people to forget even about the greatest pride of China! But then this forgetfulness is only one-sided. It may be the Mausoleum was forgotten, but the memory and covenants of Confucius continued to live; for China without Buddha, Lao-tse, and Confucius will no longer be China.

Whatever new cognitions may enter into life, for all that the bases of the ancient wisdom remain immovable.

The Mongols may come to recognize many new things, but the name of Genghis Khan and his precepts will live in the hearts of the people, and the very name is uttered with particular reverence. Likewise, precisely as we have sometimes written about the sonority of nations, so, too, memorable names and places will all live.

Indeed, it must be assumed that the Mausoleum of Confucius cannot again be allowed to fall into neglect because in its development the country will more profoundly and loftily preserve forever the living covenants of the sage. And in reality, whatever of the above-mentioned covenants we remember, it will, similarly, concern our time also.

Only very backward minds will not understand the difference between the outlived and the eternal. Granted that up to now the best commandments are not being fulfilled—this does not mean that they did not have to be given and now reiterated. What is simpler? "Do not kill," "Do not lie," "Do not steal," yet each day these imperative Covenants are not obeyed. What then? to abandon them as inapplicable or to continue to stand by them? to fall into savagery or to persistently swim out on the crest of the wave? In the precepts of Confucius, there is no hopeless condemnation. How near to life are all the good admonitions spoken by him! If he abandons something, it is only for the purpose of drawing out something better and more useful. Occasionally, the precepts of Confucius have been considered unjustly, and a meaning has been attributed to them that obviously had nothing to do with their contents. This means that someone had taken up examining his covenants with a certain prejudice.

But in studying a great man, any prejudice or exaggeration is decidedly out of place. Let there be taken into consideration his actions and words in their full significance. Indeed, speaking about the ultimate meaning, we ought not to forget that in all languages, and especially in Chinese and Sanskrit, are untranslatable expressions that may be understood and expounded only by becoming fully familiar both with the language and with the essentials of the local life. How many misfortunes have arisen out of translations, out of interpretations!

All evil interpretations and intentional perversions, of course, must be judged as deliberate offenses against another's property. Sometimes these willful distortions are equivalent to an attempt at murder. From the biography of Confucius, it is not at all evident that he lapsed into despair or fear. The fact that he was obliged to keep his carriage harnessed signifies merely his foresightedness for the greater usefulness of future actions.

"I already, long ago, began to pray"—thus replied Confucius on one important occasion. Repeatedly in biographies of Confucius, the expression is used that his life was unceasing prayer. In triumph, he swam the ocean. That is why, turning to the Great Wall, we again recall Confucius as a sign of China. We are convinced that the proposed day of Confucius will result in an actual triumph of culture.

LEAVES OF CHINA

IN Shantiniketan a Chinese hall was recently opened that was dedicated to Sino-Indian friendship. Rabindranath Tagore indeed builds way-signs on the noblest paths. Remembering China, first of all there always comes to mind the Chinese wisdom embodied in the Teachings of Lao-Tse and Confucius. One remembers the grandeur of the Great Wall and innumerable ancient Temples. But at the moment, I want to recall not antiquity but the beautiful achievements of modern China, when, despite the difficult times, there are being created excellent cultural centers. I want to dedicate this leaf to the Fan Memorial in Peking. May this diary leaf remind one of the leaves of botany.

Confucius enjoined his followers "to study as much as possible all birds, animals, plants, and trees."

In Peking, not far from the picturesque north lake where towers a beautiful white *suburgan* on a hill, alongside the Peking Library, there can be seen the new and spacious building of the institute in memory of Fan, a Chinese leader who repeatedly occupied ministerial posts and was a patron of the sciences. Fan was always highly interested in natural history and organized a Museum of Natural History in Peking. It is written that he took an interest in the fate of this institution even during his illness. Therefore, the Society of Chang-Shi and the China Foundation have named the institute in memory of this great Chinese savant. The institute has been in existence since 1928, and since this time there have been some very important works carried on in it. Primarily, the institute has devoted its occupations to Chinese flora and fauna. At the formation of the institute, it had the comparatively modest annual budget of $30,000 Mexican dollars and was lodged at first in the old residence of Fan himself. Doctor Ping was named the first director, [along] with one professor, two assistant professors, two assistants, and one artist. At present its budget has grown to $66,000 local dollars; besides the director and professor, there have entered into the staff of the Institute five assistant professors, twelve assistants, three artists, and two taxidermists.

The institute proposes, through its fellows, to carry on the work of establishing a national herbarium and to concentrate especially on the flora and fauna of the Hupeh province. Besides this province, botanical and zoological collections are being made in Szechuan, Yunnan, Kwantung, and other localities. The herbarium already contains more than 38,500 items, not counting the many necessary duplicates. In the technological laboratory, there are more than 3,000 dendrological forms, of which 1,826 belong to China. In the zoological section are more than 105,000 items. In addition, in the botanical section there is a collection of more than 17,000 photographs of plants.

The publications of the institute are contained in four series of bulletins of the institute—Chinese plants, Chinese fauna, and Chinese shrubs. In addition, there is printed a series of popular reference books in the Chinese language. The institute works in closest cooperation with the Kiangsi Provincial Agricultural Institute and with the botanical garden of Kuling. This botanical garden looks after the raising of an enormous number of Chinese plants of economic value, in order to cultivate for domestic use a large number of important Chinese flowers that are highly esteemed abroad but comparatively little cultivated in China itself.

This garden pays much attention to the planting of trees in order to promote, in this direction, the forestation of Southeastern China. There likewise enters into this work the crossbreeding of Chinese flowers—which is an enormous field for investigation with large economic significance.

Thus, there enters into the immediate program of the Fan Institute: (1) to collect the richest herbarium of China, devoted principally to the most important provinces; (2) to carry out the fullest investigation of Chinese dendrology, publishing illustrated books on the trees of China; (3) to make the Lishan botanical garden a center of dendrological studies in China; (4) to enrich the collection of birds, fish, and mollusks; (5) to investigate the biology of sea and fresh waters, and to promote fisheries.

The Fan Institute, in its brief six-year existence, with its small budget and the few members of its scientific staff cannot, of course, be compared with such well-established institutions as, for example, the Royal Botanical Garden at Kew near London or the Biological Bureau in America; but it is a pleasure to see that within the few years of its existence, the Fan Institute represents in itself an already large, nationally founded institution with all the elements for rapid and vigorous development.

Each institution primarily expresses in itself the ability and enthusiasm of its leader. "As is the shepherd, so is the flock." In this respect the Fan Institute has been fortunate in having as its director Hsen-Su-Khu, an outstanding Chinese scholar, who brings to the institution that genuine patriotism that is manifested as a true pledge of success.

In the *Natural History Bulletin*, Doctor Hsen-Su-Khu, writes: "Living in a country that is rich in flora and fauna, we Chinese are born as innate naturalists; our forefathers, long before Confucius, had already studied and put into use the vegetation and animals of our country. Besides the legendary sage, the Emperor Shen Nung, the father of the Chinese Pharmacopoeia, who in his extraordinary talents tested a hundred remedies, we find among the thirteen classics of the pre-Confucian vocabulary "Erkh-la" a great number of names of plants and animals written down and explained. Confucius himself enjoined his followers "to study as much as possible the kinds of birds, animals, plants, and trees." The great lexicographer Khan-Shu

Shen, in his great dictionary, *Svekh-Ven*, included many names of plants and animals. The first herbal, "Fen-Tzao," refers to the Tao-Khun-Chin—the Taoist scholarly dynasty of Qin. Since that time, many editions of herbals have been written, together with treatises on the mountain peonies, oranges, teas, and the plants and trees of South China, including funguses and mosses. The great research worker on plants in the Ming dynasty, Li-Shi-Tzin, went over the old herbals and compiled from them his famous book, *Pen-Tzao-Khung—Mu*. Finally, the scholarly statesman, the governor Bu-Chin-Chun, living in the early period of the Manchu dynasty, completed his great work, *Chi-Bu-Ming-Shikh-Tu-Kogo*, the first purely botanical treatise, in which he described several thousand kinds of plants, accompanied by many finely executed illustrations. These illustrations were so beautifully done that many of them can be fully used for the identification of species, even in the case of such technically difficult types as orchids. Thus, thanks to the assiduous labors of our illustrious forefathers, we Chinese are more amply provided with botanical sources than any other people in the entire world."

"The progress of the botanical sciences in China, being based on the brilliant attainments of our ancestors, inspires bright hopes. As you know, biological science as understood at present has only recently been established in China. Botanical researches even up to fifteen years ago were almost unknown. But now we have twenty-three universities and higher schools throughout China, both governmental and private. Each of them has a biological department with trained personnel, adequate budget, and completely equipped laboratories. In addition, there are six institutes for investigations in which the study of botany is excellently conducted." Then follows a description of the problems and attainments of the previously mentioned scientific institutions, in which you see a genuine optimism based on the contemporary patriotic feelings being manifested in present day China. At the end of the report, the author tells about the botanical society organized last year. In the society, some seventy experienced botanists participate who are well known for their investigations in various branches of this science. A popular journal is to be published. In each issue of the journal, there is proposed a botanical-horticultural article to acquaint the readers with the priceless treasure of the beautiful ornamental plants of China, so highly esteemed everywhere, yet, strange to say, so little cultivated by the Chinese themselves. The activity of this society ought to propagate botanical information between amateurs of this subject throughout the country.

"Looking at the latest progress of botany in the country, I rejoice at the excellent progress of the attainments of professors of this science; to a certain extent, I am dissatisfied with the comparatively small cooperation of the amateurs. We must understand that in Europe progress in the botanical and zoological sciences is supported to a noteworthy degree by the endeavors of amateurs."

"Chinese scholars are celebrated for their researches in archaeology; indeed, they can also attain as much in natural history if their hearts turn to it. I believe that the progress of the botanical and zoological sciences in this country will be incomparably more rapid if it is not solely supported by the professors of biology."

One must fully agree with the conclusions of the venerable author. Science must indeed invite all amateurs into its reserved fields of science. Precisely, love and hearty solicitude create those brilliant sanctuaries that move future generations along the path of culture. The deduction of the true scholar shows how much one can rejoice at the latest strivings of the Chinese societies. In place of a cold seclusion, we see in his words a broad, benevolent summons to cooperation. It is pleasing to see how the ancient temples and the beautiful, most refined structures of creativeness are not torn away as something remote but serve as the basis of a new and living cooperation.

THE PREDESTINED MOUNTAIN

ACERTAIN peasant in Shansi (China) was feeling very unhappy. From his father he had inherited a plot of land that was entirely unfertile. Most of it consisted of such a stony hill that even unpretentious sheep could not find any grass on it.

It is true, the grandfather used to say that this plot was exceptionally good. The peasant sighed. "But who can trust an old man who believes so many queer stories?"

If the earth were indeed good, the family who owned it would not now be in complete poverty. And yet the peasant was, by no means, a lazy fellow and applied all of his labor to procure for his family at least a little comfort. But these cursed stones! This naked, stony mountain! How could it bring anyone a living? "There is nothing to bite off a stone." Thus, the poor peasant complained and dreamed how he might get rid of this miserable place.

One day the peasant was visited by a relative who went to see the ill-considered hill. Amid the stones something glittered like silver. He took a piece and had it analyzed. Further exploration showed that the so-called "cursed hill" was a mountain of silver and represented a fabulous fortune. Thus, precisely the very spot that the whole family considered the source of all misfortune turned out to be the source of huge wealth. Often people thus regard as their ill luck that which will bring to them the highest success and fortune.

Do not think that I have told you a parable of the time of Confucius. The above episode had just taken place in Shansi! How often people, with all of their strength, reject the fortune knocking at their door. This happens not only in the lives of individuals but even of entire nations. If we ask our acquaintances whether in the past things they rejected that afterward would have been beneficial, many would have to confess that often they had not paid attention to something most important and near.

Not only was the most valuable neglected, but it was even ridiculed and insulted and considered useless.

One of the excellent thinkers of India, Swami Rama Tirtha, has said, "Hidebound are the civilized nations: they separate themselves from fellow beings and exile themselves from free, open nature and fresh, fragrant natural life into close drawing-rooms—dens and dungeons. By arrogating to themselves airs of superiority, prestige, respectability, honor, they bring themselves to stagnation." And beautifully it was proclaimed by the Western poet Wordsworth:

"The world is too much with us; late and soon,
Getting and spending, we lay waste our powers:
Little do we see in Nature that is ours."

Precisely—what is already ours, already predestined, already given.

ANCIENT MEDICINES

D R. Bernard Read does highly beneficial work. From yellowish, forgotten, and often ridiculed records of ancient Chinese pharmacopoeia, he rediscovers for the scientific world many considerations, which attract the attention of contemporary knowledge. For us, the works of this scientist are especially valuable. We have often stressed the necessity of studying ancient pharmacopoeias, and various popular home medicines, amid which one can no doubt find results of experiments of many ages.

Because of such affirmations we have often been scoffed at. Certain scientists of today fear that they may be considered out of date, and may thus lose a leaf from their laurel of modernism. I was recently accused that my considerations may support old-fashioned scientists instead of refuting together with modernists everything that was accomplished before. And I had to explain that we never asserted that everything contained in ancient pharmacopoeias is fully good and useful. We only affirmed that ancient pharmacopoeias should be studied, as one more source useful for certain conclusions of excellent scientists of today.

Of Dr. Bernard Read's researches we have heard long ago. Our friend, the Hon. Charles Crane, had some years ago recommended this excellent scientist for cooperation with our institutions, and this took place. And now we follow with increasing interest how even the newspapers dedicate entire columns to the researches of Dr. Read. It sounds paradoxical: the most modern achievements based upon the most ancient sources! And yet it cannot be expressed otherwise, because Dr. Read, through the knowledge of ancient sources, confirms the most modern discoveries of contemporary science. For a historian these strictly scientific deductions are most instructive, since through them it is affirmed once more how carefully one should approach the past of human life, in which so many observations had already been manifested. In such cases we have to deal not only with civilization but with culture in its entire originality.

It may seem to many that the healing use made of donkey skin, sheep's eyes, deer's horn, dog's brain, odd herbs, etc., all interwoven as they are in folklore, is just so much empty Chinese superstition, and that it is unfortunate that such great faith is placed in such absurd remedies.

However, an extensive survey now being undertaken by Dr. Bernard Read, Head of the Division of Physiological Science, and his associates at the Henry Lester Institute of Medical Research may greatly diminish popular skepticism.

It is the attitude of the Lester Institute that before today's medical science of the Western world can be imposed on the Chinese people, due regard must be given to the empirical observations, which form the basis of the old Chinese medical practice.

Reason has suggested that when certain therapeutic practices have been in constant use for a great many centuries not only in China but in India, and with no apparent relationship to the still more ancient civilizations, as revealed in old manuscripts, it becomes evident that some real benefit is derived.

The work of Dr. Read with his associates and staff is to put such empirical practices upon a rational basis by employing the highly technical skill of modern workers and a more fundamental knowledge of the principles involved to evaluate them by new standards, which emphasize in proper balances, deficiencies and faulty assimilation, and thereby to find fresh avenues for research, which may yield results of value in modern medicine.

Dr. Read has been working in this field for thirty years in China and has been rewarded by his success in chaulmoogra oil and ephedrine—first produced in his laboratories in Peking—among his other important contributions to medical science. Now working under the excellent facilities of the Lester Institute in Shanghai, where he came two years ago to head the divisions of physiological science, more valuable data on the Chinese Materia Medica are being contributed to modern medicine. There is now in progress an investigation into the chemical composition and vitamin contents of a tremendous variety of local Chinese drugs and foods.

The phenomenally widespread use in China of boiled-down donkey skin, called *Ah-Chiao*, as a blood regenerator and internal styptic, and a general nutritive for weak people, especially those suffering from tuberculosis, has led to an investigation into its particular character both chemical and physiological. Dr. T. G. Ni finds that it contains a large amount of glycine, cystine, lysine, argenine, and hystidine. Administered orally it improves the calcium and nitrogen absorption, and raises the calcium level of the blood. This Ah-Chiao used intravenously was found to be effective in restoring a depressed circulation after hemorrhage and shock. Further work is proceeding on its beneficial effects in muscular atrophy. In Hangchow last year, there was a quarter of a million dollars' trade of donkey skin in one store alone.

It has been shown by dietary surveys that large numbers of people live on deficient diets such as may lead to latent or subacute scurvy. In old medical practice, such symptoms as weakness of the knees and general lassitude were treated with numerous remedies that for their action may depend upon the presence of vitamin C. Hence, 120 Chinese foods and drugs purchased in Shanghai markets, as they appeared for sale in ripe condition, and also collected in the country close to Shanghai, have been subjected to a chemical study with a view to ascertaining the vitamin C content. The results are given in value of Pumels report written by Yuoh-Fong-Ghi and Dr. Read.

Among the citrus fruits, pomelo was found to have the highest vitamin C content, being superior to grapefruit and all of the various types of oranges. Many sorts of leaves that are eaten regularly and used medicinally, such as dandelion, mulberry, nasturtium, poplar, shepherd's purse, and amaranth, yielded interesting data. Green amaranth, little known by foreigners, grows in great profusion in the country, and has been found to have a very high vitamin C content and to be superior to spinach in its content of iron and calcium. The high vitamin content of willow and poplar leaves and shepherd's purse suggests good reason for their use in ancient medicine.

Dr. Read states that ancient medicine in China needs considerable clarification before forward or backward-looking people are able to estimate its true worth. As a historical record, it is of worth to the anthropologist, the naturalist, and the physiologist. Dissected from outside influences, it has a vast amount of honest observation of Chinese fauna and flora, their habitat, preparation, and uses as foods and remedies in treatment of disease, suggesting important paths of research.

In China's great classic, the Pen T'sao Kang Mu', common foodstuffs include such extremely toxic seeds as the bastard anise and poisonous terodent fish, and drugs include oranges, gelatin, and licorice. Thus, for practical purposes, no distinction need be made between foods and drugs. The voluminous old Chinese medical literature embraces the whole field of Chinese natural history, a remarkable record of observations for thousands of years.

Dr. Read feels that, apart from its applied value, Chinese medicine needs a more intelligent and sympathetic understanding on the part of modern medicine. It is universally believed in. There is need in Asia for a widespread application of scientific methods to enable people to evaluate ancient medicine at its true worth, and to heighten appreciation of modern ideas in medicine in all of its relationships.

"It is of interest to note [states Dr. Bernard Read in his report on "The Newer Pharmacology and Ancient Medicine"] that the modern medicine of the British Pharmacopoeia only included nine substances of animal origin, and of those, nearly all were quite innocuous things like lard and wax. While modern science is turning to liver, stomach, vitamin A from the eye, adrenalin, etc., it is remarkable to find the use of so many animal tissues in ancient medicine."

In this report Dr. Read presents a table showing twenty-six parts of six domestic animals used in old Chinese medicine. These animals include the cow, horse, pig, chicken, sheep, and dog.

When bitten by a mad dog, the brain of the same animal is applied to the wound. This suggests a connection with modern Pasteur treatment and is worthy of investigation.

The velvet horn of the Skia deer and other species is taken as a drug in powder form and is very highly regarded by the Chinese. Recent studies by Russian scientists show that the male sex hormone is present.

The iris and the lens of the sheep's eyes were given for dimness of vision and conjunctivitis. The eyes of the hawk, parrot, and mackerel were administered for blindness. Recently Wald has isolated vitamin A from the iris of sheep, pigs, cattle, and frogs.

In old Chinese medicine pig's liver was recommended for blindness, beriberi, constipation, etc., and has fairly recently been found to be rich in vitamin A, B, C, D, and E. A great many instances of this sort are cited. Shepherd's purse is given as an excellent example of a medicinal herb cast aside for its apparent lack of potent principles, which has been shown to be moderately rich in three of the vitamins, and well justifies the old Chinese use of it for a number of maladies.

Native remedies claiming to have a power to increase human fertility are often associated with magical ideas, but

Dr. Read believes that in view of the increasing volume of recent scientific work in this field, there is hope that information may be forthcoming whereby these claims can be properly evaluated.

Some people suffer from a deficiency of iodine. Many centuries ago in China, seaweeds were used in the treatment of goiter. It is now believed that these old remedies were often quite efficacious.

Dr. Read says that further extensive reference might be made to a host of other remedies, but that enough has been cited to show that science may progress by looking backward as well as forward; that probably the most suggestive path of progress may be gained by studying the records of old empirical medicine; that the scientists need, more than any other, to keep an open mind regarding the claims of ancient medicine, so that with the aid of modern knowledge and modern technique, an unprejudiced study may be made of the customs of our forefathers, who were engaged in the same life and death struggle against disease.

In China there have been preserved, for something between thirty and fifty centuries, remarkably accurate records of human experience in the field of medicine. These records are not accumulations of divine intuitions but empirical findings which up to the present have only been sifted with the very coarse sieve of last century science.

Thus without destroying anything, without unjust scoffing, one may find new useful possibilities, accessible to all. Dr. Read's experience of many years but confirms that when scientists go along the path of honest goodwill, they discover much of that which would remain concealed to the evil-doubting eye. Honest investigation and self-conceited skepticism are two entirely opposite things, and the way of suspicious disbelief is obscure and crooked.

In all ancient records one can find remedies that merit thorough investigation. The particles of Truth remain everywhere indisputable. Sometimes the formulae of ancient wisdom remain enigmatic for the superficial student—but yet truth remains truth when these hieroglyphs are studied without prejudice.

The path of negation is always branded as the path of ignorance. The latest discoveries but confirm the continuity of human thought through all ages. The obscure formulae often were due to the peculiarity of the language or to a deliberate desire to retain, but in certain hands, the precious knowledge. Such caution should not be condemned, for "one should not throw pearls before swine." This ordainment has been repeated in many different ways. "There is no prophet in his own country"—this sad truth also was given for the benefit of future humanity not without deep reason.

There will come a time when ignorant, self-conceited negation, in all walks of life, will be replaced by a radiant unprejudiced research. One should especially rejoice at every benevolent study—in it is contained true goodwill.

Guru Charaka,* the great Ayurvedist, still wanders along the blossoming Himalayan uplands. Wisdom knows in its straight-knowledge how many innumerable precious remedies were given to humanity.

There is no old or new age, there is no antiquity, nor modernism for the ever life-giving Panacea.

---

* Prof. N. Roerich's painting *Guru Charaka* is in the Roerich Hall in Benares (Bharat Kala Bhawan).

MONGOLIA

DO you wish to fly? Why not fly over Mongolia? What about landing fields? Mongolia has natural landing fields for "iron birds" everywhere.

Would you like to speed by motor? You can speed over all the roads and across the entire plain. Rarely can one cover such distances without interruption.

Would you care to cross the deserts by camel? You may continue endlessly without an obstacle ahead. And you will find bristling brush for the camels to eat everywhere.

Would you like to gallop on horseback? Gallop ahead. The Mongols conquered immense spaces, as the hordes of Genghis Khan may testify. These spaces seem like waterless deserts—yet very often the water is very close to the surface, sometimes within two or three feet. Besides, as I have often written, there are subterranean currents that even to this day may be heard through the pebbles and boulders. If one wishes to bring the water to the surface, the possibilities are there.

Many vegetables may be cultivated in the forest lands and on the sandy soil here; if one cares to occupy himself with it, he can have results. If one wishes to breed better horses, it is only necessary to cross the local breed with the Turkestan and Afghan horses. In two years of breeding, you will begin to see results. The same applies to sheep and cows because there is nothing to prevent the possibility of obtaining the best breeds here.

Future forests are also possible. Not only in ancient times were all these sites covered with virgin forests, but even within a decade were there trees everywhere. The cruelty of ignorance destroyed them because the cruelty of ignorance does not consider the future. Nor is there anything to hinder the organization here of model farms, under the direction of people of understanding and experience. How much cultivation and planting of grasses could be introduced here in a very short time. And how simple it would be to introduce the best methods of cattle breeding. Schools could also be organized in connection with these model farms, thus permitting the nation to progress along modern lines without losing any of its traditional virtues. In this way, all kinds of handicrafts may be encouraged and labor cooperatives also introduced. During the great frosts, blizzards, and the spring *burans*, a vast amount of useful objects could be created by the hands of the people coupled with their creative gifts. However strange it may seem, when you see the inborn artistry of the Mongols in their weaving and designs, you realize how simple it would be to demonstrate to those who have not yet realized it, how much of value could be created here. And this creation would be possible without sacrificing the fine traditions or imitating foreign importations but by working along the traditional and native lines.

In fixed amity with the Chinese government, the autonomous government of Inner Mongolia is being organized. Its capital is in Batu-Khalaga, which is nearest to the railroad station of Koko-khoto or Guihu-achen. The head of the government is the local prince, but the actual moving spirit is the Prince of Barun Sunit. All the princes come together at stipulated times to decide the current problems. By agreement with Nanking, autonomous Inner Mongolia decides all of its own inner affairs.

Although the mineral wealth of Mongolia is unexploited, the salt revenues from the great salt lakes in themselves afford a vast revenue. It is widely known that Mongolia has a profusion of high-grade hard coal, oil, iron, and gold. Certain ridges of Mongolia are especially famed for the latter; and in our travels we had occasion to see great nuggets of gold as well as gold sands washed down in the river beds. We also had occasion to see many deserted gold mines, although it was difficult to ascertain whether they had been deserted because the gold had been removed, or through ignorance of methods in mining, or because of the military movements here.

Not long ago, we had occasion to write upon the subject of the "Brimming Chalice"—just such a brimming chalice is here before us in Mongolia. In various walks of life, opportunity comes to each man to encounter circumstances that for some reason seem strangely concealed. Although it may sometimes seem that a mere accident contributed to these concealments, in reality there is no accident, and it is far more probable that these circumstances have been hidden in some great design. Special caution and goodwill must be exerted when such hidden possibilities disclose themselves, and help should not be withheld. The thought of help and mutual cooperation becomes a vital and humanitarian responsibility, although help should be at the proper moment and in the proper direction. In this case, the help needed is not great—merely that of preventing a child from burning itself at the fire, and permitting it to gain experience along the proper channels.

Medical work in Mongolia is thus far in the hands of Swedish, Belgian, Japanese, and American physicians, as well as in the hands of local Mongolian lamas. I have always been exceedingly interested in local folklore and the native pharmacopoeia, but there should be attentive research and study into these subjects. Of course, the people have great need of established medical help.

The many hundreds of *dzeren*, which trot beside the horses, indicate that the destructive work of human hands has not yet touched these spaces. From the humane point of view, it would be especially regrettable if some new forces were to enter here only to apply the deadening conditions of mechanical civilizations. Only with the proper realization of local conditions and with sincere benevolence and constructive efforts will mutual response be aroused. The heart is the one infallible indicator of the proper, benevolent mutual efforts.

Recently a rather detestable joke was told to us of some travelers who taught the labor-loving Mongol women to rouge their lips. Such perversity among travelers is despicable. If certain conventions have become part of our civilization, it is hardly necessary to contaminate these simple people with these unfortunate customs. Thus early is contagion spread. It is necessary to find the way of good thinking, good vision, good action. Each traveler should spread along his path a helpful benevolence. Although he may be traveling with some special aim, still the help of benevolence is without limits.

ERDENI MORI

(Mongolian Epics)

I

IN folklore and sagas we meet with the white steeds of heroes. We know of the white steed of St. George. We know of the white horses of St. Flora and St. Laurus. We have also met with the white fiery Pegasus.

We have seen the white horses of the Lithuanian ancient god Svetovit. And the Germanic Valkyries also were riding on white steeds.

We have heard of the white horse of Isphagan in ancient Iran. We have seen the huge steeds of Arjuna, the guardians of the Temple.

We have heard of the steed of Ghessar Khan, the great hero of ancient Asia, and we have seen the trails of its hooves on the rocks in Tibet. We knew of the steeds from Himavat, with the blessed treasure Chintamani.

Erdeni Mori—the white steed—is the Mongolian carrier of the same treasure of happiness.

Still another Sadhu has been buried alive for many days; another swallows various poisons without any harm. Here is a Lama, who can levitate himself; another Lama by means of *tumo* can generate his own heat, thus protecting himself against snow and mountain glaciers; there a Lama can give the death stroke with his "deadly eye" to a mad dog. A venerated Lama from Bhutan relates, how during his stay in the Tzang district in Tibet, a Lama asked the ferryman to take him across from Tzampo free of charge, but the cunning man replied: "I will gladly take you over, if you can prove that you are a great Lama. A mad dog is running about here, doing great harm—kill it."

The Lama said nothing; but looking at the dog, he raised his hand and said a few words, and the dog fell dead! The Bhutanese Lama saw this himself. One hears frequently in Tibet and in India of the same "deadly eye" and the "eye of Kapila." And on a map of the seventeenth century printed in Antwerp, by authority of the Catholic clergy, the country of Shambhala is named!

* * *

Today Mongolia is on everyone's tongue.

Let us listen to some Mongolian prophecies.

Listen to the prophecies of the wise Mongolian seer, Molon Baksha, as written down by his grandson Sangey Zibikoff, and translated by the Mongol Shagdoroff and Shagdor Dabayev.

"In the year of the cycle of the pig, there will be an earthquake. In the year of the dog there will be confusion amongst those who have power. A great hero will be born in a little hut. And a great Khan will pass by, attracting no one's attention. Near the house troops will pass. People, who have no claim to nobility, will become rulers, and will govern the people. Honest people will withdraw, and will take a place near the threshold; whereas liars will take possession of homes.

There shall come a time when truth will be overpowered by hypocrisy. The spotted serpent will eat its own head, and the red-spotted serpent will devour the flesh of his own body. The horse, eating its body, shall also consume its head. Hence a chief, who embezzled the people's property, shall pay with his head.

And there will come a time when a wooden cart will cost as much as a horse. For the bad horse the road is long, and for a miser a friend is far. As the dead one has no title, so the poor one has no property.

You will fell timber with an axe that has no handle.

An iron serpent will obscure the earthly light—and the whole world is a fiery serpent.

In 1904 there will be a great event.

In the year of the ox there will again be a great occurrence. In the year of the tiger there will be destruction. The year of the hare will be the year of patience and endurance.

On the eastern boundary there will be robbery, because the chiefs will let the wolf upon a herd of sheep enclosed in a yard.

There will come a time that will be called "neither mine nor yours," a traveling brass kettle and a leather *yagtan* will be needed.

The fiery serpent will dominate everywhere during the time of migrations.

From the side, where the sun rises, will appear a miraculous white stone with an inscription. If you try to obliterate the inscription with an axe, it will appear again.

Beyond this stone will be the desert, which you will reach. Those who can reach this region will again become human, and the animals will again turn into animals. It will be hard for the senile ones, and for children. Loads will be carried even on oxen, cows, and horses. Images and books you will have to carry yourselves. For the old ones you will have dry meat and fried barley. To drink black tea is nourishing.

And further Molon Baksha foretold that later there will come two to four men who will subdue unrest and will construct a religious, righteous state."

Molon Baksha died at the age of eighty in the year of the ox. His song was:

> Why does the reed wave
> On the right side of the Selenga?
> Why does the reed wave,
> On yonder side of the Kudara?
> And foreseeing sufferings in life
> Why do I already feel sorrow?

When singing this song he used to cry.

* * *

And there is another prophecy:

"The great people of Kidan will not perish. They will meet the people of Shambhala. They will carry most reverently the sacred images and will honor the country's laws.

On the white stone they will read and will call for the great Teacher to reveal the word of truth.

From great bonfires the inscription on the stone will shine. What is coming? Why does the steppe grass move? Who is coming?

Erdeni Mori itself comes. Erdeni Mori itself approaches. And the people will not remain in their previous state.

What shines above the steppe grass? Why do the holy obo (cairns) radiate? Why is the great *suburgan* already alight?

There, where Erdeni Mori has passed, the steppe grass glimmers. There the wolves become silent.

And the falcons hasten their flight."

* * *

From ancient times Erdeni Mori appears, and its treasure radiates. At sunrise and at sunset everything is submerged into silence, this means that somewhere the great white steed, carrying the treasure, is passing. As long as the people know of the ordained treasure, they will remain on the righteous path. Their path, although long and unusual, is inevitable. As inevitable as is the service to perfection. For someone it may be a fairy tale, and for another it is a reality. And someone will become afraid. And others will unfold the pages of the given book.

The book of doves also came from heaven. And the treasure came from above. And not soon was a wise man found to read the book. And many peoples remember these given great gifts. And to all evil ones the light is unbearable. Why are they so horrified? They are afraid of themselves, they have not read the great book, and they have turned away from Light. And having turned away from a small light, how can their eyes stand the brilliant radiance of the Great Light!

Menhe Tengri! . . .

. . . the great blue sky that Chengiz Khan worshipped! Endless are the plains of Mongolia. Boundless are the steppes! Numberless are the mountains, hills, ranges, and ravines, where the glory is hidden!

It seems that the desert is lifeless, but suddenly there appears a camp on the slope. Behold, many *yurtas* rise, and unexpectedly there shines a white monastery or *suburgan*. And a small blue lake glimmers in the distance.

And again the desert becomes lifeless. And again riders in bright kaftans and in yellow *kurmas* and red-topped hats approach with the speed of the wind. The saddles are sil-ver-laid, just as they were in the times of Chengiz Khan. But where are the arrows and bows? Long are their rifles on the back.

And again there is silence. But the dark outline of the caravan proceeds. The steppes are spotted with herds of black yaks. Droves of fine horses are scattered over the desert. Like snow the herds of white sheep glitter in the sun. Antelopes rush along the hillside. A marmot disap-pears in a hole. Camels, wolves, foxes, hares . . .

Where are the birds? Only an eagle circles in the heights. Black ravens appear here and there. A lark sings its beautiful song. A partridge and a quail fly up. And from the lake comes the noise of geese and ducks. A bustard runs along swiftly. Cranes and herons are flying in forma-tion. . . . Many birds!

From where comes thy great silence, beautiful des-ert? Does it come from thy boundlessness? Does it come from the high blue heavenly dome, from the great Tengri, which was always benevolent toward Chengiz?

At night all starry signs shine. The beautiful stellar runes are awakening. The book of Glory is open. Beyond the hills a ray of light flashed.

Who is there?

Who passed there?

Erdeni Mori!

On the rocks of Shara Muren are the signs of the treasure. Naran Obo guards the miraculous stone. Everywhere Erdeni Mori has passed.

II

The banner of Chengiz Khan was white. In different campaigns he used various symbols—the lion, the steed of happiness, the falcon, or the panther. Fundamentally the color of the Mongols is blue.

The laws of the Great Khan are extant even to this day, and we may recall many that are applicable to our present life. His severe penalties for theft, murder, adultery, and other offenses could be placed upon the pages of our law even in the present times. Similarly with his other official acts, his orders to his officers, and his steps for the progress of his country were broadly introduced by the Great Khan.

In order to prevent pride and vanity among the khans, Chengiz Khan forbade the adoption of pompous titles. Freedom of religion and speech were observed and the love of God acknowledged. Clergy and physicians were freed from public taxes. Capital punishment was prescribed for spies, perjurers, sorcerers, and those who accepted bribes. The marriage laws forbade marriage between the next of kin. And to raise the sense of honor, it was forbidden to employ one's next of kin as servants. To abolish intoxication, Chengiz Khan constantly discountenanced the use of strong beverages, and urged his people to eliminate the use of these entirely.

A regulation is also known to have aimed at the abolishing of excessive superstitions. The ordinances of Chengiz Khan encouraged hospitality among his nomad population and insured the safety of travelers throughout the vast extent of his empire. Rules were given in regard to camp sites, and divisions of *yurtas* were made into tens, hundreds, and thousands.

Along the caravan routes, military stations with guards were established, and at intervals of a day's journey, posts for horses were set. The army was divided into divisions of tens, hundreds, thousands, and ten thousands. Capital punishment was meted out to all officers who deserted their posts.

Judging by everything that has come down to us, Chengiz Khan was a great leader and organizer.

"The Lord preserve us from the Mongols!" Such were the inscriptions found in destroyed cities of Asia. Danish fishermen did not venture into the open sea for fear of a Mongolian invasion.

This is one of the earliest descriptions of the Mongols, presented to Europe in the thirteenth century, which was created by fear and terror:

"Lest human joys be especially prolonged, and the world's benevolence endure too long without tears [wrote Matthew Peris in the year 1240], reviling creatures of Satan himself, the countless Tartar hordes broke loose and swept out of the boundaries of their encampments surrounded by mountains. Swarming like locust over the earth, they brought terrible devastation to Western Europe, and by fire and sword reduced it to a wasteland. They are inhuman, bestial, more monsters than men. They thirst for blood and gorge themselves with it. They rend and devour dogs and human flesh, and dress in skins with their chests and backs naked except for armor. They are small in stature, stocky, hairy, invincible. With zest they drink the pure blood of their herds. Their horses are stout, strong, and eat branches, and even trees. Due to their short thighs, they have to mount these horses with the aid of three-stepped ladders. . . . They know no laws; they are completely lacking in any idea of comfort, and are more ferocious than lions or bears. . . . they have pity neither for age nor sex nor position. . . . they know no language to converse in besides their own, which no one understands, because up to recent times there was no contact with them, and they themselves never came beyond the boundaries of their country. Thus there is no information available about their customs and personalities, such as is gained through the mutual intercourse of people. They travel with their herds and wives, and the latter are accustomed to fight as well as the men. To the destruction of Christendom, they suddenly appear, and with the speed of lightning ravage and annihilate everything on their way, terrorizing everyone, and arousing terrific hatred everywhere."

This was the reputation of the Mongols when their name first reached Europe, accompanied by the sensational terror that usually preceded their attacks. The very word Tartar aroused terror; they were considered the scourge of God. The old writers called them the "plague of God"—demons sent against men in punishment.

Europe did not regard the Mongols as human beings. It denied them the honor of being enemies or customary adversaries, and considered them some sort of superhuman creatures. In those times Europeans sincerely believed that Mongols had dogs' heads and devoured human flesh. This was the sort of wild terror that gripped Europe before the appearance of the Tartars. The danger, which threatened humanity, was regarded as so extreme that even Danish fishermen did not venture into the open sea for fear of Mongols.

The same picture is apparent at that time within the boundary of the Far East as well as in the Far West—on the shores of the Pacific as well as on shores of the Black Sea. One of the Chinese historians of that period exclaims with dismay that "since the creation of the world, no nation has been as powerful as the present Mongols. They devastate entire countries more easily than we pluck grass. Why do the heavens permit it?"

Another writer, describing the consequences of Mongolian supremacy, significantly remarks that "in Asia and Western Europe a dog can hardly bark without the permission of the Mongols."

After overwhelming all Asia, and reaching the threshold of Europe, the Mongolian invasion seemed such an ominous threat that the rulers of Europe began frantically to take council with each other as to ways of meeting the threatening danger. It was decided to undertake united resistance against this human deluge, as no single country could cope with it alone. No proof is more evident of the fear that these Mongol hordes inspired, even within the limits of the greatest European countries of that period, than the call of Frederick II, Holy Roman Emperor, to the entire Christian world to repel the invasion of the dreaded Mongols. Just imagine an appeal addressed to "Germany, ardent in battles; France, nursing at her bosom a fearless army; militant Spain; England, powerful in men and ships; Crete; Sicily; wild Hibernia; and cold Norway," asking them to organize international crusades against the nomad conquerors who came to Europe from far-off Mongolia.

Once during the conquest of Persia by the Mongols, a few Mongols met some Persians, and not having any arms with them, told the Persians to keep sitting by the roadside until they go to fetch their swords to behead them. And the Persians calmly obeyed. Thus history tells us.

Excerpts from the manifesto of Frederick II eloquently describe the "Mongol Terror" that surrounded Europe in 1240:

"These people [wrote the Emperor] have emerged from the far ends of the world, where they have long been concealed in an atmosphere of terrific climatic extremities, and have suddenly and brutally swept upon the Northern countries, swarming like locusts. No one knows whence this fierce race has gained its title of Tartar, but one thing is certain, it is apparently God's will that this race has been preserved from prehistoric days as a weapon to scourge people for their transgressions, and mayhap even for the fall of Christendom. This brutal savage people has not the least conception of humane principles. They have a leader whom they revere, and whose command they blindly obey, calling him the earthly god. They are small in stature, stocky, strong with great resistance, and have unbreakable faith. At the least sign from their leader they throw themselves with reckless valor against the most incredible perils. They have broad faces, slanting eyes, and emit the most terrifying shrieks and outcries, which indicate vividly the savagery of their hearts. They know no other raiment except the skins of oxen, asses, and horses, and up to now their armor is only crudely and badly soldered iron plates. But now—and we cannot mention this without a shudder—they begin to improve their armor by looting that of the Christians. Soon the Lord's wrath will descend on all of us, and these barbarians will begin to kill us, to our shame, with our own weapons. The Tartars already are learning to dress richly and elaborately, and at present they eat the most savory food. They ride beautiful horses, and are inimitable archers. It is said that their horses, when they have no other fodder, eat foliage, bark, and roots of trees, and yet preserve their courage, strength, and agility."

Thus Europe estimated the Mongol conquerors.

In later times these estimates become more exact and more detailed. For instance, Timur, instead of the former evaluation of a destroyer, received from the French savant, Grousset, a completely different estimate. Grousset says that Timur "who combines the subtle strivings of Iran-Hindu culture with the austere mold of an ascetic, appears as one of the most colorful figures of the Indo-Iranic world." Thus the great son of Chengiz Khan in the clan of Barlass is presented in a new light by the reflective scientist Grousset. Similarly, many rulers of the world, who were hastily condemned, as quickly revealed themselves in a completely different light. Is this not the case in Russian History with Ivan the Terrible and Peter the Great?

In recalling the description of Grousset and the notes

of Plano Karpini about the interest in arts and sciences of Mongolia, we may consider that the Mongolian apotheosis reached the zenith in Akbar the Great. Of course, there have been prejudiced judgments of him as a bloodthirsty tyrant, but there has finally emerged a brilliant picture of the resplendent unifier and cultured ruler of a great country. And to this luminous image of Akbar, already apparent, new studies can only add new valuable signs. And the wisdom of the people, which is just at its base, will add the aureole of a saint to the image of the Great Emperor. Thus through the centuries the people can revere a consistently great service. In regard to the characteristics of Mongols, I also recall other notes by contemporaneous travelers. There are many valuable and benevolent tokens. One should likewise remember the sacred Mongolian books, with their covenants about the Bodhisattvas, and their admonitions to compassion, self-sacrifice, and help to one's neighbor. Let us also recall the Nestorian times. In short, let us not in any way disparage that which was so real a factor in the life of this strong and courageous people.

How many beautiful hours we recall from our own travels in Mongolia. I remember the hearty greeting of welcome of the Mongol Rin-chin. How much we valued also the fiery exclamation of the grey-headed Buriat, "Light conquers darkness!" I remember how valiantly the Mongols acted in our encounter with bandits. I remember the building of the *suburgan,* and the gracious offering of their treasures. If we go by the marks of benevolence, we will find many of them. No matter how often a nation finds rebirth, its foundations still prevail. The same may be observed with many other peoples. Circumstances may change, bringing happiness or ill-fortune, but the soul of the people remains. And one may trace this folk-soul by its ancient songs, its sayings, and its parables. In these indestructible folk mementos, one can find the worthiest characteristics.

In the laws of the Mongolian Khans, in the heroic epic

of these people, is reflected a nature that is firm, courageous, often ascetic, patiently enduring the vicissitudes of their time.

And perceiving these covenants of the past, which have not been lost in the currents of the present day, should we not help this people who desire peaceful progress?

There was a time when the circumstances of life, and the yearnings of their heart enticed the Mongols into far-off places, because man often thinks that the beyond is more alluring—"splendid are the drums beyond the mountains." But contemporary thought has directed the Mongols toward the treasures of their own lands. To appreciate our own possessions, to learn to evaluate that which is defined by destiny, is a great accomplishment. It so happens that the Mongols as such, having concerned themselves with remote places, did not as yet exhaust their own inner treasures. Not to use means not to waste. Therefore, it is but just to direct attention to Mongolia with benevolence and friendship.

No one will make the error of exclaiming again, "Lord preserve us from the Mongols." On the contrary, thoughtful persons will send hearty wishes for the peaceful regeneration of their people.

Rigden Djepo himself, in resplendent armor, is galloping on. The Mongols do not forget the visions of the Great Lama in 1927. So it is also said in the prophecies:

"On the slope toward the sunrise, a white stone will be revealed with an inscription. . . . and though you hew out this inscription, it will never disappear but will forever emerge again."

Greetings to our Mongolian friends. Greetings to Mongolia!

* * *

Tzong Kha Pa in his Teaching "Lam-Rim-Chen-Po" ordains:

[87]

"As the shadows of birds flying in the sky move together, so also good and evil deeds follow the living beings.

Do not neglect even the smallest sin, thinking that it may be harmless. The accumulation of drops of water by and by fills even a large vessel.

Habits for good and evil deeds constantly dominate over man. Deeds, even over a hundred world-periods will not disappear but will accumulate; and when the time is ripe, their consequences will arise for the reincarnated.

How happy are the travelers who have taken care to carry along sufficient food, so also living beings who have done good deeds ascend to a blissful life."

* * *

The Lama proclaims:
"Let life be firm as adamant, victorious as the banner of the Teacher, mighty as an eagle, and may it last for eternity."

Callingly resounds the conch shell over the vastness of Mongolia!

OLUN SUME

OLUN SUME means in Mongolian "many temples." And this is the name of a place of an ancient, ruined city, situated in the domain of Prince Yun-Wang, the ruler of the Darkhan Beile Khoshun. Not far away from here is the place of the future capital of Inner Mongolia, and this place has been selected by the Panchen Rimpoche himself.

It is not customary to excavate in Mongolia ancient sacred sites. Only from the outside can one study such significant remnants of the past, which evoke deep thoughts.

There are certain wiseacres, who think that, at present, there may not again occur such destructions as have happened in the past. For such shortsighted people, the past is a synonym for barbarism and cruelty. And they think that today such bestial customs are quite impossible. Yet if you remind them of the deplorable ruins of St. Martin's Cathedral in Ypres, Belgium, and bring them to Spain to the charred ruins of the Cathedral of Oviedo, or if you show them the cuts on Millet's painting *Angelus* in the Louvre, then perhaps they would somehow think differently.

Or one may take such people into any of the numerous ruined cities in Central Asia, to prove to them what minute chips and fragments the once beautiful cities and strongholds have now been reduced to.

We walk amid the ruins of an ancient city, the name of which has already long been forgotten, but which the Mongols of today call the city of many temples—Olun Sume. On a vast square, surrounded by the remnants of a wall, are huge mounds of stones, bricks, and multicolored tiles of buildings of several ages. Around is the endless plain of Mongolia. Along the wall runs what is now but a shallow stream.

Studying these ruins, one sees how Nestorian tombs, decorated with Byzantine ornaments, were used for the foundation of later buildings. It is strange to see how a huge marble turtle—a beautiful carving of the Ming period, which once served as the pedestal of a *stele*—now remains lonely on a deserted place. No doubt many times the people used the excellently burned bricks for their newer constructions. It is stated that the entire palace of the local prince is built with these ancient stones.

It is even stated that some golden images had been discovered in the ruins. People mention the discovery of a statue of Avalokiteshvara in this place and many other holy Buddhist images.

On the scattered slabs and *steles,* one can see Chinese and Mongolian inscriptions concerning the chronology of the history of the ancient rulers of the place; one can see the carving of the wheel of life and sacred foot and hand imprints on stones. Not far away, in the rocks, are caves of a destroyed Buddhist monastery. Even now one can chance to find clay images and offerings. Nearby you may find remains of ancient prayers in Tibetan and Mongolian. One of our coworkers insisted that he had heard in the depth of a cave the subterranean sounding of monastery drums. So deep is the impression received in these ancient sacred places.

On the large, slanting hillside there are widely scattered, innumerable fragments of various kinds of household vessels, as if the whole hill consists of many strata of such broken china and ceramics. Many thoughts cross the brain when one picks up these broken chips. From every broken bit seems to come the wailing of a housewife, in the presence of whom her household had been destroyed. The owners of these fragments of pottery belonged to various centuries, from the twelfth and mayhap even earlier, up to the eighteenth. It is evident that we are in the presence of many strata of life and that repeated destructions have taken place and accumulated in one spot the proof of an awful annihilation of peaceful households.

Among the most ancient primitive ceramics, one can discern almost Neolithic ornaments—imprints of string and fingernails. Next to them, there may be lying barbarically broken chips of the most beautiful porcelain of the best Chinese periods. The durability of this porcelain is such that one can hardly break these fragments. What an expense of evil efforts must have been applied in order to destroy into such small fragments big vessels, pots, and cups, of all sizes and shapes.

Realize! One such hill—what a rare treasure this could have been for future generations, if it were not for an evil will, long since dead, which reduced to fragments the priceless creations of human genius. Among these remnants one can find fragments of the most beautiful Chinese craftsmanship, which is so highly valued in museums nowadays. For museums of ceramics or for ceramic workshops, even such small fragments would represent fine specimens of the technique of many centuries. It is quite inexplicable how such a mixture of different periods could have occurred in one place. It means that, at these places, there must have raged repeated destructions.

The wiseacres sit in their studies and probably have never seen ancient ruins in their entire, awful nudity. The tourist-ified towers of castles on the Rhine and in Tyrol, with their cosy *bierhalles*, will not convey the same impression as these ruins in deserted vastnesses, full of fragments and chips, as if a fiendish hand had only yesterday cruelly devastated them. Such material cemeteries are the best proof of how human hatred can ravage. And who will dare to assert that the malice of the thirteenth century was viler than it may be now. Hatred is hatred. Treason is treason. Anger is anger—above ages and nations. However, mercy and untiring creativeness should also be above time.

To speak of the advantages of travel seems already a

truism. For much evidence of the epochs will never be adequately recorded either in books or in selected museums. Only on the spot, amid all natural conditions, can one realize with special convincingness the particles of truth. Thus, people of different nationalities render an entirely different impression when at home or when under alien circumstances. At present, there already appears to be an interest in acquainting themselves with songs, music, and other expressions of foreign folklore. This is imperative. On this basis the best friendship and mutual understanding are woven. One should in every way welcome friendly intercourse. But let us not forget that even a song will resound differently in a concert hall in a foreign country than amid the hills and waterfalls of the motherland. It is as if nature itself accompanies such creative manifestations. And the bards and minstrels themselves sing differently in foreign surroundings. Therefore, the more human relationships are conducted under natural conditions, the deeper and more real will be the impressions and the more valuable will be the consequences.

A single desert hill filled with remnants of many ages can stimulate many creative impressions and conclusions. The most inspired lecture illustrated by fragments of pottery will never give such tremendous impressions as those obtained on the very spot where human hatred ravaged. One must evoke the most convincing testimonies that would compel humanity to ponder once more that hatred and malice, as such, must be condemned. Malice enraged by the scarlet arrows of destructive anger will always be the abominable shame of mankind.

Those who tried to prove that the saturation of humanity with hatred is already a matter of the past only show their own sheer ignorance. For are there not, at this very moment, people somewhere who are killing each other? The daily newspaper will prove this. Darkness is still prevailing, if it has not become even denser in many places. The lamentations of peaceful housewives deprived of their last household treasures still sound in the tinkling of broken vessels. And these vessels were acquired with great difficulty. Perhaps they served as a true adornment of the entire hearth. And suddenly, owing to somebody's hatred, this treasure is broken, which leaves in the hearts of the owners who managed to save themselves an ineradicable feeling of the loss of something near and precious. If today in every home, there would be kept as a terrible memento at least one old fragment of some maliciously destroyed beautiful object, then it may perhaps remind humanity how carefully should human creativeness be guarded as a sign of culture.

I wanted to collect as many fragments as possible to send them all over the world to all the good people as mementos so that even in their everyday life, they should be reminded what to guard in best goodwill. Tunes of sorrow still live in the sad sounds of fragments, of what was once beautiful craftsmanship. If people could hear the sorrowful lamentations from the depths of the past, they would more clearly think of the reconstruction of life in order to escape, in the future, tears of unhappiness. Every wailing is an outcome of violence. For it was not predestined for humanity to moan and sigh. It was ordained to create and rejoice, to raise above the signs of sorrow. Therefore, through the realization from experiences of the past, let the hills of sad wailing be transfigured into the heights of joy for the future.

Again, across the Mongolian steppes, we return to our *yurtas*. Wayside grasses are nodding to us. In the evening the lama from the neighboring monastery will come to our bonfire. Again there will be narratives about Shambhala; of its Ruler, Rigden Djapo; of the miraculous treasure, Chintamani—in Mongolian, called Erdeni-Dzo, and of the wondrous migrating Stone! Even about the appearing of the Chalice of the Blessed One, there will be a message at the bonfire! These sacred words raise above all human failing—they invoke a beautiful, radiant future!

DARKHAN BEILE

YUN-WANG, the Prince of the Hoshun Earkhan Beile, is the official head of the autonomous government of Inner Mongolia. We received an invitation to visit him at his headquarters, which is within two hours' riding distance from our camp. We traversed many dry riverbeds and passed the place of the future Mongolian capital. Bricks are being burned there at present. It is especially touching to pass this way and to think that there will be built and founded the capital of a people with such a great past. You know how near to my heart is every building, even the very possibility of upbuilding. First we traveled northeast and then turned to the north, where in a distance of forty to fifty miles lies the border of Khalka.

Along the way, our car scared several herds of excellent horses. One is astonished to see to what extent local grasses, without the addition of any grain, are sufficient to keep horses, as well as other cattle, in good form. Rare *ailes* (settlements), here and there; small groves and solitary trees of the elm "Karagatch," the popular tree of Central Asia, break the hill-lines of the horizon. Here and there, one finds the high, sharp desert grasses and the usual low spiny shrubs of Mongolia. It is remarkable how not only local camels but cattle as well have become accustomed to the spiny fodder.

Between low-lying hills appeared the headquarters of the Prince—a square of white walls crowned with dark teeth—like a fortress. Within the walls can be seen the roofs of houses in the Chinese style. Upon the gates are painted colorful Guardians of the entrance. Nearby, in a similar square of walls, stands the *yamin*—the secretariat of the *hoshun*. Apparently rain has just passed over this place, and everything is covered with water. We approach the *yamin* first in order to hand in our cards. We are asked to enter. A large crowd of friendly, smiling officers and soldiers surround us. The pointed straw helmets of the soldiers, crowned with a red spray, involuntarily suggest that a similar shape of helmet could be easily adopted for modern steel helmets, preserving thus the age-old traditions.

One must sit down in the friendly *yamin* and wait to be announced to the Prince. We exchange questions about the road, good health, and other benevolent subjects. In a corner stand old Russian rifles. Manuscripts as well as Mongolian books can be seen on the shelves along the walls. An officer wearing a hat adorned with a colored ball above the spray, to signify his higher rank, enters and asks us to follow him. We pass a brightly painted gate along a paved road and enter the palace. In a clean building of the Chinese style, we find the Prince seated, and we are invited to sit down in the same manner. Along the walls beside the sacred images are hanging portraits of the officers and leaders of Inner Mongolia. A large portrait of the Tashi Lama also occupies one of the central places. The Prince himself is sixty-six years of age. His friendly, experienced, and wise face reminds us of the images of the benevolent rulers of old. Through George and Chamba (the more interpreters, the better), a friendly talk begins, which runs from local matters to religious themes. The Prince is a very spiritual person and a friend of the Tashi Lama. On mentioning Shambala, his face takes a befitting, solemn expression. It is mentioned that a nation can prosper only with firm spiritual and administrative principles. The Prince speaks of the desire of the Mongolian people for peaceful development. It is especially joyful to see the representative of his people emphasizing with all of his heart a desire for peaceful upbuilding.

We exchange presents. On our part a gold enameled watch of French workmanship; on the part of the Prince, two Tibetan carpets. The Prince intends to visit us as soon as his car is able to run on the badly flooded roads. He invites us to participate in the annual festival in the Batukhalka monastery, where the sacred dances, "Tsam" of Lamas, take place. On leaving we also visit his private chapel, situated in the same compound. The temple is kept in full cleanness, and one sees the desire to make everything as good as possible. In the temple there are, besides several Burkhans, a statue of Chenrezi and the White Tara, and on the walls is a large fresco of the battle of Shambala. Offering lamps burn callingly, and everything shows that the temple is close to the heart of the owner. When departing, we took into our car a soldier, with a red spray on his helmet, to show us the road to the ruins of an ancient city situated within the Prince's domain.

Neither excavations nor any scientific description of the place has been made, but it deserves serious research. The city is destroyed—razed to the ground. One remembers the texts of old chronicles, in which they speak about cities condemned by the conquerors to looting and devastation. The typical details of the ruins and bases of columns and numberless chips of broken vessels and fragments of ceramic architectural ornaments at once indicate the different periods of the city.

The latest period, according to the ceramics, belongs to the Manchu dynasty. Then there are obvious signs of the Ming dynasty—for instance, a huge turtle of white marble, which probably serves as base for a *stele*. But still more interesting are the remains of the Mongol-Nestorian times of the twelfth and thirteenth century and perhaps even earlier. One sees sarcophagi with Nestorian crosses, which, according to their ornaments on white stone, could be found either in the Byzantium, or San Marco, or Verona. On these monuments one can discern inscriptions, somewhere in Uigur glyphs and elsewhere in old Chinese. On the latter, George at once deciphered a very characteristic name, which in Chinese pronunciation means Elijah. This name is often repeated in Chinese Nestorian records.

Nearby, one may also see on huge heaps of ruins nicely carved capitals, which remind [one] of the lost, snow-white temple. Not in vain is this place called, in Mongolian, "Many Temples."

George suggests measuring the ruins and to make a map of the city, and to copy inscriptions for deciphering. One feels that such research may disclose many interesting discoveries. Who knows, perhaps this city belonged to the well-known Mongolian Prince George, a Nestorian who, according to chronicles, fell in a battle at the end of the thirteenth century. This period deserves serious study as it can give important pages of Central Asian history. Let us hope that future finds will take a place of honor in the Mongolian museum of the new capital. Besides governmental buildings, there immediately should be built schools and a museum to preserve the best specimens of national creativeness.

At a time when we rejoiced in studying the ancient city, dark clouds gathered around, and one could see here and there torrential rains. But the clouds did not touch us, and on our return trip, the road, which had turned into lakes, proved the result of heavy rains, which were so welcomed by the Mongols for their grass. The hillside became greener. The herds of fat, wet horses were shining, and the up-to-then dry riverbeds suddenly changed into swift torrents. We remembered the flood that took place unexpectedly during our previous expedition, at Sharagolchi. In Asia everything is unusual and sudden.

The ruins of the city once more confirmed how many rich surprises may be hidden in the Asian vastnesses. Sliding and slipping along the hillside, we reached our camp near the rock Timur. The very name suggests concealed ores—iron, coal, gold are mentioned—and in the south even oil is known. Many lakes give salt, which is a resource of much revenue. It was a joyful journey. We met a remarkable person and visited impressive ruins and saw useful grasses and other riches of nature. If one is to add to these riches constructive goodwill, then how much that is beautiful and instructive can be written again into the history of Mongolia. May this good hour come! Blessed is every upbuilding!

[98]

NARAN OBO

ABOVE all surrounding mountains stands Naran Obo. *Naran* means "solar." Verily the high white *obo* meets and bids farewell to the sun. According to narratives, this peak is surrounded with many sacred legends. From its lap to the peak—like upon the plate with the golden apples as is found in the fairy tale—all surrounding lands can be seen. From behind the hills, one sees the roof of the monastery in Batukhalka. Further on, a row of hills and then the sand—the forerunners of Alashan. To the southwest and west, sandy expanses are stretched—all these *gobis*, or *shamos*. To the south runs the path to Koko-khoto—there is already the tumult of crowds. To the east are the lands of the Sunits, and to the northwest runs Urat. To the north is Mumingan, which means "The Daring Thousand." No one remembers where this standard has shown its daringness. And from where does this daringness come——from evil or from valor?

Naran Obo itself stands on the lands of Prince Darkhan Beile. In the north one can discern the ruins of a Mongol-Nestorian ancient city. Besides Chinese and Mongolian accumulations, there can also be found, under the foundations of these ruins, Uigur inscriptions; and who, after all, knows the original antiquity of these desert stones? To the west, so people say, are the ruins of Genghis Khan's camp. One should not miss the opportunity to visit them. This place is apparently nowhere described. And after all, how could one expect for an eminent locality to do without the great name of Genghis Khan? There, amid some ruins, can be found stones with carvings. Perhaps these signs—*tamgas,* or inscriptions—of Genghis Khan, will give the key to their identification.

In the same direction, in one day's ride, is the border of Khalkha. Many diverse and conflicting stories reach us from there. Twenty miles away is an entire settlement of Khalkha refugees. To judge by the stories, it may be one way or another. One has seen one thing; another thought he saw something else.

Our camp stands among fantastic volcanic rocks, at the foothill of Timur Khada, which means the Iron Rock. Again, this great name of Mongol history did not get lost. And Genghis Khan, the great conqueror and builder, and the iron Timur—and above on the hilltop shines Naran Obo. At the base of the mountain, not far from our camp, is the site of the future Mongolian capital. The site was chosen and predicted by the Panchen Rimpoche, the Tashi Lama of Tibet himself, who is now at Kumbum. It is quite clear that for the new Mongolian capital, the new place has been chosen. This is because Batukhalka, with its ancient outlived monastery, cannot be a new beginning. And the new autonomous government naturally wants to be in new surroundings. At present the government stays at Batukhalka in *yurtas.* But, of course, this can only be a temporary solution.

According to old examples of history, the Mongolians want to build. And the place chosen by the Tashi Lama himself is not an accidental one. The same mountains that surround Naran Obo were at one time the capital of the famous Hun leader. Even at present, one may see near the rocks certain stones, which were not placed there by accident. A great deal has taken place on these sands. There is before us, amid green ash trees, the dried-up riverbed. There was water here once upon a time, but it had left the place and remains only in nearby wells and isolated springs. Of course, two or three artesian wells would give a new vivifying stream. Among future construction, one must think in the first place of water replenishment.

There is no need to complain about the soil. Everywhere

there were forests, now cruelly destroyed. We ourselves recently observed at Tzagan Kure that a willow beam of a fence sprouted before our very eyes. It means that wherever there is the least sign of life, the soil will permit it to manifest itself.

The living power of the Mongolian autonomous government is Prince Te-Wang of Sunit. His task is not easy, for he desires to bring life into new governmental forms around the ancient Mongolian banners. Quite recently, during his trip to Piking, Prince Te-Wang made a touching speech addressed to a crowded auditorium of the university, telling them that their every advice for the benefit of Mongolian upbuilding will be received with gratitude. Truly, who wouldn't help the peaceful, cultural upbuilding of a historically great country! Who could show such ignorant cruelty to contradict and impede a peaceful, enlightened beginning? On the contrary, every cultural heart will resound to this sincere address. Who would refuse to give friendly advice there, where it will be so necessary and where it will be so eagerly listened to?

In a country where the people are understanding, where the depths are preserved, where improved cattle breeding and agriculture as well as various industries are possible, could there be such heartless people who would desire the destruction of all these obvious possibilities? Of course, the whole world is in turmoil. Every day can bring staggering surprises. Everything is as tense as during the completion of a tower or during the launching of a giant liner. Above all the confusion and turmoil, it is evident everywhere that there is a search for a new world, for a new life, for happiness. Much has been outlived; much has become obsolete and requires new construction. The best minds understand that one can no longer live on old *valutas*. The most practical people already renounce the centuries-old idol of humanity—gold. Just as tensely are being sought-after forms of cooperation. Cooperation is the motto of the day. People understand that each isolation, like a prison, does not lead to enlargement, does not lead to light and sun.

In such days of an unusual worldwide tension, every desire of a peaceful cultural upbuilding resounds callingly. Mongolia wishes to build today. That same Mongolia, which contributed so many startling pages to the history of humanity, now wishes to arrange its life peacefully and culturally. Of course, it would be a pity if in the process of this building, the basic foundations of the Mongolian nation were to be forgotten, and someone would try to force upon it something entirely alien. On the contrary, one can see how valuable it would be to make use of local materials, and one must utilize all creative friendliness in order that the new structure is erected on truly befitting lines.

Studying the surrounding possibilities, we see that if Samarkand, the entire Choresm, and all flowering *kishlaks* could have for centuries maintained their brilliant fertile level, it means that the soil here is also capable of producing as well. The very fact that the soil has been resting for so long will only help the new upbuilding. Every field must rest, and Mongolia has rested long enough in order to rise again with greater force for its construction.

One must see with what inspired enthusiasm every Mongol pronounces the name, which for him is sacred, of Genghis Khan; how the Mongols recall Timur, Ugedei, Kublai, and other builders—stern, peace-loving—who held the attention of the entire world.

References to Marco Polo have already become commonplace. Not he alone, but many travelers have recorded in their writings the flourishing of local places. I have already had occasion to be reminded of how accurately and exhaustively were described these apparent deserts of today. In their day these places were truly blossoming. From excavations we become convinced that they truly could flourish. The easier it is to imagine that the new epoch of regeneration and a still greater prosperity are possible.

To those who will point out the severity of local conditions, one may reply that severe conditions so often serve as an impulse for upbuilding. The conditions of Scandanavia are often very severe, but it is precisely there that the unconquerable spirits of Vikings were forged. And in both Americas, despite all the threatening tornadoes and dust storms, the great Mayan culture was formed. The human spirit does not know physical obstacles.

Mongolia wishes to have schools, means of communications, telegraphs, hospitals—is this not to be welcomed? Mongolia wishes to have a stabilized administration, wishes to have cooperative societies, desires its own industrial companies—is this not to be welcomed! Mongolia wants to have model farms, wants to improve its agriculture, cattle breeding, forestation—is this not to be welcomed! Mongolia wishes to establish the exchange of goods and financial stabilization, and to strive toward peaceful relations—is this not to be welcomed!

There are at present in the world so many out-of-date, confused circumstances. The more so should one rejoice when one sees the desire of the people to organize themselves, to overcome difficulties, and to develop peacefully. For this is not easy. There is much malice and evil thought. And therefore, every seed of good should find sincere help and friendship. And then it is joyful to help every constructive beginning. It has been pointed out, quite recently, that I like so much the French proverb: "When construction proceeds, everything goes forward well." I do not deny that I like this proverb. I feel that, indeed, in the striving of constructiveness, many daily misunderstandings and difficult problems are solved. Therefore, I call everyone to help in the building up. Every upbuilding is not only a national task, but it also truly belongs to the world, for it increases the welfare of the world and strengthens universal achievement.

When we hear these touchingly friendly invitations of the Mongols to help them in their upbuilding, one wants to transmit to all the distant friends of culture the same wish, the same request—to unite in active efforts for the new upbuilding.

New constructive beginnings should not only arouse desire for egoistical attempts for gain or for the suppression of individuals. On the contrary, the banner of upbuilding should also be a light-bearing, unifying, and benevolent concept. Mongolia is not attempting to build a utopian Tower of Babel. The country wants to develop and stabilize itself in a natural way. No exorbitant funds are required for this upbuilding. The richness of the country itself is quite a sufficient guarantee for possible prosperity. Every cultural man will only rejoice, hearing that in our difficult days one more improvement and ongoing construction takes place.

High upon the mountain glistens the *obo* of the sun—Naran Obo. It reminds one of those spiritual possibilities, which must cement the stones of the new Mongolian upbuilding. At the foothill, bricks are already being burned for the construction of the future capital. All this preliminary activity prior to construction reminds me of my painting *Building a City.* There where there is upbuilding, there is no destruction. Every construction is an increase of Good.

"When construction proceeds, everything goes forward well."

Naran Obo, June 30, 1935

SONGS OF MONGOLIA

SONGS reveal the soul of the people.
Let us listen to the meaning of the Songs of the Mongols, which resound over their vast steppes.

* * *

"The flower of Bondorva, which grows on the Budala mountain, if even it rains, will yet wither away.

Although Yogacharya is like the Burkhan, but if he will turn away from the Truth, he will be plunged into darkness.

The petals of the buckwheat blossom, once opened, will be scattered when the wind blows.

Although Yogacharya is like a High Guardian, but if he will turn away from the Truth, he will perish."

* * *

"Rich and white—such is the golden Universe. Vast and pure—such is our motherland.

What grove on the mountains are the grapes; through what the people are glorified, this is a resounding song.

In the running water of a spring, is there any mud? Can you consider the ordainments of the saints untrue?

The water of the well is precisely holy water. Can you name the Commands of the Blessed One false?"

* * *

"A scribe takes a brush in his hand, goes to Peking, and becomes the son-in-law of a khan.

Instead of becoming a son-in-law of a prince, let us better be merry with our beloved.

It is better to be happy with the beloved from Khorchin, than to be the son-in-law of the khan.

Every mountain has a summit, every meeting with the beloved is preordained; afterward one must call with greetings."

* * *

"Will the stork ever cease to gather the fish of the diamond sea? Is it easy to cross one's sufferings—the results of previous incarnations?

Can one expect that the crane can swallow all the fish of the crane's lake? Is it easy to evade arisen sufferings—the results of previous deeds?

When you want to fell a knotty tree, take care not to cut your feet. Beware when wishing to conquer another kingdom not to lose your own subjects.

When you want to fell a willow tree, beware not to destroy your own fate. Beware when desirous to plunder another country not to lose your own welfare!"

* * *

"My steed, coming from beyond the Bayan-Khangai mountain! My steed, you roused the admiration of all the warriors of Badaragultu.

Like a beautiful cloud, you who have created clouds of dust behind yourself, my tall white steed, *hélas*, whither have you disappeared?

Your eyes are like apples and your hooves like cups; your height is seven feet. What a wonderful steed!

With two ears like a wolf, with two eyes like stars, of a cloudlike color, you are a beautiful steed!

Has no one seen it in the steppe, in a hidden place? Has no one seen how evil thieves have led it away?

If anyone has seen him, I will present him with a *kurma* (coat) of fox skin, and to him who has caught my steed, I will give a *kurma* of tiger skin."

* * *

"He who builds firmly and well, has all chances to become rich; when a firm government will be established, this will be the sign that you will be Leader.

Prosperity and happiness are bliss.

It is pleasant to be well off. It is pleasant to arrange merrymaking. We belong to the *khoshun* (district) of a glorious Prince.

Prosperity and happiness are bliss."

* * *

"Through the glory and mercy of the Lord, we, having found the highest bliss, flourished peacefully. Amid various desires and an aimless life, one should be careful not to lose the highest Bliss.

If one heeds attentively to the rules ordained by the enlightened Sages, then one enters upon the holy path of salvation. If even we are burdened by evil, let us strive in order not to lose the rules of eternity.

That They imbue us with strength is Their merit. Thanks to having become human beings, we became better—thus one should strive not to lose the rules of reverence.

If one ponders over the firmness of faith and if one will always refute inadmissible foolishness, and if one will follow the precepts of the saints, then how pleasant it will be to contribute to the means of the Holy Path.

It is pleasant that, having realized the laws, he who has contained within himself the roots of babbling, malice, and falsehood, upon purifying his nature and becoming enlightened, multiplies his happiness and holiness.

If one will give himself up to contemplation and meditation, and study the deeds of living beings of the past and the change of cycles, then it will become evident that now one must intensely learn."

* * *

"Rejoice, for ages one cannot forget to be grateful that You have consented to guide us, those that have lost their way in this earthly world, to lead us by the nearest path of the Diamond Chariot.

If following the rules of the Saints, then even despite all of our bad habits, when attentively striving along the path of perfection, we will never lose the ordained place.

Even Arhats, who have already attained through the weight of mercy this Bliss, who abide in peace, even they have to beware in order not to lose the highest Bliss in the midst of earthly turmoil."

* * *

"Bestow upon us bliss and happiness, filled with the true blessing of the three sacred Jewels. Protect the righteously established rulers and princes, and strengthen their beneficial, peaceful rule.

You Who possess the rules of the finest, mysterious, fundamental reason, who govern eternally over the sun-like faith and jewels, You remain invariably pure as the bright moon."

* * *

"Near the spring of the subtle river, there falls a light rain; during the eighth moon, leaves and flowers unfold.

Many clouds obscure the rising run, the highest reason and wisdom can be suppressed by hatred and ignorance.

The shining *Chelmon* (Venus) is the sign of the Dawn. Cloud-like white hair is the sign of wisdom."

* * *

"On the summit of a high mountain, from north and south, there grow trees and shrubs and herbs. At this time they are pleasant for the eye.

When from those beautiful trees in autumn there

comes the son of the birds amid the green foliage, this is a great and pleasant joy.

In summer various flowers blossom on the green meadows. When one observes their unfailing color and eternal vitality, this is pleasant for the eye.

Verily we are living beings of many clans, during our continuous, united life we have glorified and sung praises to the peaceful ever-beautiful flowers."

* * *

The Mongolian warriors sing the song of Shambhala. In the same manner as centuries ago, at the time of Genghis Khan, so now thunders the sacred song.

"Let us even die, but for the sake of being reborn in the holy host of Shambhala!"

Songs reveal the soul of the people.

Tzagan Kure, 1935

HOLY GUARDIANS

THUS said the Mongolian Lama:

"The Holy Keepers also visited our *yurtas*. Nobody knows when They shall appear. It is not known from where They come and whither They go, but They are usually in haste. It is told that They lay foundations for monasteries, where these are necessary. Sometimes the place of their visitation is being marked by *suburgans* or by ordinary *obos*. When the news of Their approach passes through the desert, then people rejoice in all *yurtas*. It is said that there are no illnesses in those places. And all plans and deeds are successful."

We asked: "Perhaps such success is due to mental suggestion? Such beneficial thoughts and ordainments are known."

"We know of this force and we ourselves believe that success is sent. Once the Holy Keeper was asked, 'Is it true that according to His thought many benevolent deeds are done? And how does He suggest them?' It is said that He replied: 'This happens in many ways, but the main thing is that you act as is necessary.' And they hasten in order to give to the people more good thoughts, in order that people everywhere can do the best within the needed time."

We asked: "Are They at once recognized by the people?"

"To say the truth, only a few recognize them. And the others become aware, only after Their departure. And then they again begin to wait. Stupid people!

When something is given, they do not agree; and when it is taken away they again begin to wait for it."

We asked: "And when They come, where do They stay?"

"Sometimes in Their tents, but usually They go away somewhere, and no one knows properly, from beyond what mountains They come and where Their path lies. But wise people expect Them, and expect Them very much, especially for the day of the Blessed One. And when the news of Their arrival comes, joy radiates everywhere. From *yurta* to *yurta,* messengers gallop at full speed. And hardly have the people time to gather, when He has already left. People, of course, say that They use some subterranean passages, but no one knows anything definite about these. When They suddenly appear amid the desert, people wonder how such a long waterless path was accomplished. We ponder whether somewhere there are hidden roads. Even very deep and endless caves were found, and no one knows whither they lead. And in the darkness of these caverns no one was able to find his way."

We asked: "Do you narrate all this about the ancient past, or does it happen now?"

"It was, and is, and shall be. They guard the people. They keep justice. They send new thoughts. And not long ago, and may be even now there may appear a Rider. Either alone, but sometimes two, and no one knows Their ways."

We asked: "And are there any signs of Their coming?"

"No, never. None!" Everything great and wonderful comes unexpected. So sudden that human thought cannot anticipate. But the heart perhaps may feel. When the time of Their approach comes, the heart longs and strives and flies to meet Them. Sometimes, the heart flutters as a bird, and perhaps at that moment They pass nearby. How often does a steed neigh, no one knows why; perhaps it sensed Their steeds. Very often dogs appear watchful apparently without reason, but never will a dog bark at Them. Sometimes it happens in caravan, during night-camping. It seems as if someone rides past, and when they listen—there is nothing to be heard. Sometimes a wonderful fragrance, as if from the best flowers, arises over the desert. It is said that this is due to Their approach. Some have seen an unusual white dog, like a Borsoi. Old people say that this was Their dog, and the dog runs alone, but as if with some purpose, and does not respond to calls: no doubt it hastens. Others have seen in the desert white birds—like doves, and believe that these were Their messengers. There are many inexplicable signs in our desert. Sometimes we find most remarkable stones. No doubt someone has placed them there. They are carved, sometimes with unknown inscriptions, sometimes round like eggs."

We said: "There, you see many signs in the desert, but for foreigners the desert appears boring and dead."

"That is because they do not know the language of the desert. The foreigners cannot judge the wind, nor do they smell the fragrance; and even should they meet Them, they will not recognize Their greatness."

We said: "What are They like? Some people must have seen Them."

"As circumstances require, in order not to attract the people's attention unnecessarily. I was told that in one camp They were taken for traders, in another as shepherds, and yet in another as warriors; everyone judges by himself. But They are not offended at our remarks. One, who recognized Them, tried to find what he should do. And He replied: 'You will do as is necessary, don't worry about it, but always do good deeds, everywhere and in everything.' They always teach to do good."

Again we asked: "But why do They tolerate these dead deserts?" The Lama looked at us very cunningly, and said: "And this will come in time. And the rivers will rise, and forests will grow, and grass will cover everything. Everything comes in time. As it left us because of human sins, so it will come, thanks to the Keepers' thoughts. They will send, when necessary, when we shall be able to recognize and to accept."

We asked: "And has no one any signs or tokens from Them?"

"Perhaps some have. No doubt they have. But only if anyone receives them, he will never say so."

We questioned: "And does anyone know Their names?"

"They can assume different names, but again, if anyone was lucky to hear Their name, he will never repeat it to anyone else. No one will transgress this law."

Our friend became silent and piercingly followed with his eyes a moving point on the far-off sandy hills. Perhaps he pondered whether his luck had come. In his eyes glimmered the long-waited-for expectation. We felt that he knows, has heard, and seen much more. But much longer must one sit at the bonfire, until the heart opens up. Even if the heart would be ready to reveal, the will knows how far these gates can be opened toward foreigners. To passersby, many mysteries of the desert remain close. The desert can only entrust them to their own—only to him whom it can fully trust, to him who thinks quietly about the past and the future, to him who is content with the little that is incalculable for contemporary luxury.

The desert has assumed that aspect, in which it appears to the passerby, in order not to show its significance and magnificence. The heart of Asia is hidden with all its wealth, with all deeply buried signs, and the sons of Asia know how to guard the ordained, they guard the Teaching of the Blessed One.

Perhaps tomorrow the Lama will tell us about Shambhala.

THE STONE

CHAMPA, half-Tibetan, half-Mongol, from Kokonor, has returned to our camp from the bazaar, and whispers mysteriously:

"They say, that somewhere here is hidden some stone on which is a bronze belt."

"What may this be? And where could one find out, where the stone is?"

"Who knows, perhaps one can find out from the Lamas. Only this is very difficult as they are not communicative about the stone."

We think that the matter concerns some newly discovered Hun burial mounds, or some treasure trove, or finally some legend. Firstly, the interesting point seemed to be not so much the stone, but the belt. A belt has from antiquity been the symbol of rulership. Often we find in history that the robbing or the insult of the belt led to serious consequences.

Thus we discussed around the evening bonfire the strange news about the stone and the bronze belt, and thought that it will probably be difficult to discover any more details. If this concerned a treasure, then it would be still more difficult, as people are always reticent to speak of treasures.

Indeed one can hear often of treasures and legends found in sandy *barkhans*. Sometimes they will be connected with great names of ancient legendary warriors and rulers. Also the name of Chingiz Khan will repeatedly be mentioned since this glorious name is heralded at every opportunity.

Several days pass. New interesting herbs have been found. George is busy with the Buriat Lama, who is a famous medicine man. Unexpectedly a high official arrives from the local Prince. The Prince sends his cordial greetings, and requests that we should not touch and break the stone with the bronze belt. What a mystery—again the same stone! We make inquiries, thinking that means some special ore. We ask: "Where could it be and who has found it?" The reply arouses certain recollections.

"The stone moves about and appears near sacred and famous places. Here, where your camp is, near Naran Obo, the hill is sacred. The Prince knows that you collect useful herbs and flowers. This is very good. But do not disturb the stone, which may appear here and there. You are great people, and the stone may come your way."

This reply proved that the chief significance is not so much in the bronze belt, but in the stone itself. And this stone turns out to be the legendary fabulous precious stone, which visits important regions at preordained dates. Thus the Prince's messenger asked us in quite official tones not to disturb the miraculous stone. And we, of course, ask him to transmit to the Prince that he should not worry. We shall not disturb the stone; we will not break it or otherwise violate it.

One can well imagine how surprised the local Mongols would have been, if we were to tell them all the well-known legends and sagas about the wandering stone—*lapis exilis*—which is glorified throughout centuries from the Pacific coast to the medieval Meistersingers, to the famous Wolfram von Eschenbach. In our case the circumstance was new that not a legend was narrated to us but we were asked not to harm the very stone itself. It means that not a folklore saga but the knowledge of the very stone was living without any doubt up to our days.

Another new detail about the belt on the stone may mean that the stone possesses power. In other variants there was no mentioning of this belt. It is true that one may find in legends indications about signs on the stone, which appear and disappear. It is said that the stone warns his temporary owner of various significant events. On special occasions the stone emits cracking sounds, it may become very heavy, or on the other hand may lose weight considerably. At times the stone radiates light. The stone is usually brought to the new owner quite unexpectedly by some strangers. Numerous are the qualities of the stone. Not without cause are so many sagas and songs dedicated to it. The stone is also mentioned in medieval scientific and historical chronicles. On the Himalayas, in Tibet, and Mongolia, one constantly comes across references to this miracle. In the same connection the name of the mysterious King—Prestor John—is also often cited, and even the Holy Grail is identified with this stone.

It is strange to coordinate the remarkable sagas, which are imbued with deep symbols and signs, with the arrival of the official, asking not to injure nor to take away the stone. Here is an especially sacred place. It is said that near Naran Obo, the miraculous stone has already been seen. It is prohibited to kill any animals in this place. The Tashi Lama himself ascended Naran Obo, and has blessed the place.

"The Tashi Lama gives passes to Shambhala."

Of course, this information is also interpreted in many different ways. But nevertheless up to now some people come to the Tashi Lama with the request for such a permit.

Again old signs coincide with modernity in such unexpected forms.

We have also heard how certain people scolded and stopped the narrators about such signs. Ardent guardians of secrets will whisper, and the bard will at once interrupt his story. And if the listeners still insist, the bard will conclude with some stereotypical joke, which in no way corresponds to the inspired beginning. This means that up to now the ancient rule about the keeping of secrets still exists. And people know how to guard these great mysteries, they know how to divert the conversation to some ordinary routine matters, and they suddenly draw the attention to some insignificant outside event.

And we again remember, how once a Hindu said that he would never reveal a certain secret, and that he would rather admit the assertion that nothing of the kind exists. As in ocean waves one may discern several different currents, so also the depth of human consciousness may treasure many secrets.

Some may scoff at such a steadfastness, at such a guarding of the foundations. But others will revere it, seeing how people conquering their selfishness remain firm and adamant.

"Oh, Stone—thou precious treasure—thou art known to many people." They preserved and kept the knowledge of the stone in the most sacred treasury. If an official arrives and requests not to harm, and not to take away the stone, thereby he does not reveal the secret. He himself never said what stone he had in view. It was but his duty to warn that such a stone sometimes appears in the vicinity. It means that by such a warning he did not reveal the meaning of the stone.

The messenger was happy to have our assurance that we shall not harm the stone. Who knows, perhaps in the intonation of our reply he felt that we know more of the stone than he anticipated? Anyhow, our promise not to harm the stone was received with sincere gratitude.

To know how to guard secrets already means to prove a high quality of the spirit. Who can undertake to draw the dividing line between reality and fantasy? Recently some scientists proved that epical heroes were actually living persons, creators of life, lawgivers, whose deeds, transgressing the boundary of human consciousness, were crowned with wonderful inspiring legends.

Do you know, whether or not that the Stone exists, which is glorified by so many people?

Timur Khada

TIBET

"THE grandeur of nature in Asia reveals itself in the endless forests and tundras of Siberia; in the waterless deserts of overwhelming grandeur; in a wide, flat upland that forms the southern half of the central part of this continent." Thus does Przhevalsky speak of Tibet.

Everything that is said about Tibet is full of significance, whether it is by Plano Carpini, or Rubruquis, or Marco Polo, or Odoric of Friuli, or any of the many other travelers. They all saw some of the unusual in Tibet, and Tibet has remained an unusual place.

It is said the Lhasa will now have a radio. Roads for automobiles are being mentioned, as well as airstrips. In other words, an interesting mystery is being approached from all sides. It is long since Waddell attempted to tell us about Tibet, but he did not say very much; Mme. David-Néel said more, but primarily stressed the tantric side.

At present, many countries are divided as if into two distinct existences. One is mechanical, robot-like, technocratic—contained within the conventional bounds. Machines are climbing the mountains, and above the highest peaks hover airships; various apparatus, more or less exact, calculate and measure; paper is substituted for precious metals. In other words, the old bazaar has become a modern bazaar with all of its "improvements." And yet in all these newly technological countries, the old country also remains with its fundamental treasures, achievements, and strivings intact.

In our day, the world's demarcation lines are very unclear. There was a day when one could speak of regressors and innovators; there was a time when the Stone Age was clearly followed by the Bronze Age. But now everything has become much more complicated. The Stone Age has contacted the Iron Age; regressors have absorbed the mechanical conventionality, while innovators have lovingly contacted the ancient wisdom. For this reason, in technological countries it is only with difficulty that one can draw the lines of demarcation.

In Tibet, the radio will make its voice heard and the mountain air in many places will be polluted by factories. And yet Tibet—The Unusual—will remain.

We have just spoken of hidden things; there may be many types of things hidden. We have met visitors from remarkable places who have never noticed anything. There once existed a game in which the players unexpectedly asked each other, "What do you see?" And the unprepared answers were at times very strange. People usually noticed what seemed to be insignificant nonsense, and this simple game sometimes became an interesting psychological exercise.

If people would notice everything significant, no doubt a great many more treasures would have been studied on earth. And yet it is only now that the Roman Forum is being studied; only now Egypt, Palestine, Greece, and Iran are opening up their treasures. And what will we say of other, less frequented places: even the *kremlins* are as yet unexplored. Known frescoes have not as yet been studied in detail. And how much has been passed by unrecognized, as yet unnoticed!

Technocracy is especially strong at present. It has calculated everything on paper, but as soon as it contacts actual life, its most exact formulas are drowned in the midst of non-applicability. In everyday life the telephone rings unbearably; the howling of jazz music drills the brain; the noise of the prizefight resounds. And yet all this commonplace triviality does not affect that Unusual, that extraordinary, to which the human heart is striving.

We have seen people who were deeply disappointed not

only by Tibet but also by India, Egypt, and the entire East. Just as unlucky travelers cannot see the radiance of the mountain peaks on misty days, so also were these travelers not fortunate enough to contact the places and circumstances of importance. One can see beautiful, historical Paris, but one can also see in it its repelling modern aspect. You may see one New York, or you may see its most unattractive quarters.

These two aspects, often mutually exclusive, are everywhere. Thus, there is nothing to fear that the Tibetan uplands—unusual as they are—will become vulgar. Even now, in some Tibetan bazaars there is nothing extraordinary except colorful folk products. How can one penetrate beyond these appearances? Of course, the language is needed, but the mere physical language is not in itself sufficient. One must possess an inner language; if it is found, much will be revealed; but if it is not found, then no concordance will result.

It is said, especially in the Orient, that the language of the heart is required, but no doubt it is necessary everywhere. No matter with what technology people may cover themselves, they will always converge and separate along other paths, paths that—through the Tibetan uplands, through the highest mountains—will always remain unusual.

The statements of wise travelers over many centuries must certainly have a foundation. These self-sacrificing searches were real experiences. Many of their statements remain fully convincing. The diaries of these travelers are even now read with great attention, so accurately did they record that which they saw and experienced.

Franke reported that beyond a certain place in the Himalayas, the guides refused to go, stating that beyond those mountains there was something unusual; this serious scientist recorded this statement in full earnestness. And we find similar statements by that remarkable man of the past—Przhevalsky.

The new Dalai Lama has still not been found—it has

been an unusually long period. One remembers the great Fifth Dalai Lama. No one knows of the last years of his life, when and whither he went. How unusually secret was his departure! This too lends to the mystery of Tibet.

IRAN

"THIS I ask Thee, tell it to me truly, Lord,
      Who the Sire was, Father, first of holiness?
Who the pathway for the sun and stars ordained,
Who through whom is't moon doth wax and wane again,
This and much else do I beg, O God, to know."
Thus spoke Zarathustra!
Many deep thoughts reverberated on the Iranian upland.

Over a year ago we entered into our diary: "From March on, Persia will cease to exist. Iran will be in its place. It is difficult to judge from afar the true reasons for this change of the name. At times these changes seem epidemical—so much has been renamed nowadays, geographically and socially."

As if in some great migrations, people move from old places to new ones. Perhaps they try to find earth where less blood has been spilled. Or they recall some ancient paths. Or striving into the future, first of all these travelers want movement as such. They dream of something rejuvenated and mighty.

We do not know why Iran instead of Persia. We do not know why precisely from March. But anyhow, the ancient name "Iran" sounds majestical—there is great scope in it—many great remembrances and promising aspirations. From our very heart, let us wish to Iran that which so beautifully resounds when this ancient concept is pronounced. Let us thus express our wishes to the valiant Shah of Iran—Riza Khan Pehlevi.

We do not know whether our "Himalayas" reached Persia, or as of now, Iran. Precisely, let the unsurpassed Himalayas transmit their greeting to the snowy giants of Iran. Let them remind of the ancient and always glorious songs of heroism.

Perhaps the old songs are not still resounding everywhere. The picturesque garments have begun to disappear. But will not the reborn concept of Iran remind the people of the beautiful treasures inherited by them from past ages? Will it not remind one of the two and a half thousand years of history during the waves of which the Empire stood and now with renewed might is ascending the steps of self-realization?

Is not "Shahnama"—the "Book of Kings"—really beautiful, expressing, as it does, the entire Iranian magnitude? And was not this immortal poem created by the thought of the great poet! The primordial struggle of Light and darkness, the symbol of the participation of man in the increase of good and evil is expressed in the beautiful images of Iran. Now when the country wishes to reveal, even through its name, glory, strength, and depth of thought, then one can consider such a change of name as a sign of inner growth.

Many beautiful pages have been recorded in the history of Iran. Let us remember the heroical names of the satrapies: Media, Elam, Parthia, Haraiva, Bactria, Sughd, Khwarazm, Drangiana, Arachosia, Thattagush, Sindh, Egypt, Armenian Cappadocia, Sparda, Ionia, Skudra, Kushiya, Machiya, Karkas! The names alone already convey a fairy tale of glory! Who did not dream of Passargadae, of Babylon, of Suza, of Ecbatana, of Persepolis! Whose imagination was not uplifted by the sight of the gorgeous images on the rocks and colossal statues—guardians of the entry into the ruined palaces? Even in such remnants you feel the greatness of the past; even the chips of the beautiful ornaments of the floor, even the smallest fragments of magnificent necklaces—they all speak of the inspiring scope and quality of creativeness.

The name of Khorsabad vividly reminds us of one of the founders, Sargon, with all the legends and myths that surround him. The beautiful bas-reliefs again bring to life these semi-mythical heroes. Nimrud, with the ruins of the palace of Assur-nazir-pal! Also the Kuyunjik and the palace of Mineherib and the ruins of the gorgeous dwelling of Tiglatpalassar in Kalat Pergat! And the famous gates with reliefs of the deeds of Shalmaneser. And the marvelous dyorithian statues, vessels, and Babylonian bronzes! And the palace of Artaxerxes! And finally, the unforgettable library of Assurbanipal—such eternal treasures transmute remote antiquity into a majestic reality. Even in the last century, all these memorable places were still lifeless burial mounds. And even in our presence, so many significant scrolls were still unrolled. Only in our days were found the most important Babylonian sagas of the biblical flood and parts of the epos dedicated to Gilgamesh. All these treasures will be unveiled by the incantation of one word—Iran—and will give wings to new thoughts. Iran! Iran! Iran!

And Zarathustra, Who brought the Fire; and Mani, and the Bahaists; and the living Messian mystery of the Great Imam . . . From the ancient Sumerians, through Babylon, through to Achaemenides, and up through the time of all the inspired Iranian poets on the wings of the miraculous Al-Borak "sparkled the rays of highest knowledge and highest culture"! Does not all this uplift the imagination? The wizard of the mountains—the rock of Alarnut, crowned with an unconquerable citadel on its summit! And the Kitab-al-Agani! And the snow-white Demavend! And like Guru Charaka, upon the blossoming meadows of Hamadan, the famous philosopher and healer Abu-Ali-ibn-Sina searches for wonder-working herbs; who in the West does not know him as Avicenna? His works are, at present, being published with great reverence in Europe.

From the same flowery meadows are born the unforgettable Isfahan and Ardabil carpets. No one can forget the artists of Iran: Bihzad, Riza Abbasi, Ustad Muhammadi,

Aqa Mirak from Herat with all their pictorial wonders from Shahnama, with the entire epic of Iskander, with the popular images of King Bahram and Asad. Also like an immense meadow in full bloom!

And even now, do they not still live among us, those sonorous verses of such poets as: Rudaki, Ferdowsi, Anvari, Qatran, Omar Khayyam, Sa'di, Rumi, and Hafiz—sonnets, odes, elegies, poems, in which the beloved heroes of Iran proclaim unforgettable words of valor, achievement, devotion, and love?

Countless are the images with which the history of Iran is imbued. Everyone remembers the valley of Shiraz, of the roses of Shiraz.

A famous ode, in which Hafiz sums up the charms of Shiraz, begins:

> *Khusha Shīrazu viz' i bī misalash*
> *Khudavanda nigah dar az zawalash.*

> "Fair is Shiraz and matchless her display.
> O God, protect her ever from decay."

ATTRACTION

LIVINGSTONE could only be taken away dead from Africa, so much did he love this part of the world. Casati was forcibly removed from Africa, the only place in which he felt himself at home. All the remainder of his life, which he passed in Italy, his native land, he felt unhappy.

There could be enumerated a great number of diverse examples of such, as it were, incomprehensible attractions to a definite part of the world or even to a definite place. There are Spaniards by blood who cling to Havana or South America. There are Britons who have become forever attached to Australia. There are Swedes, French people, Russians who can only breathe the air of Asia.

In human life it is so difficult to explain attractions, from the loftiest to the most every day. On the one side, we see attraction to the place of one's birth. There are many explanations for this. But how then can we divine an inexplicable, overpowering attraction to some far-removed place on the earthly globe. Often people strike out thither as if accidentally. And all at once they find themselves, as it were, anew in their native setting. Of course, no one has expelled them from their birthplace. No offenses or crimes have driven them beyond remote seas and mountains. Consequently, there must have been some other basis, some other magnet, which compelled them to strive with their whole heart to a place that no rational process could have counseled.

Such attractions are entirely distinct from the proper desire of youth to set out somewhere, to get away somewhere, to spread their wings somewhere in new air. In the hour of such decisions, the youthful searcher does not even give a thought as to precisely whither he wishes to go. He knows only calls, perhaps cries of the heart, which draw him to finding out about something. Noble characters are usually found in such seekers. They are voluntarily searching for some testing. These first days of independence will forever remain for them a beacon of stimulation.

In thought we send greetings to one of our American friends, who now, in the twilight years, with especial animation and tenderness, recalls his first boat journey as a youth. This wise old man has related to me how, in his turn, he sent his only grandchild on horseback from the Pacific Ocean to the Atlantic in order to accustom the ten-year-old to complete independence. Probably somewhere on the marked-off route, there was unseen care for the young wayfarer; but for all that he had to carry out his task, he was left to his own resourcefulness and reliability. Of course, travel in America, unusually complex and crowded with movement, can sometimes be full of all sorts of surprises. Besides, there was the stipulation that the young horseman not only preserve his own health, but that he keep his mount in good condition. Doubtless such a trip will remain in his memory as long as he lives.

Likewise we have all read about young people who have rushed off to America in quest of a new life. And in such cases, the journey itself drew them, the search for new solutions of life; but for all that, this was not always the discovery of the desired place in which they would like to localize their work and life.

Otherwise, there sounds the story about a five-year old Tibetan lad who repeatedly and unrestrainedly went off to his own mysterious home. The boy dressed himself, as it were, for the road. He tied on his back a supply of food and a sacred book, and at a convenient moment he disappeared from the house. When they rushed off to search for him, they found him going along a mountain pathway.

They tried to persuade him to return home. They told him that he ought to get back to his own house. But the lad assured them that he was going to precisely his own real home, that the house where he had lived up to that time was not his, and that he must hasten to his real home, where he must remain. We passed this place just as the boy, for the fourth time, had left, and we do not know how it ended up.

In any case, this was some sort of irresistible attraction, and it is quite possible that if it remained unfulfilled, the little one would wither, as a blossom without moisture. It was amazing to observe how the five-year-old urchin explained so seriously about his real home to which he must go.

Here are Livingstone and Casati and all the countless wayfarers [going] to their real homes, where they would wither if they could not succeed in reaching their destination, which was so clear in their hearts. Besides, this circumstance is especially striking, how these aspirants were not only seeking the salubrious conditions of nature, they were also not striving for some well-ordered place of abode. On the contrary, their home, their real home, involved much hardship. Such a longed-for home was often almost unendurable for their bodies, but for all that, their spirits exulted and they felt themselves at home.

"Beauty lies in the eyes of the beholder."

This adage shows deep insight. In it is emphasized an inner significance that surpasses everything external. If such a wayfarer has found his home, it would be ruinous to tear him away in accordance with some external circumstances. No official advancements, no tempting advantages can compensate a man for the home that he has finally discovered. He need not be made a member of the nation or tribe among which this inexplicable home of his is located. He is attracted thither, not so much by the people as by all the other circumstances of existence. Of course, when such is good for a man, it is usually not even possible to explain in words why it is good for him.

Sometimes this feeling of well-being arises even under very arduous circumstances.

Precisely likewise when a man encounters his fellow wayfarers or his opponents, often he cannot give himself any rational explanation; yet through his eyes and his heart, he knows much that cannot be expressed in words. People ought to refer with all care to such attractions. They should grasp them in their very inceptions in order not to extinguish or shatter them by the fettering action of reason. If such an attraction has awakened in a man, his nature may alter, and he may be forever corrupted; but nothing will succeed in expelling from his consciousness that which his heart, his spirit knows.

We also know people who have been permanently wounded. Someone has sometime not admitted them to their recognized home. Or someone or something has deprived them of a discovered fellow traveler. The ignorant consider such attractions nonsense, a preconception that should be terminated by any means. These ignorant ones never reflect whither, from what cause, this knowledge emanates. But on the other hand, it can be seen what an enormous significance for the entire life of a man is produced by the discovery of this, his recognized home, by the finding of his destined, formerly encountered, fellow traveler. Even if for some reason, for some good, the man should be voluntarily separated for a time from his home and his companion, nevertheless, all of his activity in the course of the temporary separation will proceed under the sign of the achieved realization.

The man has found his home; he has found his companion; he has been fortified by long-established magnets; and thus the more clearly and resonantly can he produce great usefulness for his fellow man. The heart knows when it is again fitting to make contact with some other homes, and when the hour approaches to inspire some other fellow travelers. Such straight-knowledge of the heart does not weaken a man; it merely transforms his activity. Many ask whence are such forces, such assurances to be taken?

They proceed from realization of the desired home, from the mutual strengthening of the longed-for companion. The family and teachers must deal very carefully with such a manifest attraction. The home may be very near, or it may be beyond mountains and valleys. And the companion will be found when nothing is allowed to obscure the true, destined attractions.

Tzagan Kure, April 27, 1935

MOBILITY

LAMA M. has begun visits to monasteries. Undoubtedly he will again collect much significant information both about old traditions and about all medicinal matters. It is very good that he goes. In this mobility is contained precisely that quality that I always recommend to our coworkers. The Tibetan physician D.T. also departs into the mountains. If he does not renew his supplies, if he puts off meeting with other doctor-lamas, his store will be quickly impoverished. Also, two other coworkers are setting forth—one into Lahore, the other beyond the ocean.

When we founded the institute, we had in view first of all a continuous mobility of labor. From the time of its foundation, each year there have taken place expeditions and excursions. It would not be well to depart from this already established tradition. If all the coworkers and correspondents were bound together in one place, how many excellent but unexpected possibilities would be confirmed. Of course, people do not gather together in order that, seated in one room, they continually feed themselves with information sent to them. This would be only a halfway form of labor.

What is needed is that which Hindus so heartily and significantly call the "ashram." This is the central point. But the mental nourishment of the "ashram" is procured in various places. Entirely unexpected wayfarers come to it, each with his own experience. But also, the coworkers of the "ashram" do not remain sitting there. At all new possibilities, they go in different directions and augment their scientific supplies. Not without reason was it told long ago that when the brethren went abroad, a prior of the monastery said, "Again our monastery is being broadened." It seemed that the brethren were scattering, but the prior actually considered this circumstance an extension of the monastery. And so, at present, every exchange of scientific forces, all expeditions and journeys become an indispensable condition of all progress. In this, people learn and extend the limits of their own specialty. The traveler sees much. The wayfarer, if he is not blind, involuntarily perceives much that is remarkable. In the same manner, the single, narrow profession, which once had such a hold upon humanity, is again replaced by a broad cognition.

Often even domains, apparently far removed from each other, become beneficial coworkers. And it must precisely be thus, because the final striving of humanity, based upon collaboration, upon cooperation, first of all learns synthesis. Still, not so long ago people were very much afraid of this unifying concept. Let us recall how Anatole France and many other enlightened writers were subtly ironical about inordinate specialization. Actually, in nature all thus cooperates: everything is so blended and balanced that only the conscious collaboration of peoples respond to these basic laws of all that exists.

The usefulness of travel and manifold discernment has probably, as never before, so occupied the minds of people as at present. The earthly globe will be quickly crisscrossed with traversed paths. But this, nevertheless, will be only a primary degree of realization. And on each of these paths, it will be needful both to gaze loftily upward and to penetrate deeply within in order to appreciate the multiformity of possibilities that generally went unnoticed not long ago.

One thing is dangerous, that amid all the traveling, there are too many sporting trips and contests being developed. In these purely external, mechanical competitions, much is lost that would be especially needful to compensate for in our day. All contests of strength, endurance, and speed need to be turned into contests of quickness and depth of thinking, of discernment. Each one has a store of anecdotes of school misunderstandings and peculiarities; we need not repeat them. But let us very steadfastly remember that one-sided technical education should not be striven for.

All limited, conventional technical schools are already manifested as outmoded before the repeated, imperative, and ascending concept of synthesis. If a technical school somewhere relies on a robot, the deeply comprehended synthesis gives a new breadth of horizon. In founding sections of establishments in different countries, we had precisely in view that sometime and somehow there would result the closest communication of all coworkers. They enrich each other; they encourage each other; and they exchange with each other the most undeferrable, useful concepts. If, then, there is manifested in the establishments some possibility for new cognitions, expeditions, visits, then let not this possibility be thrown aside.

Let us continue the already formed tradition of mutual acquaintances. Let us look upon each new visit of places by our coworkers as a true development of instructive work. Yet for this let us first of all develop true mobility.

When we speak about mobility, let us not forget that it is not near to many. Not a few people like to talk about mobility. Seated in easy chairs at the evening table, they are very easily ready to dream, to rise up and depart, to create and labor in new places. But as soon as the matter reaches the point of carrying out these musings, many will find ten reasons that prevent them. Each of us can call to mind, even in the recent past, instructive episodes of how those already entirely prepared to set out on a distant path feebly sink back, detained in their easy chair. The reasons for the retreat were, of course, numerous, and, as it were, worthy of vital consideration.

When a man wishes to justify himself for not doing something, you may be sure that he will find a great number of justifying causes. In this, immobility will be praised by very many. Yet mobility, that is, desire of new work, of new cognition, will be very easily censured. People will speak about empty dreaming, about unrealizable aspirations, about gullibility; few fail to show a resourceful ingenuity when they wish to avoid something whispered by the heart.

How many times have we read letters full of aspiration at a distance, full of readiness for renewed work, but as soon as you ask the writer when he can set out on a new career, he falls into a very strange silence. Obviously, all the dustiness of life has beset the tongue of the heart and reduced it to silence. All the horned doubts have crawled forth; all the absurd considerations have been listened to; and still another possibility has been lost. It is not only that it has been lost to the individual, but that it could oppress and injure a great number of people far and near.

For the sake of visionary help to a few, there has been forgotten cooperation and assistance in very great matters. The basic cause, however, has been proved to be immobility, attachment to one's easy chair. And, too, beyond immobility rises up the specter of fear in general before any novelty. This specter leads to decay and senility. When, then, such dissolution encroaches, by no external means can it be helped. Yet so many times nothing else but some wretched things have made people immobile. We ourselves have seen absolutely deplorable examples when people, apparently intelligent, have doomed themselves to the saddest sort of existence due to attachment to things. Ah, these things again! These rough tags of a dusty way of life. Sometimes they begin to rule to such an extent that the voice of the heart sounds not only improbable but even, as it were, irrelevant.

I always rejoice when I see mobility in coworkers.

MUSCAPHOBIA

OUR dog, Nokhor, is sick. In English the canine plague is called "distemper," that is, disorder or derangement. The definition is entirely correct. Indeed, there takes place in the dog complete disorganization, both physical and psychic. Besides a queerness in eating, walking, and in relationship to his surroundings, all kinds of fears have been displayed. To all these varieties of fear has been added still another curious manifestation. We have noticed that Nokhor suddenly turns himself around impetuously as if to some invisible thing, jumps up, and, tucking his tail between his legs, flees into some corner. Knowing that dogs often see things invisible to us, we attributed these inexplicable movements of terror to something not understood by us. The explanation proved to be a very prosaic one. In the springtime, there appeared the first tiny flies, and it turned out that these were precisely the cause of this fright.

Certainly in a normal condition the large dog would pay no attention to these first tiny flies. But the disorder of distemper obviously made out of these small insects some imagined monsters. Anything may be expected from a sick dog. All of us merely regretted that the disorder could inspire absurd ideas to such an extent. Of course, the most unimaginable considerations are manifested to people during insanity. Moreover, the preciseness and concreteness of these imaginings is always striking.

Whoever has heard how sincerely a sick man describes something as if seen by him is amazed at that inexpressible conviction that permeates all the details of the description.

Even when you yourselves distinctly know there was not and could not be anything like it, nevertheless you experience an unpleasant sensation at the heaping up as of actual details.

Recalling all the tales about fear that agitate people who are considered normal, you are involuntarily reminded about the muscaphobia of the dog. Indeed, our time is full of all kinds of confusions. Indeed, in such tense times the imagination is in an especially painful mood. But for all that, when you encounter obvious muscaphobia, you are always sincerely sorry for such people—these biped rational beings who so shamefully doom themselves to illusory terrors.

Among these terrors is conspicuous the egotistical surmise: What do they think about me? Moreover, it is to completely lose sight of about whom precisely the suppositions are being made. Is it what the fly thinks, or the pig, or the wolf, or the dog? Is it what the lowest rascal or the worthiest man thinks? The consideration is completely lost that one cannot occupy one's attention equally with either the opinion of the lowest rascal or with the thought of the worthiest man.

In moments of illusory terror, people completely forget that the thinking of the lowest criminal scoundrel does not coincide with the judgment of the worthiest cultured thinker. On the contrary, it would be unnatural if low, mean thinking could go along the same paths as the thought of the loftiest being.

In illusory terror, people forget that either they would wish to be considered from the viewpoint of the criminal dregs or else they wish to base themselves upon the judgments of pure and lofty minds. Of course, both do not coincide by any means.

One has had occasion to see people deeply distressed by the fact that some base, evil person spoke abusively about them. When asked, "Would you rejoice then at words of praise from the mouth of this scoundrel?" They immediately reply, with a shudder, "That would be even worse than the abuse." And in reality, this would be worse than abuse. In fact, by such praise they would be classed with him who did the praising. Actually, they would show themselves to be the recognized criminal scum of humanity, and this would be the worst that could happen.

Yet in order to be able to reflect clearly about this choice, one needs first of all to cure oneself of fear. In this cure one needs to render a full account as to precisely where the powerful monster is and where are those flies of which the miserable sick dog is so afraid. When a man is fearful, when he has allowed terrors to take possession of his very essence, then everything surrounding him begins, as it were, to cry out about all of his fears. In the course of time, in another frame of mind, under other conditions, the man sees that the monsters that frightened him were tiny flies already stuck in a sugared flytrap. The formerly terrifying flies have themselves rushed at the sugar, which betrays them, and will be thrown out with the other rubbish.

The plague of fear prevents a man from advancing freely. In the fear of things, the man prefers to rot in the cellar rather than to look up at the Divine Light. When someone tells these frightened ones about strong people, who though only as cabin boys saw the world, such a courageous decision appears to the frightened one as insanity. Indeed, fear prevents them from even thinking about movement. And here our Nokhor, miserable, has buried his nose in a dark corner and probably fears the tiny flies more than anything in the world.

It is related that certain travelers in Central Africa, among tribes of cannibals, have seen a cage in which were being fattened some captives from a neighboring tribe for the table of the local chief. Naturally, the travelers wished to help these doomed ones and so bought their freedom. But the captives had no desire to leave their cage because they were afraid they would not be fed so well and would have to move elsewhere. Either they were devoured or they were not—but this remained for them the only question;

whereas ready food for every day was more important to them than any other consideration. About the future they probably did not, in general, even know how to think. But the smell of food enchained them more strongly than any shackles.

We are reminded of another story, this one from the Middle Ages. A certain great lord received evidence of treachery on the part of his chaplain. There were no limits to the amazement of his retainers, who knew about the offense of the chaplain, when they found out that not only was he neither cast out nor executed but even received an especially savory food. When finally they asked the lord what this meant, he said, "One should not kill a priest. You see how fat he is. If we add to him still more succulent viands, this will deprive him of all mobility and activity." And calling to his chief cook, the lord said to him, "See that the chaplain does not grow thin, and if he doubles in weight, you will receive a handful of gold from me."

This means that the fetters of today, the shackles of luxury, prove to be very powerful. Yet in the base, nevertheless, will lie an animal fear for the belly and self-gratification.

If on the one side, we confront the immobility of self-enjoyment, and on the other, remember the example of terror at the flies, then it becomes perfectly clear that by some sort of admonishment, people need first of all to be freed from fear.

Poor sick dog. He fears the flies. And all of us regret seeing such senselessness. But surely, people are not distempered dogs, and it would seem they should be able to render themselves an account as to where precisely are the flies and where actual danger—in the full significance of this word.

Muscaphobia is not worthy of people.

THE DESERTS SHALL BLOSSOM AGAIN

FROM time to time, humanity fittingly reminds itself of the need of revitalizing the deserts—those malignant and leprous spots of earth. It is true that these efforts occur only sporadically. Somewhere, something must be done for reforestation! But the native inhabitants of a locality themselves, with the most predatory instincts, try to deforest the land—in other words, they impair their own conditions of existence. In this regard, it is extremely encouraging to see the reforestation of various countries. At times in our own schools, we celebrate Arbor Day, but the occasion remains a superficial outing, while the serious implication and entire purpose of this celebration is overlooked.

If the rural populations, however, are so indifferent to the questions of reforestation and forest reserves, which seem so obvious, they are still more indifferent to the subject of drought-resistant grasses and plants.

A curious episode was related to us by our expedition botanist, Professor T. P. Cordeyev, in regard to the planting of grass: he once tried to explain to a peasant the importance of methods of sowing grass so as to insure fertilization and strengthening of the soil. The peasant listened to him very morosely. Finally the botanist asked him, "Why do you not begin this practical work on your own land?"

"You mean me?" the peasant asked sternly.

"Yes, you," the botanist said.

The answer was even more austere, "God creates the grass!"

The botanist again tried to find additional, obvious

proof. And again came the same exchange of conversation: "You mean me?" . . . "Yes, you."

And still louder came the reply, "God creates the grass!"

And for the third time, the botanist tried to explain the benefits of sowing grass. But by this time, the result was a threatening outcry from the peasant, "*God creates the grass!*"—after which it was evident that it was safer to stop the conversation.

This phrase, "God creates the grass," synthesizes the rural psychology—or, as one might even say, the universal psychology. In spite of due instruction and information, the great mass of the population still holds to the idea that trees as well as grass grow by themselves. And having cut away his forests and destroyed the grass without restraint, man is astonished at the ominous manner in which dead sands begin to overtake him and personal disaster becomes the anguish of the entire earth.

During our excavations in the completely dead sands of Asia, it was enlightening to unearth the roots of age-old forests. Strangely enough, precisely on those sites one may find excellent dwelling sites and bits of woven grasses, indicating that life once flourished here. The ancient Chinese Chronicles, with their meticulous notes of early Chinese travelers, describe these now-eroded sites as picturesque cities and villages that flourished amid plenty. We cannot attribute these changes entirely to cosmic actions. The hand of man has been especially reprehensible. For instance, the picturesque Kangra Valley in the Punjab, during the comparatively recent times of Emperor Akbar, was regarded as one of the most thickly forested localities; at present this locality is beginning to suffer from a lack of trees. Although the local government is doing everything possible to fight this evident misfortune, the initial misstep was taken long ago, and the successive tasks have become increasingly burdensome. The man who cuts away a tree is generally quite indifferent to the need of planting another immediately to take its place, or at least of taking some care that the ugly remaining stump should not impede the young seed trees. As for regulating the crowded seedling—this is out of the question!

In the dead deserts of Asia, one may often hear the murmur of underground streams, which at times give rise to the beliefs in subterranean life. Not seldom have these streams been driven under stones and pebbles by human hands that have rapaciously destroyed the vegetation.

The expanses of sand in Central Asia, Lithuania, and America are limitless; thus, in the most diverse parts of the earth, one finds these same soil maladies that worry husbandmen. It is, therefore, readily understood why President Roosevelt and Secretary of Agriculture Wallace also worry over the rescue and revivification of the desert, not only through reforestation but also through the discovery of the best drought-resistant grasses. In this sense, the steppes and *gobis* of Asia provide wonderful material for study. Upon these sand dunes, upon these endless mounds is still preserved the original vegetation, which has withstood all types of catastrophes. The dunes of Barga—a part of Mongolia where "God still creates the grass"—provide opportunity for the most diverse, practical observations. There one still finds remnants of the great forests; there still are found great quantities of feather-grass and other steppe grasses that are at once strongly resistant and useful for forage. It is especially fitting that the study of these grasses, which withstand drought and other climatic catastrophes, is now being carried on along broad channels. Because such experiments require years of work, the sooner attention is paid to this imperative need of the earth, the sooner and more effectively will the panacea be found.

People who in the simplicity of their souls still think that "God creates the grass" should also remember the other proverb, "Trust God and do your own share."

Whenever I see the irrigation of the Egyptian desert, I always realize how comparatively little is needed in order to transform the seemingly dead surface to new blossoming. And in this regard, everyone—whether specialist or well-intentioned citizen—should cooperate equally in aiding the entire country. This will provide one of those anonymous, benevolent movements by which human existence is carried on.

Crossing the endless desert spaces, I always realize the countless possibilities still preserved in these virgin steppes, these rich vistas, these expanses where the best breeds of cattle could again be raised for universal benefit. I do not even venture to speak here of the vast store of medicinal plants scattered throughout these regions, verily by divine grace, and still utilized so little by men. And science has only now begun to pay attention to these treasures, which have been known for centuries but have been forgotten in the bustle of life.

Also, only now are people beginning to study with utmost exactness the local languages in order to avoid the errors that so often arose through lack of precise translation. In many conventional and symbolic expressions of the Tibetan and Ayurvedic pharmacopeia emerges the profound significance of the ancient experiments. From the medical point of view, Barga and the slopes of Hingan offer excellent *materia medica*. Together with the discoveries, one's path here is enlivened by the peaceful Mongols whom one encounters and whom the entire sympathy of one's soul goes out to. Of course, only knowledge of their language will draw from them the secrets of their souls. On the way we visited one of the greatest Mongolian monasteries—Ganjur. The name of the monastery has itself been preserved from the eighteenth century, when the Chinese Emperor donated to it the complete collection of the sacred books of the Ganjur. We saw these volumes and admired the excellent edition made in Peking; unfortunately, the wood bindings were destroyed in one of the recent catastrophes.

In the Ganjur, George found, in the possession of one of the old lamas, a Tibetan medical manuscript and succeeded in copying it; it is most fortunate that he possesses a complete familiarity with Mongolian and Tibetan because for this work, it is invaluable. In the monastery there are numerous images, and the lamas speak of the coming "War of Shambhala," adding, "But a man of great heart is needed for it." We were present in the monastery during the discourses of the pupils, when the little ones, clapping hands, ask each other the most extraordinary questions. How illuminating are these ancient traditions!

During our trip, we realized again and again how necessary it is to preserve these irreplaceable treasures. And how often today, with all of our relative civilizations, do the most dreadful barbarities occur. Yes, we must learn to safeguard not only the treasures of man's handiwork but to extend this caution to all the true sources of light. For this reason, the revivification of the deserts, literally as well as in its sublimated spiritual implication, becomes one of the most noble responsibilities of humanity.

May all the deserts blossom again!

AFFIRMATION

THERE are before me two communications: one from South America, the other about Siberia beyond the Arctic Circle. The news is quite different, and still the essence is the same. Up to quite recently, the inquisitors of science would have condemned both suppositions. But life does not tarry to vindicate the boldest guesses.

Only recently the word "Atlantis" came again into use. Only recently, the ancient communications with the American continent were still considered fairy tales. Only during our generation was the Siberian tundra beginning to show, instead of its deadliness, its subterranean riches.

Life itself revealed the frozen ancient Vikings and mammoths preserved under the cover of ice. Life revealed the temples of the Mayas and the Aztecs, disclosed Taxila and Harappa, and presented to humanity new scripts and hieroglyphs. Generously, these treasures were given out. Lavishly were the treasuries opened.

The communication says:

"The Brazilian archaeologist Bernard da Sylva Ramos, who for many years has been excavating in the Centre of Brazil, recently published a book, *Inscriptions of Prehistoric America*, in which he proves that America was known to the cultured Asiatic nations over two thousand five hundred years before Columbus discovered this continent.

The main proof consists of an inscription on the rock of Gávea in Brazil, which up to now was regarded as undecipherable, and which Ramos has now succeeded in reading. The text, according to him, is as follows: "Tyre, Phoenicia. Badezir, Firstborn of Jethbaal.""

Badezir, or otherwise Baltazaar, was the King of Phoenicia in the ninth century B.C. His father was Itobal or Ishbaal. The inscription on the rock of Gávea was probably carved by subjects of Baltazaar, who came to Brazil for commercial purposes. According to Ramos, the Phoenicians conducted a brisk trade with America, crossing the ocean on sailing ships, availing themselves of the ocean currents, and stopping at an island en route between Africa and America.

Some settlements in South America up to now bear Semitic names. This circumstance greatly baffled scientists, but the inscription deciphered by Ramos explains this enigma. The Phoenicians not only traded with the aborigines of America but founded there their own settlements, something in the nature of factories and concessions and, of course, gave them Semitic names.

From another part of the world, it is announced that in Siberia, near Salegarda, in the Valley of the Ob and beyond the Arctic Circle, there have recently been discovered ruins of two ancient cities.

"Last year, an expedition of the Academy of Sciences of the U.S.S.R., under the leadership of Adrianov, started excavations in the delta of the Poluya River near Salegarda (in the Yamalo-Nenetzky district of the Omsk province), which revealed cities of unknown people who lived there in remotest antiquity, in the Transpolar Ob region.

During the excavations the expedition found artistic objects that prove the high cultural level of the inhabitants of this city. The excavations continued and a second city, 40 km from Salegarda, was unearthed.

In both cities, about thirty-six thousand different objects were collected, which evidently belonged to the Scythian culture. The excavations definitely prove that at the time of the existence of these cities, the flora and fauna there were different. The bones of birds and animals discovered in these cities show that there were abundant vegetation and large forests there, where now a barren icy desert stretches itself. It was also possible to define the type of buildings—they were light structures, surrounded by a ditch and an earthen rampart.

So far, what kind of people lived in this transpolar region in remote antiquity remains a historic problem that scientists have to solve."

Such communications are extremely significant. From South America and from Siberia, one justly expected revelations about the distant past. And now these regions of ancient settlements have begun to give up their mysteries. It becomes clear once more that the discoveries are not only not exhausted, but that it is more correct to say that they have not even been properly started.

It is strange to remember how recently much was considered impossible. People scoffed at Schliemann's "fantasies" about Troy. People shrugged their shoulders when statues of Astarte were found in Kiev (Russia). The remarkable animal style was ignored. And not only was all this unknown and neglected, but forerunners of these discoverers were rejected.

To such historical confirmations, there also should be added signs of other domains of science. People laughed when someone said he could receive radio waves without a receiver. People laughed when a pipe in the kitchen suddenly began to broadcast music from the radio. Now there is food for more "laughter."

The press announced: "The so-called 'anomaly of the atmosphere,' recorded periodically every fifty-fourth day by radio stations in all countries, has lately become a matter of serious scientific research. The M. T. Telephone and Telegraph Company is conducting uninterrupted investigations, trying to solve this mysterious manifestation."

And as a result of these investigations, some new facts were revealed. Thus it turned out that the phenomena took place as a rule on the fifty-fourth day but sometimes as an exception on the forty-third day. All radio stations of the Far East were completely paralyzed for a certain period of time on February 8, April 2, May 15, and May 27 to 28. This phenomenon placed before the radio and astronomic investigators a most interesting problem. It was found that the phenomena coincided with the passing across the sun of the most intense solar spots.

The culminating point of the maximum and minimum phase of the phenomena was established over a period of twenty-seven days—that is to say, just that period during which the sun completes its full revolution around its axis.

However, on May 15, the phenomenon occurred on the forty-third day and the reckoning from April 2, and this was an exception in the established periodicity. On May 23, that is to say, on the fifty-fourth day of the previous regular anomaly, the phenomenon was not observed, and it took place only on May 27 and 28; and, moreover, on May 28, the anomaly was witnessed twice, at noon and at 3 p.m. The indicator of the saturation of ions of the upper strata of the atmosphere on May 26, 27, and 28 also showed the presence of obvious irregularity of the state of the ion strata.

Taking into consideration the mentioned facts and also that the year 1936 is the culminating point for the period of the increase of the sun's activity, which manifests itself every eleventh year; and taking into consideration that the radio irregularity takes place only during the daytime, there can be no doubt that this phenomenon depends on solar activity.

On the base of scientific observations, the hypothesis has been construed that the said phenomena are called forth by the active influence of the sun, which increases the density of the ion strata "E" to such an extent that it prevents the conductivity of short-frequency electric waves.

This also explains the fact that this phenomenon does not interfere with the long waves, which do not penetrate the ion strata but are transmitted in the immediate neighborhood of the earth's surface.

Results of research during the full solar eclipse may, to a considerable extent, reveal the enigma of the ion strata of the atmosphere, which extends some hundred kilometers above the earth.

Such observations compel us once more to ponder upon a great many inexplicable conditions and possibilities that arise before every searching eye. In the heat of disputes, many phenomena are attributed to solar spots. Many "spots" should be investigated!

* * *

There is a story of how a certain ship was once instructed to fulfill, at midnight, a secret sinister mission. The captain of the ship took every precaution to approach the indicated spot as quietly as possible; all lights were extinguished, and not a single sound betrayed the presence of the ship. It seemed that every possible human precaution had been applied. But at the very moment when the ship had reached the destination, not having been heard or seen by anyone, there suddenly flashed up on the entire rigging the fires of St. Elmo—some power had upset all the human machinations!

PLAGUES

IN the past year in the United States of America alone, one hundred thousand people perished from cancer. Add to this shocking figure all the other victims carried away by cancer in Europe and other countries, and the total sum resulting is the loss of an entire war. The misery of cancerous illnesses differs externally from other epidemics. People are terrified by cancer. They build still another hospital. They announce in the newspaper about the means of completely curing cancer, yet the number of victims not only does not diminish but, I dare say, grows more menacing.

Cancer is not so tempestuous as The Black Death or cholera, but it will continue to advance so long as actual prophylaxes are not taken and attentive and lengthy investigations are not begun. By this we do not wish to affront those self-sacrificing physicians who are striving unceasingly to put an end to the deadly grip of cancer. There are well-known examples of the really amazing self-abnegation of some medical men.

The matter lies not in physicians alone but in people themselves, who for the sake of conventional habits do not destroy certain harmful features of their way of life. Already it has been repeatedly made known that statistics everywhere have fixed upon meat eating as one of the causes of cancerous illnesses. Precisely, the general shock to the nervous system amid the unhealthy conditions in contemporary cities is likewise manifested as a contributing factor to this frightful disease.

Meanwhile, there are certain localities where cancer

is generally unknown or appears only in imported cases. It is also known that higher altitudes are, as it were, manifested as a principle guarding against cancer. This would appear to mean that it is needful, first of all, to begin investigations in localities where cancer is generally absent and to ascertain precisely what local conditions are distinctive. It is also known that Tibetan Lamas have cured certain cases of cancer. In this treatment, the cure, of which we have been witnesses, is produced by vegetable substances under conditions used in definite mountain localities. This circumstance at once calls up the necessity of different researches into the remedies themselves and the special conditions of the prescribed locality. It may be the quality of mineral waters or of the soil, or the nearness of glaciers abounding in meteoric dust—who knows what conditions may be influential besides the purified mountain air and sun.

It would seem that these indicated circumstances must impel those who are either ill themselves or filled with philanthropic purposes to assist in these investigations. But the outcome of the matter is not altogether so simple. People are interested, but beyond inquiries and aimless wishes, the matter does not progress. Let us even admit that such researches would require considerable time. Let us admit that among them would occur partial disappointments. Nevertheless, statistical data and the already observed possibility of a cure for cancer, though only in certain forms, must be manifested as reason enough for the awakening of hearts to investigations of this kind.

The very shocking number of victims must compel people to reflect about increasing the means of research. The city laboratory method alone is not always successful in grasping the tortuous trail of the viper. If there is manifested even a hypothetical possibility of enriching methods of investigation, then surely this should be employed without losing a day or an hour. In such a manner, prophylactic conditions can be found that will render the very way of life healthful. On the other hand, it is possible to point out those already existing natural conditions that are manifested as a preventative against the frightful disease.

Why lose any time when a bold progressive work could be going on? Why be abstractly terrified at the numbers of victims, while something somewhere could be done upon the paths of salvation?

Such investigations are required immediately and not for cancer alone. I hear there is impending still another new scourge bearing the name of the Spanish influenza. Many physicians consider this form exceedingly close to a pulmonary plague. According to certain symptoms, this is actually something entirely analogous. Each year there can be seen a wave of such attacks flowing into different countries. In any case, there is in this some new form of disease. If that which we call a cold has formerly existed in deadly forms, then, too, on the contrary, that which has long been known as the *grippe* has grown into dangerous forms of the Spanish influenza.

Just now we read about the fact that at present many people are gravely ill with a strange form of inflammation of the lungs, which are being attributed to recent dust storms of unprecedented strength. Even animals breathe with similar symptoms. China has been passing through a grave form of similar illnesses. It is thought that from the valley of the Yangtze, whirlwinds are bearing infectious dust with clearly defined bacteria.

In one way or another, we are again encountering an enhanced form of lung and throat disease. If, then, we take into consideration all the increasing cases of heart disease, of a strange increase in blood pressure, of meningitis, and the other nerve-heart forms, then again can be seen the plague rising up against humanity, which is not noticeable in the cinema or at dancing parties, at horse-races or prizefights.

"Orgies during the plague," in the words of the gifted poet, always calls to mind those follies that so easily lead to irreparable consequences.

Since the Great War, among all the peace conferences,

the nations have expended sixty billion dollars on armaments. Right now, mobilizations are rumbling again. The possibility of war impends in various parts of the world. It would be instructive to know how much in the same period has been spent in the conflict with the monstrous plagues of humanity, such as cancer, heart diseases, forms of influenza, and other menaces. Let us not count in this figure already existing hospitals and other scientific and medical establishments. These attainments have already been accomplished. It would be significant to examine the amount of the figures spent in new researches and to compare them with those spent on armament.

It is said that up to the fifth month, children produce their own vitamins, but that after the fourteenth month, this quality is lost. Then, a particular prophylaxis is required. Why, then, not think about this, even within those limits that are easily within the range of thinking of each man? Indeed, one should not be intimidated by the infectiousness of diseases. Of course, it is newly recognized that cancer, as well as pulmonary diseases, is infectious.

It would be just as senseless to fill the consciousness with fearfulness and in that very way give access to any and all infections. Original thought about prophylaxis must not be a sign of fear. This should simply be the economy of life in order that it may be fulfilled in an excellent and harmonious tension of energy. Where it is possible to foresee a diminution of sufferings, they must be foreseen, and it is needful to achieve this with all humane measures.

It is impossible to charge physicians with the entire task. All people must be coworkers in the matter of the broadly conceived Red Cross. Thus, it is often the custom of those assembling for the famous cup of tea to bestir themselves with spoon and tongue, and then separate without any results. It is indispensable that each discourse bring in something effective. From these seeds, though they are small, is put together that which is greatest and undeferrable.

The scourge does not rise up by itself; the hand upraises

it. It is needful that the hand should not raise up the scourge. It is needful that the course and successful progress of peoples be in no need of scourges, when so much that is beautiful has been ordained.

[153]

FOOD

IN descriptions of the flora of the Far East, we read: "In addition to garden vegetables, the Chinese, Koreans, and others make use in their diet of many wild plants, which take the place of the cultivated varieties. In this there must be seen an adaptability of the people to the local conditions of life, where unexpected floods often inundate fields and gardens; or where tribes who live mainly by the hunt have no time to be occupied with garden culture, and yet in the village in spring, there is not enough green stuff. A local population that uses almost no meat in its diet must vary its table; but the poorest of them, thanks to an acquaintanceship with wild plants, never sit down without food. Early in the spring when rains are usually lacking and there is no green stuff in the gardens, cultivated vegetables are replaced by young leaves of ferns, by sprouts of marsh plants, and by the stems of the white peony. White goosefoot is used in the diet and wild sorrel, young stalks of wormwood, spring leaves of dandelions, sow thistle leaves, and many others.

"People living in marshy country or along river valleys eat the young shoots of the bullrush, tubers of arrowleaf, leaves of water lily.

"Among the known wild vegetables of the most nutritive value should be recognized the bulbs of different kinds of lilies, wild garlic, wild cherries, lily blossoms, martagon bulbs, and bracken leaves.

"Of the ferns, the young leaves of Aspidium felix are made use of in the diet. Leaves of the lily are usually gathered, dried in the sun, and stored away for winter.

The lily petals contain starch and have proved to be quite nutritious.

"Young greens, the winged seeds of the small-leaved elm, which grows everywhere, go into the diet in raw or cooked form. It is interesting to note that the bloom's chakomka are cooked and used for food."

Then there go on descriptions of edible nuts and mushrooms, as well as of nutritious seaweeds, varieties of beans, coriander, Colocasia, batata, inyam, wild yams, edible burdock (gobo), Perilla, Dolichos, and other useful and nutritious plants, which have long been esteemed by the local inhabitants. If, then, there are added to this long list all the strawberry, raspberry, lime, and other local teas and vegetable beverages, and it is remembered that even ordinary couch grass yields a nutritious decoction, one obtains an entire inventory of useful natural plants.

In this connection, it unwillingly strikes the eye that local people actually eat little meat, yet long experience has taught them to find a natural substitute for this universally current food. Compared with the lengthy roll of wild plants suitable for nourishment, the list of cultivated garden vegetables seems a relatively short one. People who often experience hunger and the harsh conditions of nature have actually begun to seek out all the possibilities for a food supply. For them it is too common an occurrence when an onrushing, unexpected flood, in the course of a few hours, turns fields and gardens into sandy hillocks. They know early and late frosts, and for centuries they have felt the destroying power of tornadoes. Indeed, all such necessities have directed attention long ago to the possibility of finding nutritive, sustaining food in the vegetable world.

When hunger breaks out, at first there usually begin to be complaints about the lack of generally used grains and meat. But altogether many other possibilities attract no attention. They are simply lost to view, for no one ever remembers about the natural gifts of nature. Science has established the fact that vegetables are more nourishing than meat. Indeed, science has once more whispered that ancient truth that a meat diet is not needed at all, except in cases of unavoidable necessity. In the study of vegetable vitamins, science is usually occupied with cultivated garden vegetables. Now for such investigations, it should turn to all the plants that grow in the wild state and thus are so readily obtainable.

Both tropical and Arctic climates yield a great number of nutritious wild plants. How useful it would be and how necessary to conduct researches upon these nourishing helpmates in the life of man! Indeed, outside of their unquestionable nutritive qualities, undoubtedly these plants also have medicinal properties that could unite nutrition with a direct aid to healthfulness. Among the cultivated garden vegetables, their medicinal properties are far from always investigated and applied. It could be so easy to combine both a nutritive and medicinal diet. As for that, in the most ancient covenants we see how a weekly change of food was proposed by which was foreseen not only the nutritive factor but also the remedial. Instead of a great number of patented surrogates, the most natural solutions of many problems have been placed at people's disposal in nature itself.

If the imagination is not stimulated as to the paths along which to seek the solution of such problems, then let us turn once again to history, to ethnography, to the study of the ways of life in all their details, even to those that are apparently strange at first glance. For the treatment of animals, rural doctors and healers first of all ascertained what herbage the animals were eating at the time of their falling ill. By such a natural, experienced way were found many useful remedies.

Among many peoples we have learned of articles of food not only useful but also most excellent, such as young bamboos, rose petals, and other unexpected but nutritious adaptations of the surrounding nature. We are not intending to compile a vegetarian cookbook, but through many travels, each one has been struck by the employment of wildly growing plants. Each one who is acquainted with their broad usage involuntarily advances a question as to why such plants should not be investigated scientifically from all their points of usefulness.

We see that, up to this time, new forms of flora are continually being disclosed. Even from this side, the investigations of the vegetation of the planet are far from concluded. It goes without saying that in the sense of the study of nutrition and medicinal properties, the question is likewise far, far from being elucidated. But for each keen-sighted one, it is obvious that the age-old experiences of many peoples can be broadly and usefully applied.

OUR LESSER BROTHERS

IN China it was considered especial good fortune to be devoured by a tiger.

There is narrated a remarkable method of hunting the lion in Africa. Having tracked down the king of the desert, the hunters go out after him without guns but with a large pack of small, vociferous dogs.

Hidden in the brush, the lion endures the clamor for some time, but at last among the branches begins to appear his menacing paw. The experienced hunter then says, "Now he's going to jump," and, sure enough, the terrible beast leaps high in the air and lands in the next thicket.

A new, fresh pack is then added. The barking of the dogs increases. Experienced hunters say, "He won't stand this for long." Then comes a strange moment, when the dogs in their consuming rage rush into the brush. The hunters say, "Let's go, he's already finished." The desert king cannot endure the barking and ends up dying from heart failure.

In India we have had occasion to observe a tribunal of monkeys. On a lofty rock is seated in a circle a full Areopagus of the oldest, grizzled judges. In the middle of the ring is placed the accused. He is obviously much alarmed and tries to prove something both by gesticulations and outcries, but the tribunal is inexorable. Some decision is reached, and the condemned, with his tail between his legs, whimpering pitifully, is taken to a steep cliff and cast into the roaring torrent. Thus it happens in the foothills of the Himalayas.

Indeed, if we listen to stories about the great apes living around the snow line, we can compile whole books. We have had occasion to see these mountain dwellers sitting sedately in a family circle in the open space around their cave. Observers have remarked, "Do they still not have flint implements?" In them is much similarity to men.

Here is still an animal perception, akin to man. In the cold wintertime, on the Tibetan highlands, the forage has disappeared under the snow. For three or four days, the camels have been sent by a route where exposed herbage has been reported. This hope has proved futile; deep snow has fallen there, and forage is not to be found. In the course of two weeks, all the camels have perished. We recall a clear winter morning in our camp, on the glittering, snowy upland, seeing some animal moving in the distance. A camel! Without men.

Slowly and with dignity the lone, emaciated camel approached our tents. Its manner was assured. With its last forces, it hastened to the place where it had formerly been fed. It recognized the camp unerringly as its home. In fact, it was fed with the last remnants of grain. Pack saddles were ripped open in order to procure the tufts of straw. Nevertheless, it lived through it all, this sole, faithful camel. It survived and later went with us through all the mountain passes, by the cornice-like trails, to Sikkim. We presented it to the Maharajah of Sikkim, and perhaps it is still living on his lands. This was the first two-humped camel that had entered India from Tibet. All the neighboring inhabitants came running to stare at it, and it calmly shook its head; and its deep and lustrous, wise eyes were like dark agate.

Very likely the eyes of a deer, beclouded by tears, are also full of expression when the hunter hastens to dispatch it, having wounded it. The more sensitive hearts, once gazing into such eyes, viewing these tears, will never again use a knife upon a dumb animal.

If only people would decide upon the killing of animals only when extreme need presses them, the need of food. All longing to kill must be abandoned. Medical treatises about the spread of cancer show that this scourge of humanity has been especially developed where a meat diet is on the increase. An experienced physician always forewarns that sooner or later one has to renounce meat if there are undesirable stones in the liver or similar adverse affections. From the standpoint of nutrition, one reads almost continually in scientific journals conclusive articles about vitamins that far transcend the necessity for meat. It must be hoped that the time has passed when brutal physicians prescribed raw meat and blood. How horrible it was when they even recommended blood drinking!

If even the question of preserving health, and the scientific experiments, and the counsels of physicians are not convincing, then will it not finally persuade one if one gazes into the eyes of animals?

The friend of the home is the dog. The eyes of a faithful dog can tell so much; moreover, they see more than ordinary people. How many times could it have been observed that a dog senses something invisible, bristles up, and warns one by growling! It is possible to recall very many narratives of such perceptions of animals. It appears to us that dogs sense more than other animals, but perhaps this only seems so to us—we observe the dog more than the other beasts. The dog has entered more into our way of life, and people have been accustomed to canine expressions.

One sheepdog asked for coins, collected them in its cheek, and went into the bakery and demanded a loaf with a bark. In Paris we knew a dog that went to fetch the newspaper. There are so many known examples of the self-renouncing behavior of dogs, when they themselves were prepared to freeze, giving warmth to their masters.

Everyone can remember the touching expressions in animals' eyes. People could learn much from them.

Today we got a new dog—*Nokhor,* which in Mongolia means "friend."

II

SCATTERED BEAUTY

BEAUTIFUL UNITY

COLOR, sound, and fragrance are cornerstones of great synthesis. From time immemorial, people have felt the great inner meaning of these expressions of the human soul. Quite recently people have again begun to remember how close are color and sound, and that the three are the basic remedies against human diseases. Thus he who thinks about the conception of color does not at all associate it with paint as such, but he has in mind one of the greatest concepts of our existence.

The color value of a painting, indeed, does not mean the mere value of paint but of its harmonic correlation, as the French say *valeur*. What does such correlation mean? Again we must say, that for him who is ignorant of the concepts of synthesis and symphony, such correlation will be an empty word.

Let us not dwell here on the deep significance of art for human life—this axiom should be clear to everyone. But nowadays we must especially stress the meaning of synthesis and the symphony of life. Synthesis will be understood by everyone to whom is close the concept of Culture. If human thinking were to remain but on the level of elementary civilization, then it would be too early to mention sacred synthesis; but where the human spirit has traveled toward Culture—that is to say, the Cult of Light—there one may already find cooperation and understanding on the basis of synthesis.

If civilization has not saved humanity from disunity and mutual hatred, then Culture has opened the beneficial gates of synthesis, behind which we can find a true cooperation.

The artists do not rest on primitive considerations of paint, but the very understanding of sonority of color leads them to such beautiful gardens from where may be seen superb vistas of the glorious future. When we speak of synthesis, and of the symphony of life, we shall not avoid powerful and enthusiastic expressions. All these domains of synthesis and symphony are uplifting and lead to the summits. Often the human eye can hardly stand the radiance of snowy peaks, and it is not for the human eye to judge the splendor of these summits. But we have not been called into this world to criticize, but to labor, to admire, and to follow these leading summits in continuous creation.

Create, create, and create! Create in daytime, create at night; for creation in thought is as essential as our physical expression. In this creativeness you shall overcome the most hideous habits of vulgarity, triviality, and quarreling. People sometimes think that creators are very selfish and conceited. But these ugly properties belong to the domain of darkness. When a person "climbs" to the Light, then such an abhorrent husk drops off by itself, and man becomes enlightened. His "I" is changed into the conception of "We."

On the same path toward the summits, man will understand the true meaning of *"Guruship."* From the depth of darkness one can hear at present disgusting cries: "Down with culture," "Down with heroes," "Down with teachers." It is a shame on humanity, but one witnesses such outcries of crass ignorance even nowadays. But he who thinks of such a refined conception as color and sound, culture and harmony, he will understand the infinite Hierarchy of Beauty and Knowledge; and having ascended the majestic stairs of achievement, he will lead also the pilgrims of life following behind.

It is splendid that you all are young. Some in age and some in spirit. Around creativeness there must be this perpetual feeling of youth, which gives incessant striving toward heroism. Countries measure their glory not by captains of industry but by artists and scientists. Such a requirement of history places upon us the duty of incessant perfectioning. He who never ceases in this ascension never becomes old.

I send you my heartiest greetings on this path toward the radiant summits, and I trust that you, forgetting all petty divisions and small human moods, will progress in continuous creation, cherishing the glorious traditions of your great Motherland, India!

Nolini Kanta Gupta writes in the *Triveni,* in the course of his article on the "Beautiful in the *Upanishads*":

"Art at its highest tends to become also the simplest and the most unconventional; and it is then the highest art, precisely because it does not aim at being artistic. The aesthetic motive is totally absent in the *Upanishads;* the sense of beauty is there, but it is attendant upon and involved in a deeper strand of consciousness."

Verily, Art at its highest does not tolerate any conventionality, nor violence. In the very foundations of Be-ness lives the concept of Beauty, in all its convincingness. We, as builders, do not deny, nor reject.

"In Beauty we are united!
Through Beauty we pray!
With Beauty we conquer!

"OEUVRE INCONNUE"

EXHIBITIONS were lately held, demonstrating the idea of which I had already the occasion to write and speak several times. From the point of view of the history of art, it is always most important to reveal the so-called unknown artists. The names of great masters are very often in public judgment collective conceptions. When looking over the standard handbooks on art, we will find, in addition to the well-known celebrities, numerous names whose creations are not commonly known. And yet these artists lived to an old age, worked incessantly, and had as their teachers, great masters.

About an exhibition in Paris, the press reported the following: "An exhibition of sixty paintings, acclaimed by connoisseurs as the highest works of art but bearing the signatures of unknown artists, was organized in Paris under the patronage of Georges Huysmans, and was heralded to be the most remarkable of the series of thirty exhibitions of the Parisian season."

An exhibition of unknown artists reminded old collectors and critics of many episodes concerning mistakes of judgment committed by the best authorities on art.

One of them narrates: "Thirty years ago I got the idea of submitting to the jury of an exhibition a small Roman landscape painted in light-yellow and bluish colors, and also a pen drawing representing a peasant with a large hat. Both paintings were flatly refused. And yet the landscape was by Corot, and the drawing was nothing less than one by Rembrandt himself."

Another art critic added that paintings by unknown

authors were now and then acquired by the largest art museums and believed to be by known great masters. On a recent exhibition of old Italian art in Paris, there was exhibited the famous *Open-Air Concert*, previously cataloped by outstanding authorities as a Titian and now regarded as a masterpiece of Giorgione.

Such anecdotes remind us of the famous saying of Toulouse-Lautrec: "A painting should be perceived by the heart." In other words, a painting should be valued on its merit, and not because of the signature. This French artist adds: "What would it matter if an image of an Evangelist turns out not to be by Velasquez, if its high quality ranks it equal to the brush of the latter!"

We can remember many facts from life that prove on what quicksand conventional judgment is based. In the Metropolitan Museum of Art in New York, there is a painting attributed to Matsys, which is actually a painting of the very interesting but completely unknown master of the Netherlands, Hasselaer. His signature, which I and the well-known authority on art, Senator Semenoff-Tianshansky, have seen was evidently removed by its previous owner. On the market it is, of course, an entirely different thing to sell an unknown Hasselaer in order to have the opportunity to offer a famous Matsys.

I myself have seen a written certificate by a well-known authority stating a painting to be a Rembrandt. Yet from this painting there had just been removed the name of Jan Victors, a distinguished pupil of Rembrandt. I also remember a landscape of the eighteenth century, under which was visible an older signature of the seventeenth century. One may cite many stories that eloquently prove that a painting should be judged not by the signature but on its merit.

There are two types of collectors. One group requires, first of all, only the name. The other demands an artistic quality. For the collectors of the former type, there have been created innumerable fakes. A rather rude art dealer used to laugh: "A signature costs but a couple of shillings!"

Many tragedies and dramas in the art word are due to the conventional judgment. Again, if we take the largest encyclopedia on art, one is struck by a multitude of completely unknown names, which apparently left no result of their activities, yet they were connected with the greatest masters. They were commissioned to adorn cathedrals and public buildings, which proves that they were en vogue. Besides, their names were cited by old historians of art, who obviously had cause to esteem them greatly. Verily judging by the rare signed painting, one is convinced that these artists, although unknown to us, were great and excellent masters who fully deserved their page in the history of art.

If even today, before our very eyes, there disappears a signature from a painting, then evidently such sinister episodes also took place in the past. It is said about a well-known collector that he always carried with him a phial with alcohol, and while bargaining for a painting, he washed off the signature to decrease the value of the painting. Many tragedies indeed have taken place around art objects. We ourselves were once horrified at seeing how a restorer reduced a beautiful painting to a seemingly dilapidated condition in order to purchase it cheaply.

After all, one can write a most instructive story about the life of paintings and other art objects. Who knows, perhaps some dramatist will someday take as his subject not a human being but the tragedy from the life of a painting. A long procession of dramatic, tragic, and highly joyful and solemn episodes is depicted around the works of art, weaving their aura.

Everyone has heard of the destruction of masterpieces of Leonardo by religious fanatics and cruel invaders. I remember how a beautiful sketch by Rubens was used as cardboard for the binding of a book. An excellent portrait by Bryullov was covered by an ugly landscape. Under the excellent painting attributed to Ingres was discovered the signature of his collaborator, Carbonniere. In all countries there has always taken place intentional or involuntary shiftings of names and definitions. Together with revaluations and fashions, every century had its own conventionalities. Instead of true revaluation, new concealments are taking place.

But let us not dwell on old art only. The problem of contemporary art is still more acute. May the examples of the past teach our generation to open their hearts to young artists! And after all, who can affirm who are the unknown and the known artists, and to whom are they known or unknown?

I have been told of a most remarkable collection of "unknown" French artists of the recent period. A collector from Marseilles began to collect paintings of artists who died very young or who, in despair, discarded art. A large collection was assembled. A visitor who did not know the names might have thought that they were paintings by Degas, Monet, Manet, Rafaeli, Menard, LaTouche, and other celebrated French artists. This collection also contained some strongly individual conceptions. It became quite clear that at some time, an enterprising person may arrange from such a collection a most striking and significant exhibition. Besides paintings of artists who died early in life, there were those of artists who considered themselves *decouragés*. And it is yet another question whether they were all right considering themselves failures. Sometimes a terrible injustice brings people to this entirely undeserved self-estimate.

A friend of ours when saying "unknown" always used to add "unknown to me." And in this he was quite right. How can anyone say that a person unknown to him at the moment, and in a certain place, may not be greatly revered by other people elsewhere? Such a consideration should be understood by many people nowadays. Otherwise, in self-conceit, some people may imagine, that if they do not know something or do not accept it, then all other people also do not know and do not admit it. Such is the usual vanity of the ignoramus. Besides, the question of being known or unknown is one of the most conditional.

This definition is based on many casual circumstances, both conscious and unconscious. Many excellent geniuses received recognition only after their death. For some curious reasons people seem to value only the factor of death in their judgments.

Hélas! Because of crass ignorance, so often the ugly Danse Macabre replaces the beautiful predestined Dance of Life. May exhibitions of "unknown" artists remind us once more of the conventionality of human judgment, and may they create one more act of justice in the contemporary world.

Verily in every academy, institute, and school of art, besides the artistic technicalities, there should be instilled the true sense of beauty. The sense of beauty, even if it is inborn, still needs educating for unfoldment. In the same way, though every human being has been given the gift of thought, yet the art of thinking also needs education. The classical Museion—the home of all muses, was precisely that Temple, where the sense of beauty was developed and glorified. In the same manner, people should welcome every upliftment and refining of the human spirit, which takes place in such unifying noble temples, reminding us of the glorious academia of ancient Greece. These beautiful hearths were the sign of a true renaissance. In the all-unifying academia, people will learn to become more kind, honest, and just. These qualities also belong to the same great concept of the Beautiful.

"The beautiful is scattered through the universe like the auriferous sands."

It would seem that in the history of art, there are many convincing examples of how people who devoted themselves to Beauty expressed it in a multitude of ways, choosing that which at the moment appeared to them the nearest. How beautifully they combined painting with architecture or with sculpture, not to speak of mosaics and the various graphic arts.

Precisely, as priests they served Beauty, finding the most persuasive expressions for the beneficial influence upon the broad masses and refining the consciousness of the people.

We all know of the martyrdom of scientists like Copernicus, Galileo, Paracelsus, Lavoisier, and other innumerable sufferers for truth. There exist entire books dedicated to these martyrs of science, and next to them there should also exist volumes on "Martyrs of Art and Culture." However, once we know that artists are priests of the beautiful we also know all unavoidable attributes of attainments.

We know not only of ancient Herostrates who destroyed the beautiful. Even in our days, Sargent's painting was barbarously cut in the Royal Academy in London. A vandal slashed Millet's *Angelus* in the Louvre, and another brute in 1912 stabbed Repin's *Ivan the Terrible* at the Tretiakoff Gallery in Moscow. Much has been written about vandalism. We introduced the Banner of Peace as a Red Cross of Culture to protect real treasures of humanity. And now let me mention another hidden but cruel vandalism that quietly existed in the life of many nations.

When studying Old Masters, we often find that many very good paintings were, for some reason, overpainted by inferior artists with entirely different subjects. It is obvious that the old paintings had become old-fashioned, and the artists simply used the wood as material for his modern and more fashionable creation. One should not think that only paintings of secondary importance were subjected to such barbarous manipulations. On the contrary, among the recorded cases we find some very important names which today occupy a place of honor in the history of art.

I remember how once in Italy, while studying a beautiful painting by the master Virgo inter Virgines, we were surprised at the exceptionally good condition of this painting. When expressing our amazement at this, we received the following unusual but characteristic explanation: "Apparently in the beginning of the seventeenth century, this beautiful painting was already considered old-fashioned and therefore, despite the religious subject, "Ecce

Homo," it was covered by another religious subject, which had remained all the time in a certain monastery. And this second painting was by far inferior to the original masterpiece. It was noticed comparatively recently that through the second painting there had become vaguely discernable the outlines of a different composition, and the person who had purchased this inexpensive painting from the monastery decided to remove the upper layer, thus revealing a beautiful masterpiece." Now this painting adorns the Art Institute of Chicago.

I have personally seen an old replica of the well-known painting by Correggio, which is in the National Gallery in London; and on this replica I could clearly see the outlines of an ancient portrait, and indeed the panel on which it was painted proved to be far older than the replica.

Once we had occasion to witness how from beneath paintings of the seventeenth and eighteenth centuries, there appeared in good condition beautiful originals by Lambert Lombard, Rogier van der Weiden, Adrien Bloemaert, and other artists equally renowned. And in the Bulletin of the Museum of Fine Arts in Boston, we find a most instructive story about the portrait of Sir William Butts, by Hans Holbein the Younger. Let us quote a few lines from this article:

"On November 17, 1935, the museum purchased the striking portrait by Hans Holbein the Younger. . . . Connoisseurs, seeing the portrait, refused to believe that Holbein could have done it, and with good reason. As it had appeared for about three and a half centuries, it was certainly not Holbein. In very recent times, however, a young friend of the Butts family, who had retained possession of the painting from the time it was done until it passed to the museum, a painter by the name of H. M. Jonas remarked that the hand seemed painted in a manner somewhat different from the rest of the portrait and suggested an earlier style. He was permitted to have an X-ray made, and the result was the discovery of a portrait underneath. The X-ray showed a different outline to the cap, a full beard, a different chain, and a suit puffed with white silk. It also revealed the existence of an inscription on the background. Next came the difficulty of restoration. The first restoration was undertaken by Mr. Nico Jungman. It was an extremely difficult task, since the overpainting was of very nearly the same period as the painting underneath. It is obvious that the sitter caused his portrait to be repainted later in life. When this was done we cannot be sure, though probably in 1563 when Queen Elizabeth came to Thornage and was elaborately feted. It is likely then that Sir William, an older man, holding high offices, demanded that he be shown with different garments and ornaments added, and, therefore, had himself repainted, presented in regalia, and brought up to date, but unfortunately by a very inferior artist."

This interesting story has two meanings. First, we must pay tribute to the administration of the Boston Museum of Fine Arts and to the restorer, who has completed this most difficult restoration so successfully and thus has revealed to the world the original masterpiece of a great artist, without any later inferior additions and overpainting. Second, this instructive historical episode shows to us once more that vandalism is committed not only by the hands of an infuriated mob but also secretly in highly distinguished dwellings for the sake of vanity and prejudice.

Beauty cannot be guarded by orders and laws alone. Only when human consciousness realizes the inestimable value of beauty, its power of creating, ennobling, and refining, only then will the real treasures of humanity be safe. And one should not think that the vice of vandalism belongs but to past ages, to some notorious invaders and conquerors. We see that vandalism of many kinds takes place even today. Therefore, the endeavor to protect and save beauty is not an abstract, nebulous move but is imperative, real, and undeferrable.

Verily, education in art and beauty is a necessity. And although it is a "beautiful" necessity, yet it is a necessity with all its duties and obligations. We always rejoice when we see that thoughts are being transmuted into action. Such transfiguration is manifested by a true *oeuvre*, a clear yet at the same time almost untranslatable word. One can say "creative work," yet something more profound and summarizing is expressed in this French concept.

About art in all its manifestations, people are accustomed to judge very light-mindedly. Some have read two verses and already speak with authority about the poet. Some have seen three or four paintings or reproductions, and already pass judgment on the artist. From one novel they fix the position of a writer. One book of sketches is enough for an irrevocable opinion over a cup of tea.

More than once it has been noted in literature that the celebrated "cup of tea" binds one to nothing. And perhaps the pronouncements at the dinner table likewise are not binding, yet they often have very profound consequences. In such conversations, over a "cup of tea," people do not think about the fact that the separate productions are only as the petals of the entire *oeuvre*. Even an experienced horticulturist or botanist would hardly undertake to form a judgment about an entire plant from a single petal of its blossom.

Each one has had an occasion to listen to a definite opinion about an author, yet it has been proved, upon verification, that the speaker had read only one volume of his writings. This is not to mention those, in general, who do not take the trouble to do any reading themselves but pronounce their judgments according to the newspaper critics. But the concept *oeuvre*, the concept of all a person's creative work, should be set forth with special clearness. Not only a full acquaintance with all the creativeness of the author is needed, but for making a just estimate, it is necessary to assimilate his productions in the chronological order of their creation.

The whole creative work is like a necklace put together in a definite order. Each production expresses this or that psychological moment of the creator. The life of the artist has been composed of such moments. In order to understand a result, one must know the cause. One needs to understand why such and such a sequence of creation took place. Whatever external or internal circumstances were stratified and produced fragments of the whole creativeness, this would mean to form an opinion about the design of a necklace from merely one or two links of it.

In all kinds of creativeness—in literature, in music, in the graphic arts, everywhere—an attentive and careful correlation is decidedly necessary. It is well known how much has been attributed to authors that which was entirely alien to them, based on incomplete quotations from some train of thought. You know that not only casual people take it upon themselves to pass judgment. In each domain dwells a self-appointed judge.

It is said that the valuation by critics changes three times in a century, that is, by generations. To observe these deviations of evaluations is very instructive. How many irrelevant considerations will influence public opinion! The competition of publishers or greed of the dealers in artistic productions, finally any of the various forms of envy and enmity are so complexly reflected in appraisals, that for the future investigator-historian it is often completely impossible to discriminate. A great number of examples of this could be adduced.

Let us recall how two competing publishers tried to disparage an author, whom they had in view, in order to secure at a lower rate the right of publishing his work. You know that such specific belittlements are to be found in any annals. Let us recall how a certain dealer in pictures tried by all means to depreciate for a time the value of an artist, with the end in view of buying up enough of his productions and then commissioning someone to resurrect anew the forgotten or discredited artist.

Let us not bring up certain episodes out of the world of collectors, when competition led these people to most unworthy conduct. It is only important to remember that appraisals of creative work are singularly tortuous and personal. We recollect how a certain music lover warned a well-known musician not to play on a particular day because an influential critic had a toothache. But when to all these mortal chances there is united the wish in general not to acquaint oneself with a man's entire work, then his situation becomes truly tragic.

Let us recall any prolific author. Can one form a judgment about him without knowing the sequence of all his works? One can, indeed, estimate separate productions of the author, but then this will be an opinion which concerns the production itself but not all the man's creative *oeuvre*. It is not alone the biography of a great personality, for it is still more valuable to follow the accumulation of creative power, and all the paths of its expression. Thus once again we see how significant in its meaning is the word *oeuvre*. It impels one to out-"oeuvre"-line the entire manifestation, and comprehensively to examine its influence and consequence.

History, passing from a personal *oeuvre*, appraises also the *oeuvre* of an entire nation, of a whole epoch. If the historian does not teach himself in the small and accessible, then by what means can he draw near to and encompass broad problems? Before thinking about such comprehensive tasks, it is necessary to reflect about the conscientious judgments of parts, of individuals. He who sets himself the task of always staying within the bounds of truths learns to discriminate in all fortuities and to compare causes and effects carefully. It is a pleasure to rejoice at the whole beautifully composed necklace in which are found many natural colors in unexpected combinations.

Just now when there is so much destruction and upheaval, each clear, honest, exhaustive understanding of a subject will be an especially needed contemporary task. We have read how Stokowski has definitely expressed himself about the harm of mechanical music for true creativeness. Stokowski has justly reminded us that even between the very vibrations transmitted directly or mechanically there is an enormous difference. Certain instruments are generally imperceptible in mechanical transmission.

In a time when music and science design and the graphic arts have been subjected to mechanization, precisely then must the appraisals of creativeness be still more precise, profound, and well-grounded. At this very moment, when it is the modern practice to strive for the brief, the staccato, and the casual, it is especially necessary to aspire for evaluations on the basis of the entire *oeuvre.*

Greetings to all true lovers of the beautiful, who help to make the masterpieces known and revered.

MIGRATION OF ART

AT the end of the last century, we arranged traveling exhibitions of French and American art, which,
besides previous international exhibits, were among the
pioneers of the modern migration of art. Great migrations
of nations, as in the past, so also in the present, have many
analogies. At present, of course, one of the first messengers
of such movements is, as was to be expected, art. When
we wrote on the coat of arms of our institutions about
the universal significance of art, we likewise had in view
the mutual understanding of nations by means of the language of art.

During the last years, a great deal has been done in this
direction. Various institutes of art, societies, and leagues,
each in its own sphere, tried to sponsor the exchange of
art and mutual understanding through the best universal
language—creativeness.

Even into the most remote countries penetrate the
traveling exhibitions, lectures, and concerts. During the
period following the Great War, one could have observed
remarkable, peaceful conquests through art. The names of
writers, painters, artists, and musicians, both composers
and players, as well as the news concerning the development of science, traveled colossal distances. During journeys, one may with joy realize to what an extent, and sur-
prisingly widely was spread, this peaceful, inspiring news,
even in the most unexpected corners of the world.

Some time ago, haughty politicians and leaders of
governments probably did not even admit the thought of
how potent may be such untiring messengers of culture.

Undoubtedly, many such political leaders would be sincerely surprised would they had heard what helpful, powerful factors have irresistibly grown up in the world. Truly, no matter how hard certain bipeds would try to darken the significance of creativeness as a universal, moving power, no mechanical intellectual calculations can overthrow the authoritative facts about the growth of cultural relations. And let us also not forget that these relations in the majority of cases originate not from governments but from private social initiatives. Thus, the people themselves take part in the widest world constructiveness, strengthening the foundations of culture. This private social initiative must be greatly emphasized. It is a radiant sign that above all confusions and misunderstandings, universal wisdom builds its paths of achievement by means ineffable.

In many departments of creativeness—in literature, in the pictorial arts, in theater, and in the newest forms—everywhere, at present, there may be noticed the most curious circumstance. The migration of art takes place not only by spreading or by becoming acquainted with its art but also in the desire to work within the forms of the neighbors' art. One may observe, for instance, how in the theater, the East dreams of Western forms, and the West is often inspired precisely by Eastern originality. In the theaters of China and Japan, one can notice at times various imitations of Hollywood. Besides, how may attempts in the Eastern style take place among the exhibitions of Paris and America? It is just as if narrow nationalism is mutually condemned. And it is rather questionable whether anyone has seen a successful Chinese or Japanese Hollywood and whether the excursions into the East as manifested by Western hands continue to be convincing. Among the multitude of such attempts, comparatively few are really persuasive.

Of course, let us not consider those cheap superficial stagings, which are not even concerned with the questions of inner convincingness and character. Even in many, better cases, where a very respectable striving is evident, there is often a lack of inner persuasiveness. And yet, this is a fundamental condition of all the arts. No emphasized imitation will lead to desirable results. And in this sense, only a kind of mechanization or technocracy of purely external methods is attained. It is true that one often notices an author trying to acquaint himself with the museo-archival side. No doubt he had consulted some specialist, but one can easily see whether the author came to like the essence of his own creations or whether some other objects and desires predominated in him. Artificial intellect does not carry convincingness, which comes from knowledge out of love.

The authors will probably not always give themselves an account when they were directed by a special problem ordered by extraordinary contemporary conditions or when their creativeness arose from the unrestrainable song of the heart. Also in this respect, some peculiar divisions into civilization and culture will take place. In other words, conventional contemporary problems will appear to be as if bound by civilization, but the convincing song of the heart, all-conquering and unforgettable, will already be in the realm of culture.

When in various countries one meets such conventionally borrowed forms of creativeness, one has mainly to doubt the correctness of the so-much-desired paths of the migration of art.

Especially now, when many nations have consciously opened their eyes upon their past and at the same time have mastered the latest achievements, one can expect that the migration of art will again find a correct course between the shores of the true concordance of nations.

The charm of these truly national resoundings is understood with difficulty in distant countries, which are so different psychologically as well as climatically. Why should we admit any imitations when the discovery of the true sources of people is possible? We see that in India, China, and Japan, each has its own refined theatrical art. Why then does it need Hollywood, which in its own way will say those words of creativeness typical for it?

Everywhere lately, a most remarkable phenomenon can be noticed. The most unsuspected countries have manifested their own artists, creators, and executors. We are not surprised at this in any way, for we always knew that this is so and must be so! But for many, this simple circumstance was a revelation in itself. Such revelations only show the ignorance of many and the unjustified haughtiness, as if much is above the understanding of some one. Such limitation of thinking is mere ignorance. There are many beautiful circumstances that people do not wish to admit. And in the matter of the exchange of art, special care and refinement and all true love must be applied, which will kindle and give convincingness to creation.

The great pilgrims of antiquity believed in their migrations. They were not only driven by trying circumstances, they moved according to some great creative decisions. Of course, they loved these migrations, and the best of these travelers accepted, with the greatest attention, the peculiarities and beauty that they met on their way. We see it from the heritage that they left us. The migration of art will also widely fulfill its world-unifying mission. On these glorious paths, CREATION will always remain the true resounding of nations, with all of their inexhaustible treasures. In the wake of the great travelers has remained intact the picturesque mountain ranges and limitless seas and rivers crossed by them. Likewise will remain intact the convincing sources of national beauty, transmitted through creativeness with care and deep love.

The paths of exchange of art and science will, of course, become longer and broader. In the history of our time, this peaceful cultural achievement will not only be recorded but will be appreciated in full attention.

It is the time of great migrations and profound mutual understandings! Let it be so!

ANCIENT SOURCES

"WHEREIN lies the truth of ages? In laws and commands or in proverbs and fairy tales?" In the first the will is intensified and in the second is the imprint of wisdom.

The shortest proverb is permeated with reverberations of place and age. And in the fairy tale, as in a buried treasure, is hidden faith and the strivings of people. The proverb may be sad, but it will not be destructive, and likewise one will not find distasteful fairy tales or repulsive folk songs. The proverb, and the fairy tale as well, are for the good. But the sources of the commands are different. How many commands become obsolete and quickly evaporate! Yet try to eradicate a proverb or legend. They may go underground, but they will persistently emerge again.

"Know how to catch the smallest devil by the tail and he will show you where his superior hides." This old Chinese proverb points out the significance of the smallest details for revealing the most important. Truly, the minute detail will be the best key to a great achievement. It is wrong to think that details are unimportant for the path of ascent. Even some most excellent heroic acts have rested upon details that were foreseen in time. How carefully he who follows the Teacher notices all the stones! He will miss nothing extraneous. Only a poor disciple will say, "Guru, in my exaltation I broke my nose." Such incommensurateness will only show how far the disciple is from being observant. This Chinese proverb means, furthermore, that the greatest criminal is more easily detected by the smallest details of his conduct.

It is wonderful to observe the subtlety and correctness of all details in proverbs, legends, and fairy tales. Of course, sometimes in an inaccurate translation something may appear superfluous and clumsy, but one need only turn to the original to find that the old proverb "One cannot omit a word in a song" has a deep meaning. And not only can a word not be omitted, it even cannot be transposed. And from this point of view it is instructive to observe the chiseled conciseness of folk language. As the best seeds are separated by repeated winnowing, so in the furnace of the ages the tongue of folk wisdom is forged.

In all ages and nations there will always be short periods during which all these accumulations will be haughtily rejected. Like buried treasure they will go underground for the time being. As in forbidden catacombs there will remain only the whisper of prayers. Thus somewhere, and yet in full care, will be safeguarded the signs of people's observations, and later on they will be unearthed from their hiding places. Again, with renewed fervor they will be studied. And again, precisely from these inexhaustible sources will the founts of culture be renewed.

Some thoughtful explorers will again go deep into the unravelling of the sense as well as the forms of ancient heritages. Again they will admire the refined details of these forms, so well forged, so well chiseled, born of long patience in bygone rhythms of life.

Precisely, one wishes to emphasize that in these ancient heritages the meaning and the structural form can give equal joy to the explorer. Perhaps superficial people will speak of an "old-fashioned" language; but a true revealer of the runes, an inquisitive scientist, will recognize how remarkable, how simple and fitting are the definitions and in what combinations the greatest emphasis is brought out, correctly drawing the attention, just where it is needed.

Take any ancient proverb and try to change the sequence of words in it. You will see as a result that much of the sense will be lost. We have seen many distortions of sense due to poor translation. Only recently have languages be gun to be studied without prejudice, and therefore in certain well-known monuments of the past, modern translations reveal new and significant details. The historical names themselves have undergone in the various translations such a multitude of changes that at times it is difficult to realize that one and the same person or place was meant. Especially guilty of this have been the textbooks of the secondary schools. A great number of children in a hurried course of study, at times learn terms which later, in mature years, are met again, but with an entirely different connotation, giving rise to unnecessary complications. But now, in many branches of science, we turn inquiringly to the original sources, with an open mind. Thoughtful study will help again to appreciate the most characteristic, the most minute details and definitions.

And what could be more profound and all-embracing than the observation of thought itself and its structure? People speak, not without reason, about the art of thinking. Precisely in the structure of thought is expressed the same general concept of creativeness. Lovers of art for art's sake always will emphasize especially not only that which is said but also how it is said. The way things are said, the way they are done, the way they are thought—all this is a source of delight for every true observer; and now, when so much must be spoken about the loss of quality in all of life, precisely the quality of all that is created is especially significant.

All problems requiring a quick solution are in need of a high quality of expression. The famous "somehow or other" is more than out of place. Everyone must realize his responsibility for his way of thinking and acting. Let us not imagine that the mode of thinking is unimportant; as in all creativeness, the manner of expression, of technique, have an enormous significance. A painting is convincing only when it has been executed in such a way that it cannot be changed, when the observer feels that it could never have been otherwise and that what is presented to him has been composed as was necessary. What great observation of all details is necessary for this convincingness!

What a wonderful school of convincingness is contained in the true creativeness of peoples—anonymous, full of character, and ever living.

Peking, January 3, 1935.

CREDO

LYSIPPUS was a blacksmith's apprentice before he ever became a sculptor. The heart of a great artist has never been withered by anguish of a reflective spirit or distress of a hungry body. There is no drought that can destroy the seed of creativeness once it is ready to sprout. Amid the most burdensome labors the folksong sounds a call to renewed creativeness. It is implanted in the quality of each task. Art, knowledge, labor—these are sons of that same creativeness that guides and uplifts.

From the most ancient times, the aims of art have been characterized by the most diverse words. However multiform these definitions may be, everywhere their essence is perceived to be one and the same. First of all from art is demanded persuasiveness. It is said that to be convincing, one must see through beauty. And so it is. To view with the eye of beauty, this means one must comprehend the very best in composition. What sort of composition is this? Much has been said about conventional premeditated arrangement, about a tendency to pretentious subjectiveness. Many times people have tried to express their just indignation at something that in their opinion weighed down the lofty concept of creativeness and rendered it incapable of soaring flight.

Such in reality is conventional composition. In the last analysis artificial composition will always provoke boredom and weariness. But there is also another composition that is natural and yet indefinable in words. The artist may see so clearly and constructively, so to speak, that you do not miss a word of his song. It is precisely as in nature, when the most varied elements are combined in complete harmony. When one examines a cluster of crystals, it is forever amazing how, even when unexpected forms are encountered, they always make up a harmonious, conclusive whole. Thus it is in all artistic creativeness. Its productions have crystallized so naturally that any argument about composition simply falls to the ground. In such a crystal of creativeness is expressed that convincingness that can be definitely felt, but words will be powerless to define it or to give any recipe for it.

When a picture has been naturally built up, you can add or subtract nothing. You cannot shift its parts, and this, not for the reason that you must not violate "symmetry," but that you must not deprive the picture of its vital balance. You have the desire to live with such a picture because you will find in it a constant source of joy. Each object that sheds joy around it represents a veritable treasure. You are indifferent to what school or trend it belongs as an *objet d'art*; it will be a persuasive guide of the Beautiful and will bestow upon you many hours in which you will feel a love for life. You will be grateful to him who has helped you meet life with a smile, and you will take good care of this hieroglyph of Beauty. And you will become better, not at the dry command of morality but from the creative radiation of the heart. In you will awaken the Creator, which is latent in the depths of the consciousness.

In its best disclosures, science proves to be art. Such striking scientific syntheses are forever imprinted upon the human brain as something overwhelmingly conclusive. Then science ceases to be a conventional synchronization of facts and advances triumphantly into the domain of new cognition, leading humanity along with it.

Creativeness, whether it be in symbols or in art, or in any of the realms ruled by the Muses of the classical world, will be attractive, that is to say, convincing. Science is already entering such immense fields as thought. Now it is coming to light that thought acts according to some sort of laws not set down in human words yet already perceptible in series of experiments being carried on at present. The mind of the thinker will be a creative one.

It has always been required of art that it be creative. This demand is no more than just. After all, art cannot be other than creative. Be it a most intricate picture, landscape, or portrait, once this work emerges from the hands of the true artist, it will be creative. In the complexity of present-day concepts, it may be that the very idea of creativeness has fallen to pieces. Sometimes people begin to assume that creativeness must be expressed in forms having nothing in common with reality. Some may still remember the joke originating at a French exhibition, where a picture turned out to have been painted by a donkey's tail. In their quests of creativeness, instead of liberation (for creativeness must always be free) people begin to seek some new limitation and conventional recipes. In this is forgotten the most fundamental condition of creativeness; first of all, it does not tolerate anything conventionally imposed and self-restrictive.

For example, let us cite Gauguin. Can one possibly call his pictures conventional or tendential? Precisely in the freedom of creativeness, Gauguin strode over all the limiting frames of his subject as well as any sort of restrictive technical rules. He always remains a creative artist, that is to say, a true and convincing master craftsman. The power of persuasiveness of this artist is not in any recipes or rules devised by reason. He has created just as a bird sings, which cannot but sing because its song is the expression of its essential nature. His persuasiveness lies in the fact that he has been capable of viewing each of his pictures as a part of creative nature.

This inner vision of a picture, to the extent that it is requisite and convincing, will always be far outside the methods of technical rules. Creators of all times and peoples have created their productions not only by intuitively seeing them in their best form of expression but by extending their creativeness to the very material in which they worked. The sculptor having inspected the block of marble creates from it the best possible. The master woodcarver employs each quality of his piece of wood in working it into the forms appearing to his creative eye. The painter intuitively selects colorful material for each of his expressions. The artist would probably be unable to explain afterward why precisely he employed oils or tempera or watercolor or pastel. And so it must be. Why does an orator raise and lower his intonation? Why does the musician discover those ineffably enchanting harmonies, which even he cannot always repeat?

Intuition is being much discussed at present. Volumes are being written about intuitive philosophy. The solution of problems is being sought not only in calculations but also in intuitive synthesis. One artist has said: "Do thus, in order that people may believe you." Another, discussing a certain realist, asked: "Does he have to depict all the wayside filth just because it exists in reality?" Yet at the same time let us not condemn realism. Of course, it is only in striving for the actuality that in turn produces that convincingness, for the sake of which one must see with the eye of beauty.

Recently much has been said about the synthesis of art. In all the arts, synthesis is nothing but a condensation of all good possibilities. Once Brulov[*] said, in jest, that art is extraordinarily easy: "One has but to take the right color and apply it in the right place." In essence the master and great technician spoke truly. Precisely one must do what is needful in applying the color, and something whispers what this "needful" is. The master knows when it would be impossible to do otherwise, yet when you ask him by what canons and rules he has done exactly so and not otherwise, no artist can explain to you what laws he followed in doing as he did.

Comparing the works of art of different times and peoples, we see that frequently the most apparently diverse

---

[*] A famous Russian artist of the mid-nineteenth century.

productions go together excellently in a common grouping. One can easily picture to oneself how certain primitives; Persian miniatures; *objets d'art* of Africa, China, and Japan; Gauguin and Van Gogh can all appear in one collection, and even hang on one wall. Not the material or technique but something else enables these entirely different examples to live together in harmony. They are all truly products of creativeness. Moreover, all kinds of art and sculpture, painting, mosaics, ceramics—in a word, absolutely all things in which have been expressed the creative outburst of a master—will be friends and not mutually exclusive antagonists.

Each of us has often listened to contradictory pronouncements. One says that he understands only the old school. Another vehemently raises the objection that all must be in movement and, therefore, he finds joy only in the modernists even though their works may be harsh and strident. Some esteem only oil painting, while others admire the delicate watercolor. Some affirm that they like only "finished pictures," while others assert that they treasure sketches most highly, as the first inspired impulses of the creator. Some can be enraptured only by monumental works, while others feel warm affection for miniatures. Some limit their taste to the grandiose; others find repose of the spirit in small artistic *bibelots*. Do all such limitations denote limitedness of soul on the part of the art lover, or rather, may it not be that these amateurs have simply dammed up their possibilities?

Very often one's preferences and one's collection depend upon some accidental initial impulse. Perhaps some time a man has heard that a picture is painted with oils, and this expression took root in his brain. Perhaps in the family circle a child has been impressed by a word spoken about watercolors, or he may have been given a set of them and from this chance beginning has followed his interest in precisely this medium. In all manifestations of life and particularly in the matter of artistic impulses, one often has occasion to encounter initial fortuity. Indeed, these "accidents" often prove to be for matters of chance. A man has begun to respond precisely to one thing rather than another and, in this, may have been expressed his dormant accumulations. Spring has come, and buds open out naturally, which have long been asleep through the winter cold. New creativeness has begun!

What a beautiful word—"creativeness"! In various languages it rings out appealingly and convincingly. In its own way it speaks about something latently possible, about something triumphant and conclusive. So mighty and beautiful is the word "creativeness" that all conventional obstacles are forgotten in the face of it. People rejoice at this word as a symbol of advancement. The command of creativeness covers over all whisperings of the limited mind about rules, about materials, about all that is so often answered with the suppressive word "impossible." To creativeness, all is possible. It leads humanity along with itself. Creativeness is the banner of youth. Creativeness is progress. Creativeness is mastery of new possibilities. Creativeness is peaceful conquest over stagnation and formlessness. In creativeness has already been implanted movement. Creativeness is the expression of the fundamental laws of the universe. In other words, in creativeness is expressed Beauty.

It has been said that Beauty will save the world. People have smiled at this formula with sympathy or with derogation, but no one can refute it. There are certain axioms that may cause wonder but which one cannot overthrow. Humanity dreams about freedom; it inscribes this great hieroglyph upon the facades of buildings. At the same time, mankind exerts every effort to restrict and reduce this concept. Great freedom of thought is manifested in true creativeness. That will be true that is beautiful and convincing. In the secret places of the heart, for which man himself is responsible, has been implanted trustworthy judgment as to what true conviction is, what creativeness is, what Beauty is.

As Velasquez said: "Not a picture but truth itself."

Let us recall two excellent passages from Anatole France's *Garden of Epicurus.*

"Whatever wins its vogue only by some trick of novelty and whim of aesthetic taste ages quickly. Fashions change in Art as in everything else. There are catch-words that come up, and pretend to be new, just like the gowns from the great dressmakers in the Rue de la Paix; like them, they only last a season. At Rome in the decadent periods of art, the statues of the Empresses showed the hair dressed in the latest mode. Soon these coiffures looked ridiculous, so they had to be changed, and the figures were given marble wigs. It were only fitting that a style as rococo as these figures should be re-periwigged every year. The fact is, in these days when we live so fast, literary schools last but a few years, sometimes but a few months. I know young writers whose style is already two or three generations out of date, and seems quite archaic. This is doubtless the result of the amazing progress of industry and machinery, which sweeps modern communities along. In the days of MM. de Goncourt and railways we could still spend a fairly long time upon a certain form of artistic writing. But since the telephone, literature, which depends upon contemporary manners, renews its formulas with an altogether disconcerting rapidity. So we will merely agree with M. Ludovic Halévy that the simple form is the only one adapted to travel peacefully, not down the centuries, that would be assuming too much but at least down the years.

"The only difficulty is to define what the simple form is, and one must admit this difficulty to be a great one.

"Nature, at any rate as we can know her, and in milieux adapted to life, offers us nothing simple, and art cannot aspire to greater simplicity than nature. Yet we understand well enough what we mean when we say that such and such a style is simple, and such and such another is not.

"I will say this much then, that if there is no simple style, there are styles which appear simple, and it is just these which carry youth and longevity with them. It remains but to inquire whence they get this fortunate appearance. Doubtless we shall conclude that they owe it, not to their being less rich than others in diverse elements, but rather because they form a whole in which all the parts are so well blended that they cannot be distinguished separately. A good style, in fact, is like yonder beam of light which shines in at my window as I write, and which owes its pure brilliancy to the intimate combination of the seven colors of which it is composed. A simple style is like white light. It is complex but does not seem so. This is only a simile after all, and we know what such parallels are worth when it is not a poet who draws them. But what I wished to make plain is this; in language the true simplicity, which is good and desirable, is only apparent, and it results solely from fine co-ordination and sovereign economy of the several parts of the whole."

"If you would taste true art, and experience a profound impression before a picture, examine the frescoes of Ghirlandajo in Santa Maria Novella at Florence, depicting the *Birth of the Virgin*. The old master shows us the room of delivery. Anna, upraised on the bed, is neither young nor beautiful, but one sees immediately that she is a good housewife. She has ranged at the head of the bed a jar of sweetmeats and two pomegranates. A serving-maid, standing between the bed and the wall, offers her an ewer on a platter. The babe has just been washed, and the copper basin still stands in the middle of the floor. Now the infant Mary is taking the breast; her wet-nurse for the nonce is a young and beautiful lady of the city, a mother herself, who has offered her bosom to the end that this child and her own, having imbibed life at the same fount, may keep the savor of it in common, and by force of their blood love each other as brother and sister. Near her stands another young woman, or rather a young girl, like her in features, perhaps her sister, richly dressed, wearing the hair drawn away from her brow, and plaited at the temples like Aemilia Pia; she stretches out her two arms toward the infant with a charming gesture, betraying the awakening of the maternal instinct. Two noble ladies, clad in the Florentine fashion, are coming in to offer their felicitations. They are attended by a serving-maid bearing on her head a basket of water-melons and grapes. This figure is of a large simple beauty; draped in flowing garments confined by a girdle, the ends of which float in the wind, she seems to intervene in this pious domestic scene like a dream of pagan antiquity. Well, in this warm room, in these gentle womanly faces, I see expressed all the life of Florence, and the fine flower of the early Renaissance. This goldsmith's son, this master of the Primitives, has revealed in his painting, which has the clearness and brilliancy of a summer dawn, all the secret of that courtly epoch in which he had the good fortune to live, and which possessed so great a charm of its own that his contemporaries themselves were wont to exclaim: 'The gods are good indeed! Oh, thrice-blessed age!'

"It is the artist's part to love life, and to show us that it is beautiful. Without him, we might well doubt the fact!"

Leonardo ordained:

"He who despises the art of painting, thus despises a philosophic and refined conception of the universe, because the art of painting is the daughter, or rather grandchild of Nature. Everything that exists was born from Nature and has borne, in its turn, the science of painting. This is why I say that painting is the grandchild of Nature and relative of God. He who blasphemes the art of painting, blasphemes Nature.

"The painter must be all-embracing. O artist, may thy multiformity be as infinite as the manifestations of Nature. Continuing what God has commenced, strive to multiply not the deeds of human hands but the eternal creations of God. Never imitate anyone. And every creation of thine, be a new manifestation of Nature!"

History records the manifold remarkable achievements of Leonardo da Vinci in all domains of life. He left amazing mathematical writings; he investigated the nature of flying; he conducted medical researches and was a distinguished anatomist. He invented musical instruments, studied the chemistry of paint; he loved the wonders of natural history. He adorned cities with magnificent buildings, palaces, schools, libraries; he built large military barracks, constructed one of the best ports in the Adriatic, and planned and built great waterways; he founded mighty forts, constructed war machinery, sketched military plans. . . . Great was his versatility.

But after all these remarkable achievements, he remained in the memory of the world as an artist—as the great artist. Is this not a true victory of Art?

Himalayas, 1938

TAGORE AND TOLSTOY

"**B**Y ALL means visit Tolstoy," thundered the gray-bearded Stasov, Director of the Slavonic Department of the St. Petersburg Public Library. This happened during my visit to him, after graduating from the Academy of Fine Arts in 1897.

"I do not care much for academic diplomas and distinctions. But let the great writer of Russia recognize you as artist. That will be a real distinction. And no one will appreciate your *Messenger** better than Tolstoy. He will at once understand with a message your envoy is speeding. Don't delay, in two days I am going with Rimsky-Korsakov** to Moscow. Come along with us. Elias (the sculptor Hinsburg) will also join us. Come along, come along!"

Thus we are together in the railway compartment. Stasov, a septenarian, took the upper berth, grumbling that otherwise he cannot sleep. His long white beard was hanging down. A heated dispute starts with Rimsky-Korsakov about his new opera. To a realist like Stasov, the entire epic of "Grad Kitej" does not appeal.

"Just wait, you have to discuss this matter with Tolstoy. He says that he does not understand music, but he weeps when he hears it," says Stasov jokingly to Korsakov.

At that time there was much talk about Tolstoy's *What Is Art?* and *My Belief.* All sorts of fables about Tolstoy and his life were whispered, as is usual around great men.

---

*   *Messenger* is the name of Roerich's first painting, which is now in the Tretyakoff Gallery in Moscow.

**   Rimsky-Korsakov, a famous Russian composer of national operas.

Gossipers had a wide field for their imagination. They could not grasp how Count Tolstoy could plough the field or make shoes. Absurd anecdotes about Tolstoy's so-called godlessness were in circulation. These slanderers concealed the fact that a godless person could never have written the beautiful parable about the three hermits.

I regret that I do not have at hand the actual text of this narrative, but everyone who wishes to cognize the great personality of Tolstoy should know at least a short summary of it.

On an island there lived three old hermits. They were so simple that the only prayer they used was: "We are three—You are three—have mercy upon us!" And great miracles were manifested during this simple prayer. The local bishop came to hear about these hermits and this inadmissible prayer, and decided to visit and teach them the canonical prayers. He arrived on the island, told the hermits that their prayer was undignified, and taught them many of the customary ones. Then the bishop left on a boat. And he saw that across the sea, following the boat, was a radiant light. As this light approached, he discerned the three hermits, who were holding their hands and running upon the waves hastening to catch the boat. When they had approached, they asked the bishop: "We have forgotten the prayers you taught us, and have hastened to ask you to repeat them." When the bishop saw this miracle, he said to the hermits: "Continue to live with your old prayer."

Could any godless person give such a remarkable image of hermits, who attained illumination in their simple prayer? Indeed to Tolstoy, the great seeker, everything basic and truthful was near to the heart.

Everyone also remembers also his *Fruits of Enlightenment,* which is full of sarcasm about ignorantly interpreted spiritistic séances. Certain people wished to see in this the negative attitude of Tolstoy toward the entire metaphysical domain. But the great thinker only scourged ignorance.

In his epic *War and Peace, Anna Karenina,* and many other

essays and parables, there was manifested a wide comprehension of psychology in its highest sense. In the heat of argument Tolstoy may indeed have asserted that a simple folk dance for him is equal to the highest symphony. But when one had an opportunity to witness how deeply Tolstoy was moved, especially by symphonies, one understands perfectly well that in his paradoxes was contained something by far finer and broader than the public may have wished to see in its own interpretation. Tolstoy, the great teacher, before his very end, started out to the Optina Pustyn,[*] and did not this spiritual act signify a remarkable apotheosis of his wonderful life!

The morning following our arrival in Moscow, we went to Tolstoy's home in Homovniki. Each of us brought something: Rimsky-Korsakov, his latest compositions; Hinsburg, a bronze statue of Tolstoy; Stasov, some new books; and I, a photograph of my *Messenger*.

Those who know the quiet side streets of ancient Moscow, the old residences divided from the street by a ward, and the special atmosphere of those historical dwellings—they will understand the whole unforgettable impression of those surroundings. There was the fragrance of apples in the air, mixed with the aroma of libraries and old furniture. Everything was simple and yet refined. We were welcomed by Countess Sophia Andreevna, the wife of the great thinker. Stasov took command of the conversation, and Tolstoy himself only joined later. He appeared in his typical *tolstovka*,[**] quite in white, and there remained forever the first impression of his radiantly white appearance.

Only in great men can this simplicity be combined with majestic convincingness. I know that his definition of "majestic" would not please Tolstoy, and he would probably have interrupted it with some harsh remark. But he was never against simplicity.

---

[*]   Optima Pustyn is a well-known hermitage in Russia.
[**]   *Tolstovka* is a kind of workman's overshirt, which Tolstoy liked and usually wore.

Only such a gigantic philosophical and literary talent and unusually expanded consciousness can create that grandeur, which was expressed in the entire figure, gestures, and sayings of Tolstoy. It was said that his face was a simple one. This is not so; he had a strong, typically Russian face. Old, wise peasants and so-called old believers, who sometimes live far away from cities, have such faces. Indeed, the expression of such faces may be severe. But in them there is no mean irritation; on the contrary, there is expressed a mighty thought. India also knows such faces.

Tolstoy admired the work of Hinsburg, making some abrupt remarks to the point. Then my turn came, and Stasov had been quite right supposing that the *Messenger* would not only be approved but would even call forth some remarkable comments. On my painting, a messenger is seen hastening in a boat to some ancient Slavonic settlement, carrying the important news that some tribes had attacked their neighbors. Tolstoy said: "Did you ever cross a swift river in a boat? You must aim higher than the desired destination, or you will be carried downstream. So also in the domain of morality, one should always steer much higher—life anyhow will carry one down! Let your Messenger aim very high—then he will attain!" Very often in life this advice of Tolstoy was remembered by me. Then Tolstoy dwelt on folk art, on certain paintings from peasant life as if wishing to direct my attention toward the people. "Know how to suffer with them" was also one of Tolstoy's ordainments. Then we talked about music. Again there flashed some paradoxes, but behind them there was such a love for art, such a searching for Truth, and such a care for the people's education that all those disputes merged into a beautiful symphony of service to humanity. And from morning till evening there resounded an unforgettable *Tolstoviana.*

On the following morning, starting on our return journey, Stasov said to me: "Now you have been bestowed with the true distinction of an artist!"

Amazing is the whole life of Tolstoy as a great writer and greater teacher of light. Every event of his life increased the deep veneration of the people to him. And when his excommunication from the Church took place, the undivided sympathy of the masses was with him.

Besides the many published works of Tolstoy, there circulated everywhere in Russian society many banned essays and letters. The causes and effects of Tolstoy's excommunication were discussed in whispers, there were rumors about his private meetings with the Emperor. Also certain prophecies of Tolstoy were discussed; later these remarkable predictions were widely announced through the press. In these the prophetic writer already foresaw the great war, and many other stirring events.

All news about Tolstoy's sayings was attentively received; as if above official authorities, Tolstoy's mighty thoughts dominated. Besides his thundering statements about non-resistance to evil, about pan-human love, about true education for all, there were also such touching descriptions, as for instance, on the death of a tree. India would especially value these simple, truthful words, which contained a deep thought about life omnipresent. Through one of his feminine heroes Natasha, Tolstoy exclaims, "Yes, I was thinking that we are hastening, and think we are hastening home. But God only knows whereto we are going in this darkness. And perhaps we shall arrive, and will find ourselves not in *Otradnoye* (estate) but in a fairy-tale kingdom. And then I thought . . ."

The sacred thought of a beautiful realm lived in Tolstoy's heart, when he followed the plough like the true ancient hero of the Russian Epos Mikula Selianinovitch; or when like Boehme, he made shoes; or when like the great Carpenter, he stood at the bench, seeking contact with all phases of labor. Untiringly this sower cast in his precious seeds, and they took firm root in the consciousness of the Russian people. Innumerable are in Russia the homes in the name of Tolstoy: Tolstoy museums, Tolstoy libraries, and reading rooms. And can one imagine a more glorious end for Tolstoy than his departure to the Optina Pustyn and passing away at a small railway station? A significant end for a great traveler! This passing was beyond all imagination, and Russia at the first moment could not even believe it. I remember how Elena Ivanovna[*] brought this news to me, repeating sorrowfully: "It is unbelievable, it is unbelievable. As if something basic, some part of Russia itself, has left us. As if an epoch is closed. . . ."

And now, as I write these lines there suddenly appears a radiant rainbow across all the purple and snowy ridges of the Himalayas, from the very earth to the very sky. A blessed sign from Heaven to Earth.

Again Elena Ivanovna brought news, but of a quite different kind. She often, through her great intuition, found in bookshops something new, needed, and inspiring. Thus she brought Tagore's *Gitanjali* in a translation by Baltrusaitis. These beautiful, sonorous poems radiated like a rainbow; and in the Russian translation of Baltrusaitis, they sounded as a clarion call. Until that time, Rabindranath Tagore was not known in Russia in his entire scope; it was known that Tagore's name was acclaimed all over the world, but we Russians had no occasion to cognize the depth of the heart of this great poet.

Gitanjali came like a revelation. The poems were read at gatherings and at private "at homes." Only true talent could create such a precious mutual understanding. The quality of convincingness is mysterious. The foundation of Beauty is ineffable, and every pure human heart rejoices at the reunion with Light. This realization of Beauty, this universal response of the soul was brought by Tagore. What may he be like? Where and how does this giant of thought and beautiful images dwell? The inborn love for the wisdom of the East finds its application in the touching, calling, persuasive chords of the poet. Now everyone at once became imbued with love for Tagore. It was evident how even the most contradictory people, the most

---

[*]   *Elena Ivanovna* is Madame Helena Roerich.

irreconcilable psychologists were united by the call of the poet. As if under the beautiful dome of a temple or in the consonances of a majestic symphony, the inspiring song victoriously united all human hearts. Just as Tagore himself proclaims in his uplifting *What Is Art?*:

"In Art the person in us is sending its answer to the Supreme Person, who reveals himself to us in a world of endless beauty across the lightless world of facts."

Everyone knows that Tagore does not belong to the earthly world of petty facts, but to the world of Truth and Beauty. And the persistent desire arose: "How and where to meet?" Will not fate bring about a meeting here, on this plane, with him who so powerfully called toward Beauty the Conqueror? Strangely, Providence transforms imperative dreams into reality. Indeed unforeseen are the paths. Life itself weaves the beautiful web as no human imagination can visualize it. Life is the best fairy tale.

We dreamed of meeting Tagore, and there he himself appears in my studio on Queen's Gate Terrace in London in 1920. Tagore had heard of my Russian paintings and wanted to meet me. And just at that time I was painting a Hindu series *Dreams of the East*. I remember the amazement of the poet at such a coincidence. We recall how beautifully he entered, and how his spiritual appearance impressed us. Verily, the first impression is the true one.

At the Luncheon of the World Fellowship of Faiths in 1934 in New York, Dr. Kedarnath Das Gupta recalled our first meeting with Tagore in the following words: "This occasion had its beginning about fourteen years ago in London. At that time, one day I was at the home of Rabindranath Tagore, who said to me, 'Today I am going to give you a very great treat.' I followed him, and he took me to South Kensington to an apartment filled with superb canvases and paintings, and there were Nicholas Roerich and Mme. Roerich. As Mme. Roerich showed us the paintings I thought of our beautiful ideal of the East: *prakriti* and *purusha*, man revealed through the woman. That visit has never been out of my mind."

Just as unforgettable for us remains this visit of Tagore, with his inspiring talks on art; his letter about paintings also remains as a cherished memento. Then we met in America, where the poet lectured so convincingly about the immutable laws of beauty and about mutual human understanding. In the rush of the leviathan city, the words of Tagore sometimes sounded as paradoxical as the fairy-tale realm of Tolstoy. The greater was the attainment of Tagore, who untiringly traveled all over the world, with the imperative call about Beauty. The poet said in China: "Civilization expects the great culmination of the expression of its soul in Beauty." One may quote at length, from the books of Tagore, his prayers and ordainments for a better life, which are so easily carried out in the beautiful domain of the poet's heart.

Are these calls far from life? Are they but the dreams of a poet? By no means! This whole truth, in its entire essence is preordained and realizable in earthly life. Ignoramuses will assert in vain that the worlds of Tagore and Tolstoy are utopian. This is thrice wrong! Is it a utopia that one should live beautifully? Is it a utopia that one should not kill and not destroy? Is it a utopia that one should learn to imbue one's surroundings with knowledge? These are not utopians but reality itself, as real as the fact that one should help wherever possible. If the light of Beauty would not penetrate at least through dimmed sparks into the earthly plane, life itself would be unbearable. What deep gratitude humanity should render to those giants of thought, who self-sacrificingly taught the eternal foundations of life! Without these laws of the Beautiful, life would turn into such bestiality and ugliness that every living breath would be choked.

Horrible is the curse of ugliness. Terrible is the persecution that throughout history tried to destroy true seeking and cognizance. When an ignoramus orders that everyone should think according to his code, this is tantamount to the demand of nonsense and imbecility, for it is destruction. Majestic are the gifts of Tolstoy and Tagore to humanity. They are not selfish misers but most generous donors; they give and give endlessly. Tagore's heart strives to spread real education. Santiniketan—this stronghold of enlightenment—is forever linked with a host of great names. So many artists and cultural leaders of India and many foreign coworkers participate in the ideals of Santiniketan.

The ploughland of Culture is not easy. People sometimes believe that the accomplishment of colossal historical events was always crowned with laurels. History sometimes records entire periods of difficulty in but a few stingy words. Yet how many thorns were met on the way, and how much priceless energy was expended in order to lay the steps of human achievement despite all obstacles, enmity, and ignorance. The more joyful is it to witness how esteemed are the harvests of Tagore's sowing. In Tagore we see a wonderful synthesis of the thinker, the poet, the bard, the artist, and the teacher of life. From the depths of ages we heard that such coordination of happy manifestations is possible. But when it takes place before our very eyes, here on our *terra dolorosa,* against all attacks of chaos, then such attainments verily open for us new vistas. The human hearts become filled with gratitude when witnessing such glorious deeds. The giants of thoughts are not in need of such gratitude. But it is necessary for space, as building material for a more radiant future.

One cannot name any sphere of Culture to which Tagore is indifferent. With everything educational, creative and constructive, Tagore will not only sympathize but he will find forceful helping suggestion. It is but natural that Rabindranath Tagore responded cordially to the pact for the protection of the world's cultural treasures. Whose soul could vibrate with greater ardor for the safeguarding of the fruits of creativeness than Tagore's? But he knows the difficulty of the present moment. He feels what malice and hatred hover above the world at present. Not from newspapers but through his wise heart, he comprehends what danger to peaceful labor threatens during the present

Armageddon. Tagore does not conceal these dangers. As always he speaks daringly of questions of peace and education. One can imagine how ignorance is hissing somewhere at his call for peace.

The last letter I received from him recently sorrowfully defines the present world situation: "My dear Friend, the problem of peace is today the most serious concern with humanity, and our efforts seem so insignificant and futile before the onrush of a new barbarism that is sweeping over the West with an accelerating momentum. The ugly manifestations of naked militarism on all sides forebode an evil future, and I almost lose faith in civilization itself. And yet we cannot give up our efforts, for that would only hasten the end."

The heart of the great poet is filled with grief at the current confusion. The thinker knows that every worker of Culture should valiantly defend his post and self-sacrificingly stand up for the treasures of the world. And in this self-sacrifice is also manifested the sign of Tolstoy's service to humanity. As Tolstoy was never a politician, so also Tagore stands adamant as the mighty teacher of life.

One cannot name anyone, who with such convincingness, combines modernism with the ordainments of ancient wisdom. Such a synthesis to the majority of people seems even irreconcilable. Even the esteemed philosophers often state their forbidding "or"—"or," as if life is not of one source and as if the cosmical laws are not immutable. Even the most ancient ordainment proclaimed through the *Rig Veda:* "Truth is one—men call it by various names." I often had occasion to hear how even educated people said that it is old-fashioned to quote Confucius or the Vedas. They suspected a certain lack of progress when someone studied ancient wisdom. Only now is science, in the person of some advanced research workers, beginning to reaffirm the value of knowledge that has reached us from the depths of antiquity. In Tagore such wisdom is inborn, and his deep understanding of modern literature and science gives that equilibrium, that golden path, which to the majority seemed a utopia. But this attainment is right in front of us, one has but to admit it in full attentiveness and goodwill.

On the seventieth anniversary of Tagore's birthday, we wrote: "*Vijaya, Tagore!*" Difficult is such a victory, but the more precious it is to admire the radiant hero in the service of humanity.

To the superficial outside observer, Tolstoy and Tagore may seem different. Some people who like to revel in contradictions will no doubt also try to apply their wit in this case in order to separate. But if we shall analyze both the thinkers benevolently, and without prejudice, we shall but regret that there exist no portraits of Tolstoy and Tagore taken together—in a hearty talk, in deep wisdom, and in the desire to bring good to humanity. On the occasion of Tagore's seventieth birthday, we rejoiced to see Tagore's portrait in the Latvian newspaper *Segodnia.* The renowned poet of Latvia, Rudzitis, has beautifully characterized the great Tagore in a monograph, and now from Praha Prof. V. Bulgakoff sends me a beautiful postcard of Tolstoy and himself, taken in 1910 in Yasnaya Poliana. And again the great images of Tagore and Tolstoy rise before me in their great service to humanity. Together on one picture, I would like to see these two giants of thought.

Deep homage to Tagore and Tolstoy!

GORKY

THE great Russian writer Maxim Gorky passed away in Gorki, near Moscow, on June 18 [1936].

During the last months, three great Russians have left this world: the great physiologist Pavlov, the composer Glazunov, and now Gorky. All three were known to the entire world. Who has not heard of the famous experiments in the field of reflexes, conducted by Pavlov? Who next to Tchaikovsky and Rimsky-Korsakov did not also admire Glazunov? And who has not read among other Russian classics the works of Gorky, who has recorded unfading images of Russian life?

Over half a million people went to pay homage to the remains of the great writer, and over seven hundred thousand accompanied the funeral procession. The representative of the Union stood as a guard of honor and carried after the cremation, the urn to the Kremlin Wall, where it is immured. The entire diplomatic corps was present. Gun salutes thundered in honor of the great writer. Some French papers were amazed at the way a whole nation paid tribute to its national hero. There were wreaths from the French and Czechoslovakian Governments. The foreign Press unanimously hailed the achievements of Gorky.

It had been resolved in Moscow to erect monuments in honor of Gorky at the expense of the State at Moscow, Leningrad, and in Nijny-Novgorod, the latter already bearing his name now.

The Municipal Council of Praha decided to name a street in the Czechoslovakian capital in his honor.

Benes, the President of Czechoslovakia, sent the

following telegram to Moscow: "The death of Maxim Gorky will compel the entire world, and Czechoslovakia in particular, to remember the progress of the Russian people during the last fifty years and of the Union since the revolution. The participation of Gorky in this process was in the spiritual respect and convincing. For me, personally, Gorky and all other Russian classics were my teachers in many respects, and I remember him with gratitude."

H. G. Wells sent a hearty message from England, and Romain Rolland telephoned from Switzerland to Moscow the following letter: "At this painful hour of departure, I remember Gorky not so much as the great writer, nor even his colorful path of life and mighty creativeness. I remember his full, saturated life, which like his motherly Volga, flowed richly in streams of thoughts and images. Gorky was the first among the world artists of the word, who cleared the path for the people who gave them his strength, the prestige of his glory, and his wise life experience. . . . Like Dante, Gorky emerged from Hell. He brought out with him and saved his friends in suffering."

The Paris papers, which have reached the Himalayas, record many signs of a worldwide esteem to the deceased. He was honored not only by friends but by all sections of cultural life. Even the most reluctant obituaries highly comment upon Gorky's works, such as *The Lower Depths, Mother, Letopis, Childhood, Artomonov's Business, Chelkash, The Town of Okarov,* and conclude: "a man and an artist has passed away, whom we all loved." Thus art has united both friends and foes.

From the very beginning of his vivid literary career, Alexis Maxim Peshkov, whom the whole world knows better by his pen name Maxim Gorky, achieved an exclusive position amid Russian classics. About every great ma there are many legends; also around the name of Gorky, there was woven much truth and invention. Some tried to represent him as a severe cold-blooded materialist; others based themselves on single abrupt words, by which it is impossible to judge a man and his work. But uncorruptible history will depict to the full extent his great image, and people will find in him many unexpected traits.

About his last minutes, Dr. L. Levin writes in the *Izvestia* of June 20th: "Alexis Maximovich died as he lived, a great man. In these painful hours of illness, he never once spoke about himself. All his thoughts were in the Kremlin, in Moscow. Even in the interval between two oxygen cushions, he asked me to show him the newspaper with the project of Stalin's new constitution. During the short periods of relief from his illness, he spoke about his beloved subjects: literature and about the possibility of a future war, which worried him very much. The last day and night he was unconscious. Remaining constantly at his bedside, I discerned the following abrupt phrases that he said: "There will be war. . . . One should be ready. . . . Fasten up all buttons!"

N. Berberova writes in the Paris press of a characteristic episode in the life of Gorky:

"This was on the day when the current issue of *Sovremennye Zapiski* (*Contemporary Review*) was received with the concluding chapter of Bunin's novel *Mitia's Love*. Everything was put aside: work, correspondence, newspapers. Gorky locked himself up in his study and was late for lunch and absentminded. Only at tea it became clear: A remarkable work . . . truly remarkable—in these words he characterized *Mitia's Love*. . . . It is difficult to believe that Gorky could cry with real tears when reading the poems of Lermontov, Block, and many others. . . . "

Further, N. Berberova quotes from a letter she had received from Gorky, in which his devotion to poets and poetry was expressed: "I am deeply enchanted by the broadness and multifacetedness of themes and subjects in poetry. I consider this as a real quality, as a good sign. It shows the broad outlook of the author, his inner freedom, the absence of chains with any conventional moods, with any preconceived ideas. It seems to me that the definition: 'the poet is the echo of world life' is the most correct. Of course, there are and should be ears that perceive only the bass tones of life, and souls who hear but the lyric of life. But Pushkin heard everything, perceived everything and, therefore, has no equal. Can there be anything higher than literature—the art of words? Certainly not. It is the most astounding, mysterious, and beautiful in this world!" Those who do not know the groups of Russian literary thought should be told that Gorky's praise of Bunin shows his broad judgment, for Bunin belongs to another camp.

Many valuable traits of Gorky will reveal themselves in the course of time. I happened to meet him on many occasions in private talks and at numerous committee meetings, gatherings, etc., and I cherish his friendship. On all occasions I could trace some new remarkable details of character, which very often did not correspond to the outwardly austere appearance of Alexis Maximovich. I remember, how once during the organization of a great literary enterprise, when an urgent decision was required, I asked Gorky for his opinion. He smiled and said: "There is nothing to argue. You as an artist will feel what is needed. Yes, yes, precisely you will feel—you are an intuitivist. Often above reason, one should reach the very essence!"

I also recollect how once at a friendly gathering, Gorky revealed, quite unexpectedly for many, another interesting side of his character. We spoke about yogis and various psychic phenomena whose home is India. Some of the guests looked suspiciously at Gorky, who kept silent, and they apparently awaited his severe criticism. But his resumption amazed many. Filled with an inner radiance, he said: "The Hindus are a great people. I will tell you of my personal experience. Once in the Caucasus I met a Hindu, about whom many remarkable stories were circulating. At the time I was rather inclined to doubt. At last we met, and what I will tell you, I saw with my own eyes. He took a long thread and threw it up into the air. And to my surprise, it remained hanging up in the air. Then he asked me whether I would like to look at an album and what picture I would like to see. I said I would like to see pictures of Indian cities. He gave me his album and looking at me, said: 'Please, look at these pictures of Indian cities?' The album contained polished brass sheets, on which were reproduced beautiful views of different cities, temples, and other views of India. I looked over the entire album, attentively studying the pictures. Then I closed the album and returned it to the Hindu. He smiled and said: 'Well, you have seen views of India. Then he blew at the album and returned it into my hands inviting me to look at it again. I opened the album and to my surprise found only polished plates without any pictures whatsoever. These Hindus are indeed remarkable people. What refined thought!"

Does not this characteristic trait of Gorky prove his all-containing and broad consciousness?

He very much wanted to have my painting. He selected from those that I had at the time, not a realistic landscape but one of the so-called pre-war series, *The Doomed City*. This painting precisely corresponds to the mood of a poet. Indeed, the author of *Storm-Finch* was a great poet. Coming from the depth of the people, Gorky fearlessly walked across all obstacles of life—he went the path of the Russian people, encompassing its multifacetedness and the richness of the Russian soul.

The Moscow newspapers of June 21st, under the title "Gorky in the role of Harun-al-Rashid," tell the following story accompanied by a photo of Gorky dressed as a tramp: "This was in 1928. Gorky wanted to see what goes on in public bars, what kind of people visit them, whether he would find there any types similar to his old novel *The Lower Depths*, what became of them, what the new visitors are like, etc. But how to arrange such an expedition? Gorky decided to disguise himself as a tramp. With a huge beard, well he entered into intimate talks with the people there and as a result wrote a new novel, which forms part of his *Across the Soviet Union*.

"Those who know Gorky will understand that this episode is indeed typical of him. Being a true realist in the broadest sense, he considered it necessary to convince himself in life, not so much in order to enter into his diary leaves sketches of new types, but in order to affirm a synthesis for an actual expression of his consciousness.

"He was trustful and he trusted. He loved to trust and he was often cheated. . . .

"Once he came out from his study singing and his face expressed utter joy, so that everybody was amazed. It turned out that he had read a newspaper report that somewhere, somebody has discovered some new microbe. Gorky thus expressed his enthusiasm at the prospect of helping humanity through combating yet another disease.

Once I met Gorky in business relations when the publishing company of Sytin in Moscow and the Niva were merged into one big concern. A colossal, unifying program in the literary and educational field was in project. It was interesting to witness how every conventionality and formality tortured Gorky, who wanted to overcome all formal obstacles without delay. He knew how to build on a broad scale. Take, for example, the three mighty cultural institutions outlined by him: The House of World Literature, the House of Scientists and, the House of Art. All these three gigantic ideas show the creative scope of Gorky's thought, who was striving to find across all difficulties the eternal words—words of enlightenment and culture.

He carried his chalice of service to humanity throughout life unspilled.

In the name of the League of Culture let us offer our sincerest, heartiest thought to the great memory of Gorky, which will remain forever radiantly affirmed in the Pantheon of World Culture.

WOMAN'S DESTINY

"THE women's movement in India is undoubtedly one of the major, vitalizing forces in our national life. . . . But the movement in India has only just begun; and in this initial stage, it is difficult to venture on a prophecy about its future, except that like all movements born of necessity, it is full of hidden possibilities. For taking facts as they are, it is notorious that a nationwide women's organization with a definite aim and operative standards did not come into existence long before."

Thus speaks Lakshmi N. Menon about the feminine movement, and as she concludes her interesting and significant article:

"Now it is up to the men of India to help this movement. It is not merely the women's cause; it is also the nation's cause and, I will add, humanity's. But even if they, the large majority of them, do not, the movement will go on and will succeed. The past is full of warning; the present is full of hope. Destiny and the future beckon to us—dogs may bark but the caravan will pass."

Thus was said in the *Twentieth Century* in June 1935. It goes on to say how impossible is delay when fearful events are again oppressing the world, and how already long ago, we summoned women to unite their forces for the effective carrying out of good works.

Lakshmi N. Menon speaks correctly in her article about the many difficulties that obstruct the speedy development of the feminine movement. We are in complete accord with her about the quantity of all the prejudices and superstitions, which, outside of questions of absurd atavism and self-conceit, hinder seeing what has already been established and what apparently should have stood out clearly and indisputably from the beginning.

It would seem ignorant and nonsensical in our day to still speak about woman's equal rights. In view of contemporary civilization and more so of culture, about which so much is said, surely it is impossible to be in any doubt about this, that complete woman's equal rights are such a truism that it should be taken for granted. Indeed, how can it be otherwise? Surely, the present is not the time of the troglodytes. Of course, only an ignoramus would dare to speak just now about the difference of men and women's rights.

In fact, it is even shameful to talk about any distinctions, yet so often legislators of so-called cultured countries still fail to rid themselves of this unthinkably monstrous prejudice. It is difficult, even hopeless, to glance into the distant past, seeking the causes there. Indeed, in such quests there can be found a multitude of misunderstandings, misinterpretations, and misuses by means of partial cases and all the other inadmissible peculiarities. But surely, for the present, each moment of which is already manifested as a part of the future, it is only needful to intensify all forces in order that here on the Earth equal rights are first of all enthroned as the most primary condition of human merit and dignity.

There will be precisely an epoch of culture when laws will no longer be either feminine or masculine, but will actually be human and, primarily, humane. Then, too, organizations will no longer be divided according to sex but to other, different characteristics of cultural tasks. Such a time will indeed come because human paths, through all agitations and convulsions, will nevertheless proceed in these directions. Not without reason is the current age called the Age of the Mother of the World. In this magnificent concept is also included the recognition of woman as not only worthy of equal rights but as a being invested with a special trust for the fulfillment of undeferrable world tasks.

Among these really urgent, impending problems will be first of all the introduction of goodness into the world; that is, the introduction of the broadest and deepest creativeness of good. Already the world has become very evil. Explain this situation however you will; nevertheless, the absence of goodness is manifested as an international fact. It is precisely as if people have lost all knowledge of how to conduct themselves with each other. The concept of the heart has so often been crushed, as it were, reduced to ashes. If among the lofty world tasks of the Mother of the World, She first of all establishes the earthly activity of the heart, then verily this will be the opened gates into a garden of beauty.

Also, the Mother of the World takes to Her heart the matter of the peace of the whole world. Through all the manifest obstacles to peace, nevertheless a strong woman's union will precisely and imperatively enunciate this concept, which is sacred to human dignity and merit. For what then must people contend and overcome, boil and blaze—surely, it is all for the same earned, enlightened peace.

This means that we must not only think about equal rights, understanding them as something already inalienable. Beyond this attainment rise up great world problems offered to woman by the epoch itself. The author of the cited article regrets the fact that up to now there is still no national woman's union in India. Of course, this also needs to be said not only about India but, after all, about the whole world. For such an effective and beneficent union, there must be produced the possibility of feminine cooperation flowing broadly throughout the world.

If for some reason it is impossible to create one great union, then surely it is possible to gather together in thousands or perhaps in hundreds of thousands of cooperative groups. It is immaterial how these cooperatives would be standardized. Perhaps according to specialty, perhaps according to spiritual problems—there may be a great many solutions about such working cooperatives. The essential thing is that they rise up immediately. It is needful that they come into being not only in large cities but also in every village, carrying everywhere the vitalizing force of toil and heart and striving for culture. Since we began with the example of India, let us continue with the example of that blessed country. Hamid Ali, chairman of one of the departments for the improvement of rural life, relates:

"In our district there are thirteen hundred villages. Four times a year we organize courses, both for women and for men. . . . Women come, the Hindu school mistresses and many others, without religious distinction. In the district are seventeen castes, from the Brahmin to the untouchables. Muslims, Mahratta, Christian, Jain—all work together. We teach them kitchen work, sewing, laundering, soapmaking, weaving, dairy work, carpentry, nursing, gardening, the care of children, and the combating of diseases. We give them instruction in veterinary science, about laws concerning women, and laws about loans—in a word, everything that should make life in the village better and happier. In the evening, after classes, we have music, pictures, games, the smile of joy. Of course, our poor people have forgotten how to laugh. Of course, it is difficult to be merry, having food only once a day. But you should hear them on these evenings when they sing, listen to the radio, and laugh together. Many also come without invitation. I have seen up to two or three thousand gather in a circle in order to join in and listen awhile. . . . The farmer is changing and abandoning old, slow, and narrow methods. Under the influence of our movement concerning the betterment of rural life, many villages have already brought improvement to their lands, and some have even unified their farms along cooperative lines."

And so precisely, this useful beginning closes with words about cooperatives. In the wisely constituted cooperatives, it is least of all possible to expect quarrels, disagreements, perplexities. Constructive work and the urgency of labor problems tie the consciousnesses together. People busily occupied have no time to quarrel and argue. It is necessary to work; it is necessary to succeed. And it is so attractive to convince oneself of the obvious success that cooperation produces.

The great task of the Mother of the World is first of all one of unifying and persuading. No one in the world can impede the rise of working collaborations. Against cooperatives likewise no one can make any objection. At present in all governments, this form of partial collaboration is being broadly accepted everywhere, for it is not needful to devise new laws that are disturbing to some people. This means that it is only necessary to be united in the most heartily compacted groups, and though in small measures at first, to approach the multiform task. I emphasize the point that every seed is small, and therefore one should not strive all at once for enormous, overburdening dimensions. On the contrary, precisely the small dimensions at first can promote and make easy mutual understanding. Then later, it is not difficult, in a businesslike order, to find the points of contact between the already strongly welded cooperatives. Everywhere one has occasion to hear about the most unexpected and original forms of the cooperative. Not long ago one could read about entire enterprises based on the exchange of manufactured wares. If an exchange of handiwork is possible, then just as precisely is it possible there to awaken an intellectual and, beyond that, a spiritual heart exchange.

Among the imperative tasks of our days, first of all will be work. It is precisely "work" that cloaks itself in many perplexities. Noticeably among women now is a sincere desire to work, as the basis of independence. Indeed, let us repeat, work must be most diverse, from that of the hand to that of the lofty brain. We are tired of accounts that work must first of all take place in some sort of factory. Every constructive spirit is everywhere possible and everywhere valued. And women know how to work. Of course, freedom is not in beginning to smoke or to commit excesses with any other narcotics. On the contrary, just at present there is required an unusual temperateness in all branches of life. Faith and loyalty come in sobriety. As it has been said: "Unfaithful in the little, unfaithful also in the great." But truly beautiful is the labor of the Mother of the World. Inspirer, creatrix, everywhere producing the creativeness of good—can anyone possibly argue against this?

When equal rights are spoken about, something offensive is felt in any premises to the effect that there may be some who are of unequal rights. Of course, only criminals should be deprived of any rights. But all are members of the human society; they are first of all people. Therefore, can there possibly be disputes about equal rights in our twentieth century, which thinks not only about civilization but also about culture? Has not the human heart all rights? Does not the possession of human blood convey equality of rights?

The author of the above-cited article ends it in a call for assistance. Is it possible to speak about assistance where there is already clear, realized, competent cooperation? Surely, all should strive for justice. Surely, all should aspire to the creative power of good. All must strive for peace, for constructive labor. One must be a traitor to humanity to oppose these axioms. One must be a betrayer of nature to rise up against the unity of the human heart.

Each of us sees two definite types of people. Some welcome the good, while others draw up in some sort of convulsions at any mention of the creative power of good. Let us not forget that the evil adversaries against good are at times highly organized. Does this not mean that those who are united together for good, for justice and mutual respect—that these too must be strongly unified?

I do not know if many answered the call contained in the article quoted about the feminine movement. I do think that increasing numbers must respond to it as they would to urgent questions that most vitally concern them. Just now the world is in great confusion, and, therefore,

every unification in the interest of justice and the creativeness of good should be undeferrable. The Age of the
Mother of the World cannot be something commonplace.
Let us listen with sensitive alertness for the decree of the
betterment of life.

FATE

"REMBRANDT from the first steps of his activity surpasses the limits of a certain local significance, and his entire creativeness has a pan-human aspect. The grim tragedy of his life loses its routine and historical meaning, and becomes, like the tragedy of all great martyrs, a universal symbol. At the same time the symbolism of the art and life of Rembrandt carries a fatal character. Everything that happened to him—had to come, according to some higher laws. The horror of his life acquires a grandiose beauty precise owing to its enormous scope. This is a true Golgotha, a cross, unbearable for average people; a test, for which only the Great Ones are chosen.

"Studying this tragedy, which is so logical in all its details, one realizes its inner harmony. Witnessing the awful finale of Rembrandt's life, when one sees him as an ailing old man, forgotten by everybody, indulging in wine, living in deep poverty, one shudders, but yet understands that such an end was the most majestic, the most dignified for a genius. From the point of view of Highest Justice—it was more worthy and beautiful than the plague of the centenarian Croesus Titian, or the parting of Rubens from his beautiful wife or the oversatiety of Velasquez with pompous court functions. Rembrandt was glorified by the crown of martyrs and contrary to reason, one sees in this the highest reward."

Thus the art critic, Alexander Benois, describes the apotheosis of Rembrandt's life in his essays. Alexander Benois found convincing characteristics for many artists, but this criterion of the life of Rembrandt—of the martyr's wreath, of beauty contrary to reason—proves his great understanding. "Contrary to reason"—this simple, convincing expression no doubt seems to many to be out of place and ill-fitting. The weary last physical days of Rembrandt or Franz Hals (who closed his life story as a watchman in an almshouse) may appear to many average minds an unworthy end.

The knighthood of Van Dyck at the Court with its luxurious garments will no doubt seem a more befitting consummation of the life of a great artist. But behind this ephemeral apotheosis, one may distinguish something far greater, the glimmer of which is so intensely saturated that not every eye can conceive it. Precisely in the same way, an electric spark in its greatest tension becomes imperceptible to the human eye.

Also, if you will try to substitute the tragically majestic fate of Leonardo da Vinci for the gorgeous fairylike end of Raphael, then again the highest harmony will be destroyed. Even the fact that the forgotten grave of Leonardo, near the monastery of St. Florentine, has forever been leveled with the ground, even this gesture of fate remained in the style of the great artist.

Beethoven in his Symphony *Eroica* deplored the fate of the consul Napoleon, but if instead of the tragic end, one would imagine the picture of a gradual decay of the Emperor, then the symphony would have lost all its grandeur.

And the great Boehme?—A shoemaker!

During a discussion of the fate of Joan of Arc, someone tried to visualize what final chord would have been the most glorious finale for the triumphant warrior-virgin. Many suggestions were advanced, and one even went so far as to propose crowning her the Queen of France. But after many long disputes, the decision was arrived at that the apotheosis preordained by the Highest Laws was undoubtedly the most magnificent. Of course, no one will vindicate the treacherous judges of Joan of Arc. Similarly no one will justify those quasi-connoisseurs of art who condemned the now-famous painting by Rembrandt, The *Night Vigil*, or his other painting, which was rejected by the municipality, but now is one of the greatest treasures of the Royal Museum at Stockholm.

The evil condemners, ignoramuses, and traitors will forever remain as such. They by no means intended to make the martyrs' crown. They, as true servitors of darkness, will remain in its sinister abysses. But quite above their machinations, beyond all earthly understanding, the Highest Justice transforms carbon into sparkling diamonds. No doubt everyone could add to the above-cited examples many others from all parts of the world. From the highest to everyday testimonials one may see how some unforgettably glorious crowns are being manufactured for some future cosmic needs.

Only to know the untold paths and to be aflame in their realization! Rembrandt could have closed his life as the owner of a curio shop, or as the head of the local Guild, or even as the captain of the society of musketeers. Many different bourgeois solutions may be found. Rembrandt was a collector, and such a great connoisseur could easily find a way to deal in art objects. He was a rich house-owner, and could have, in time, increased his real estate. He could have indulged in many things, and could have "peacefully" rested in his native city. But apparently, such a trivial end was not his fate. The great treasures that Rembrandt gave to the world were weighed on entirely different scales, unseen to the human eye.

Joan of Arc could have "peacefully" remained in her village as an esteemed prophetess and healer. She could have concluded her life as a venerated abbess or just as a respectable citizen. To everyone the path was open. But the Great Law expressed through her one more testimony of truth. The flame of her heart, the fire of the pyre—this flaming crown was far above all common laws. It was quite beyond human imagination.

People speak much about fate. But from what links is so-called fate forged? From a peaceful herd to a devouring fire. From the highest welfare to the greatest poverty. And by what human definitions can this Highest Plan be expressed? One cannot find words to express them, but one can feel them with one's heart. And one must acquaint oneself with such subtle feelings, because through them the new world is perceived.

Confucius, who was misunderstood and persecuted, ordained:

"When we study manifestations, we can achieve knowledge; when we reach knowledge, we acquire goodwill; when we reach goodwill, the heart is purified, and man becomes cultural; when man becomes cultural, order reigns in his home; order reigns in his country; when order reigns in every country, then peace will be attained in the whole world."

This also looks like an easy path—from everyday routine to the peace of the whole world. In this path, which looks so easy and obvious, is expressed the highest universal Law, which is not accessible to many. This law hints by some superhuman language at predestined fate. Every man, every member of the human family carries the responsibility for the peace of the whole world. No one has the right to refuse the beautiful duty of goodwill. No one has the right to burn Joan of Arc at the stake. Who has the right to bemean Rembrandt? In fates, which seem complicated to the earthly eye, resound the Highest Laws which demand extraordinary expressions.

The poverty of Rembrandt is majestic. The pyre of Joan of Arc is beautiful. The thorns of Confucius are great. The Thorny Crown leads the world.

For indefatigability let us remember an advice of Leonardo da Vinci:

"Patience is for the insulted ones, as a garment for the freezing ones. As the cold increases, dress more warmly, and you will not feel the cold. In the same way, during terrific insults, increase your patience, and the offense will not touch your soul."

LAUDABLE ENEMIES

I N the American monthly *Inspiration*, there has appeared an article under the thought-provoking title "I Was Kicked Upstairs by My Enemies." The author tells us how his actual success in life was due to his feud. The story begins:

"Have you ever noticed how opposition sometimes is the making of a man? How enemies sometimes succeed only in 'boosting' the man they try to 'break'? As president of a successful company in the office equipment field, I am what I am largely because some business enemies of mine hatched a plot to throw me out of their way and start me 'on the toboggan.' It is all very pleasant now to contemplate serenely the course of events, from my vantage point in the president's office; but it was a far cry from pleasure during the miserable years I spent when I was their near-victim. I was a half-demented man for a few months, while I thrashed around as helplessly as a trout caught squarely on the hook of a beautifully colored fly. Yes, beautifully colored fly is a good parallel. My enemies did a very good job of it. They won their game with me in every way for several years. But, as I say, I can now sit here serenely and ask: 'Where are they?' They got what they wanted and found it different from what they expected; whereas I got what I didn't want and have made a lot out of it—more than I had ever hoped for."

And the author concludes his instructive narrative: "I regard these 'enemies' simply as chessmen in the game of life, who, by attempting to checkmate me, were themselves relegated to the rear. I sharpened my wits on them and used their villainy to step forward. I am firmly convinced that opposition and impending disaster frequently draw qualities out of a man that he did not know he possessed; and sometimes as I look at my sixteen-year-old son and feel inclined to shelter him from troubles and from enemies, I wonder whether this is not a complete mistake. Throughout nature, one sees how opposition develops qualities, and I doubt whether man is an exception. I can say with a significant meaning: 'Thank God for my enemies'; they most magnanimously kicked me so far upstairs that I now stand far above them."

How many such significant cases take place continuously! One can always say to the enemies: You will impede and we shall build. You will delay the structure and we shall temper our skill. You will aim all your arrows and we shall uplift our shields. While you will compose subtle strategies, we shall already occupy a new site. And where we shall have but one way, you will have, in persecution, to try hundreds. Your trenches will but point out to us the mountain path. And when we direct our movements, you will have to compile a voluminous book of denials. But we shall be unimpeded by these compilations.

Truly, it is not pleasant for you to enumerate all that is done against your regulations. Your fingers will become numb, as you count upon them all cases of forbiddances and denials. Yet at the end of all actions, the strength will remain with us because we dispelled fear and acquired patience, and we can no longer be disappointed. And we will smile at each of your grimaces, your schemes, and your silences. And this, not because we are specially anointed but because we do not love the dictionaries of negation. And we enter each battle only on a constructive plan.

For the hundredth time we smilingly say: "Thanks to you, enemies and persecutors. You have taught us resourcefulness and indefatigability. Thanks to you, we have found glorious mountains with inexhaustible beds of ore. Thanks to your fury, the hoofs of our horses are shod with pure silver, beyond the means of our persecutors. Thanks to you, our tents glow with a blue light.

You yearn to learn who we are in reality, where are our dwellings, who are our fellow voyagers because you have invented so many slanders about us that you yourselves are hopelessly entangled. Where is the limit?

At the same time, several keen people insist that it is not only useful but highly profitable for you to go our way, and that no one who has walked with us has lost anything but has rather received new possibilities.

Would you know where is our dwelling place? We have many homes in many lands, and vigilant friends guard our dwellings. We will not divulge their names, nor shall we probe into the habitation of your friends. Nor shall we seek to convert them. Many are travelling with us and in all corners of the world, upon the heights flame friendly beacon fires. Around them the benevolent traveler will always find a place. And verily, travelers hasten to them. For besides the printed word and the post, communications are dispatched by invisible forces; and with one sigh, joy, sorrow, and help are transported through the world fleeter than the wind. And like a fiery wall stand the battlements of friends.

This is such a significant time. You need not hope to attract to your cause many youths, for they also are the designated ones. In the most varied countries they also are thinking of one thing—and they easily find the key to the mystery. This mystery leads youth to the glorious beacon fire, and our youth now is aware that the cruel every day can be transformed into a festival of labor, love, and achievement. They have the consciousness that something glorious and radiant is ordained for them. And from that mighty fire, none can repulse them.

We have known those who after their hours of labor, come silently, asking us how to live. And their hands, reddened from toil, nervously twitch over the whole list of necessary, unuttered problems. To these hands one does not give a stone instead of the bread of knowledge.

We remember how in twilight they came, beseeching us not to depart. One could not tell these young friends that it was not away from them that we were departing, but for their sake we were going in order to bring them the treasure casket.

And now you denying ones, you again ask how we can understand each other without disputes. Thus a friend contributes that which is most needed; a friend does not waste time. Thus is the quarrel transformed into a discussion. And the most primitive sense of rhythm and measure is being transformed into the discipline of freedom. And the comprehension of unity, which doubts not but searches for illumination, transforms all life. And then, there is still some word that you can find only yourself, consciously unwavering and righteously striving.

Often you are angry and lose your temper, but you should be just the opposite. You slander and condemn, and, through this, you fill the air with boomerangs that afterward snap your own forehead. "Poor Makar" complains at the cones which painfully strike him, but he has strewn them himself.

You do not object to becoming important and to surrounding yourself with presumption, forgetting that self-importance is the surest sign of vulgarity. Now you speak of science and yet new experiments appear suspicious to you.

Now you laugh about seclusion and you yourself do not realize the most practical usages of the laboratory of life. You yourself are seeking to escape as soon as possible from an overly smoky room.

You often hide yourself and express doubt, while doubt is the most insidious poison invented by vicious beings. Now you doubt and betray, and do not wish to learn that both of these negations are the product of ignorance, which is in no way akin to children—on the contrary, it grows with years into a very ugly garden.

Now you are shocked if you are accused of prejudices, while your entire life is crowded with them. And you will not concede one of your customary habits, which are obscuring the most simple, practical understanding. You fear so much to become ridiculous that you provoke smiles. And you are shocked at the call: Be new! Be new! Not as on a stage, but in your own life.

You value property as highly as if you were preparing to take it with you to the grave. You do not like to hear the talk of death because it still exists for you, and you have given to cemeteries a great portion of the world. And you carefully outline your ritual of funeral processions as though this procedure was worthy of the greatest attention. And you eschew the word attainment because for you it is linked with conventionalities. According to your ideas it is a strange and improper matter to be occupied in life with these ideals of attainment in service for humanity.

Nor let us even mention your deep reverence for financial matters. It is not only a necessity with you, but a cult is contained for you in the sham formulae of the contemporary world. You dream to gild your rusty shield. But while you will evoke the destruction, we will turn toward creative Lakshmi.

Just now evil is active and the Star of the Mother of the world surrounds the earth with its rays of future creations.

You accuse us of nebulous inconsistencies, but we are occupied with the most practical experiments. And how silently are our friends working, searching for the means of new experiments for good!

In irritation you named our discoveries "panther's leaps." You were ever ready to judge us utterly without knowledge of what we are doing. Although you pretend to condemn those who speak of that which they do not know, yet you yourself are acting so. Where is that justice for which you have sewn such clumsy theatrical togs for yourself? When, to your joy, you believe that we have disappeared, we will be again approaching by a new path. However, let us not quarrel; we must even praise you. Your activity is useful to us, and all your most cunning schemes give us the possibility of continuing the most instructive of chess-games.

And if a constructive goodwill shall be promoted even by you, laudable enemies, let this be so, if only the blessed construction benefits thereby.

Light conquers darkness!

DANGEROUS DISEASES

THE Chinese Hospital Dialogue advises:

"Doctor, when I have formed a habit, is it hard to break?"

"I think if you are in earnest, it can be done. As the proverb says: 'There is nothing difficult in the world except the fear of an insincere heart.'"

It is most touching to see that a modern hospital book closes on such a wise proverb. Verily, remove fear and insincerity, and at once the heart will recuperate. How many dangerous diseases have been caused by ignorance and its children: fear, covetousness, and malice. As the next progeny of these, we find the creeping asp of slander.

Slander is the transmission of a lie. It makes no difference whether the lie is transmitted in light-mindedness or malice or ignorance—its seeds will be equally destructive. I recall the remarkable reply of Kuindji, who himself was against every form of lying. Kuindji was on bad terms with Diaghilev. A certain artist, knowing this and probably anticipating that Kuindji would enjoy a bad report about Diaghilev, told Kuindji some ugly gossip about Diaghilev. Kuindji listened patiently and then interrupted the artist with a thunderous exclamation: "You are a slanderer!" The man who had transmitted this gossip, after such an unexpected defeat, tried to justify himself by saying that he did not make up that gossip, but that he only transmitted it "for information, without even a bad thought." But Kuindji was adamant, he continued to look grimly at the unfortunate informer and repeated: "You brought me this vile news. Consequently it is you who are the slanderer!"

How many of such self-justifying slanderers intrude upon an atmosphere of creativeness. They scatter the most poisonous seeds and try to cover themselves with the shield of non-responsibility. They, as if, did not think of any consequences; they only repeated it for information, as if every slander and lie is not being repeated "for information" only.

It is not sufficiently emphasized that slander and lies are ugly. It is not pointed out that these fragments of darkness encumber and poison space. It would seem that people should know well how anger and irritation poison the system, but then every liar and slanderer in some measure sinks into lethal hatred and first of all poisons himself. Hatred also lives around jealousy and ignorance and around that same perversity of the thinking apparatus, which is so difficult to heal. A child may be unsociable, queer, suspicious, but it is not born hating; this evil quality is taken up from the many examples set by the elders.

"Slander, slander—something will always remain!" What malicious care is expressed, in order that something hateful should remain. In this manner certain people are more concerned with the preservation of evil than of good. The good in some measure will always be selfless; whereas evil, first of all, is egotistic. And if a man will begin to assure that he has committed something evil for the sake of good, believe him not; undoubtedly he wanted to justify his selfhood or tried to distinguish himself selfishly in the eyes of a superior.

One has to be surprised how weak are the laws that punish slander. In some countries the persecution of slander is almost impossible. One can convince oneself only that not by laws that persecute slander but by preventive measures, one may considerably weaken this poisonous asp. This also may be attained in schools; but still more so, this can be achieved in home life. Exclude from the family circle all trifling gossip, and you will save the younger generation from committing great slander. If youngsters do not hear from childhood any mutual accusations nor any seeds of gossip and slander, they simply will not respond to this type of "recreation."

If at home there is no card playing, then the first foundations of their character will form themselves without the necessity of murdering the most precious time. The future of family life very much depends upon the parents themselves. Perhaps precisely now one is led to remind of the hereditary possibilities of the family, for very often instead of an attractive principle, the family creates but a repulsive element. And there, wherein lies repulsion alone, there—because of the absence of attraction—lies the beginning of chaos.

Gossip and slander—what an infamy!

There are many epidemics. It has gradually become evident that not only the generally accepted scourges, such as the plague, cholera, and the other infectious diseases, but also many other illnesses are contagious. And what if slander also represents a contagious manifestation and moreover an epidemic one? There are many forms of very contagious psychosis. History continuously mentions facts of mass psychosis, which at times took really threatening dimensions.

If one were to investigate the sources of slander, one would no doubt find that in a pure, worthy, and cultural atmosphere, slander does not thrive. Observe the home as well as the social atmosphere of notorious slanderers, and you will find the real seat of this dangerous psychosis. Even ordinary falsehood is not pronounced everywhere. There are such places in the world and such persons in the presence of whom the slanderer and liar feels himself so uncomfortable that he will not dare to resort to his favorite *mal* parlance. But where slander is pronounced lightly, there look for an old, established evil. The microbes of slander feel themselves there greatly at home.

Let us not feel astonished if among works on psychic diseases there will appear real medical treatises on slander, on its causes and methods of propagation and, let us also hope about preventive measures.

One thing is clear—that, if life is in need of newly affirmed foundations, then first of all, all fatal epidemics must be overcome. Among these scourges of mankind special attention will be paid to the multiformity of psychosis. Curing drunkards, drug-addicts, thieves, and all criminals in the field of sexual perversity will no doubt lead also to the cure of one of the worst perversities—the vice of slander.

It will be noticed how different perversities manifest themselves simultaneously. When observing a slanderer or a notorious liar, you will find that the rest of his life is not pure. Undoubtedly he will be subject to other forms of criminality. In the future, state hospitals, besides the wards for drug addicts, drunkards, thieves, and other criminals, there will be one for the most dangerous infectious disease—the ward for slanderers.

And old English law provides that precisely slanderers are punishable by flogging. But let us leave it to the *psychiaters* to decide, what measure of healing is best suitable for such a dangerous and abhorrent disease.

When one acquaints oneself with the Pasteur Institute, one will probably be asked not to remain too long in one of the laboratories. You will be warned: "Here are especially dangerous microbes." In the future, psychiatric hospital visitors will be asked to leave a certain ward more quickly, and it will be added: "The microbes of slander are very contagious!"

THE SCHOOLTEACHER

AT the last session of the English National Union of Teachers, the honor of being president had been conferred on the schoolmaster of a small country town, Mr. J. W. H. Brown of Somerset. In his presidential address, he made some wise and significant statements, which are of importance in the widest international aspect. It is also of great interest that a schoolmaster from a far-off country place was elected the President of the National Assembly. The following are some quotations from his address:

"It must be a state in which there is a more equitable sharing of the 'Common Good,' whether of wealth, leisure, happiness, health; but further and more important, it must be a state in which all contribute and more fully and more intensely cooperate in creating and increasing that 'Common Good.'

"This cannot be done in a generation. It needs wise planning and sustained effort; it needs to educate the people—propaganda if you will—and to arouse enthusiasm.

"There must be legislative planning, industrial planning, planning for commerce, for health, and, above all, for education in its widest meaning—that is for making people fit for the world in which they live and giving them the desire and the ability to improve it. It is for this planning ahead for education that I appeal.

"When will some political party or all political parties put education not merely in the forefront of their programs but in the forefront of their practice? Instead of this futile tinkering with the present, why cannot they plan boldly and nobly for the future?

"The average men and women of this country want a better life for their children than they themselves live; they would make an overwhelmingly favorable response to the right appeal from the right quarters. Enthusiasm for a great educational advance could be readily aroused. The means are available. They should be mobilized and used. Religion, art, science, common sense could all play their part. From the pulpit and the platform, in the Press, on the screen, and by the broadcast, reason could be convinced and feelingly awakened.

"Hitherto public policy in education—when we have had one—has been the conscious policy of adjusting the next generation to the needs of the present. But surely, it should be concerned rather with giving each new generation 'the ability to face new issues in new ways.' If we really desire to educate for a true democracy, this must be recognized.

"In other ways, too, there must be a change of heart as well as of policy. The idea that children of different social classes must be educated in different types of schools perpetuates caste and renders democracy unattainable. It is mostly sheer snobbery. You cannot produce a democracy by an education based on class prejudice and on fostering class distinction.

"One can say that, on the whole, the kind of education given in the primary schools is given by the best methods and is calculated to train the whole person—body, mind, and spirit. It is hampered by very imperfect conditions and does not go far enough. Remove these disabilities, and it would be an education that would fit our future citizens to live fuller and better lives, and be fit to play their part in evolving it."

I do not know whether we would agree with Mr. Brown on other details, but these fundamental thoughts expressed by him should be near to the whole world. Truly, even primary education should not tie students only to the past but should arm them well so that they can joyfully meet the future. Precisely this thought we affirmed in our advice to the Master Institute of United Arts and to the International Art Center. We said, "Humanity is facing coming events of cosmic greatness. Humanity already realizes that all occurrences are not accidental. The time for the construction of future culture is at hand. Before our eyes the revaluation of values is being witnessed. Amid ruins of valueless banknotes, mankind has found the real value of the world's significance. The values of great art, knowledge, and labor are victoriously traversing all storms of earthly commotions. Even "earthly" people already understand the vital importance of active beauty. And when we proclaim labor, beauty, and action, verily we know that we pronounce the formula of the international language, and this formula, which now belongs to the museum and stage, must enter everyday life. The sign of beauty and action will open all gates. Beneath the sign of Beauty we walk joyfully; with Beauty and Labor we conquer. In Beauty we are united. And now we affirm these words—not on the snowy heights but amid the turmoil of the city. And realizing the path of true reality, we greet with a happy smile the Future."

And reality itself compels humanity to seek for true values.

The worst is to turn someone's head backward—this means to strangle him. In medieval times it was said that the devil, taking possession of a person, finally kills the parson by turning his head backward. The same principle is expressed in the parable of Lot's wife, who was turned into a pillar of salt. Instead of striving into the future, she turned back and, therefore, both mentally and bodily she became fossilized. The same thought is expressed in other folklores in most striking symbols. And despite all these warnings in practical life and in school education, this striving into the future is hardly ever applied.

One should greet every voice, which, in one way or another, directs us into a radiant healthy future. The schoolmaster is also right in stating that primary education should be uniform. In the same way, from very childhood, young hearts should be imbued with the positive foundations of the past, but apply them toward the future. The true son of his motherland is he who desires his country's improvement and perfection and who understands that without progress there can be but retreat and regress. Either we advance or go back. It has been said and repeated that it is impossible to remain static.

The main thing is to affirm oneself mutually in progressive intentions of goodwill. Details can always be settled. If from childhood a person will be imbued with true tolerance, then he will always find the basis of esteem for his fellow coworkers. One has but to realize in one's heart such a constructive and progressive ideal, when all other problems will appear as only technical details.

I have already more than once praised the beautiful decisions of teachers in Europe, India, and America, which they reached during various congresses and conventions. And with regret we had to point out the unfortunate oppressions to which educators were so often subjected. And in this struggle, one has to find a common front in order to overcome all evil obstacles.

The schoolmaster correctly points out that not only should legislation be improved, but benevolent changes should take place in the hearts of all connected with education. Without these healthy strivings of the heart, all laws will remain but dead ballast. But in order that such a wonderful transfiguration of human hearts may take place, it is necessary for all who work in the field of culture to unite and to support each other in such beneficial educational movements.

Public opinion should be nursed and educated. Public opinion is formed in schools from the very first school hours. Hence, if all the teachers of the world will unanimously ponder over that which is so undeferrably needed for the whole of mankind, then that temple of public opinion will be erected, that "museon" of all muses, which will always serve as a radiant beacon for all who wait impatiently, search, and strive to perfection.

Salutations to the English teacher; greetings to all teachers who ascend the same summit of labor, tolerance, and progress!

Mr. H. G. Wells justly says, "No conqueror can make the multitude different from what it is; no statesman can carry the world affairs beyond the ideas and capacities of the generation of adults with which he deals; but teachers—I use the word in the widest sense—can do more than either conqueror or statesman; they can create a new vision and liberate the latent powers of mankind."

Striving to a peace for the whole world, the educators can accomplish a conquest—peaceful and magnificent.

Tzagan Kure, 1935

TACTICA ADVERSA

GENGHIS KHAN frequently resorted to feigned retreat in order to draw the enemy into pursuit, and thus the more easily to smite him in the rear with his reserve forces. Thus is it told. It is likewise said that the tireless conqueror sometimes set fire to the steppe behind his hordes in order thus to speed the movement of his army. Perhaps such tales of the versatile military technique of the great conqueror are true, but in any case they are plausible, because in his great campaigns Chenghiz Khan undoubtedly made use of the most diverse technique unforeseen by his enemies.

It is also attributed to him that, wishing to maintain a healthfully austere way of life, he ordered his high officials to tear their expensive silken garments on thorn bushes in order to demonstrate the inapplicability of such clothing. It is said that he simulated indisposition from imported beverages in order to attract people to the local milk products.

In ancient history can be found many examples of the most unexpected countertactics that produced the most conclusive results.

In battle, man cannot discriminate precisely when he is exposed to the utmost danger. During the impact itself, it is impossible to examine which circumstance was most perilous or most beneficial. What blow saved one from a still greater blow? A falling horse, by its fall, protected one from an unexpected overthrow. A casual outcry caused one to turn around and thus avoid a deadly arrow. Therefore, right was the ancient wisdom that paid attention to the final result, to the effect of all that takes place.

It is impossible to fix the end premeditatedly, but from the end it is possible to see from what was composed much that has preceded. For these observations, well-tested attentiveness is needed, but likewise requisite is knowledge of what countertactics consist of. This latter circumstance, so salutarily effective in many historical events, is not often examined. True, people like to repeat, "No luck, but misfortune helped"—yet in this speech there is assumed, as it were, an accidentalness of some sort of misfortune; but, of course, countertactics do not know bad luck. They know only systematic actions, which it is difficult to calculate in close proximity to them.

Each traveler knows how clearly and beautifully is outlined a snow-covered peak at a distance, and how much it loses form during the severe and hazardous approaches to it. Likewise in events, it is difficult to make a proper estimate in inordinate proximity to them. But countertactics say reassuringly that where there is a pure fiery striving, there all accompanying manifestations are also shown to be systematic. But a much refined consciousness must be applied in order to evaluate the unusual actions of countertactics. True invincibility will always be concomitant with extreme resourcefulness. People cannot recognize the upward-leading paths and, for their part, must apply all sensitiveness of resourcefulness and mobility.

Each worker knows the value of mobility. How far must this true mobility be from the petty fidgeting that can only complicate proper movement. When a worker is asked how he walks, he will reply that he does not know precisely how, but whither he knows steadfastly from the hour of setting out. In the same way, no sort of "unexpectedness" of the path confuses the true doer of things. He has already assumed the premise that in everything that happens will be the element of utility.

He likewise knows that certain encountered actions must be brought to the opposite extreme because only then is their meaning manifested and in the same way are panaceas found. Each senseless attack thus acquires greater evidence of absurdity if it is helped to roll along to the limit. Then is unrolled the whole abominable absurdity, and even a casual observer will apprehend the degree of hideousness.

So many times, an experienced leader, having an opportunity to cut short a stream of absurdity, has held back his followers, saying, "Let it roll on." The wise leader calls up his hidden troops only after necessary measures have been carried out. What sort of a leader would he be if he summoned his secret reserves prematurely? The enemy would not yet be fully disclosed. The hostile forces still would not have attained their utmost intensity, yet his reserve troops would be fully engaged. Therefore, countertactics know, first of all, such a practice of economy.

But the inexperienced watcher cries out, "Stop! Why? This is senseless!" But the experienced worker corrects him, "It is not only foolish but also ugly. Wait a minute and you yourself will see this intolerable degree of ugliness and ignorance devour itself."

The history of various peoples does not by accident continually repeat to us about different manifestations of countertactics. These repetitions allow us to memorize examples of the victorious expedient of the counterblow. You know how people say, "Give a thief enough rope and he'll hang himself," or "Don't wave, he's coming." Yet the same popular wisdom proposes that the rope must be given; yet the awaiting of the coming also goes on, not in carelessness but, on the contrary, in full attentiveness and tensity.

So many times the best covenants speak about smiting darkness. This means the overthrow of darkness must come to pass and therefore countertactics must be only a means of conflict but in no wise a permissible inaction. When people say, "Give a thief enough rope and he'll hang himself," in this is foreseen a whole series of actions. The thief must be discovered. The rope must be at hand, there must be enough of it, and it must be given. The thief must carry out an action, for he must hang himself with this rope.

History does not relate how Judas found his rope. It is thought that he found it in some special way because his unheard-of evildoing led him to self-destruction. Only observe, and you will see how evildoing defeats itself. I have already had occasion to write about many observed cases of diverse forms of the overthrow of villainy. Actually in this multiformity of automatic retribution is contained the singular refinement of the laws.

Here we speak about justice, yet you know that around this concept cling the countertactics, and by their often inexpressible reactions, they help in the discovery of every step of evil. For a structure, a clean place is needed. Each builder is first of all concerned about the ground on which the foundation is to stand. He sees if there are any fissures or dangerous crevices. By all the best measures, he avoids corroding moisture, and first of all he fills up any cracks.

After the erection of a structure, no one pictures to himself what deep underground labors have taken place for the solidity of walls and towers! Before beginning his upper structures, the builder directs his attention to all the deep-seated unexpectedness. If moisture should appear, he will not suddenly abandon the sandy ground but will carefully observe what are the ultimate quantities of moisture and where [is] its source. We know how sometimes even urgent structures have been delayed while unexpected underground conditions were put in order.

"Blessed are the obstacles, by them do we grow." He who said this knew all the dimensions of the obstacles, and by his experience could appraise them and apply them beneficially. Construction in goodness is tireless, prudent, attentive. What beauty is contained in this inexhaustible creation!

Peking, February 20, 1935

REAL VALUES

IN the *Narada Silpa Sastra*, high ordainments about the significance of art have been given:

"We will speak of the manner of construction of the art gallery. According to Usinara, the art gallery is to be erected in the central part of the city, on a site where four roads cross, in front of palaces and houses or in the center of the main street."

"Pictures are to be such as to captivate our minds and give joy to our eyes. They must be of several colors, brilliant with various color shades. . . ."

"Divine Narada says that we will speak here of the manner of decoration by painting. According to Usinara, painting is for the pleasure of the gods, for the satisfaction of the presiding deity of the building, and also for beauty."

Thus spoke Narada.

And in another age, in other expressions, but similarly uplifting, Leonardo da Vinci praises the great meaning of art. The same solemn homage we find amid the Chinese classics, in Japan, in Persia, and everywhere in the world; this is told by the best people in the highest terms.

Art is not destruction. In art is contained the seed of construction, not destruction. This was felt always; even the Minister of Finance will find new convincing formulae. Without exaggeration, the treasures of culture are the stronghold of a nation. The entire upbuilding—all enlightenment, all spiritual inspiration, all happiness and salvation—will be born upon the foundations of cultural treasures. At first let us realize and safeguard culture, and then the designs on the banknotes of the country will also become attractive. Along the innumerable paths of communication, creativeness will surge forward in all its noble multiformity.

Likewise, it will not be an exaggeration to say that the language of the heart has many times proved in the history of mankind most convincing and attractive as well as unifying. Not only are the names of Apollonius, Rubens, Velasquez, and many others immortalized in art but also their unforgettable advice in the field of statesmanship. Objects of art themselves have, many a time, been the best ambassadors, introducing peace and friendship. We already have pointed out that the exchange of art treasures even prevented misunderstandings and was ahead of verbal agreements. If the world, according to Plato, is ruled by ideas, then noble seeds of art will always be that beneficial sowing, which will give the best, well-remembered harvest. Therefore, it will not be commonplace to affirm again and again the wide meaning of art and the true value of the beautiful. Thus let us safeguard everything that is beautiful with all the care of our heart.

For the establishment of our Pact for the Protection of Cultural Treasures, first of all, one has to acquaint oneself with the history of the origin of the Red Cross. The founder of this noble idea, the famous Swiss philanthropist, Dunant, and his self-sacrificing friends, for seventeen years have tirelessly knocked at the hearts of mankind in order to tell of the undeferrability of such a humanitarian project. Everyone should remember the history of the Red Cross, which had so many troubles and difficulties. Likewise, in the question of the protection of art treasures, let us always keep in mind that these great treasures are being destroyed not only during times of war but also during the manifestation of every human ignorance. Alone, the protection of cultural treasures will awaken many dormant paths of creativeness and entire countries will again remember that therein lies their strength and unconquerable dignity and value.

Let us always remember how beautifully such great men of India, Vivekananda and Tagore, spoke about art.

Said Vivekananda: "Don't you see? I am, above all, a poet." — "That man cannot be truly religious who has not the faculty of feeling the beauty and grandeur of art." — "Non-appreciation of art is crass ignorance."

Rabindranath Tagore concluded his article "What Is Art?" with the words: "In art the person in us is sending its answer to the Supreme Person, who reveals Himself to us in a world of endless beauty across the lightless world of facts." Who else now could define art better than this glorious poet of India!

In *Leaves of Morya's Garden*, Book One, we read:
"Pure art is the true expression of the radiant Spirit. Through art, you gain the Light!"
"True Art is the expression of the radiant Spirit. Through Art, thou hast the Light!"

SUCCESS

D R. CANNON, professor of physiology at Harvard University, not long ago gave a lecture in Peking on "The Role of Chance in Discovery." After citing many examples from different scientific practices, the professor came to the conclusion that "success follows only those who take advantage of it."

An excellent formula. It is absolutely correct and applicable to all branches of life. In fact, in addition to conscientious, farsighted labor, one should further manifest the capacity to observe the signs of the inception of success. So many times one has had occasion to read about the fact that it is necessary to know how to apprehend success, as it is an "easily frightened bird."

So many times one comes upon old sayings to the effect that "nothing ventured, nothing gained," which among different peoples in their own tongues is interpreted variously but all in the same direction. An endless number of stories and legends speak about unsuccessful simpletons, who in their foolishness let the *Zhar-Ptitsa*, the Firebird, escape.

Precisely, they have let the *Zhar-Ptitsa* slip from their hands. It had already been found. Wise admonishments have said, "Take the Firebird, but take not the golden cage. The fool has invariably reached for the golden cage and thus let slip the precious gift contained in the Firebird. The fools have been forewarned: "Seize the Fire-Blossom—look not back." But right at this moment, something began to happen, and all that had been found vanished. Verily, success must be taken and grasped firmly, instantly, single purposedly. In this unique striving is expressed that faith will already be bordering upon great and real knowledge.

In the same warning stories, there are always deduced many circumstances that promote the discovery of success. Beginning with gray wolves or unknown well-wishers, mendicants and passersby, many circumstances are manifested as helpers in success. Great attention should also be paid to this inspiring assistance. Not only should one discern such prearranged helpers, but also in the social order, one should create contributing circumstances. Precisely, such circumstances have to be created.

The germination of success is not a personal matter, it is state prosperity. Of course, cach private, beneficial success is also state progress. Consequently, the state must consciously concern itself that such successes are made attainable. The attainment of all the best takes place through all the loftiest. Hence the state, as such, must give its citizens all the best, all the truly cultural.

And as always, we are speaking not about quantity but about quality. What of it, if periodicals come out in editions of many tens of pages, when from the standpoint of quality, they could be improved by being cut in half. What of it, if all sorts of questionable restaurants and cafés chantants grow as funguses and foul the thinking of people. Not without reason does the East fail to understand the difference between a "chantant" and a "Shaitan." Last evening in the midst of the desert, we listened to the radio. We listened for about two hours. We tried out various waves and visited in them the most diverse countries. What did we hear? True, somewhere there flashed out a fragment from *Lohengrin*, but all the rest was so much on the order of restaurant fox-trot tunes that once again I was obliged to feel horror at what space is being filled with. Of course, all these sounds, manifested and unmanifested, have an influence on the human consciousness.

It is well enough known that space has been filled, but evidently it has been insufficiently assimilated that the filling of space is the greatest responsibility of humanity.

The essence of quality is that multiform, constructive material of which is built the success of civilization and, beyond that, culture. The man who has been civilized by the fox-trot is lost on the paths to culture. To him, the blessed paths already prove to be unattainable.

What is there for us? Impulses have been ordained for us, yet it has not been given to us to accomplish. Here is to what pessimism can become addicted, the consciousness, which is not bad but which has been overburdened by the baseness of everyday routine. He who utters such negative, pessimistic words thus renounces constructiveness. Whatever signs of beneficial successes would be shown to such a man, he will wave them all away as unattainable and go to drown his sorrow in a neighboring tavern.

In this famous "drowning" of sorrow is expressed the same cowardly pessimism. You see, it is needful for this biped to drown in violence. He thinks that he is drowning his sorrow, whereas he either drowns or smokes up his own attainment. If right now, space itself is rumbling with the horror of vulgarity, then surely it is the business of each administration to replace vulgar triviality with manifestations of lofty quality.

We have been obliged to speak repeatedly about the fact that there is no point in slandering people, that they exclusively demand vulgarity and baseness. Both are the result of one's childhood. But give beautiful harmony, beautiful song, beautiful words, and people will be drawn to them pure-heartedly.

There are evil forces everywhere. Everywhere they carry on their work of dissolution, and they dream of depriving people of those successes that have already been ordained. Indeed, it is possible to considerably postpone what has been ordained, but for all that it will be manifested. Each such postponement is an abominable offense against humanity. Anyone who has a desire to harass someone into darkness and deprive him of light is by that fact a coworker of darkness. Of course, people, as such, are not at all collaborators of darkness. Provided the servants of darkness cannot draw them into the loathsome and the vulgar, sooner or later they will become sober. Revolts of entire peoples will rise up against all the drownings, smokings, and poisonings. Success follows that a government understands that it is impossible to keep the people on a low level by giving them products of low quality. Then, too, space will not roar and shriek but will be confluent in the Beautiful.

Whether successes are in scientific discoveries, whether they are in ennobling creativeness, whether they are in simple, everyday life is a matter of indifference; everywhere successes must be recognized and accepted. Enough has been told in stories about gaping oafs and simpletons who let good fortune escape. The age of construction of the new culture must be an age of successful people, each of whom, in his own way, will discern his treasure, his ordained success.

"Success follows those who can receive it."

LUXURY

I

THE book *Fiery World* indicates:
"It has been said that humanity must abandon luxury. Not without reason have people themselves so isolated this concept. Luxury is not beauty, not spirituality, not perfectionment, not construction, not benevolence, not compassion; no good concept can replace it. Luxury is destruction of resources and possibilities. Luxury is dissolution, for all structures without rhythm mean only disintegration. One can see clearly enough that worldly luxury has already been shaken, but, as a cure, harmonious cooperation must be found in order to rid the world of the plague of luxury. Egoism will raise the objection that luxury is an earned abundance. It will also be said that luxury is regal. This will be slander. Luxury has been always a sign of decay and eclipse of the spirit. The chains of luxury are most terrible too for the Subtle World. Needed there are advancement and continuous perfectionment of thought. The encumbrance of luxury will not help one to the next Gates."

Were these words said for some hoary antiquity? Or are they needed today in the same measure as then? It is very deplorable if commands against the ignorance of luxury are also needed today. But be this as it may, who will dare to deny that precisely now luxury must be eradicated? How often has the world been told that luxury is a sign of extremely bad taste! How often were examples of the fall of Babylon, Rome, and many other empires pointed out, when instead of beauty, education, and enlightenment, humanity became obsessed by vulgar luxury!

Let us not forget how Genghis Khan, wishing to

avoid the possibility of the spreading of luxury amid his warriors, carried out in front of all the people the most instructive demonstrations. He told some of his closest friends to dress themselves in the finest Chinese silk robes and went with them through thorny bushes, dry tamarisk, and other sharp, prickly plants. When they arrived at the meeting place of the people, naturally their silk robes were torn to pieces. And the leader pointed out to his people the uselessness of luxurious dresses. He also showed with the help of his friends, how luxurious food only causes illness, thus teaching them to return to milk and a simple healthy diet.

Such examples of endeavors, to turn the consciousness of the people to a beautiful, sound living, one may quote in plenty, from all ages. But it appears that even now a sound foundation has not been realized, and the machine, revolting against weak human common sense, overpowers the wise distribution of forces. Just at present, it is especially necessary, without fearing derision and mockery, to remind again about healthy beauty and goal-fitted living. Some countries already announce premia for handicrafts and home industry, and this is not a retreat from civilization. In this way wise leaders try again to attract attention to the necessity of a high quality of workmanship and to applying one's leisure time for skillful self-perfectment.

Even recently, vulgar luxury was ascribed only to the ignorant nouveaux riches. Of course, these newcomers to the golden calf, often complete ignoramuses, are easy prey to the dark whisperings of luxury. But let us not close our eyes that far beyond the circle of nouveaux riches, there grows the desire for easy earnings and for vulgar forms of the luxurious perversion of life.

The book *Fiery World* wisely reminds that precisely egoistical ignoramuses will always defend luxury, and the same book farsightedly points out that there are many signs that luxury in the world has already been shaken. This means that one must very attentively watch that the next step of existence is really surrounded by truly noble creations.

But this necessary condition of life must be watched not by some official inspectors but by the population itself, in order to create as soon as possible a conscious understanding of the harmony of daily life.

II

Luxury in objects must also leave humanity for that reason, that this abhorrent conception treacherously involves people in spiritual luxury, which is still more harmful and infectious. In self-centeredness people become careless toward the workers in the field of education. The excesses of luxury have created similar hideous excesses of enticement for outer physical strength, all sorts of races and competitions, and admiration of muscular force. One abnormality always leads to another. The growth of the material side of life calls forth a doubtless downfall in spirituality in all countries and in all creeds. More than that, every striving toward spirituality and the sublime problems of "be-ness" is considered inadmissible in the daily life of materially "civilized" society.

It is true, some nations, and among them mainly India, keep to ethical methods of thought; but even among these nations, there are already just complaints that the young generation is losing the understanding of the high foundations of life. From other countries there comes the most deplorable news about the growth of militant atheism and about unhealthy idolatry before crass materialism. The real workers of spiritual education are pushed back into the back rows. People are not ashamed to state that, at present, there is no time altogether to speak about living ethics. And one may add many examples of similar horrors. Of course, from ancient history we also know that Confucius, the Just One, was prosecuted by unwise rulers. And Plato was sold as a slave. We know also that Aristides, who was given the byname the Righteous, was expelled by his co-citizens from his native town. Such records sometimes seem like slander upon humanity. It is too difficult to imagine that Aristides the Righteous could have been so maltreated by bestial ignoramuses, who dared to commit such a strikingly harmful step for the state as the expulsion of their best citizen. But during the latest excavations in the Acropolis of Athens—what a shame—there were found ceramic tablets that represented votes against Aristides. How terrible is it to witness the actual tablet with the inscription "for the expulsion of Aristides!" This corresponds to the most awful vandalism, when absurdly and as a shame for the whole of humanity were destroyed irreplaceable treasures of great beauty!

When we read about the destruction of the most remarkable libraries, when we see lists of already non-existent creations of art, will not even the most shameless heart shudder? Some Herostrats of antiquity and their followers of our day proudly announce that they want to destroy museums and temples. We see such insane statements in print. But not one of these Herostrats will realize that he follows the commandments of most ignorant luxury. If luxury is the destruction of means and possibilities, if it is decay, then every barbaric destruction of great creations will already be a luxury, a vile luxury. Herostrat, when burning great monuments, of course did not understand the high meaning of creativeness. In the same way, the servitor of luxury, surrounding himself by hideously pompous, gilded encumbrances, is like the same Herostrat in regard to noble, true art. If we think of new forms of life, if we want the happiness of our near ones, then is it not our duty to replace ugliness by lofty, noble forms of living, be this in the material or spiritual respect?

III

With great difficulty people begin to understand such axioms that friendliness opens the gates to cooperation. But when we have to fight in the days of Armageddon against selfhood and rudeness, this may be achieved only by consonance of cooperation. In this incessant and joyful cooperation, we will cognize that the best people so beautifully understood the meaning of beauty in the whole complex of life. The great Teacher Swami Vivekananda tells us: "Don't you see that I am, above all, a poet?" "That man cannot be truly religious who has not the faculty of feeling the beauty and grandeur of art." "Non-appreciation of art is crass ignorance."

Rabindranath Tagore finishes his book *What is Art?* with such words: "In Art the person in us is sending its answer to the Supreme Person, who reveals Himself to us in a world of endless beauty across the lightless world of facts."

The *Fiery World* ordains: "One should avoid prejudice both in the great and the small. Many possibilities have been cut short by prejudice. Indeed, the fiery energy is very sensitive to prejudice. But, being aware of this quality of the energy, one can counteract prejudice by means of suggestion," and "A benevolent thought is the basis of a good action. Thought is luminous before action; therefore, let us count the camps of good according to the lights of thought."

These reminders about the harm of prejudice and about the bliss of light-bringing good thoughts are so needed now when the battle takes place with all the dark phantoms, with ignorant luxury, and with vile treason. The refined heart will make it possible to distinguish where is the borderline between the noble search for beauty and the self-devouring, wild luxury, which decomposes even powerful empires.

Let the Banner of Peace, as a symbol of realization and the construction of Beauty, remind and warn where begins the dark kingdom of spiritual cannibalism.

Verily, luxury must depart from humanity.

O QUANTA ALLEGRIA

"WHERE is vast ancient Rome?" And only then he recognizes it, when little by little from all narrow nooks and corners begins to appear ancient Rome—here as an arch, there as a marble cornice built into the wall, there as a discolored column of porphyry, there as a facade of an evil-smelling fish marketplace, there as a whole portal in front of a modern church, and finally, far away, where the living city ends, as a colossus lifts itself amid thousand-years-old ivy, alone and open plains, as the immense Coliseum triumphal arches, remains of endless palaces of Caesars, imperial baths, temples, tombs, scattered over fields; and the foreigner is no longer aware of the narrow streets and lanes, and is completely surrounded by the ancient world: in his memory arise the gigantic images of Caesars, and shouts and acclaims of the ancient crowds resound in his ears. . . ."

Thus narrates a classical description of Rome. And it is just, when an old Italian recalling the former life exclaims, *"O Quanta Allegria."* How many similar exclamations about the coloring, the characteristics, the solemnity of various manifestations of the past can be heard even now! Well-wishing and inquiring visitors will always find the rhythm of antiquity, obscure for many, in all of its multiformity. And again we will see that the dark pages will be covered with benevolent recollections.

What a wonderful quality of human memory and consciousness that in the end good considerations will prevail in us! Truly it is evident that evil is finite, while good is infinite. We can turn to numerous historical examples and check their reflection in human memory. Even the most terrifying becomes solemn. Even the most ferocious wraps itself in patient attention. As if in all imperfections, there was some seed, which in its own way gave a positive coloring to them.

We began by mentioning Rome. How many attractive, positive traits are pointed out in these descriptive lines, which end in an accord of great beauty! Some other author, more limited, would undoubtedly have spoiled his description with some unnecessary and harmful details. But our artist follows only the fundamental truth. Everything negative and superficial is unnecessary in his broad characterization. Perhaps someone may say that such a characterization is not objective. And probably this critic would pile up so many considerations that everything expressive and necessary would be covered with the dust of all kinds of belittlements and smoothing.

For the expression of true solemnity, the composer carefully picks out the combinations. Nothing that is small and rattling will bemean his powerful solutions, and this integrity will retain that convincingness that gives joy to many centuries.

"When the blue sky came into being and below it came the dark earth, then appeared between them man." Thus speaks an inscription of the eighth century, found on a stone near the Orkhon River.

One feels in the shortness of this hieroglyph that the virgin steppes are as yet not tilled. The virgin taiga has not yet been desecrated. The depths of the earth are intact. And in these untouched vastnesses, in the entirety of a broad imagination, the great Mongolian Kurultai, in the year 1206, proclaimed Genghis Khan as the Emperor of the Universe.

This was possible. This was as natural as the flight of an eagle of the steppes. Just as natural were the messages of Archpriest John to the emperors—rulers of Europe. These writings, up till now, are preserved in archives and are again diligently studied by searching scientists. It sounds

like a fairy tale and, at the same time, the heart resounds
to the past. To many people was ascribed the personality of Archpriest John and the description of his fairylike
country. At times it seems all is but a legend, but again,
on a shelf in the archives, are preserved the messages, are
safeguarded the documents of embassies, and somewhere
is recorded the beautiful page of life.

Very likely, the true personality of Archpriest John
will, after all, never be known—this leader of a great country, carrying on negotiations with emperors of the world.
It does not matter in what way someone may solve this
historic problem. One thing remains certain—that something beautiful occupied many minds. And the very subtlety beckoned the possibility of new developments.

Note that while the saga of Genghis Khan, the way
to Shambhala, and the kingdom of Archpriest John
remained within the bounds of legends, at the same time,
certain searching scientists attentively listened to these
elusive calls of antiquity. And again some one, feeling
exalted by them, exclaimed, "What joy! What life! What
boundlessness!"

An old woman healer tells the youth about ancient
medical compounds. Silvery laughter and jokes interrupt
her convincing talk. But the experience of ages has taught
the healer calmness: "Laugh, laugh! But go and ask all
those whom my herbs have helped." From his early youth,
Saint Panteleimon commands recognition as a healer.
Over useful, good flowers and herbs, the Ayurvedic physician bends down. Every grass of the steppes is full of
ancient lore. Is this in a fairy tale? How can it be a fairy
tale when everything is of great benefit?

Likewise, the beautiful voices of antiquity built the
great saga of life, and a valiant Gallahad, not afraid of
fieriness, gathers sparks of fire into a design of Eternity.
The searcher is not afraid that instead of kingly cities,
before him lies only a hilly field. For in every hillock there
may be a casket with some message of the Archpriest John
or with a ring of Genghis Khan. When everything seems

to have been read in this world, then from the depths of the earth appear complete, new, and as yet unread alphabets. From Harappa in India the attention of the scientist in futile searches directs itself to the Easter Islands, and such unusual decisions begin to correspond to as yet undeciphered riddles.

Life with all the overtaxed and burdened contemporaneity again matures into the simplified hieroglyph, if imagination is yet vivid. What vigilance, what subtlety of thinking when it is alive with the searches of Truth!

In this same great Rome, the stone head of the Statue of Truth bit the hands of liars. Truth does not tolerate falsehood. The heart knows wherein lies falsehood. The Heart is the Gate of Truth!

YOUTH

THE youth is attacked from many sides. It is whispered: "Youth is absorbed by sport"; "It has turned away from humanitarian sciences and is engrossed in materialistic technicalities"; "It neglects the purity of language and spoils the speech with horrible slang"; "It has deserted its family"; "It prefers jazz"; "It avoids lectures"; "It does not love the book and does not like to read." A lot of awful things are said about the youth. Of course, in every single case there has been some reason for such accusation. Even in the daily press, one may find facts as if supporting them. Let us even admit that to some extent, this is so. But if we look at the causes, we find that, before accusing the youth, we must first call to answer the elder generation.

Is there much sincerity in the family? Is the home life always attractive? Is it possible to express serious striving under contemporary conditions? Is there much upliftment and high aspiration in the routine housework? Does the elder generation devote itself to humanitarian ideals? Who laid the first path toward materialism? Who filled the home with poisonous tobacco smoke? Was it the youth that introduced alcohol into the home? Has the family time to listen to the quest of the youth? Does the family strive into the future? Where is born indifference to good and evil? Where is the birthplace of slander, bad language, and gossip? Where has the youth heard for the first time blasphemous jokes? Where did they hear for the first time of destruction and not of upbuilding and creativeness?

Hence, instead of accusing the youth, let us realize where the hotbeds of this misfortune are hidden.

Let us ask ourselves: "Do we know the really hardworking youth?" Of course, we do.

"Do we know the self-sacrificing youth who gives to the family all of his earnings?" Of course, we do.

"Do we know the youth who is sincerely and ardently dreaming of a beautiful future?" Of course, we do.

"Do we know the youth who craves for serious books and inspiring discussions?" Of course, we do.

"Do we know the youth who knows how to live in harmony and mutual trust?" Of course, we do.

"Do we know the youth who has consecrated himself to the service of the Beautiful? Of course, we do.

Thus pondering over the best heights of humanity, we shall also find on every summit some of the best young souls. And this radiant ascension of youth takes place not only in one country—they symbolize our present age all over the world.

Greetings to all young coworkers! We rejoice to witness many most enlightened associations of youth, who struggle toward Light in strenuous efforts. How heartily they strive toward the highest aims of mankind. We know what hardships they have to overcome. We know how they have to rise above local and family circumstances and yet they find inexhaustible strength to go by the higher path. And on all their trails they affirm blessed milestones. And all this common good is accomplished amid indescribable difficulties. And still attainment takes place; and when one wishes to think of something touchingly joyful, one recalls these affirmations of the young generation.

Another instance of harmony among youth comes to mind. I remember how in a huge, stern city, the young, after hard work for their daily bread, gathered gaily in the evening, dressed in their best, hastening to partake of the living water of philosophy, science, and art. They were so accustomed to joint activities that they even tried to live in small communities.

We recall three rooms. In them live eight girls. All of them are hard workers. One is a shopgirl, one a secretary, one a stenographer and, the others work in factories. We asked them:

"For how long have you already lived together?"

"For three years."

"And how often did you quarrel?"

They laugh . . .

"Never!"

It is not a miracle! People of various professions can live harmoniously together, can after the day's difficult work, despite being tired, gather together; and they do not fight, but they revive and enrich each other through an exchange of lofty ideals. What inspiring and convincing affirmations one can hear from the youth. Who strives in highest enthusiasm to truth and is indignant at injustice if not young hearts! For thirty-two years at the head of schools, I am connected with the youth and no unhappy recollections have marred my contact.

If we shall judge the young without prejudice, we shall find many beautiful signs of self-sacrifice, striving toward knowledge, love, and beauty. Those who are in the habit of condemning youth should beware of senile babbling. These desperate condemners see that life today is in confusion and ugly misunderstanding. But when they try to find the guilty, they usually, excusing themselves, look for the easiest scapegoat. They see only the results but avoid thinking of the causes. These causes are quite curable if properly treated by the entire society.

If every unprejudiced observer would find the many numerous, beautiful, and touching examples in favor of the youth, then it would not be difficult to arouse public opinion to appreciate precisely these manifestations of good. The young people, even though inexperienced, yet courageously and self-sacrificingly oppose the dark forces; and, therefore, those who consider themselves wise should sincerely support every noble effort of the youth. But one can support only through examples in life. No abstract nagging will give a harvest. Only actions and deeds, living examples, can convince.

If youth itself realizes the joy of work and inspiring communion, then the more so should the wise elders encourage exactly this joy. One should not coldly condemn that which has given such beautiful evidence. If because of our times, everybody finds it difficult, then one should jointly try to transmute these difficulties into joy. The young hearts understand this. Therefore, let us help in every way that the youth may meet on the path of bliss and inspiration.

One may equalize everything by the lowest, but such equality is tantamount to degeneration. But, every equalizing by the highest will be true progress. In many parts of the world, there exists a legend that because of one righteous man an entire city was saved. This legend, which is so beautifully and multiformly expounded, shows that in everything, quality is valuable and not quantity. Consequently, every good example outshines the negative suppositions.

The seal of the age is created by all nations and, therefore, the easier it is to gather good signs. In various languages, in various customs, these hieroglyphs of good are highly inspiring.

A child tries to reach a postbox to push a letter into it. A passerby wants to help him, and notices on the envelope, which was obviously made by the child itself, the scribbling: "To Saint Nicholas," and asks: "What is this?" — "Mummy is dying and nobody wishes to help her."

In such an amazing way, the heart of the child prayed to Saint Nicholas and received a response and help. Thus the young and youthful find the way to the highest.

STEADFASTNESS

I RECALL an unforgettable episode from my first exhibition in America. In one of the large cities, a local collector of art and wealthy patron arranged a festive dinner in my honor. Everything was luxurious and on a large scale, and the best people of the city were present. As usual, many speeches were delivered. The host and hostess, both already gray-haired, joyfully and cordially entertained the guests. Everything was magnificently arranged, and the hostess drew my attention to die rooms which were decorated in blue and purple flowers and said: "It is precisely these shades that I adore so much in your paintings."

After dinner one of the lady guests present said to me: "This is indeed a remarkable reception," and added confidentially: "Probably this is the last dinner in this home."

I looked at my neighbor in the greatest amazement, and she, lowering her voice, continued: "Don't you know that our host is absolutely ruined and just yesterday he lost his last three millions?"

Naturally I was shocked, but my neighbor explained: "Of course, it is not easy for him, especially considering his age. He is already seventy-four."

But the apparent steadfastness and calmness of the host and hostess and all the surroundings were in obvious contradiction with this revelation. After this conversation I began to take special interest in the host's fate. Three months after this dinner, they had already moved to their former garage. It seemed that everything was lost; but after three years, this art patron was again a millionaire and again lived in a palatial home.

When I spoke to his friends about my astonishment, asking why his numerous acquaintances and after all the city itself, to which he had donated such huge sums, did not help him, I was told: "First of all, he would not have accepted any help, and secondly, he is used to such financial storms."

This last conversation took place in a large club, where near tall windows in easy chairs were sitting many distinguished members, reading newspapers and talking. My friend, pointing at them, said: "These are all millionaires. Ask how often every one of them ceased to be a millionaire and then became one again. Just guess who of them is at present on the top of the wave and who is nearing the abyss."

And the club members continued to read quietly and to chat joyfully, as if no troubles ever disturbed them. I asked my friend how he explained such a remarkable state of mind. He shook his shoulder and replied with one word: "Steadfastness."

Verily, the concept of steadfastness should be greatly stressed amid other basic principles of life. Virility is one, goodwill and friendliness is another. Desire to work is a third. Perseverance and inexhaustibility is a fourth. Enthusiasm and optimism is a fifth. But amid all these foundations and many other necessary creative conceptions, steadfastness always remains as a firm cornerstone, giving impulse and success to all progress.

Steadfastness is the result of true equilibrium, which has Libra as its symbol. Such equilibrium is not a heartless calculation, neither despising the surroundings, neither conceit nor selfishness. Steadfastness always stands in relation to responsibility and a sense of duty. Steadfastness will not lose balance, will not slip nor waver. Those who advanced firmly up to the last hour are always steadfast.

In our days of confusion, disillusion, and narrow distrust, the quality of steadfastness is especially blissful. When people so easily become panic-stricken, only a steadfast person can lead with a healthy understanding and can thus save many from the horror of drowning in chaos. When people try to convince themselves of all sorts of prejudice, mirages, and other nonsense, only a firm person can decide in his heart where there is a safe exit. When people become crazy, then even a short squall appears to them like an endless horrible storm. And only steadfastness will remind one of true co-measurement.

Perhaps someone will say that steadfastness is nothing else than common sense. But it will be more correct to say that from common sense, steadfastness is born. The concept of steadfastness is already an expression of reality. Steadfastness is required precisely here on the earthly plane, where there are so many circumstances against which one has to hold out. Therefore, it is so useful, amid many concepts of goodwill, cooperation, and progress to understand the value of steadfastness. Not without reason is it always appreciated how firmly a person stood against certain attacks, strain, and unexpected blows. In such cases vigilance and presence of mind are praiseworthy, but steadfastness will also be acclaimed as something positive and victorious.

As an example of steadfastness, I recall a story that I heard in San Francisco.

A foreigner had arrived. Apparently he was wealthy. He was received everywhere in society. He acquired many friends. He won the reputation of being a good, wealthy, and kindhearted fellow. Once he asked his new friends to lend him ten thousand dollars for a new business. Something curious, though very usual, happened. All of his friends found sufficient reason to refuse his request. More than that, everywhere people showed coldness toward him and some even turned away. Then this foreigner went to visit another person who from the very beginning had been rather formal toward him. He explained his project and asked for a loan of ten thousand. This time the checkbook appeared at once on the table, and the required amount was handed over to him. The next day the foreigner again came to see the same person. The latter asked: "What has happened? Did you miscalculate the amount? Perhaps you need more?"

But the foreigner took the check from his pocket and returned it to its previous owner saying: "No, I need no money. What I need is a partner, and I invite you to join me." And they founded a company that became very prosperous.

And to all other so-called friends, who again smiled most friendly, the foreigner said: "You have fed me with your dinners. Remember, my table is always served for you."

Dr. J.L. knows this story.

How many instructive experiences are given by life itself! Imagination is nothing else but recollection.

ASSISTANCE

IS it necessary to render help?
It is so imperative that words cannot express the
urgency of giving help to others by thoughts, councils, labors, and in every possible direct and indirect
way. Because the chief cause of the world crisis may
be attributed to a lack of mutual assistance, it becomes
increasingly clear that the present crisis is not basically
material but precisely spiritual.

Of course, there exist many philanthropic societies and
centers where one may apply for assistance. But here I do
not refer to organized help but precisely to the desire of all
humanity to render mutual help. In this universal desire,
true progress may be expressed.

Many times it has been stated that the development
of a means of communication, in addition to its obvious
functions, should chiefly contribute to the development
of friendliness, mutual protection—in other words, to that
widely varied, mutual help that becomes the real enhance-
ment of human existence.

Because of the poignant universal crisis, one too often
hears expressions about innumerable fortunes that have
been destroyed and with them the possibility of help. Such
expressions consider only the one sided possibility of mon-
etary help. But if we assume that money is the only basis
of help, then we are erecting the so-called golden calf to
denounce that which many excellent pages of the world's
literature are devoted. What a circumscribed and truly sor-
did criterion would be humanity's if it found a place only
for money, with its tinsel and relative valuation.

Evolution needs those true values out of which must also emerge the good life; and for such world cooperation, the first necessity is an evidence of benevolent, mutual assistance. If there would be enough cordiality and people would share the gains of their life's experiences, what a bounty of new constructions could arise! If only all the visible and invisible ways of intercourse would carry with them not only personal acquisitiveness but benevolent help, how much more blessed would the new wings of humanity seem!

Consciously or unconsciously, the same thought is being felt in various parts of the world. If only one could infuse into this universal current—if not love—at least the benevolence of mutual help. In numerous countries large departments of tourism have been organized. All types of movements for intellectual cooperation and societies for cultural relations are being organized. One must assume that such societies are planning not only casual tours through museums and universities but also fundamental efforts for mutual assistance and a common understanding toward that benevolence that is needed now in the world. We cannot imagine that Ministries of Tourism are being organized solely to satisfy casual curiosities or for the successful disposal of railroad tickets. This would be unspeakable.

The numbers of scientific expeditions of all kinds are being increased. Trade missions of various kinds are penetrating into far-off places. "Iron birds" speed through the air, at times with tidings and at times solely in the service of speed. It is with good reason that these symptoms are increasing. Let us also presume that it is with good intent. Tourism, travel, is in fact the living university that inspires people to new or reborn possibilities. One should say to each traveler, "Give help to all things on your journey. Give help with all your possibilities, with all your tokens and experiences. Many hearts will stretch out toward you, in word and thought, because for them you are not the usual person. You are unusual, and they will listen doubly to your advice." Such advice to travelers is not abstract advice; everyone who has visited remote countries knows with what eagerness they long for the tales of distant travelers, in these remote hearths, campfires, tents, *yurtas,* or walls. This respect for far-off experience is the same in all countries. In all countries, the traveler is listened to—in some places, prayerfully; in another, with curiosity; in a third, with avarice—but everywhere, with attention.

The responsibility of the traveler is great. Let his heart not become hardened and reject those who seek his counsel. Let the traveler not believe that due to a specialized profession, he cannot have an open eye and practical experience. It is the traveler, along all paths, who is best able to gather the most varied knowledge. It is impossible to imagine such a degree of petrification that a man should know nothing beyond the limits of his own specialty. The more learned a man, the more he knows and the more practical is his advice. Nor will the knowing man be penurious with his advice because his heart has partaken of these riches of knowledge for the sake of the Common Good.

To all travelers, one may say, "Many useful counsels will be expected from you. Gather all of your knowledge, and do not be reticent in giving this benevolent help. Your useful advice will be awaited in diverse countries; hence, apply them to diverse tongues and diverse understandings. But principally, do not be miserly. Your practical counsels will be deeply and heartily valued. From them will be born cordial, mutual understanding between the nations. The practical advices of travelers will divert many misfortunes, will impel useful self-activity, will cure despair, and will contribute to healthy construction."

One should not think that such great tasks are created only at peace conferences. Many results of the greatest significance are created upon the paths of the travelers. Sometimes, as is known to us, a callous and shortsighted person will caution against helping others. There are such, and a dreadful oblivion awaits those who refuse to help because of egoism. One may explain such a forbiddance of help by mental deficiency, but one must have great limitations, indeed, who denies help to others because of fear.

All sacred writings ordain the giving of help without restriction. It has been sufficiently stated that casual differences between those in need should not serve as obstacles. It is no longer necessary to quote the commonly known parables and scriptures, or to repeat that which has been printed in the world thousands and millions of times. Let us only say that those who forbid the giving of help to others doom themselves to oblivion.

Let us assure each other that in the name of the common welfare, we will help along all paths. Let us remember that he who forbids the giving of worthy advice is already an unworthy destroyer. When numerous unfortunates, whole races and nations ask for advice and help, let it be regarded as a guarantee of one additional step toward benevolent understanding.

Let travelers look upon this possibility as an enlightened duty. Let them fulfill it with all cordiality, bringing to it their accumulated experience. A sincere desire of benevolence will bring conviction to their advice, which will flourish like a fine harvest, giving life to much human waste. Every person should help in all ways, along all paths. Eastern wisdom states: "Silver that is buried turns black."

Be worthy councilors; help and love heartily the work of help.

HEAVENLY GIFTS

JOYFULLY, we followed all the news and articles about the glorious celebration of Sri Ramakrishna's centenary. How wonderful it was that, here on our confused and disturbed earth, there was such widespread devotional reverence and admiration! And this recognition of the Great Attainment came from various countries, from different peoples. All dedications to the Blessed Bhagavan were permeated with a profound love from the heart, which means that the message of the Paramahamsa deeply touched the very soul of humanity.

People should rejoice at every manifestation, for in it is expressed the striving toward the Good. In this common bliss is contained a real heavenly gift that mankind should cherish above all ages and nations. Did not the Bhagavan himself, in his goodness, show the example of tolerance, of compassion? If people would only manifest more care and reverence for the heavenly sendings that continuously illumine our dark earthly life!

Heavenly gifts are always connected to human consciousness with lightning speed. Everything from the Highest, everything from Above, naturally directs human imagination toward Light, toward sparkling urgency. And so it is. The greatest realization can come like lightning, instantaneously. But yet another condition has to be recognized in our earthly understanding: in these high conceptions is revealed a heavenly language, for which we have but poor expressions in our earthly tongue.

If we gather all of our conventional definitions around

the concept of Heavenly Gifts, it will be but a weak and limited expression of the Ineffable.

Only the heart can give life to such expressions as solemnity, greatness, ecstasy, awe, joy. Without transfiguration through the Heart, all these lofty words are but dead sounds. Thus it has been ordained since antiquity that the highest gifts should be reverently accepted and introduced with dignity into earthly life.

Love, too, is like lightning, but it must be informed and affirmed by a full consciousness, or even this worthy feeling will be but a shimmering mirage.

Many epics tell of the sending of Heavenly Gifts into earthly surroundings. Such legends offset human light-mindedness and introduce an understanding of higher concepts into the consciousness.

Heavenly Gifts, if not introduced lovingly and with care into earthly life, will be as wings torn off, which, despite their magnificent beauty, are useless. But the Highest Will provides wings for blissful flights. Without a genuine, ardent striving toward the spiritual, humans will forget about the wings, which will become dusty with disuse. The God-sent magnificence will be changed into morbid grayness.

Stuffed birds with motionless, spread wings always arouse a sad thought: the symbol of movement and flight has been stilled and is thus condemned as worthless.

The cultivation of Heavenly Gifts in earthly conditions is a difficult science. Difficult, for it is born of labor, and a science, for the many experiments and tests that preceded the heavenly blossom's unfolding, unharmed and perfect in its predestined grandeur.

Not only are the rare chosen ones called upon for the blossoming of Heavenly Gifts on earth, but every home can have a sacred garden into which Heavenly Gifts are brought with great love and surrounded by the highest offerings the human heart can render.

At times, people in their despair imagine that Heavenly Gifts have ceased to flow. But they do not consider that their own eyes may not be able to discern the Invisible Light in the glare of the sunshine. Do people not take refuge from blissful rain under an umbrella? And do people not flee into a shelter, even into dungeons, from purifying thunderstorms and from majestic waves of Light? Do people not try to make a small thing of the Greatest. How sad it is when Heavenly Gifts—these generous, beautiful treasures—are derided or locked up in the safe of a miser!

The deniers will invent all imaginable excuses in order to shift their own ignorance and rudeness to others. Little physical effort is needed to destroy a beautiful flower; in the same way, a very little, coarse force is needed to defile the highest Heavenly Gift. But if anyone will argue that this is already known, let us reply with the words of Vivekananda: "If you know what is good, then why don't you follow the Ordainments?" In these significant words thunders a direct challenge to all who violate and abase the Highest. And is this question today not most imperative?

If anyone will tell you that repetition is unnecessary, answer, "If something useful is not applied, one must reaffirm it!" A discussion of whether help should be rendered at all would be immoral; everyone will agree that one should always help. This means if somewhere, something precious is being neglected, then one should endlessly reaffirm it as long as one's voice lasts. And if anyone sees that a humanitarian principle is violated by ignorance or malevolence, it is his duty to point this out, if he is secure in his understanding of the true values.

Heavenly Gifts are many and diverse. These beautiful helpers are sent to assist humanity generously and magnificently. The shower of Bliss is poured forth in benevolent generosity, but only drops of this treasure reach the earth. Yet every thought about Heavenly Gifts strengthens the heart. . . . Especially now, when human hearts are in such confusion and deep pain, one should strive toward the highest of healing agents—toward Heavenly Gifts.

Thy benevolence fills
My hands. In profusion it is pouring
Through my fingers. I cannot
Keep all. I am not able to distinguish
The glowing streams of richness. Thy
Benevolent wave pours through the hands
Upon earth. I do not see who will gather
The precious gems. The tiny sprays,
Upon whom will they fall? If only I could
Carry home the Heavenly Gift!

BENEVOLENCE

WHEN one remembers Bhagawan Sri Ramakrishna, Swami Vivekananda, and all the leaders of the Ramakrishna Mission and its centers, there always comes to mind the concept of benevolence. Benevolence is a powerful word. Both of its constituent parts presuppose an accumulation of blissful force. *Bene* means the Good in its entire constructive sense. *Volence*—volition—is the power of thought and will. And when this immense high might is directed toward the upliftment of humanity, it represents the true essence of the Sri Ramakrishna movement. In this movement there is revealed so much of a direct self-sacrificing labor. Precisely, there is a constant benefaction, untiringly and gloriously penetrating into the hearts.

All these good words are easily pronounced, but for the ordinary person, it is not easy to manifest them in life. The very thought, the art of thinking, requires education and training. And only in the process of doing good does benevolence receive its vital significance. In the same good-doing is created a better future. This is not a truism; on the contrary, at present all nations should exercise the art of thinking in this direction. Let us beware that somewhere, instead of benefaction, there should not appear the ugly grimace of malefaction.

People sometimes think about the future, yet very often it does not enter at all into vital deliberations. Indeed, it is not entirely within human forces to determine the future, but each one should strive for it with all of his consciousness. And not to a beclouded future should one aspire but to precisely a better future. In this striving will already be the pledge of success.

On days of solemnity, prayer is uplifted about the future. No misty abstractions does it affirm. In it are expressed three principles—realization of that which is most lofty, the building of world peace, and benevolence—as the fundamentals of existence. Without these three bases, construction is impossible; yet they must not be promised abstractly but in their full and undeferrable reality. It would seem that the third-mentioned principle ought to be the most ordinary feature of everyday life. Only benevolence! Only goodwill and altruism! For whom? Why, for people themselves. For those with whom the task has been set to pass over this field of life.

It is a fact that no deep studies and instructions are needed for benevolence. It would seem that it is already presupposed at each human encounter. Can it be possible to draw near to any human being without fundamental goodwill? How is it possible to meet a neighbor with hatred or suspicion, or even with plotted villainy? Where then, in what sort of covenants, written or unwritten, have malice and suspicion been ordained?

"Man is a wolf to man." Surely this is one of the most malignant aphorisms. For so much results from auto-suggestion. If one hears from the cradle about good, then it, too, will surely remain a guiding principle. Even all the confusions of corrupted life will not eradicate the concept of good. Where man has been accustomed to live in good, there he values all the remarkable significance of the word "benevolence." Surely this word is very imperative. Volition, formulated will . . . This is already something accomplished, done!

Volition cannot only be instinctive. It is promoted in full consciousness, in full responsibility. Perhaps each state council ought to be opened with the important question: "Is there benevolence?" And he who remains silent should take no part. It will probably be said that precisely the malicious ones will themselves cry out about benevolence. And here, too, an imprint of human radiations would show the truth.

Heart radiations would show the true feelings, without the mask of insincerity. How mottled would be the radiations of the false, the insincere! The man who has not pondered upon the deep significance of benevolence will not often understand in general what is being spoken about here! Why underline words known to all and which, moreover, have never improved anything? Of course such monstrous opinions are possible.

Not seldom a vendor cries out something very useful, absolutely without thinking about the meaning of the words uttered by him. Does a scribe often know the contents of what he has copied? Sometimes even one who reads aloud to another thus frees himself, as it were, from an understanding of what he reads. In such a manner often the most valuable and urgent considerations become meaningless words.

Is a better future possible without benevolence, without benevolence in all its solemnly imperative meaning? What sort of peace will there be on earth without benevolence? And where will be the "glory in the highest" without a profound and unceasing desire for good?

A better future. You must be better today than yesterday. If there is no longing for this, then surely from that which is most important and already ordained, only a negligible fraction will remain. All the great signs may be in readiness. But if there be no desire for the sake of good to follow them, then what part of them will be perceptibly carried out? Who then has the right to vitiate or belittle that which has been composed by great paths? Surely this is no empty dreaming but the responsibility of the messenger.

Even a simple postman in twilight and in darkness proceeds with caution in order not to stumble, in order that a branch may not lash him in the eye, in order to avoid wild beasts. Yet he bears someone else's letter about which he knows nothing. When, then, man thinks about the future, when he takes into consideration all its conditions and all good wishes, how much more strivingly and carefully does he proceed, ready and alert. He proceeds vigilant and imbued with feeling. He makes haste in order not to pilfer an ordained hour, and in his heart sounds glory in the Highest, and peace on earth, and benevolence for his neighbor.

Benevolence needs to be taught. Peace needs to be established. With every palpitation of the heart, one should be enraptured by glory in the Highest!

Examples of the creation of a better future may be drawn from various domains. One of them has remained in memory from early school years.

We were all tremendously impressed by the story of Schliemann—the noted investigator of Troy. We were all entranced by how he, from early years, set himself to the task of future researches, and how he began to prepare himself in all the branches of learning, and how he tenaciously enriched himself with knowledge and yet, at the same time and just as perseveringly, amassed a fortune. Of course, he maturely thought out all the resources he would need.

After many years of conscious labor, he brought to science his precious offering and remained the forefather of many brilliant investigators coming after him. One can imagine how, in his time, the businessmen shrugged their shoulders at the scholarly tasks of Schliemann. Likewise, one can see how other scholars, probably more than once, labeled him as an amateur and made fun of his undertakings. Yet with originality and persistence, he composed his own scientific future.

That which for another would have been attainment was for Schliemann only a means that had an applied relative value. In so many years of conscious labor is a large share of selflessness.

One can find in the history of the world many examples of such self-sacrificing attainments. But why dig in ancient annals when in our age we have the glorious examples of the lives of Bhagawan Sri Ramakrishna and Swami Vivekananda? In them is manifested the highest blissful benefaction and a leonine striving into a better future. And in what simple, all-penetrating words were expressed their outlines of spiritual unfoldment? May everyone be blessed who can speak of the Good in simple words. All the heaps of evil thoughts have deviated humanity from simplicity and constructive work. Every day, people are accustomed to witnessing destruction and murder. It is shocking with what indifference people imbue the abhorrent stories, which altogether do not befit humanity. With every day these horrors and cruelheartedness grow. Every place where the word "benevolence" is affirmed becomes a true shrine and stronghold of a better future.

Thus, let us again recall the beautiful word "benevolence." Verily, the conscious creators of a better future are filled with true benevolence.

THE BIRTH OF BOREDOM

IN the midst of a discussion of contemporary life, someone was bewailing boredom, but another exclaimed, "You are yourself a bored man!" The first speaker began to assert that he personally was not bored, but that the circumstances of his life were so uniform and colorless that not he but the conditions of life were tedious.

Whereupon the second speaker went on to insist that nowhere in life, in nature, could there be such circumstances as would give birth to boredom. He said, "We ourselves engender this deathliness in ourselves which we call *ennui*. We ourselves are tedious, but not at all life or nature."

A third speaker recalled from the life of the hermits of India, how without moving away from the entrance of their caves, the Rishis were conscious of the entire fullness of existence.

A fourth pointed to the life of the holy St. Sergius of Radonega remarking, "Could such ascetics have the feeling of boredom at all? Would they even be acquainted with this word?"

Thus, the first speaker, who carelessly referred boredom to the life about him, encountered resistance on all sides. No matter that he unwittingly gave the entire conversation a direction unexpected by him. There are many examples that clearly show that boredom is nothing but a decline of vital energy. This absence of energy is begotten by conventional bases born within ourselves. It happens that people wrongly employ the very expression "boredom." Sometimes they wish to express by it their impatience with something. But, of course, such impatience will already be a sign of a lack of that discipline that will always be the effect of a special tension of energy.

Two definite types of people can be observed. One loves inner discipline as a part of his own nature. He does not need to be taught this concentration of the will. The man who willingly realizes the significance of regularity is shown to be one who appreciates the value of his own and of another's time. Discerning these values, the man will always remain steadfast, observant, and resourceful. He will be a strong man. The other type of person is, by his nature, afraid, and he tries to shun any form of discipline. Assuredly, this type of person, even though he possesses certain realizations, will not take upon himself individual responsibility, nor manifest true patience, and he will, quickest of all, admit dissolute, worthless discussions. This type of person will not be strong. In addition, he will be a great lover of self, filled with egoism. He easily repeats the word "boredom," trying to impose the blame for this burdensome feeling on the circumstances surrounding him.

Such a person will try to draw those about him into the same fallacious discussions of his burdens. He does not even reflect that the engendering of boredom takes place exclusively within him.

Among the expedients for counteracting such an egotistical weak-willed state, first of all there will be, precisely, the development of the art of thinking and of knowing how to feel oneself a part of nature. Many times the art of thinking has been insistently set forth as something that must be organized and cultivated. Just so is it precisely needful to know how to adjoin oneself to nature. Each one has had occasion to see unfortunate types of people to whom the book of nature was completely closed. Before the face of nature, filled with indescribable attractiveness, they will play at cards or dream about the "charms" of city life. They will reach such incommensurateness that they will be ready to betray fair nature for the horror and subversion of the city.

One can imagine what actual perversions of the organism, what pathological convulsions take place when something precious and beautiful is obscured by the conventional and the degenerating. Of course, the human heart is painfully contorted at everything unnatural.

The heart does not tell of its sensations in earthly words, but each shock to the heart remains through many lives. One of the most painful blows to the heart will indeed be when the concept of boredom takes root. The heart cannot support this deathliness.

In all institutions of enlightenment, from children's classes on, the concept of boredom should be driven out by all possible means. And in this, the filling up of time must not be something purely mechanical. It is needful that time is not actually divided between action and thinking. What can be more attractive than thinking and creativeness before the face of nature? This joy can arise in the most diverse labors, for an actual mental creativeness only promotes the quality of each task.

So many times it has been misstated about the oppositions of East and West, which have been understood not in the geographical sense but in the sense of fundamental psychology. And yet, at the same time, each one distinctly feels that there are no oppositions, nor can be, for both here and there must be the inner striving for life-giving synthesis. In this synthesis of benignancy, tolerance, and creativeness, there is not found the least place for the weak-willed anathema called boredom.

Is it needful to speak about boredom if it is so deadly and abominable? How can it be needful since this word is so often repeated by the old and the young? Boresome types even try to assume the pose of some sort of ultra-modernity. In their foolishness they propose to surround themselves with a kind of inexplicable secret aureole, but in the very process they remain simply bored offscourings, unapplied in life. If evil be manifested in any form whatever, do not attempt to keep silent about it. This abscess will only create complete gangrene. Hasten to cut away this injurious concept of boredom as quickly and as resolutely as possible. The boresome type is afraid of being ridiculed, but at the same time, it is primarily ridiculous in its own delusion.

The tatters of boredom will be like some monstrously absurd buffoonery. Grand Guignol! And to whom then is it desirable to be in this frightful burlesque?

Thus, let not the viper of boredom dare to approach anything educational and enlightening, anything cultural. All, then, who especially feel the absurdity of this dreadful concept, let them with united efforts draw out all the germs of it. Verily, boredom is not in the surrounding circumstances, nor in life, but is in people themselves.

NARROW GORGES

A CERTAIN writer used to tell me how difficult it was for him to finish his book, in which he did not want to offend anyone. Since the book was concerned with panhuman questions, it was only natural that the author wanted to arouse interest without enmity and unnecessary offenses. And it is precisely from these good wishes that such unusual limitations arose. The writer got into such impassable, narrow gorges that he was compelled to cut out page after page from the valuable accumulated material.

In the first place, the writer checked his considerations with regard to races—a lot had to be crossed out; then came the checking according to classes. Likewise, it took out many pages. Then he had to verify the text in regard to professions. And again here, important material had to be omitted. Then the rest of the writings were checked from the point of view of age, religion, and customs; and again, entire parts of the book had to be set aside. Finally, he had to think of the conditions of education; questions of schools, social organizations, sport; attitudes toward art, of everything that is embraced by the word "culture." One had to extract from the remnants of the book almost everything that could create any interest.

Then the disappointed author tried to read for himself the polished skeleton, and he became horrified and could not admit the thought that he himself could have written such a commonplace vulgarity. Then the unfortunate author began to think. Whom did he please by depriving his work of even primitive significance and interest? And then began a curious reversal of the procedure. For the remaining fragments of the book, the author began mentally to select as readers all sorts of professionals; and from the opposite point of view, nowhere did he find a prospective sympathetic reader.

Finally remembering that the ruins of the book should represent something indisputably well-intended, the author imagined his book in the hands of a policeman. But here also he was greatly disappointed, for he understood that in this case his well-intended work represented no interest.

And thus, in the reverse order, the author gradually began to include everything that could arouse the attention of various kinds of readers, and his book grew, almost to its original size.

Thus, the very same narrow gorges, which appeared so terrible and impassable, suddenly changed into a wide-open plain, on which met people of various ages and all nationalities and positions. Finally, the author went to see his worldly-wise friend, with the following tragic question: "How should he act in order to arouse human consciousness and make them think?" His friend heartily laughed at this dilemma, and said, "I would like to [ask] a Manu, or any lawgiver, whether he would stop for a minute in order not to offend someone. In the first place, he would have to avoid hurting the feelings of all criminals. His covenants then would become some sort of instructions in thefts; and in order to make someone happy, he would have to line his teaching with vulgar anecdotes. If you really want to arouse human consciousness, remember that to offer something that is already inherent would be not only ridiculous but even immoral. And if, God forbid, your book would arouse only praise, this would be for you a fatal sign!"

How many phantomlike, narrow gorges have been built! Sometimes the mirages are so distinct that it is even difficult to establish the beginning of their formation. In general, every generation is quite beyond the reach of human earthly laws. After all, the true moment of death is likewise undefinable. One may, according to earthly standards, only suppose the time of generation or dissolution. Under such circumstances, decisions "ad adversum" are especially significant. So-called "Tactica Adversa" often helps, especially in insoluble problems.

Should our writer not have mentally begun to please all conditions, depriving his work of the most essential parts, and if he would not have done so with full force, he would not have come to the realization of the incongruousness of his actions. If the writer would have thought even in part how to please only one particular person, he would not have come to the realization in all its remarkable evidence. But he wanted to smile at everyone, and instead of a smile, there resulted a most sour and banal grimace. In his sour servility, the writer reached just the opposite result. Even the policeman at the corner of the street would have been offended in his own particular way. But when the writer pictured to himself all the existing and phantomlike gorges, he understood that one may not pass through these and that it would lead only to destruction. He fully realized this decision, judging from the opposite. And this complete decision showed him the entire incongruity of his fears.

Thus, when there are too many narrow gorges and the walls of these gorges approach one another to such an extent that one may not pass already through them, then suddenly, instead of narrowness, a broad plateau appears and that which seemed to hinder serves but as steps to broad vistas.

LIMITS

S EVERAL newspapers report simultaneously of events bordering on extremes. In one paper, under the heading "In What Crazy People Believe," one reads:

"At the World's Fair in Chicago, there took place the most savage ceremony of marriage that has ever been held.

"In that part of the exhibition, which is called 'The World a Million Years Ago,' amid the reconstructed models of dinosaurs, brontosaurs, triceratops, and other prehistoric monsters, two nudists were married.

"During the ceremony the bride wore only a smile and the bridegroom a serious expression on his face.

"The bridesmaids, the best men, guests, and so forth actually had not a single thread upon them, not even a fig leaf.

"Only the priest looked somewhat different in this ensemble, for he wore a goatskin!

"The young bride belonged to the nudist colony in Indiana and her young husband to the colony in Mirror Lake, in the state of Wisconsin."

"After the marriage ceremony, the young couple put on clothes and went to the husband's colony in order to establish their home there. They had thought of all the necessary things for their home, except for clothing, which they did not require."

Another newspaper, under the heading "Black Masses in London," quotes particulars from the *Daily Mail* about the disclosure of a black lodge that organized "black masses" in the capital:

"During these masses, black candles are lit, black bread

is served, and black wine, and so forth. . . . The participants of the mass confess to one another the good deeds they have committed and express deep repentance for having done them. Then an orgy begins."

Parallel with such sacrilegious, repulsive communications, one reads another article under the title "Do You Dance Carioca?" which states:

"Now a new dance is the order of the day—'Carioca,' a new craze. There is actually not much new in this dance, the characteristic part of it being that it is danced by leaning one against another, forehead to forehead."

Despite their diversity, all three of these newspaper articles denote one and the same madness of the world. We, of course, quoted them quite casually, unpremeditatedly, only because they appeared simultaneously; but these mournful records could easily grow into a multitude of facts, about which the press either does not write or they appear, in view of their usualness, in small type.

Unfortunately, all such similar communications appear not only in astounding variety but even in an extraordinarily accelerating progression. One cannot think that all these shameful grimaces of humanity have already become customary. To presume such accelerating abhorrence and savagery would already be pessimistic. But the discovery of an epidemic is not pessimism but the beginning of the process of recovery. When we know the enemy, then this already leads to the gates of victory. The same applies to fearless disclosures of sacrilegious and immoral machinations. Every disclosure will already be, to a certain degree, a prevention of a further continuation of these dark rituals.

Just imagine the invention of a butting dance. Up to now, people looked pityingly at butting rams, and used to say, "Truly, rams will be rams!" But now in dances people will imitate these lower creatures, and perhaps some enterprising manager will think of supplying the dancers with horns in order that they may hold on to each other even tighter. Why, then, did proud, civilized people mock foreign rituals that they did not understand? Indeed, this newly invented dance is a sufficient degradation of the pride of civilized people. Or can one imagine anything more sacrilegious than the marriage of nudists by a priest clad in a goatskin! In all these details is hidden some dark, blasphemous meaning. Could there really be found such a monstrous priest who wished to put on that goatskin? We, of course, but repeat the communication from newspapers, but is it possible to assume that they are erroneous? If so, there should have appeared some corresponding, refuting statement. But in view of the present times, can we presume at all that the communication is a lie? When reading about the goatskin of the priest, one may easily connect it with the other newspaper article about the "black masses."

Many probably think that "black masses" are the result of bad novels and other unwholesome inventions, but unfortunately there appears everywhere news about such sacrileges, and with convincing concreteness. And if one also adds to this other terrible manifestations of human degradations, then to our deep regret, this shame of our age also appears to be real.

Villainy and all the nets of darkness begin from very little, which is almost indiscernible in the hustle of everyday life. But even these smallest black seeds in their dark potentiality grow up into the greatest sacrileges. And people forget altogether that sacrilege is neither small nor big. Every sacrilege is the manifestation of greatest ignorance and of lowest savagery, and represents in itself a great, shameful crime. Not without reason was ignorance in ancient teachings considered to be the greatest crime. For an ignoramus not only harms himself, but he seduces and harms the whole of humanity; he infests the whole atmosphere. Therefore, sacrilegious ignorance is not a personal crime—it is a service to darkness; it is an active evil, which destroys the constructive achievements and pulls man down into the abyss of chaos.

Let us not think that dark chaos is something abstract; let us not forget that human gatherings should not only increase the good but ought not to be a source of degradation.

Flattering compromisers will perhaps say, "Is it right to underline so persistently some dance or the goatskin of a priest?" Let these compromisers realize what may result from one goatskin and that already a whole "black mass" is growing! Let us also not forget that human responsibility should not admit blasphemous sacrileges that lead to incurable earthly diseases.

Precisely, in our times much that seems to be a hazy abstractness has become an obvious reality. The consciousness of the heart persistently warns that the limits of erring have been reached. Ignorance flourishes, gorgeously surrounding itself with absurd conventionalities, and the human spirit wails and warns: "Let us not transgress the limits!"

EASY DIFFICULTIES

IT is especially difficult for people to change their mode of living. One cannot help remembering an old proverb that "old furniture ought not to be moved." And this saying wisely states that something old should not be moved. That means that all difficulties are relative only in regard to our consciousness. Verily, people often speak of difficulties when they create them in their own imagination and have affirmed them with a prejudiced consciousness.

The city dweller, being surrounded with conventional city comfort, considers that life in tents or in *yurts* would be the most dreadful existence. And should he find himself with such a prejudice in the conditions of desert life, he himself will actually build up all sorts of terrors. But if he will enter various conditions with the firm belief that people live everywhere and that they themselves create the conditions of life, then all the frightful phantoms will be dispersed. Not without reason do children who are uncontaminated by conventional superstition yearn for traveling, for knowledge, and they easily adapt themselves to different conditions.

Who knows? Perchance the migration of nations as a result of the Great War was nothing but a lesson—a trial, for the renovation and broadening of consciousness. I remember how an enlightened and highly spiritual lady was terrified at the thought that she might have to spend all of her life in the well-organized confines of city life. Truly, if one only imagines that all inhabitants of Earth have reached but a little well-being, then in that petty limitation is contained the great danger of petrification. And so a divine fate has pointed out that people should again travel and again shake themselves up for the acceptance of new profoundly conceived structures.

After all these years, it has become clear to everyone who has seen many people that two distinct types of people have always existed.

Some always come up to the surface amid unbelievable difficulties; and not only do they come to the surface, but they also bring much help to their surroundings. Despite various family and property complications, they always remain alert, cheerful, and friendly. The other type, even with outside help, always goes down. They cannot reconcile themselves to the change of conditions and even of nomenclatures. They not only consider themselves unhappy, but they carry that grey unhappiness into their surroundings.

Every journey is for these people like some punishment from Above. They not only are unable to understand the new local conditions, but they become engulfed in baseless condemnations of everything that is beyond them. One of the greatest consolations for them consists in mutual condemnation and mutual belittlement, as if through demeaning someone, they hope to raise themselves. Instead of learning how to adapt themselves, understand, show compassion, and move on, they prefer to slowly sink to the bottom, as it is said in an old Ukrainian proverb: "Don't spend your forces in vain, brother, sink right to the bottom.

Such cases as we have seen during recent years did not concern only one nation. They were of a purely international nature from which those who are alive in spirit could learn in life the advantages of an active optimism and the horrors of an ignorant pessimism. Of course, these two types of humanity, one leading, successful, enlightened and the other deadened, ignorant, and deteriorating, are always with us. But the years of extraordinary world disturbance have only brought them more clearly into focus.

Experienced educators have always understood that children should not be separated from nature because only in it do they retain mobility, resourcefulness, and decisiveness. A wise physician always advises city people to keep closer to earth, and the results of such wise advice are often evident in life. All sorts of organizations—Sokols, Scouts, Pioneers, hikers, guides, and other healthy movements that bring city dwellers out into nature are the most healthy manifestations of recent years. Everything that calls to the friendly bonfire, around which all must be done by the people themselves, strengthens the spirit. And not only has everything to be done by themselves, but everything has to be thought of in a new manner and perhaps in a better way.

Inventiveness must be exercised. Who knows whether such a giant of inventiveness as Edison could have appeared if he had grown up in the narrow comfort of a city! Every one of us has seen many examples where even more or less outstanding personalities were overcome by surroundings of vulgar well-being. I remember a brilliant educator who on sending his wards into life used to say to some of them, "I regret that your parents are wealthy. I hope you will not be trapped in a gilded cage." And to others, he said would say, "No metal weighs down your wings. Fly high and far!"

As if to justify this advice, all conventional values were suddenly shattered. Even such strongholds as real estate values were struck as if by an earthquake. A certain inhabitant at the time of an earthquake rushed out of his house complaining, "And this they call immovable property!"

Many such maxims are offered by life itself. Some people are doomed to fears and are terrified by them; and others take things sensibly as they are. Some are unwisely attracted by mirages, and others understand very well the difference between a mirage and reality. But in order to find one's way amid mirages and illusions, one must first of all perceive these mirages. One cannot help remembering the Indian parable about the seven blind men who describe an elephant, each from his point of view.

Likewise, you cannot describe in words the impression of a mirage to him who has never seen one. But in cities, mirages do not appear. In order to see them, one must visit the desert and there learn, on the spot, to distinguish reality from illusion.

Convinced of their infallibility, city people have great difficulty in distinguishing true impressions. I remember how a member of our expedition, who was in the desert for the first time, decided to explore a beautiful illusionary lake. All of my persuasion that this lake did not exist was to no avail. The deluded traveler summoned two attendants and, to the surprise of everyone, said that he would reach that lake within an hour and that he believed his eyes more than our contentions. After many hours the poor fellow returned exhausted and angrily refused to further discuss the question of the existence of the illusionary lake. And one must recall with what self-assertion he criticized our order to stop at a small well, instead of going an extra hour to the "splendid lake surrounded by trees!"

Mirages are always quite instructive. Only personal experience can teach the vanity of illusionary conceit, and the experiences of life are obtained best of all amid nature.

But one cannot go out into nature only theoretically, deciding upon the usefulness of such an experiment. There will be small gain in such intellectual decisions. Nature must be understood. It must be entered into as a coworker, not with condemnation but in admiration.

Everyone remembers the beautiful legend about the mines of Falun, so picturesquely narrated by Hoffman. The owner of the mines is very stern with the miner, who, not from love of the work itself but from other, personal motives, comes to carry away the hidden treasure.

The voices of nature sound for those who enter it with an open heart, benevolently. Antaeus contacted the earth for the absorption of strength, in order to renew the might of the spirit. Indeed, it was not from intoxication that he fell upon the ground, but he touched the earth consciously, and then the earth conferred upon him a healthy renewal. Antaeus was called a mighty giant. Is it not from these health-giving contacts with the earth that he received this mighty name? And could those trials, those confusions that overcome one in closed cellars, under vaults, and between narrow walls have appeared to him as great difficulties?

Probably Antaeus would consider such relative difficulties simply incomprehensible. Thus, from the point of view of nature, such "easy difficulties" become not a paradox but really a definition. "Burden me more when I go into the Beautiful Garden." Is this not an exact indication of how and where difficulties are transmuted!

When the Magi gazed into the boundless sky, they saw the Guiding Star. If they had not looked into the vault of heaven, they would not have seen the Star. Blessed is he who in his days had armed them with the knowledge of observing the laws of nature and had awakened their vigilance, thus making them watchful and turning them into wondrous messengers.

Why should we deplore any difficulties when the Guiding Star watches over us! He who said, "Blessed be the obstacles, through them we grow" also knew the Guiding Star.

Tzagan Kure, April 2, 1935

STRATAE OF LIFE

EVEN in primary schools, pupils have already heard about the many dynasties that supervened upon one another by the dozen in various countries. With epic indifference are being mentioned these radical changes as if this was the building of new and peaceful nests. No one mentioned that one could easily say either a dozen changes or a dozen tragedies.

Can one remember many completely peaceful changes of dynasties? Almost every such change is followed with upheavals, murders, and all kinds of atrocities. Precisely, a real tragedy was lying at the foundation of every such change. It did not only concern the ruler and his principal coworkers, but usually entire classes of people underwent a change, the psychology of the nation changed, and also the objects of striving.

New rhythms came into life painfully. Cries and terror accompanied them, and now, after many centuries, the schools treat quietly these changes of dynasties. Not only the pupils but the professors themselves often forget what is hidden beneath these epics. When one speaks of wars, of pestilences, of all kinds of other catastrophes, it is but natural that the tragic side is recorded in the expression itself, as well as in the word itself. But the change of dynasties sounds as something indifferent. The change of the conditions of life in the imagination of the people likewise sounds peaceful, and yet, beneath these epically peaceful words is hidden a whole tempest, often of many years with many perils of destruction.

Therefore, among even primary school courses, one

must apply a more exact and expressive terminology. The expressive definitions of ancient historical events will strengthen the consciousness of the youth. From one side they will sow the seeds of enthusiasm as well as heroism; from another, they will keep from despair.

"Every despair is a limitation, but the heart is limitless." "But there is beauty every time somebody takes part in building the New World. This is the true domain of the heart. This longed-for purification of life gives rise to the solemnity that shines forth like an inextinguishable Light."

"Where is the feeling, the substance with which we shall fill the Chalice of Great Service? Let us gather this feeling from the most precious treasures. We shall find elements of it in religious ecstasy, when the heart quivers with the Highest Light. We shall find other elements in the feeling of heartfelt love, where the tear of self-abnegation glistens. We shall find elements amidst the heroic achievements of *podvig*, when power is increased in the name of humanity. We shall find them in the patience of the gardener when he muses on the mystery of the seed. We shall find them in the courage that penetrates the darkness. We shall find them in the smile of a child when it reaches out to a sunbeam. We shall find them amidst all the flights that carry us into the Infinite. The feeling of Great Service is boundless; it must fill the heart, which is forever inexhaustible. The sacred tremor will never become an everyday porridge, but when the tremor left the very best Teachings, they turned into assemblages of empty husks. Thus, in the midst of the battle think about the Chalice of Service and take an oath that the sacred tremor shall not leave you."

The ancient ordainments about the holy tremor must be realized in their vast conception. Precisely, the warmth and heat of this tremor preserve the heart from cold, from that very terrifying, deathly cold that cuts short every communion.

How many absolutely dead bipeds, walking corpses,

may be observed, which by their very approach defile and pollute such places where something valuable and perhaps even beautiful was already heard. Precisely, not an abstract command but a patiently introduced new understanding can warn those who have contracted the dreadful disease of dissolution. Truly dreadful is the site of a decomposing corpse. But such decomposition is likewise possible in life. If purely physical means can avert such a state, then how many spiritual influences may act as the best prophylactics?

Spiritual healings will help not only to avert physical complications, they will not only arrest the decay of spirit, but in their potency they will give to the withered spirit a healthy onward movement. For the spirit as the finest substance is so close to spatial vibration, so close to movement.

If one were to whisper in time to the one who starts out in life what complications, beautiful as well as terrible, are contained in the concise formulae of epics, such a transmutation would forever fortify the direction of this traveler. If he will understand the causes of the entire tragedy of pain and sorrow, he will find in his own actions more worthy, so to say, more cultural ways of achievement. The very succession of the spiral curves of evolution will be built with a greater preservation of human dignity. In his heart, man will feel the bitterness of tragedies and the great exaltation of service and heroism.

SEALS

MUCH is said about the ancient Chinese seals that have been found in Ireland. The antiquity of these seals refers to several centuries before our era, some even think several thousands of years. On the basis of these seals, the question is debated as to the ancient relationships of Ireland with China. Others observe that there could have been an intermediary point in Egypt or Crete, which had a long-standing relationship with both the Far East and with the British Isles, the latter of which served as the source of certain metals.

Indeed, all such questions require many confirmations and complementary facts, but, nevertheless, the discovery of ancient Chinese seals in Ireland reminds us again about the extension of long-distance relationships in the remotest times. Long ago, we had occasion to find amber in kurgans from the Stone Age, in Koenigsberg, Central Russia. In Neolithic times, before the knowledge of metals, relationships were demonstrated at quite extensive distances.

All archaeological findings, the uniformity of many discovered types, and finally, the details of ornament, rituals, and the other elements of their way of life indicate not only a community of the feelings common to man but also unquestionable relationships at long distances. The similarity of the alphabet not long ago discovered in Harappa and Mohenjo-daro, India, with depictions on Easter Island, also indicates noteworthy international relationships many centuries before our era.

Without any difficulty it is possible to discern how entire protracted periods confirm the development of international relationships; and then, as it were, there comes on a strange tribal forgetfulness, a timorous immobility, and the memory of former relationships is wiped away. In itself the memory of peoples represents an extraordinarily interesting manifestation. To contemporary man, it sometimes seems perfectly inadmissible that, in any manner, entire peoples could forget about something already fully known to them. The facts and allusions in ancient chronicles indicate the possibility of just such a strange forgetfulness.

Many of the completely lost technical methods of Egypt, the existence of gunpowder in ancient China, the details of various lost techniques of Babylon, certain objects of the Mayan culture—all this reminds one about the fact that very essential discoveries, incomprehensible to us, have been forgotten in their entirety. Moreover, such forgetfulness does not always coincide with epochs of advancement or decline. It is precisely as if some other psychological or even physiological facts have altered the channel of the current of popular thought.

Amid all the misunderstandings and presuppositions, the question of the most ancient international relationships always proves very complicated, yet it is especially interesting from the point of view of peace. The discovery of objects of definite antiquity in remote countries is a material sign of some relationships, the more so when the objects are found in ethnographical strata, which actually belong to former cultures of life. Something extremely inspiring is contained in these substantial signs, which are actually embodied in these seals of national relationships.

And again at present, in certain countries inertness and immobility are so clearly manifested, in that there are inhabitants of certain cities who are proud of that fact that they have never had to go beyond the limits of their native city, or that they even succeeded in keeping themselves from crossing a river that flows through the city. There are all sorts of droll people. But among the strangest extravagances, such a prejudice of immobility always remains one of the most striking. Yet what a great number of people exist who have never glanced beyond the limits of their country! Only in recent years has travel re-entered, as it were, a program of self-education. Whereas from remote antiquity, voices have been borne to us calling out about the usefulness of travel and of international knowledge.

The celebrated, everlastingly mentioned Marco Polo must be looked upon as a collective name. Frequently by this name are meant the infinite number of travelers who have been the bearers of international relationships. The name of Marco Polo has become firmly fixed in history, but indeed a great number of names, of ancient beaten paths, remain unknown. But that is not the question. Of course, any historical name becomes not so much a name as a concept. It is precisely this, that on ancient discovered objects, we see marks incomprehensible to us, which now serve us as conventional signs, yet which formerly were the personal seals of some firms or of some definite individuals.

Each reminder about international relationships is, as it were, a new seal upon the human peace treaty. Not so long ago in London, a certain Spaniard, Madariaga, delivered quite a pompous speech about the price of peace. No bombasting abstractions are the substantial signs of peace, but, first of all, the material seals of world relationships.

People are actually thinking about peace—some self-interestedly, others selflessly. In all cases there is required some sign, the substantial seal of the fact that outside of human violence and hatred, there have been possible peaceful relationships in the different domains of business.

The price of peace is defined as living human merit and dignity, as benevolence of heart, broadly embracing and noble. Not by denials of cultural treasures but by recognition of the creativeness of good is the price of peace defined and established.

Archaeology as a science based on material memorials is manifested right now as an assistant in many scientific and social considerations. And, likewise, in the question of the price of peace, archaeology can bring many of the most precious signs. From long-forgotten ruins, from abandoned burial places and the remains of palaces and cities can be adduced material proofs of peaceful international relationships. In semi-historical writings in old hieroglyphics, the story reaches one's ears about how, in fragile boats and on wearied horses, man penetrated remote regions, not only in warlike fury but also with a good desire for peaceful exchange. Underneath these narratives will be placed, as it were, material seals, ratifying the human peace treaties.

In the creativeness of good, it is always possible to come to terms, for only in a paroxysm of malice or of dark misanthropy are peaceful advancements impossible! Long ago it was said in various tongues, "He who lifts up the sword will also perish by the sword," and he will perish in a preordained hour that will perhaps be for him quite unexpected. And so it is in each quarrel and in each dissension.

The seals did not ratify quarrelsome contracts. The seals were affixed to a document of some relationships, of some business establishments. Yet in each true business will be the element of peace. A victory through beneficial signs will be a most radiant and striking victory. It is possible to kill with a serpent sting but not conquer, for to conquer will mean to convince. In such prices of peace, let us refer carefully to all material signs. It would have seemed inordinate to connect Easter Island with Harappa, India, or, now, Ireland with China. Yet what is impossible at present? Seals or depicted hieroglyphs are fully convincing. "Peace on earth, goodwill to man" is also imperative, for goodwill is engendered in the heart. And what is more substantial than the human heart in all of its inspired ascent?

Man should rejoice at each seal of peaceful relationships. Each sign of remote international agreements is a pledge of the possibility of future treaties, heartfelt and unbreakable. At one time, savage warriors devoured the hearts of the vanquished, but now in each peaceful relationship, let people remember about the living heart. The seals of antiquity are for the future.

Timur Hada, July 18, 1935

[303]

ROBOTS

"ERIC, the robot, was exhibited for the first time in England at the Schoolboy Exhibition. It can fire a machine gun at command."

This is the caption under a photograph of a steel monster, which appeared in one of the local newspapers. In the rotogravure section of the *New York Times* is depicted a scientist from Massachusetts making some complicated calculations, and the caption says that he is inventing brains for a robot. Thus, in all corners of the world, humanity is not preoccupied with devices of self-perfection but is busy with perfecting monsters that could replace man in various fields. Thus, the very quality of man's labor is substituted in our civilized world by the conventional properties of soulless automatons.

Many millions of the unemployed and hungry ones are in search of labor, ready to apply their energy and skill to any work, only to be saved from want and hunger. But they are threatened not only by living competitors, but brains are even being invented for some robots. It is possible that all calamities and malicious confusions of man's trend of thought will be directed chiefly along the lines of soulless mechanization, forgetting the true meaning of their earthly destination!

Music is canned, art is on film, lectures are on the radio, ships run without captains, bombing airplanes fly without a pilot, and as a climax of mechanization and the crown of the annihilation of the human spirit stands a war of poisonous gases and biological extermination of all that lives. The old ordainment of "all living should live" begins to appear as something out of date. Instead of mighty symphonies and inspiring operas, the saxophone is howling and men move slowly in the mechanical *macabre.*

We want to think that this is an exaggeration. Perhaps the invasion of robots under various garbs and marks is not as threatening, but to this effect testify many newspapers and communications from all parts of the world. From everywhere reach us wailings not only about unemployment but also about the deadening of the spirit. The inspiring spiritual leader T. L. Vaswani regrets the rapidly growing tendency to cynicism. He points out that hero worship is the basis of an individual's advance and a nation's progress. Cynicism is a form of disintegration. Our need is a new integration of thought and life. He rightly refers to cynics as "crows." Hero worship is the "spring of national life."

From a different part of the world echoes: "We want heroism that is heroic in its own secret thoughts. We want heroes who slay dragons in private. We want royal courage that strangles an unworthy impulse as soon as it is born . . . . It must be in his nature to be heroic."

And we also hear: "Look around. There is depression. There is despair. We need reconstruction, regeneration, rejuvenation. The ancient book prayed: *"Tamaso ma jyotir gamaya."* "Through darkness, lead us unto light." Yes, the path to light passes through the realm of suffering and sorrow!" Verily, this path is being fulfilled. Darkness has become so dense that people, drowning in it, cease to desire light. Under the eyes of the hungry, hecatombs of grain are being burnt. Millions of cattle are being destroyed in order to clear them out of the way for some kind of speculation, and it is argued that some people who will remain will derive an unusual benefit from this procedure. But who will it be? Who will survive and remain? And will he not then encounter some long ago, wound-up robot, and will the latter not smash his head by his usual mechanical movement, while the last mechanical record finishes playing a jazz piece on the theme of Chopin's *Funeral March?*

At the same time, despite all these terrible signs, we cannot be pessimists. We know that the robots will manifest themselves in all their mechanical ignorance. Precisely, they, as it has already happened, will stop traffic. They will not deliver an urgent message; they, rusty from fog, will steer the ship toward a fatal rock. It is difficult to imagine who will prove to be more destructive—the robots wound by a mechanical hand or that anticipated, inhuman biological war that is discussed in the newspapers.

Perhaps some people hope that nothing will remain of our civilization altogether, not to mention our culture. But then the shameful pages of newspapers with their columns about crimes would decay at first turn. I recollect how H. G. Wells, making a speech at a dinner, said: "Do not be surprised if this piece of glass becomes a rarity someday for somebody!" This joke expressed a genuine irony in regard to a sad reality.

And still, above all robots, above all vipers of godlessness and dark ignorance, beautiful hearts of cooperation are born. True, they are rare. It is also true that everyone who enters this path encounters many difficulties. Black stones are showered at him. All robots and man-haters would like to see destroyed everyone who thinks of creative cooperation. There is not even a shadow of a possibility for the dark ones to convert to their faith or rather atheism, those young ones devoted to the true cognizance of the heart. Therefore, darkness condemns them to annihilation, and there is no such malevolent invention and slander that would lose the opportunity to destroy each ray of light.

But the ancient Rishis have foreseen precisely this hour of darkness, which is the testing stone for those in quest of the Light. These seekers of the good know these obstacles are not accidental and must be conquered. Amid true seekers, there are also many pseudo-seekers. There are many of those Nicodemuses of the night who whisper sweet words at night and are ready to betray in daytime.

Give them the smallest test to express their own tendencies, and at once they will disappear into the abyss from where they came.

Ask whether this Nicodemus would sacrifice for the sake of a good night's sleep, and he will hasten to disappear in order not to burden himself with the slightest effort. But man lives not for them. People live for the sake of those devoted hearts, the mere mentioning of which multiplies one's strength. Those who cling to darkness will abide with it, but those in quest of the Light will reach it despite all dark obstacles.

The book *Fiery World* ordains: "Someone says that he wishes to attain cosmic consciousness; let him better think about purifying his heart. Let him not so much imagine himself as conqueror of the Cosmos, but rather let him wish to cleanse his consciousness from dust. One cannot penetrate beyond the limits of the law without wishing to become transformed in the approach. Verily, the baker of bread, in both the spiritual and material sense, must not think only as to how to get his own fill."

"The experienced physician advises the convalescent not to think about his past illness, and urges him to think about the future and about favorable circumstances. Thus, any reminder about the past illness is cast out, not only physically but spiritually. One should apply the same simple method in all the situations of life. Particularly during fiery actions, when fire is palpitating because of darkness, one should not think about darkness and its reaction on fire. A manifestation referring to the future will kindle the heart. The most oppressive thing can be dispelled only because of the future. Fools clamor about finite life. Can eternal life possible be terminated? So many terrible things have to be preformed in order to violate life! Even wild beasts do not dare to return to the dust of the abyss."

"Among psychic maladies the most frightful, almost incurable, are treachery and blasphemy. Once a traitor, always a traitor. Only the strongest fiery shock can purify such an infected brain. If such a criminal condition emanates from obsession, this is likewise not comforting. Is it possible to conceive of cooperation with a traitor or a blasphemer? They are like a plague in the house. They are like a fetid corpse. Thus, the Fiery World has no consolation for traitors and blasphemers."

"Boldness should be combined with caution. Otherwise boldness will be madness and caution will turn into cowardice. People who can picture to themselves the entire complexity of fiery waves can appreciate the advice of caution. The Yogi does not forget full caution; in it there is respect for the great element and reverence for the Fiery World. One may understand that it is necessary to exert the utmost caution, as when passing between rows of the finest vessels. If these works of fiery labor require such carefulness, the fiery waves themselves enlarge the path of our observation of the heart." Precisely through this observation of the fiery heart and vigilance, one can unerringly discriminate where lies this life-creating striving and where the mechanical seal of the robot.

My friends, many robots are at work now. There are all kinds of conventionalities, deadening forbiddances, and rusty creakings of wrath, and all other properties of mechanization and all kinds of technocracies—all these dark evils will be conquered by the fiery heart. When I think of you who gather in friendship in the name of true peace and cooperation, my heart always fills with joy. Working all day, giving your energy sometimes to routine work, you find strength to gather in the evening with all the vitality of the spirit for uplifting spiritual deeds.

Honor to those who inspire you to strive to these achievements; honor to you who find within yourselves the indefatigability and patience to transmute the routine of life into a radiant, beautiful garden.

III

PAX PER CULTURA

GATES TO PEACE

M AN became winged. The good blue sky is scratched by airplanes. Do they carry beneficial news? Perhaps they are bringing panaceas? Or perhaps they hurry with signs of blessed knowledge? or with help? But who knows—perhaps they carry mortiferous bombs? or pernicious gases? or maybe complete annihilation? What else?

Are bombs, gases, or murders permitted? Is the extermination of humanity allowed? What kind of council has admitted murder?

Somewhere a peaceful settler, in great labor, builds for his family a hearth. And at the same time, somewhere beyond the seas, bombs and poisonous gases are being manufactured to kill his children. Who knows where evil intentions are brooding, where malicious attempts are contemplated? Has the consciousness grown so coarse that it has become accustomed to witnessing murder? As in the ancient Roman Coliseum, even people today are ready to pay for the spectacle of execution.

Someone wishes it, gives the command, and the wings of humanity carry death and annihilation. And in the smallest type, the press will mention the destruction of human lives—of women and children. Perhaps without wings, this hateful killing would not have taken place. The figures of ancient wars are not comparable with the gigantic hecatombs of our days. The scale on which destruction is carried out is also beyond all proportion; in the past, destruction was carried out primitively, but now in "highly civilized style." Where was such civilization ordained? Where is the right to trample human dignity?

Are the Gates into the Future guarded by such wings?

Well, let us assume that airplanes do not carry death-bringing sorcerers. May they bring messengers of enlightenment! Let us assume that the turning of the knob of a radio apparatus will bring not ugly, vulgar tunes but the best harmonies. Let us expel all narcotics in order that sobriety may flourish. Sophia, Vera, Nadejda, Lubov—Wisdom, Faith, Hope, and Love—are not abstractions! In the epoch of the Mother of the World, the protectress of everything constructive, women will gather into an invincible host and will become benevolently bewinged.

* * *

At random I wish to quote some statements of representatives of various countries expressed at our International Convention of the Banner of Peace in Washington.

The delegate for China, the Hon. Tswen-Ling Tsui, stated: "The project to unite all nations under a common banner for guarding cultural treasures against destruction in times of war as well as of peace has a noble purpose and is worthy of the support of every person. Real culture and true science, in their contributions to civilization and the welfare of humanity, know no national boundary lines. Their products and shrines should, therefore, be immune from injury during times of international strife."

The Persian minister, H. E. Ghaffar Khan Djalal, said, "The Banner of Peace will be a haven of refuge in times of war and tumult. It commands deep appreciation and the wholehearted support of mankind because the treasures of art and the science of antiquity are a great factor in human life. Not only do they enlighten our modern civilization on the culture of our ancestors, but they serve, at the same time, to guide and encourage us in the pursuit of that art and grace that renders life gentle and fine."

The minister of the Republic of Panama, H. E Señor Dr. Ricardo J. Alfaro, in a long eloquent speech points out: "I am a firm believer in the theory that peace is the natural state of man on earth. . . . Modern science has attained a terrific efficiency in perfecting the machinery and methods of destruction. . . . May God forbid it, but if the world has another war, there will be no combat, but only massacre. . . . What must be made intangible to the mailed fist of the warrior is art and knowledge, and it must be saved from the fury of the belligerents. For this reason, the idea of safeguarding those monuments (of art and science) and creating for their protection a Banner of Peace, which every combatant will respect, is one that cannot but deserve the most enthusiastic support from all governments, from all peoples, from all civilized persons. . . ."

Major General Blanton Winship of the War Department, Washington, affirmed: "I assure you that the organization that you represent has my wholehearted support. Educational, artistic, and scientific institutions, such as libraries and museums, and magnificent examples of architecture may well be said to be the links between the ages, and any organization that serves to protect and save them to posterity in time of war, in my opinion, performs an inestimable service to humanity."

His Excellency Dr. Esteban Gil Borges, now the minister of foreign affairs of Venezuela, on behalf of the Pan-American Union, asserted: "It is highly encouraging that in a moment when there is so much anxiety in our hearts, so many doubts in our minds, so many clouds over the future, you have gathered here to perform a great duty of preserving the heritage of thought that we have received from the past and that constitutes our common patrimony today and a sacred debt to posterity. I fervently hope that this flag (the "Banner of Peace"), above every monument of science, art, and religion, will be the banner of a crusade that will remind every man that in these places they may be aware more strongly of the ties of brotherhood through the love of beauty and the peace that comes from the possession of truth and faith in God."

The minister of the Republic of Czechoslovakia,

H. E. Dr. Ferdinand Veverka, proclaimed: "My presence here is the token that Czechoslovakia wholeheartedly supports the noble aim of the International Roerich Peace Banner Convention. . . . Peace is a state of mind. Peace is a primary state of things, not a reverse of war, not a breathing spell between struggles. When this recognition dawns upon us as a reality, then the time will come when harassed and tired humanity will conceive and embrace real peace."

Dr. James Brown Scott, director of the Carnegie Endowment for International Peace and president of the American Institute of International Law, concluded his speech as follows: "Possessors of the culture of the past, trustees of the culture of the present for the future, we will, by the signature of a universal pact, set up a universal standard for culture and humanity, past, present and future, and, at the same time, a universal standard for nations and their international relations."

Another authority on International Law, Professor de La Pradelle of the University of Paris, in wishing the Convention every success, wrote: "*Sauvegarder l'Oeuvre, c'est sauver le génie humain; action civilisatrice qui mérité bien, en effet que pour convaincre les gouvernements, et s'il le faut, le gouvernement supreme, l'Opinion, moralistes et techniciens, artistes et juristes s'enrôlent sous la Bannière aux trois Besants. Je suis heureux de saluer, avec la protection de l'Oeuvre, la défense de l'Art, source de Paix, Foyer de Fie.*"

Speaking on behalf of the Japanese Government, the Hon. Toshihiko Taketomi, said, "This symbol then, on behalf of beauty and knowledge, brings together again the East and the West."

One of the greatest military authorities, the late marèchal Lyautey, wrote: "*La mission [du Pacte Roerich] quelle s'est donnée pour la protection elective des Monument Historiques et des Oeuvres d'Art offre pour la sauvegarde de la Civilisation et de la Tradition un tel intérêt! Mais aujourd'hui, plus que jamais, il est non moins désirable de s'élever contre la guerre ellememe, Jlèau dont nous, a devonstons tous prix, nous efforcer de conjurer le retour.*"

The Hon. Senor Don Eduardo L. Vivot, on behalf of Argentina, assured: "Nothing is more precious and intangible for all the nations of the world, without any race distinction, than its cultural treasures. . . . The aim pursued by the Roerich Pact and Banner of Peace is none other than to insure their inviolability—and my country warmly applauds this idea and adheres to its aims."

These are the voices of statesmen. And now, let us remember a few of the voices of eminent social representatives.

Mrs. Franklin D. Roosevelt wrote: "I think the ideals presented by the Roerich Pact cannot help but appeal to all those who hope that the best in the past may be preserved to guide and serve future generations."

Mrs. William Dick Sporborg, president of the New York Federation of Women's Clubs, on behalf of half a million members, stated: "We are going to lend our spirits and all of our influence to such movements. . . . I want you to know that we stand foursquare back of your organization. . . ."

Leopold Stokowski exclaims, "It is a noble project!" And Prof. Edgar Hewett greeted the Banner: "Assuredly the spirit of this proposal must commend itself to all right-thinking people of the world."

Maurice Maeterlinck welcomed the Pact: "I am at full heart in accord with the signatories of the Roerich Pact. Let us group around this noble ideal all moral forces at our disposal."

India expressed heartiest adherence through the voices of Sir Rabindranath Tagore, Sir Jagadis Bose, Sir C. V. Raman, Sir Radhakrishnan, Dr. N. C. Mehta, Dr. James H. Cousins, Dr. O. C. Ganguly, Dr. Asit Kumar Haldar, and many other eminent leaders. One can also not forget how enthusiastically the Indian press responded to the signing of the Pact by the twenty-one governments of North and South America.

What a treasure trove of beautiful testimonies!

All these authoritative expressions are more than mere

personal thoughts. They are like pledges of nations, and it is most valuable to witness that in our tense times there are everywhere such fervent defenders of peace, beauty, and knowledge everywhere. If only these noble spirits would know each other and would form, in cooperation, a valiant host of crusaders for peace and culture! Indeed, humanity is tired of destruction. In every school, in every academy, in every university, there should be convincingly taught all the great, constructive humanitarian foundations.

When we affirmed our motto: *"Peace through Culture,"* we did not have in view any hazy abstraction, but expressed the conviction that this is the only real working principle of peace. If Culture is the accumulation of all the highest achievements, then truly such a beautiful pavement can lead to the stronghold of Peace.

Beautiful should be the Gates to Peace!

"MIR"

M*IR*—this word in Russian means both the Universe and peace. Not without reason are these two great conceptions united in one sound. If one imagines the Universe one also realizes peaceful labor. Beginning work, one also becomes conscious of the Universe.

People talk about peace especially when they are afraid of war. But there are different kinds of war: internal and external, visible and invisible. Which of them are more horrible remains to be seen. . . .

Indeed, the worst calamity for ancient and present humanity is that their greatest poet, the wise, blind Homer, appeared to be a bard of war and not of peace. Together with his faith in the gods, he also lost faith in peace:

> There is and there can be no union
>> between lions and men.
> Wolves and sheep cannot live in
>> hearty concord.
> Eternal foes they are—hostile against
>> each other.
> Hence, between us, love is impossible.
>> No concordats
> Can exist between us until one is
>> slain,
> Feeding with his blood the fierce
>> god Ares.

This means that "everyone will kill each other." "In the Universe there will be no end of war. . . ."

Through the *Iliad*—the war of Troy— begins endless

war, which throughout ages lasts until our days!" exclaims Merezhkovsky. There are many soul-stirring lamentations. And Dante has round, infernally burning abodes for murderers and all malefactors.

And there are also other testimonies.

On the Eastern shore of Crete in Palaikastro—the ancient Heleia, which was the capital of the island about 1400 BC—there was found an ancient hymn, one of the most beautiful and simple prayers of humanity:

> Great Cronus, rejoice,
> O Ruler of joy—rejoice!
> Thou proceedest
> Leading the spirit.
> Come to us on the mount of Dictea
> And rejoice in song and dance!
> Let us greet Thee on lutes
> With flute accompaniment,
> And let us sing encircling
> The infallible Altar.
> For here, Thou,
> The Immortal Child,
> Was hidden by shield-bearing guardians
> Who accepted Thee from Rhea.
> And many fruitful years commenced
> And mortals cognized the truth,
> And even wild beasts were tamed
> By all-blissful Peace!

Mir—peace; in this one word is expressed the whole essence. "To live in peace means never to raise arms against each other." This commandment was given in all languages, in all ages.

And on the Eastern side is Cronus, and on the Western side, Quetzalcoatl—both are messengers of peace; they both "close their ears when they hear of war." In Canaan, Melchizedek, the king of Salem—the King of Peace—blesses Abraham in the name of Adonai, the God of Peace. Thus, in all religions, the first word is "peace."

When one studies symbols and tablets, one will find in all images and hieroglyphics the same desire—the sacred prayer for peace.

"Do not do evil to animals" is the ordainment of Triptolemus, the messenger sent by Demeter to savage people after the great flood; Triptolemus was to teach people agriculture and to uplift them from the bestial to human life. "Do not do evil to animals" in Biblical language means: "Blessed be those who have pity for everything living" because "all living beings suffer together and wail up till now." They suffer together with man, they perish with man, or they are saved with him.

Should man kill animals in order to feed on meat? No, by no means, ordains Demeter, the fruit-bearing goddess. With bloody food there enters into man the spirit of killing, the spirit of war, but the spirit of peace enters only through bloodless food.

And Hesiod, the shepherd on Mount Helicon sings:

> "God made it a law for beasts, birds,
>   and fishes
> To devour each other—because they do not
>   know the Truth.
> But to man, God gave the Truth!"

The truth does not kill! For everyone, it is always possible not to kill, not to make war. If you kill, you will die; give life, and you will live. A child understands this, and yet this is the mystery of mysteries!

Should one defend culture? Yes, one should, always and in everything.

Should one help the workers of culture, the depressed and burdened? Yes, one should, always and in everything.

Should one unite around the sign of culture in order to conquer the attempts of destruction and decay? Yes, one should, always and in everything.

Perhaps culture, knowledge, and beauty are sufficiently guarded and affirmed? No, they are not.

Perhaps everywhere the foundations of culture are already strongly fortified? No, unfortunately, they are not.

Perhaps the workers for culture are especially safeguarded by law and in the consciousness of the people? We wish it were so!

And the League of Culture, as the voice of public opinion, is undeferrably needed!

We have to invoke peace—non-killing. What does this mean! Is it possible that millenniums have not taught people that which has been ordained by all Commandments? But what do we see? The further we go, the more one has to reiterate the necessity of peace. Where is evolution when a monster gun is already loaded and death-bringing poison is madly sown? People have became so skillful that poison and death already fall from the blue sky—from the same blessed sky from whence was bestowed only blissful prana, the panacea.

What has happened? Under the ground there are explosive mines and threatening gangways! From the blue sky comes poison and death! The barrels of gigantic guns are proudly raised. Soon there will probably be a "festival of the shell," when it accomplishes a flight around the world, when it will destroy everything that can be destroyed.

"People cannot guess beforehand in what terrible danger humanity stands in case of a new war"— Prof. Andre Meier. "The poison gases of the last war are child's play in comparison with what we will see if a new war breaks out," adds another expert, Prof. Cannon of Columbia University. According to Dr. Hilton Jones of New York, a newly invented gas can destroy a whole army as easily as "blowing out a candle."

Truth! The inventor of poison believes that he creates truth. The makers of guns are proud that their tools will annihilate a man even beyond the horizon. The forger of the sword anticipates that his steel will penetrate all hearts. . . . Such are the thoughts of man!

Hélas, not such a truth is needed! "Mankind needs another truth," says Gorky: a truth that will blissfully, strengthen creative energy." A truth is needed that will stimulate mutual trust and striving toward goodwill.

Others make impenetrable armor and shields. Perhaps they hope to create a defense against all evil influx? Let it be so.

The defense of culture, the defense of the motherland, the defense of human dignity does not think of violent usurpation. . . . The armor of defense is not the poison of destruction. Defense is justified and attacks are condemned.

It has some special meaning that, in Russian, *mir* is synonymous for peace and for the Universe. This synonym is not due to a poverty of the language. Indeed, the language is rich. They are synonymous in their essence. Verily, the Universe and a peaceful creativeness are indivisible. From ancient times this salutary synonym had a special mission.

Mir—the Universe and *mir*—the peaceful, universal labor; a creative sowing, the beauty of the world—the conqueress.

ON VIGIL FOR PEACE!

THE main thing is to start the movement and to give direction to the thought. Later on, thought will readily flow, assuming a world scope. Of course, there always will be imitations, repetitions, elucidations, comments and affirmations. Everything is for the good. Dangerous is only a morbid stagnation.

The friends of our Pact have again cause to feel encouraged. In the League of Nations, there have been proposed useful measures for the protection of art treasures. The League urges bombproof shelters for art, and museums are to be isolated from military objectives.

In a report recently issued by the League of Nations' International Museums Office, the building of bombproof shelters for portraits and restoration of the medieval sanctuary system for statues are recommended to all countries? It proposes that pending an agreement for the protection of art, competent authorities everywhere will put their national art on a war footing along these lines:

"For movable or easily transportable artworks, the building of reliable shelters within museums, offering the same efficacy as those designed; for example, for protection of the civil population against aerial bombardments.

"Equipment of museums with a view to the removal of artworks to these shelters in cases of impending danger.

"Drawing up drilling instructions for training museum staffs in these delicate operations. Acquisition of material that can be rapidly utilized for protection against effects of bombardment of artworks difficult to remove.

"For architectural monuments, adoption of the same

protection measures by competent departments with a view to insuring, in the event of aerial bombardment, the safety of more fragile parts (stained glass windows, bas-reliefs and other sculptural features) both inside and outside monuments. Acquisition of appropriate equipment for dismantling these parts.

"Steps to be taken with public authorities with a view to clearing in peacetime certain artistic monuments of outstanding artistic or historic value of all surrounding buildings, works, airdromes, lines of communication, and so forth used or capable of being used for military purposes.

"Lastly, and in view of facilitating and concluding an international agreement acceptable to the military authorities of all countries, construction outside urban centers and in places that give rise to no misunderstandings from a military or from a strategical viewpoint of shelters and depositories to which movable objects to be protected can be transported wherever possible, or appointment of a town or center in each country to be declared strictly neutral and to serve as a last asylum for humanity's laws."

Thus, the League of Nations also ponders on the protection of the beautiful. We will not discuss the details of these proposals; some of them are more feasible, others less. This does not matter. It is important that the thought about the safeguarding of cultural treasures is spreading all over the world. Many more Golgothas and burning pyres will yet fill the world with confusion and awe, and these horrible signs will imperatively remind the world how undeferrable are the questions of the protection of all flowers on the field of culture.

Some time back, we suggested to our Pact committees to gather and summarize all proposals regarding peace, emanating from manifold organizations. Much indexing and many catalogues have to be made in order to reveal the world thought about peace, about the protection of world treasures, about agreements possible in this direction. There is endless work to accomplish, and world events prove the real necessity of these efforts.

Similarly, to the many branches of the Red Cross, there will arise around the Banner of Peace various problems for decision. Without envy and enmity, every country will have to bring its mite into the treasury of true achievements.

In schools, from early childhood, the foundation will be laid for the saving of the Beautiful. This year will mark the thirty-fourth anniversary of our peace pact movement. During these three decades, many people have approached, many opinions were expressed, but one thing remained unalterable—the undeferrability of action. World events have but confirmed this.

Newspapers communicated that the Spanish government, with difficulty, saved the cathedral in Barcelona from its own mob. It was necessary to paste large posters on the walls of the cathedral urging its protection and to call out troops with machine guns. Is this not a striking example of how necessary it is to educate the people's consciousness? Before our very eyes, deplorable and irreparable destructions are continuously taking place, and only a powerful moral impulse can save humanity from a repetition of fatal annihilations.

The Pact for the protection of cultural treasures is needed not only as an official regulation but as an educating law, which from the first school days will imbue the young generation with the noble idea of safeguarding the true values of all humanity. The Pact has already been signed by twenty-two countries. No doubt this large number will gradually be joined by all other countries as well. Our Pact has justly been named "The Red Cross of Culture." Truly it stands in closest relation to the great Red Cross, which at the time of its inception was received rather skeptically but now has become an indisputably humanistic foundation of life.

To show the imperative necessity of all peace movements, let us listen to some statements of leading militarists: "If previously peace wished to subject war to its own laws and regulate it by legal limitations, and tried to compel war to respect its morals and values, now it is the opposite: peace should be subordinated to the demands of war, which has become the ruler of the age and has shifted peace to a mere concept of armistice. This emancipation of war, which constitutes the main feature of our era, demands for its realization the introduction of the last decisive step: the abolition of the present social order, which is based on the assumption of peace, and the substitution of this order by a militaristic one. The establishment of such a militaristic constitution is the specific aim of today."

Let us not burden the reader with too many such depressing quotations. There exist entire volumes, as for example, *Total War* and *The War for Annihilation*. They describe a war in which the whole population of the nation is to take place, with the object of the complete annihilation of the enemy by all available means and without any restrictions whatsoever, without mercy. Thus, *Total War* is directed not against the enemy's army but against entire nations as such. "War is the highest manifestation of the vital will of the people and, therefore, politics should serve military supremacy," so the militarists assert.

One can easily understand what is meant by the "complete annihilation of the enemy." This covers also all accumulations of culture. In the face of the cruel aims of *Total War*, the merciless methods of conquerors of the past will appear to be child's play. If humanity has reached such unheard of monstrosities, one must the sooner direct all efforts toward the protection of cultural values—both with artistic and scientific treasures and in the person of cultural representatives themselves.

It is deplorable that after millions of years of existence of our planet, one has still to reiterate such axioms. Hence, if at our previous Peace Pact Conferences we called for a doubling of efforts, the present condition of the world demands that our efforts should be increased threefold! On vigil for Peace!

HRIDAYA

Carozon, Kokoro, Sin, Al-kulub,
Del, Cor, Njing, Dzuruhe.

IT sounds like an invocation! But thus people call the
Heart. India, Spain, Nippon, China, Arabia, Persia,
Italy, Tibet, and Mongolia.

Heart, Coeur, Herz Serdze

In all their writings, preserve the memory, shout, and
whisper to each other the precious word of the heart.

The three hundred tongues of India and as many in the
rest of Asia, and again as many in the Russian vastnesses,
and again as many in the Americas, in Africa, and on all
the islands proclaim the same concept of fire, love, and
heroic achievement. Words fail to describe all the infamies
that have spread all over the earth. The wheels of life are
covered with mud. And yet, across all trenches, over all
obstacles and pitfalls universally resounds the word which
signifies the heart—the treasury of Light.

People have come to heartaches. People have covered
their hearts with dust and their hearts have grown hairy.
Their hearts shriveled in fear and horror. And yet they
have not forgotten the word that will remind them of the
heart—the center of life.

At times it seems that all treasures have been desecrated by man. People have slandered the most sacred. The
Highest has been belittled, but they have not forgotten the
heart—the cradle of love.

People have become enshrouded in darkness. They
have blackened their tongues with evil treason. The most

valuable vessels have been broken. They have become choked by the vilest malice. But they have kept the memory of the heart—as of the last refuge.

* * *

"Coming into a new country, first of all ask, what is the name for the heart? Meeting new people, if even you do not know the sound in which they express their thoughts, point from your heart to theirs. Almost everybody will respond to this testimony of sincerity; only a few will be surprised or perhaps will feel ashamed, and only very few will become indignant. Remember that those who become indignant are in their actions evil people. Do not expect friendship or goodwill from them—they are already decaying."

* * *

There is as yet no institute devoted to the Heart. There are, of course, entire large institutions dedicated to the fighting of the various scourges of humanity, but there are no special institutions that study this most important moving factor of life. Gradually very important experiments on the heart are being achieved. News has just been received from Italy that a heart, which had stopped beating, has been brought back to life. At Milan on February 21, a person whose death had been attested by the medical personnel of the Milan Hospital was brought back to life by an injection of adrenalin. All newspapers are full with the particulars of this case.

The patient suffered from a complicated form of heart disease and was treated by all means available to science. But in spite of all precautionary measures, he died. Although the physicians were fully convinced that death had actually taken place, yet one of them made an injection of adrenalin by way of an experiment. After thirty minutes, the heart began to beat feebly, and in a few hours it was working normally; and at present, the physicians are in a position to state that the patient is out of danger.

Similar actions of adrenalin were known before; it remains to investigate how, in itself, this powerful substance will react upon the function of the organism. Many cases are known that when a fatal issue was prevented by an injection of adrenalin, it brought but a short postponement of death. And it was noticed—I speak in this particular case of children— that nervousness increased and, at times, became difficult to control. This perhaps was due to entirely different causes, but the above-mentioned makes us think over the use of this radical remedy.

Folk medicine often reports cases of cures by most unexpected means. And usually these unforeseen and at times strange remedies remain without proper investigation and are lost in the realm of anecdotes.

I recall how in the family of a priest, a child died from suffocation following croup. The priest in despair took the body of the child and ran with it into the church, toward the altar, where he began praying in frenzied exaltation. It so happened that the child had its head hanging down and his father, not knowing it, was shaking the child violently by its feet. Suddenly a large clot of hardened mucus came out of the child's throat, and it coughed and began to breathe. The heart had slowly returned to life.

Think how many multiform manifestations of apparent death may take place! History reports infinite cases of reawakened dead. Various forms of lethargy have been observed and, after all, cannot be properly determined. Why does the life functioning suddenly stop? Why do the dead again return and, even under such unbelievable circumstances, often after burial? Of course, there are many explanations to this. But until the world of the heart will be properly investigated, until then, these will be only fortunate or sad occurrences.

Of course, the profound life of the heart is perhaps the most difficult one to be described in words. Precisely the heart must be studied, not only in pain and anguish but in its healthy state. If the nervous system of plants reacts to the most minute changes of temperature, to distant clouds, to the slightest touch, then how many more beautiful and remarkable resoundings and pulsations take place in the heart. Besides, it is difficult to say what is a healthy and what is a diseased state of the heart. It is known that many die quickly from heart attacks, having yet a so-called sound heart; whereas others, long ago given up as cardiac catastrophes, live long, very long.

The pulse does not express itself only in a number of beats but first of all in its quality, and this quality of heart-beats is but little examined and explained. When one says: "Guard your heart," that means, first of all, not to become irritated, not to get angry; and on the other hand, do not feel sad and do not fall into despondency.

Every minutest detail of life will resound first of all not in the brain but in the heart. Precisely the heart realizes and responds to the most distant earthquakes, as the best seismograph. But it is not customary to consult one's heart. It is not customary to consider it as the receptacle of the most High. And when people read direct advices about the importance of such aspirations, they are being condemned as being abstract, abstract, as being invented by some inaccessible ascetics and as being inapplicable. And yet it can be always applied to that which is taking place in the heart, if only one would listen to it frankly and sincerely.

A man who is confident that he does not notice many quite realistic manifestations, first of all does not wish to notice them. He presupposes, in his haughtiness, that nothing will take place, that he will hear nothing and that nothing will disturb his peace. Precisely conceit prevents man from perceiving reality. At times the heart beats like a sledgehammer upon a darkened consciousness. A man is ready to pour upon his heart all kinds of poisons in order to stifle it. And he will not think what may be the cause that his heart is so excited, what bad or good has taken place, what usefulness or what harm has caused the knocking.

The smallest to the highest—all is contained within the heart. It resounds to everything that lives. Touching and wise are the ancient reminders of the great significance of the heart.

"The spirit, which is in my heart, is smaller than a grain of rice, smaller than a grain of barley, smaller than a mustard seed, and smaller than the smallest seed of grain. And yet the same spirit that lives in my heart is greater than the entire earth, greater than space, greater than heaven, and greater than all the worlds.

"The messenger of all action, all desire, all perception, smell, taste, all-embracing, silent, distant—such is the spirit that abides in my heart. This is Brahman Himself. He who says, 'I follow him who exists from this world,' truly there is no doubt for him."

Thus says *Chandogya Upanishad.*

AWAY WITH CRUELTY!

THE historian records as follows the plundering of Rome by Spaniards and German Landsknechts during the days of the famous Pope Clementius:

And what no blockade could stop were the daily demoralizing, horrible rumors about blasphemous orgies and vandalism, which took place in Rome, about the fury of fanatic iconoclasts; St. Peter's Cathedral had been turned up into stables, the Landsknechts kept their houses in Raphael's stanzas in the Vatican; the remnants of Pope Julius had been thrown out of the tomb; the statues of Apostles were beheaded; the procession of Lutherans with the spear of St. Longinus, the sacrilege with the Holy Relic of St. Veronica, the intrusion into the Holy of Holies; about inhuman cruelties, during night orgies, about the mock funeral of the cardinal and resurrection from the coffin, the murder of an abbot for his refusal to hold mass to a mule. There constantly flows in news even about a crack in the dome, about processions of priests and monks led through the streets to be sold, about the nocturnal conclave of drunken Landsknechts, sacrileging the holy mass.

Another eyewitness adds:

Starvation and pest followed the plundering. The city was exhausted and soldiers already pillaged not for gold but bread, searching for it even in the beds of the sick. A sinister silence, devastation, infection, corpses scattered everywhere, filled me with horror. Houses were open, doors broken, shops empty, and in the streets I could see but brutal soldiers.

We are quoting the above lines describing one of the

many plunderings of Rome because of it in comparison with other invasions, there is usually very little known. In schools one only reads that Pope Clementius had to spend a certain time in the besieged castle of St. Angel, but the real horrors of vandalism and blasphemy are not even mentioned. The Emperor himself and kings did not even consider this state of war. When we study other documents of those times, we find that at some courts this horror was only referred to as an unhappy incident. But when the Spanish representatives arrived to save the city, they could not, even with the help of the generals of the plundering armies, take control of the situation because to such an extent had the vandalism, cruelty, and blasphemy taken hold of the Spaniards and Landsknechts.

From where could such terrible cruelty and sacrilege originate? It, of course, originated from everyday hardheartedness. But how could such an atrocity flash up instantly? This evil fire, no doubt, sprang up from habitual rudeness and cursing. We know how the infection of the vulgarity of bad language mischievously creeps into everyday life. Chaos manifests itself everywhere, where even for a minute cultural striving is neglected. One cannot for a moment remain in static condition—either down or up. Much is written in literature, dramas, and tragedies about the nature of cruelty and atrocities. From everyday rudeness, permitted and nurtured, there arises abhorrent blasphemy, vandalism, and other ugly manifestations of ignorance.

The paroxysm of ignorance, as often pointed out, is first of all directed against the Highest. Crass ignorance desires to annihilate something, to cut off someone's head, if even a stone one of a statue; ignorance tries to cut out the child to leave only from the mother's womb, to destroy life, and to leave only an "empty place." Such is the ideal of ignorance. It greets illiteracy, it welcomes pornography. It relishes vulgarity and slander. It is difficult to estimate where one finishes and the other begins. Altogether the scales of ignorance are undefinable.

Since cruelty is created by everyday vulgarity and rudeness, how carefully should one extinguish every form of coarseness. How patiently even the smallest rude expression should be eliminated from every home. Rudeness is absolutely unnecessary. Even wild animals are tamed not by rudeness and cruelty. In education rudeness has long been condemned as giving no useful results and only creating a generation of ruffians.

When we read historical examples of misery and ill-luck that took place owing to everyday vulgarity, when we see that these misfortunes continue also today, then is it not necessary to take definite measures in the schools and in the family to safeguard youth from every form of rudeness? The inexperienced youngster is so easily contaminated with the peril of rudeness. Ugly, bad language is so easily introduced in life. Such language is called improper; in other words, it is not admissible.

In opposition to proper language, there apparently exists dirty language. And if people themselves admit that certain expressions are improper, it means that they themselves consider them dirty. Then why favor dirt in life? No one will pour a pail of slops and garbage on the floor in his room. And if such a thing happens by accident, then even the most primitive people will consider it abominable. But bad language is nothing else but a pail of slops of garbage. Is not bad language just a bad habit? Children are punished for bad habits; but the grownups are not punished and even their dirty expression calls forth encouraging smiles.

The habit of rudeness, ill-language, and blasphemy has spread to such an extent that it is simply not noticed. If people remember all the blasphemous jokes, which cause a roar of laughter, it will be quite natural that today these people go to church as if for prayer and tomorrow they are nurturing their horrible bad language.

It has been said long ago: "Yesterday a small compromise, today another small compromise—tomorrow a great scoundrel." Coarseness surprises not only by its inner cruelty but also by its senselessness.

People like the Pharisees often show such hypocrisy when pretending to regret the loss of purity of language, yet they themselves sometimes sponsor the mutilation of language. Amid rubbish are born horrible microbes and they spread in colossal pernicious epidemics.

It has been asserted that Beauty will save the world. Recently we read an excellent book by the renowned Latvian poet, Richard Rudzitis, *Realization of Beauty Will Save*. Indeed, everyone will agree with this ardent call. But the very concept of Beauty compels the introduction of refinement into everyday life. Not a senseless luxury, but refined beauty is meant. And such a refined beauty does not depend on material wealth. And, first of all, such refinement should not be abused by any form of rudeness.

We speak of the protection of cultural treasures. And for the realization of this axiom, everyone should free himself from a rude attitude to higher ideals. Besides, let us always remember that when protecting cultural treasures, we must not forget the creators of them and pay tribute to them as to living monuments of culture.

Thus having remembered horrors and cruelty, let us conclude with Love and Beauty as a blissful creative force.

"Urusvati" Himalaya, 1937

MONSALVAT

IT is generally assumed that our organism can be best
developed and kept fit by all kinds of sport. Exercises
are very necessary, of course, particularly when they are
carried out in pure air. Opinions, however, do not agree as
to the nature of such exercises. Moreover, the harmonious
development of the nervous system is as important as that
of the muscles. Once the nervous system is balanced and
the nerves have regained their normal tension, we can
achieve much that muscular development alone can never
achieve.

Everyone recognizes that highly specialized sports,
which only exercise a certain set of muscles, are not the
best form of training. We have, first of all, to utilize the
prana present in pure air and to exercise those movements
that are natural to the human organism. Such movements
allow the nervous fluids to circulate naturally and are the
most fitted for the development of body and spirit.

It is a well-known fact that a man under nervous excitement can make a greater effort than a trained athlete.

Artificial tension tends to produce artificial thinking.
The golden measure can only come from the harmonious
equilibrium of the whole organism.

It is deplorable when one thinks of all the marathons
today, since they are nothing but a needless waste of time.
When we see nonstop dancers establishing records of sev-
enty-two hours, we begin to wonder who is to benefit from
it. There is certainly no beauty in it. If we were to see
couples embracing one another for hours, we would find it
both grotesque and undignified. These modern marathons

are nothing more than a caricature of the great classic race instituted by the Greeks. Moreover, after the Marathon the Greek runners were accustomed to frequent the Academy, where they could listen to the lectures of great scholars and philosophers. In this they were not one-sided.

Others will tell you that violent bodily exertion prevents a healthy development of the nervous system. We know that the Peripatetic school of philosophers in Greece always lectured while walking so as to harmonize their spiritual and physical activities.

If we compare the sport of the decadent Roman circus with the classical games of Greece, we will get some idea of the inferior character of all purely physical contests.

Unfortunately, a public execution will draw an immense crowd even today. In Germany they have again begun to decapitate women criminals, and although this takes place in the prison courtyard, if such a spectacle were to be transferred to the public square, you would find in this 'civilized' age of ours that the amphitheater would be packed. As a matter of fact the gate money would probably exceed all the sums that go to philanthropic works.

We once heard that certain ladies were vexed because capital punishment by hanging had replaced that of being burned alive. Such monstrous sentiments are due to an abnormal development of certain instincts, and a great deal of ugliness and brutality is due to a narrow, one-sided prejudice. Certain muscles have swollen, producing, as it were, an ulcer of savagery and sadism that has poisoned both heart and brain.

Against such one-sided physical culture, there is the theory that a proper education of the nervous system will do more than anything else to develop the muscles and put all the organs under our control. We know that it is our thought that sets all the muscles in movement, although there are many who are so thoughtless as not to realize this important fact, which is quite easy to prove.

We often meet with people who give little attention to

physical exercise but who are, nonetheless, quite healthy, physically and mentally.

By aspiring toward the higher life, they took a lively interest in existence and this alone helped to keep their organism well balanced.

Value the gift of life. In desiring to live a life of labor and activity, you will have acquired an impulse that will do more to keep you healthy than all the remedies, vaccinations, and massages. Conscious mental massage can pump fresh energy into any weak part. The simplest breathing exercise of pranayama, which consists of inhaling fresh air and sending the prana in it to any weak spot, is a practice that you can prove for yourself. Every day one hears of monstrous methods for curing disease or failing health. One will take to narcotics or to alcohol so as to cure insomnia; another, because of certain symptoms, begins to smoke or take drugs, oblivious of the fact that he is only increasing his troubles. We often hear about the joy of dedicating one's life to service, but what joy can there be in the use of narcotics, nicotine, and alcohol? They will not help us toward the joy of development and ascent but only lead to a shameful retreat into darkness. Doctors are well aware of the harm caused by an addiction to sport, and it is quite common to hear of heart troubles and other ailments caused by overexertion.

Cardiac neurosis and other serious heart diseases are all induced by these excesses.

A specialized athlete is hardly fit for average physical activity. He is like a hothouse plant, which can only live in artificial conditions.

The specialized athlete is far more one-sided than the professional man of business, and if one listens to the ideals of sportsmen and prize fighters, one very soon begins to doubt about the value of civilization in its present condition.

It would seem that bullfights are beginning to lose their interest, but even this is not certain since crowds can still be gathered to applaud this cruel sport.

The Boy Scout movement, however, is quite apart from professional sport, and is one of the most healthful ways of employing our leisure time. The golden measure is a doctrine that has been preached for centuries but has perhaps been rarely understood.

As we rise steadily in our ascent toward the spiritual heights of Monsalvat, we will find very few sportsmen or prizefighters among the pilgrims. Those who aspire constantly toward these heights are very different in character. Physical prowess is not enough if we are to overcome the hardships and dangers of the way.

The aspirant to Monsalvat generally has the necessary physical and spiritual strength to lead him along the beaten track, and it is not one that is drawn from a desire for prizes. The hearts of all who ascend these heights keep a healthy rhythm and one that does no harm to spiritual growth.

Monsalvat, the sanctified, is a name known to all languages. Constantly developing, let us avoid all that is dead and finite. We are mistaken, however, if we imagine that bodily achievements are the goal of life and those which deserve the crown.

It has been ordained that the spirit alone will receive the crown.

Let us remember how the principles of Monsalvat were born; let us not forget how this guiding concept emerged into life.

As we approach it, we are aware that its signification goes beyond all our limitations, as every teacher has to repeat.

To those engaged in life's daily routine, the heights of Monsalvat may seem remote and inaccessible. Many will save up their possessions, saying, "They will be needed when I wish to go there." These people are not misers infatuated with earthly possessions; they are falcons who are spreading their wings, and they know that when the time has come to go, they can go.

In the first place, they will have overcome the feeling

of solitude, that deadly cold feeling that terrifies all those who dwell in ignorance. Lofty expressions are alone suited to the heights, for commonplace words do not naturally gather about lofty concepts. Those who desire to see can behold many things; those who wish to listen can hear voices.

Monsalvat—the sanctified!

PEACE TO ALL BEINGS

"Whoever thinks evil of it in his heart,
Let his heart rot!
Whoever stretches his hand toward it,
Let his hand be cut off!
Whoever harms it with his eye,
May his eye become blind!
Whoever does any harm to this bridge
May that creature be born in hell!"

THESE lines, about the first bridge across the Indus, were written by Naglug, the Buddhist ruler of Ladakh, who ever tried to instill in the population a respect for all that is constructive.

The good king Asoka also gave first place to construction, and the Blessed One Himself never tired of sounding the call to constructive effort.

A short time before He passed away, He exclaimed: "How beautiful is Vaisali."

Such holy teachings were spread abroad by Buddhist preachers, and no one can point to destruction on the part of a Buddhist.

Enlightenment and construction are the panacea that is at the basis of all Buddhist teachings.

Is it the moment to talk of peace when wars are raging? Certainly it is now that we ought to proclaim, on all hands, the doctrine of peace, enlightenment, and goodwill.

Peace cannot be imposed by governmental decrees. True peace will only be secured when the nations realize the vanity of quarreling and mutual destruction.

Peace that results in dishonor and enslavement can never bring happiness.

Only peace that arises from tireless efforts to construction and enlightenment can bring happiness.

Some people think that as long as the cannon is not roaring, peace can be maintained. It is the roar of the heart, however, and not the noise of the cannon that provokes war.

Many never tire of repeating, "What is the use of preaching peace in these days when, as in the case of China, we see hecatombs of cruelty and bloodshed? Such calls to peace are only hollow phrases, abstract ideals."

One could answer that murderers and destroyers have always existed on our long-suffering earth, and alas! They will last for a long time yet, but, let us hope, not forever.

Meanwhile, the penal laws and commandments are not only being decreed but applied to life. And so it is with peace. Even if we allow that this blessed word "peace" is for many a mere abstraction, nevertheless we know that the order "Peace to all beings" has been proclaimed. And the order is not merely an abstract idea but something that we have to apply.

He who gave such an order knew very well the true path for humanity.

Only active enlightenment can give us a proper perception of the world.

"Peace through Culture"—we will never tire of repeating this truth. If it has not yet become a truism, this is because the consciousness of all nations has not been saturated with this sole way of reaching the highest good.

To understand the real meaning of peace, one ought to be conscious of the real treasures of humanity, for he who is conscious of such values and really understands them will know how to preserve them.

Museums and universities in which history and archaeology are taught are not enough because they only deal with the formal aspect of these subjects. What we have in mind is not the dead letter and the formal side of these studies but rather the awakening of consciousness in the hearts of the nations.

Many times we have had occasion, with our own eyes, to see these senseless ruins that are the shameful monuments of human ignorance. We have seen the most beautiful monuments ruined, the finest sculptures shattered or destroyed, and all through the criminal ignorance of their value.

Such vestiges of destructive mania ought to warn us to be careful with these irreplaceable treasures.

We have recently heard of a plan to bury all artistic monuments under sandbags. Quite apart from the practical inconvenience of such a project, we should realize that sandbags alone will never suffice, and that only culture is powerful enough to protect the beautiful. Thus, we should hasten to repeat on all hands "Peace through Culture."

Why do I speak of the protection of art treasures on this memorable day? It is not merely to avail myself of such an occasion. I have other reasons. On memorable days people recall the highest principles. When, therefore, all of our friends are ready to repeat the commandment "Peace to all Beings," let them think of the way that leads to peace. Let them remember how carefully all cultural treasures ought to be preserved because this alone can lead toward the future gateway of peace.

"Peace to all Beings."

THOU SHALT NOT KILL

BEFORE me lies an imposing volume *The First World War*. The publishers of it no doubt desired to show all the negative moments of the war and its consequences. Such books are excellent indicators amid the search and appeals for peace. If we witnessed all these horrors in the age of civilization and great discoveries, it means that the world culture is greatly shaken.

Besides its text, that book horrifies the reader with its pictorial reproductions. Let us not enumerate all such disgraces of humanity. It is sufficient to look into the eyes of a starving child-skeleton in order to feel into what abyss savagery and bestiality lead. The shameful destructions of the majestic creations of human genius also appeal to the hearts that are not yet fossilized.

The meaning of this white book on a table is similar to our white Banner of Peace, which was discussed at the Washington Convention. The more such books, the more signs of a reminder, the more the human heart will shudder and will ponder about the closest measures for the protection of dignity, for the safeguarding of the noble seal of the age. For what can be more dishonorable for such a seal of the age than the destruction of culture in its deep significance?

We must be thankful to all those who, by one sign or another, try to decrease the field of killing and destruction. It is true, we are horrified looking at some of the pages of the book of the Great War, but we exclaim at the same time: Let the school teacher, when showing such books to the students, say, "This will not be repeated." So much terror has entered life, destroying the moral and material bases, that indicators should undeferrably appear on perilous spots from which humanity must be saved!

But in order that the teacher should have the right not to conceal from the children past horrors, he must cover every page of horrors with ten volumes of the true heroic deeds of humanity. He must know how to speak beautifully about those who shed their blood for the defense of the best constructive and educational foundations. Therefore, every publisher who shows the horrors takes upon himself the duty to issue books depicting the best images of the heroes and leaders of mankind.

In the days of the world crises, the wise Commandments should be especially remembered. Among them the most outstanding and imperative is: Thou shalt not kill! During the millenniums of bygone ages, the spiritual leaders of mankind on all continents repeatedly and patiently reminded of this closest basis of life. Precisely, this commandment has in view the safeguarding of life—that greatest gift for self-perfectment. And again, this planetary command was sent out, but again the blacksmiths of the whole world untiringly forged swords and spears, presupposing attacks, slaughter, and murders.

Endless volumes have been written against the killing of the body. From all sides it has been shown to what an extent this cruel action does not correspond to human dignity. If one could collect all the sayings that have accumulated around this conception, then we would see an amazing wreath, and on every leaf of it would twinkle the tears of humanity of all ages and all nations.

But amid the confusion of life, it has become unbefitting and even shameful to speak about this Commandment. And he who dares will be regarded as an impotent pacifist of the most perverted kind. He who speaks of this Commandment will be considered, if not insane, then at least a suspicious character who upsets the social structure of contemporary conventionalities. Indeed, if in antiquity murders were counted by the thousands, then in our "enlightened, civilized" era, the number of killed exceeds many millions. If in the Stone Age, hunters with primitive bows and spears killed some animals, then now in the slaughterhouses of Chicago alone, within the shortest time, some fifty thousand animals' lives have been taken. Such is progress!

And if with all the scientific data at hand, you will try to advocate the advantage of the nutritive value of a vegetarian diet, you will again be suspected of some intentions directed against society. Civilized humanity, often reiterating the word "culture," still regards blood as something highly nutritive; and there still exist ignorant physicians who prescribe raw, bloody meat. Lamentable dicta—whatever you will say about blood, meat, about the cruel pastime of hunting, or about the so-much-liked-by-the-mob executions, all this will be permitted as a befitting conversation in the parlor rooms of highest society. As they taste a sugar-coated biscuit and dip their lips in the famous cup of tea, you can smilingly relate how during a certain execution, not only was all available space filled with excited onlookers, but even from all windows and roofs of adjoining houses, people were staring at such a "rare" sight. If you will narrate without much criticism, then the society will enrich such themes with many piquant details.

Thus, together with the amount of ordainments against killing, there also grows the very number of murders of both animals and human beings. Many wiseacres will state: "Such is the law of life." And if you will contradict, quoting authoritative Commandments, then your interlocutor will reply, "You are yet too young," as if, according to his opinion, old age is the symbol for bloodthirstiness and cruelty.

Cruel are the deeds of this world. On the one side, people try to discover all sorts of remedies to prolong life; and on the other, they, with still greater speed, invent deadly guns and poisonous gases, which, besides destroying human life, poison the whole planet and inflict much greater harm than the civilized modern consciousness wishes to admit. All this refers to the body. But let us not forget that besides the body, we should keep in mind the human spirit, consciousness, thought, and ideas that govern the world. Of this a multitude of philosophers of all ages wrote and spoke, and in confirmation of this truth, they went into the fire and onto the scaffold.

But now the enmity of the world has reached such a state that to speak of the perversion or violation of the spirit is considered merely a bigotry of bad manners. And indeed, where now can people hear about vital ethics, about the purification of consciousness, and the discipline of thought? The churches insufficiently stress it, and we all remember how guns were brought for blessing into churches. In schools there is no chair of ethics, and yet this subject, in all its historical vividness, could be one of the most inspiring. The ethics of the spirit, the teaching of the heart, has behind itself a most beautiful literature in all epochs. But it is not the custom to read such fundamental chronicles. It is not in the habit to search in characteristic old expressions something needed even today. For us who are addicted to aimless speeding to bodily contests, can there be any time to inspire ourselves with the beauty of ancient conceptions and images?

Having transplanted our consciousness into bazaars, into stock exchanges, into stadiums, into every possible kind of race and super-race, we simply lose the understanding wherein lies that self-perfectment for which we are here on this earth. One may run faster than his neighbor. One may fly faster than birds, but one may also swallow up one's neighbor more bloodthirstily than a tiger. Embitterment has generated that unheard-of negation that destroys the meaning of human achievement. We had an opportunity once to quote the most significant statement of a British engineer-inventor, who said that humanity is not ready to accept great discoveries. And H. G. Wells, not because of the triumph of culture, recently suggested building a new Noah's Ark.

Verily, in home life, in the schools, in social activities, many lessons of cruelty are taught. And in exchange, how blankly and tiresomely is repeated the withered command:

Thou shalt not kill! And in the physical body, people have ceased to understand what it means, not to kill; what higher meaning this commandment, austere in its brevity, has.

And when matters reach the stage of killing the spirit, the murdering of the consciousness and of the heart, then our contemporary dictionary comes into complete disorder and turns out to be altogether useless. But the threatening crisis of the world, we repeat, is not in the bazaar, but in our hearts. Until people understand the meaning of pre-ordained self-perfectment, they will not be in a position to value the whole practicability of the command not to kill not only the body but also the spirit.

Some dark instigators shout, "To hell with culture!" "To hell with heroes, leaders and teachers!" But precisely through these renovated conceptions can construction and betterment enter life.

Embitterment, after all, leads to poverty, to perpetual dissatisfaction, in which even wealth appears as poverty. Cruelty makes of the heart that stone that we try to throw at our neighbor, instead of illumining the near ones with the light of cooperation. In the conception of cooperation, no thought of killing will enter because cooperation needs life and not death. In the difficult days I want to greet friends with this blissful cooperation, which will bring us to a mutual understanding of the high meaning of self-perfectment.

Always when we pronounce the great commandment: "Thou shalt not kill," let us understand it not only in its physical but mainly in its spiritual sense. This last meaning will direct our attention to the heart and will help us understand the great Commandment not only in the narrow earthly way but in the whole magnificence of all higher worlds.

Cooperation, cognizance, strengthening of the spirit will again give to the world those heroes that the hearts of mankind long for.

Himalayas, 1934

FREDUM

FREDUM is the term given in the ancient laws of the Franks to the fine imposed against the violation of peace. In other words, this fine is the "cost of peace," or "price of peace." Other similar fines were "the cost of man," or "the cost of blood," or "the cost of vengeance," also known as *wergeld* and *faida*; *fredum*, among all these laws, is also one of greatest significance for our times. We should not be surprised that under current circumstances so-called civilized mankind has something yet to learn, even from the ancient Franks.

The people who considered it necessary to safeguard by law a peaceful state of life were striving to ethical legal codes. It would also be good if nowadays amid the numerous international, criminal, and civil laws, people remember the basic question of the violation of peace.

Such a law could remind people in everyday life of the significance of this imperative concept. Everyone wants peace. But—*horribile dictu*—many wish to approach it not by peaceful means. But true peace cannot be built on the foundations of insult, belittling, or self-glorification.

In all aspects of life, the concept of human dignity should always, of course, be venerated and upheld. People should not only be conscious of but learn to love the concepts of dignity, honor, and heroic attainment. These qualities should not be abstract, as on the stage or in the pages of novels. They should be manifested in all the details of daily life. They should be vital because only living is convincing.

One sometimes hears nowadays that the concepts of honor and dignity are considered as outlived. And around the word "honor," there seem to hover duels, bloody fights, and mutual assaults. But honor has nothing in common with the bloodshed of a duel. The human consciousness should, of course, be superior to the "price of blood." A righteous judgment need not be based on walking upon red-hot iron. It is never permissible to combine the living concepts of honor and dignity with certain medieval conventionalities.

It is quite possible that timid thinking is afraid to include in contemporary life many concepts, which are as if shadowed by superstition and prejudices. But the honor, dignity, and virtue of man cannot be regarded as a prejudice. Similarly, every defense of peace will be neither a sign of fear nor of superstition. In every manifestation of this noble striving, there will already be expressed that love toward peace, which is ordained in all fundamental laws and creeds. "Blessed are the peacemakers."

Certainly, every insult of peace, every violation of a peaceful life, already contradicts positive human constructiveness. If a man is, as Plato says, *zoon politicon* (a social being), then in such a social structure, mankind should be first of all imbued with a veneration for peaceful relationships. This is not impotent pacificism but a virile and conscious defense of dignity, be this around the hearth or in a clan or in the state. How could the idea of the defense of dignity be non-peaceful? One can visualize a peaceful guard or a vigil in the name of peace, but essentially, in the heart of such a vigil, there should live the ideal of peace. This beneficial peace will not be like an ill-wishing neighbor; on the contrary, it will be a good neighbor, who honestly knows his borderline.

Conquest and annexation should be considered medieval. One may convince a man in the name of honor, reason, or the heart, but every act of violence will forever remain on the dark pages of the history of mankind.

Such persuasion, in the name of honor and dignity, is possible when a man is truly like Plato's "social being," and not a ferocious beast. But to be such a "social being," one has to exercise patience and tolerance to the highest extent. No one requires self-humiliation; it is ordained since ancient times that "self-humiliation is worse than pride." Of course, neither in superstition nor in hypocrisy and bigotry can any concept of peace and honor be established. If someone heralds peace while at the same time sharpening the dagger in his heart, this will not be peace but evil hypocrisy.

In the ancient Kainourgion of Byzantium, the majestic image of the Nikopoia was surrounded by inscriptions of prayers of parents for their children and of children for their parents. Thus, the most sacred and heartiest were exhibited in cold, official halls. From the history of Byzantium, we know that such inscriptions remained as dead conventionalities. In their formality they could not inspire or convince anyone; the complete downfall of the Byzantine Empire only proves that the dead word has nothing in common with life.

Innumerable hypocritical inscriptions left their shadows on the face of the earth. Precisely, these signs of hypocrisy turned many people away from the true understanding of the great, sacred foundations such as peace, honor, and dignity. He who knows how to affirm honor would have the right to speak of real peace. Without honor and honesty, what peace is altogether possible?

The fine for the violation of a peaceful state of life is an extremely precise and universal demand. It includes not only a violation of public safety, as foreseen by police regulations, but can cover a much wider and more necessary field.

When we speak of the protection of cultural treasures, this will also be a struggle against the violation of a peaceful condition of life. When someone puts a lawful restraint against cruelty, this also will be a care for the same peaceful life. When people work for the elimination of everything harmful in human evolution, this also will be the defense of the same sacred and beautiful peace, the striving for which still exists in the depth of the hearts of mankind.

Innumerable sayings about peace exist in the covenants and laws of the East and the West. From the most ancient antiquity, there stand before our eyes the radiant images of great lawgivers—born peacemakers. In the whole classical world, one can trace many strivings to the same noble ideal. Not without reason have we now remembered the *fredum* of the old laws of the Franks. The period preceding the medieval ages was always considered the darkest epoch. But even from this epoch, despite the "price of blood," resounded the striving for the defense of peace.

In one of our last diary leaves, we spoke of peace unto the whole world. For the realization of such a broad and sacred concept, one must abide by many peaceful conditions, the violation of which, even from the point of view of primitive laws, would be considered a crime. Let us not be misled by the idea that such peaceful understanding is regulated only by pompous international conferences. They exist in all of our relationships. Therefore, first of all, let us be extremely cordial and thoughtful toward each other. Let us realize the necessity of tolerance and patience. If we were to reiterate these foundations an endless number of times, it would not be superfluous according to the present conditions in the world. From obeisance to peaceful laws, there is born a renaissance of honor and dignity. These eternal concepts can never be considered as fossilized remnants but will remain forever as the basis of a wise and enlightened evolution.

The true safeguarding of peaceful conditions will attract to itself the success of which so much is said and for which so little is done. Nothing is easier than to break a precious vessel. But even if it be glued together, it will yet remain forever a damaged invalid. Therefore, create in benevolent inexhaustibility beautiful vessels. Adorn them by the best thoughts and dedicate these vessels of life in your innermost heart to the great peace of the world.

Tzagan Kure, June 7, 1935

MEMBRA DISJECTA

SET, the god of darkness, scattered the limbs of Osiris throughout the world. Isis, disconsolate, collected the scattered parts and then joyfully set them together. We know of similar legends in other lands, and from the most remote times, people have feared dismemberment and dreamed of unity. The Tower of Babylon is symbolic; for by stimulating the people's sensuous egoism, it ended in a deplorable division of languages.

From the most ancient times, we have heard of some sort of unity, of wholeness of body. This cannot mean that all people adhere together like a single body, or that the walls of our houses should fall and all life be mingled like water in a bottle.

It is evident, then, that it is spiritual unity that has been aimed at everywhere and from time immemorial. It was long ago proclaimed, as in a dream, that if people abandoned the condition of beasts and came to trust one another with love, faith, and hope, the mother of these three, Eternal Wisdom, would guard against all senseless quarrels and misunderstandings.

It is possible, of course, to set love, faith, and hope in any order that one pleases, although there will be always those who hold that one of them takes precedence over the others. All these principles of life, however, must be taken to heart, whatever their order of sequence may be.

Without hope, one cannot advance; without faith, there is no refuge; without love, you will become a monster. Without these three luminous daughters, the mother will not appear, for upon what else is the Great Wisdom founded?

Humanity has been broken up and disunited through forgetfulness and by wandering off the highway of evolution—both of which are inadmissible.

How are we to collect the scattered limbs of Osiris, when Isis, despite her wisdom, remained disconsolate, for she was well aware of all those obstacles that had been artificially created to prevent unity.

At present, when the scattered limbs are further apart than ever and disjoined by chaos and gigantic upheavals, unity is all the more difficult to attain.

Leagues and councils have been summoned, many of them sincere in their intentions, and all have made an effort to remind humanity of what was so urgently needed. The fate of such institutions and their helplessness when it comes to a practical solution is obvious.

Messengers of goodwill are passing through the world, many of them not known to political circles, but above all such efforts for peace, we continually hear the order being given to adhere "to strict business principles."

And as a result of such principles, we get fresh rifts and further signs of disunity.

It is impossible to encroach upon anyone's soul because this home of higher feelings is not subject to "strict business principles"?

Without heart and soul, however, business principles merely degenerate into a gnashing of teeth, a dance of death, a rattling of dry bones, in which all hope of ever uniting the world into one body is impossible.

Hurricanes, earthquakes, droughts, and floods ought to recall the fact that strict business principles are inadequate and that when fires have broken out, persuasive words will only turn to ashes.

These strict business principles, in all their ugly conventionality, are most probably at the root of all of our divisions. People no longer think of mutual assistance, prosperity, or future good fortune but only of covering sheets of paper with figures, which may be relied upon to make a total but are deeply misleading in their meaning.

Something inimical to the structure has insinuated itself into the foundation of our thinking, and the building falls.

Every useless destruction, every case of mutual oppression, will only tend to scatter and isolate the limbs of humanity.

If anyone full of goodwill toward his neighbor is met only with abuse and threatening lists, then what sort of an agreement can be made?

Are not the messengers of goodwill often enough little more than tragic or comic figures? The ambassador whose speech is full of goodwill while his pockets hide loaded revolvers can hardly be admired.

Bookkeeping, with its double and triple entries has now become all important, although the budgets of almost all countries are now in deficit and the only thing that unites them is their common debt. If one were indebted to a good neighbor, all would be well, since one can always come to an agreement with what is good. Goodness and kindness can overcome all obstacles.

If all of our plans run in evil channels and are partitioned off by "strict business principles," then it will be difficult to cross these barbed wire fences, and all of our benevolent feelings are likely to dry up. One should not imagine that the withered blossoms of benevolence have no influence on the world's harvest, or that a dried-up root will not stop the growth of other roots. Evil, once it is sown, produces the most unexpected seeds and this often enough at long intervals.

May God preserve the world from such seeds!

We have often read in fairy tales of dead water and living water by which the limbs of heroes, scattered abroad by evil agents, were made whole again.

Popular wisdom, then, has always foreseen that the body of the hero will eventually be restored. Sometimes the hero is destroyed by the envy of his brothers or relatives, but in the end, the popular wisdom of these old tales always restored the scattered parts.

Historical problems are generally solved in the popular consciousness, and if not settled at the round table, they find their cultural-historic solution in the life of the people. Much has been destroyed by violence, but much has also been built from the life of the people and the solutions discovered in their consciousness.

If one speaks with the wise ones among the people, they will tell one that the scattered limbs of humanity will eventually be joined together again. The steady toil and creation of the worker is something that goes deeper than any "strict business principle." By his constant and unswerving activity, he is welding together the scattered limbs of humanity. That which is not settled within the narrow limits of the round table is decided on the immense stretches of the harvest field.

And the Mother Sophia, the Great Wisdom, how can she be disconsolate since she is the Mother, the Great Wisdom?

VANDALS

THINGS are beginning to be chaotic and unsettled on this earth. The planet has never been very stable; but at the present moment, there would seem to be, according to the reports, a sort of whirlwind of destruction.

From Paris one of our friends writes: "Today we saw a film, taken in Spain, which showed the destruction caused by air raids over Barcelona. The effect was very depressing. Immense buildings were cut in two, as if by a knife; one of these was pulverized, the other still stood with all its rooms open to view and occupied, and one could see the corpses lying everywhere. There was a school that showed how scores of children had been slain, and on the half-demolished platform, the dead body of the teacher. The Spanish Government has arranged an exhibition to show how artistic and historic treasures were destroyed, together with the measures adopted for their preservation. These consist of the exportation of transportable art treasures and the protection of the historic monuments by means of sandbags. No doubt you have also read the plan of "Geneva Refuges" for children and aged people, all of which, however, is only a palliative. Not long ago, at a banquet of the Institute of Higher International Studies, it was agreed that our Pact would be preferable to such measures because of its moral and cultural value. At the same time, everyone agreed that its eventual adversaries, whom we know by their action in Spain, China, and Ethiopia, will not hesitate to violate the Pact or the General Convention of the Red Cross."

In Red Cross circles, they are quite convinced of this. Thus humanity has so far deviated from the principles of culture and civilization that even the Red Cross is beginning to lose its significance.

And here is another letter. "All the strange discussions in matters of defense that are going on today having nothing in common with our Pact. We are speaking of an international cultural agreement on a humanitarian line while they speak of sandbags."

The idea of burying lofty cathedrals under sandbags is as absurd as to speak of abolishing the Red Cross and wrapping every soldier up in sand bags. The idea of burying national treasures, moreover, has a prehistoric flavor about it. Recently, one of the English ministers, Mr. Eden, foresaw that, in the future, terrified city folk might be obliged to flee to the caves and cellars like the troglodytes of old. Let the worldy-minded, then, adopt such primitive methods and bury their treasures.

All this, however, is so far from the spirit of our Pact that it would be a very easy matter to show our priority and the little value such measures have when compared with a cult for the art treasures of all mankind.

Caricaturists could find matter in these methods, for they might depict a cathedral smothered up to the spires in sandbags, so as to illustrate the biblical warning: "Build not upon the sand."

If humanity is to abandon all its highest principles and stake all its hope on sandbags, then it has come to a very sorry pass.

Everything today justifies us and our friends in issuing a call to defend all national treasures. It is said that when the ostrich gets wind of danger, it thrusts its head beneath its wing or in the sand. Natural history is full of such examples, and we might do worse than study the life of ants and bees who possess superb organization.

In every periodical we look at today we come across illustrations of barbarous destruction. Such documents will continue to live as a shameful witness of what has been done by the humanity of our times, although the whole of mankind is, of course, not necessarily engrossed in such destruction. But such acts are being perpetrated before the eyes of all, and when we figure the percentage of those who raise their voices to protest, it is not overwhelming. In any street accident, you will find four classes of people around you: those who make a genuine effort to help, those who congregate from mere curiosity, those who draw off in fear; and, finally, those who take a pleasure in the misfortune of others. And with vandalism it is all the same. Whether active or passive, they are the same uncultured destroyers. Toleration toward evil differs little from evil itself, and it is high time for humanity to give attention to the passive type of vandal. Before our eyes, all kinds of destruction are going on, either from the bombs of totalitarian warfare or from human poisoning of one sort or another. It is a question of which sort of poison is the more ruinous—that of poison gas or that which aims at the destruction of culture. In the so-called peaceful communities, anticultural processes are now taking place on a large scale, while people remain silent or crowds are divided, as in the case of street accidents. At such times, alas, the number of those who exert themselves on behalf of culture is extremely small, while the crowd of those who are curious or malignant takes on huge proportions.

All these curious or evil-minded people try to excuse their conduct, but they are unwilling to reflect that, in so doing, they range themselves alongside the vandals.

All who evade joining in the defense of culture enlist in the ranks of passive vandals. In passivity there is always a kind of activity, which can be very dreadful and repulsive, with consequences that may bring about the disintegration of an entire nation.

The passive vandal ought not to imagine that his silence has not effect.

On the contrary, history exposes not only the active vandal but also those who stood by idly and looked on while torture and destruction were being committed.

How heartless, how cruel are all those who feign deafness and remain silent when they ought to cry out!

We have spoken of defending everything that helps with the evolution of the human race.

Defense is one thing, but aggression is quite another. We have issued a call not to bury ourselves under sandbags but to counteract destruction through the power of thought, of culture.

Traces of culture are being destroyed, obliterated, and scattered abroad, and, in allowing this, mankind has composed a page of history that will look very black in the future.

The doings of such brutal destroyers and tortures will be recorded together with the fact that a vast portion of humanity connived and assisted in such vandalism.

There are many ways of participating in such crimes. One need not launch a bomb oneself from the airplane; there are also those who manufacture bombs and invent arms and engines of destruction. One can stand opposed to cultural undertakings and destruction, distortion of constructive thoughts, bring on a condition of savagery.

From such premeditated schemes, the dispersal, dismemberment, and annihilation of whole groups of accumulated treasures can arise. Everyone who by deed or thought contributes to such destruction must be included with the vandals who play havoc with the human spirit.

Terrible deeds are going on in the world. Devastating wars are no longer known as wars. The most dire destruction goes by the name of "change of policy" while the vandals strut around in new uniforms and trappings and look upon themselves as the arbiters of destiny. Does it matter which way man rushes to fratricide and self-destruction? Perhaps we shall have a new march composed someday for those who proceed toward criminal vandalism.

Yet there is this enormous majority of curious and malicious onlookers, this odious *tertius gaudens*, who fail to understand that they themselves are furthering all sorts of vandalism.

Toleration in participation is a crime.

Man must raise his voice against vandalism.

REQUIREMENTS

"**N**EVER become intoxicated or tell lies; never do anything that can injure another. Always be neatly and cleanly dressed. Shave each morning. Never be drawn into a disorderly competition with others. Never despoil anyone. Never enter into an agreement with merchants for a concerted fraud. Never accept a commission for anything purchased. Never do anything that could mar the honor and dignity of Turkey."

Such a document must be signed by each guide in Turkey. He not only must sign it but with all of his moral qualities must abide by it in all of his life, in all of his actions. Thus, he has finally discovered where the ideal people live. Truly, the man who is able to fulfill these ten commandments ought not to be a guide but, at the very least, a member of parliament or a minister.

Of course, it would be unseemly if the modest guide should possess valor and such other perfections as are not always assumed to exist, even in the case of higher ranks of the government. By this I have no wish to affront Turkey; I have never had occasion to be there. But in many other countries, these qualities required of the unassuming guide could be a true adornment of any citizenry.

Do not think that I am censuring in any way the document quoted. On the contrary, that country in which such an exacting document comes to life deserves both encouragement and sympathy. Even from the point of view of preserving cultural values, the document cited will be unusually noteworthy. Strange as it may be, so often the fate of cultural values rests precisely in the hands of guides. They are the ones who recite reputations.

If one recalls the different sayings of guides as well as all the statements of guidebooks and tourist brochures, one may be convinced as to how much upon them depends the reputation of historical memorials, if not of entire countries. Not so long ago, we had occasion to read that in one state there were excluded from sale some newly published atlases, in which were retained some old boundary lines that might be upsetting to the dignity of the country.

Likewise, I recall how we urgently wished to transmit a sum of money to Tallinn from a remote telegraph station but could not do so because the telegrapher was convinced that Reval was still in Russia and he knew nothing whatever about Estonia. And, too, I remember a certain guide who, pointing out in a museum an old Spanish-Hebrew armchair, assured us that it was in this armchair that Moses received the Commandments on Mount Sinai. We need not adduce a great number of anecdotes from the lives of guides and from guidebooks. It remains absolutely beyond question that not only much historical truth but also a multitude of reputations are actually left in the hands of these guides.

Meanwhile, in many countries there are established entire ministries of tourism that are certainly bound up with the existence of guides and guidebooks. Let us admit that the publication of guidebooks is under the control of competent scholars. Yet in such a case, the guides, too, ought to pass certain examinations on the subject of those historical memorials, which it is their duty to explain to the public.

Thus, to the ten rigid but just regulations for guides, there should be added one more—that they should be well acquainted with that subject that they talk about. Indeed, if to the stern requirements of the ten regulations, there should be added sound, well-founded knowledge, then the guides would likely be made the most respected people in the state. In the last analysis, this is not far from the truth. Whoever is entrusted with meeting foreigners and fairly informing them of the cultural values in his native land will be a most necessary and respected citizen.

The more so will a man deserve respect who knows the true values of his own country, in that even many of the oldest living inhabitants do not always know the noteworthy features of their native city. So many times one has had occasion to encounter people who have an official position, yet who were not only completely uninterested in the notable memorials within the limits of their province but even, in a sense, really knew nothing about their own native city. If you should make an inquiry of them about it, they would waive the matter aside, sending you either to the local keeper of records or to a society of enthusiasts of the place, the address of which would frequently be unknown to them. These local societies would not only be difficult to locate, but it would be no less difficult to find out their business hours.

Again we have no wish to condemn, since we know very many of the conditions of life and the prejudices that surround these people who are devoted to cultural work. Of course, up to the present, so often have they been obliged to be true ascetics and to be exposed to all sorts of ridicule and abuse. Each mechanic in the city will consider them parasites or, at best, needless archive members. Such individuals may even be found who are proud of the fact that they know nothing about history and all the public memorials of culture. Of course, it has been remarked many times that everything humanitarian is relegated by some to last place.

Indeed, all this takes place, to speak simply, as a result of ignorance, but there is nothing consoling in such a conclusion. Only in recent times have people crept out beyond the limits of their homes and become accustomed to travel. As to this, the Belgian King justly remarks, "People cannot lead healthful lives if they seal up all the doors and windows. It is as if a little fresh air is beginning to be sensed in the world."

Each physician can discourse about the harm of sealed

doors and windows. Therefore, so timely is the comparison made by the Belgian King. It is needful to become accustomed to this opening of doors and windows. In these preparations, the question with which we started out, namely that of guides, is a very essential one. Ministries of tourism remain in one secluded spot, but guides spread out over the face of the entire country. They give out information not only about memorials of times past but, in passing, they necessarily touch upon contemporary creativeness. And in both matters, they roust not, even involuntarily, spreading false and damaging accounts.

All this is so well understood, yet at the same time so undeferrable and indispensable.

A certain guide told a visiting foreigner about how it took several centuries to erect a certain building.

To this, the visitor replied that in his country, at the time, the building of such a structure would not require more than one year. The guide felt resentment about the memorial of his native country. The next day, when they were continuing the survey of the city, the foreigner inquired about some prominent building, whereupon the guide replied, shrugging his shoulders, "I can't say. It wasn't even here yesterday."

FEARS

"THE sun set. Forest murmurs began. The crowns of old oaks appeared as monstrous silhouettes. The gigantic pines turned red. Flowers glimmered like horrible eyes. The ravines became pitch black and the boulders protruded like huge skulls. Look, what a terrible face the forest shows!

"The crane hurried into the meadow and gabbled: "Beware, beware!" and disappeared behind the trees.

And above, in the foliage, the raven croaked: "*Finis! Finis!*"

The thrush above screamed: "Terrible! Terrible!"

The oriole whistled: "Oh, you poor fellow!"

From the top of the tree appeared a starling that took pity: "A good lad is lost. Pity. Pity."

And the woodpecker persisted: "Let him, let him!"

The magpie gossiped as if in the bazaar: "Let us rush to tell them. Let us rush to tell them!"

And even the peaceful bullfinch squeaked: "It is bad, very bad!"

"How many fears! From the earth, from the trees, from the sky—whistling, crackling, and hissing. It seemed as if all the snakes rose from the grass—no help, no escape! And on the path there was standing the bear himself. What else, if not a bear, could that black spot be? And these flashing lights are not fireflies but also something horrible.

"Under the enchanted rock, an unknown wizard had settled. And he caught birds with ingenious traps. And he taught every bird one word. And the wanderers became frightened and pale, hearing this horrible judgment of the birds. And the wizard smiled; he listened to the birds and they brought no fear to him. Only he was aware that they knew no more and could say nothing else."

Are not all horrible words like this gabbling of birds? And is not the terrible bear but a rotten tree stem? And are not the ghostly snakes but twigs in the grass? And who are these mysterious wizards who teach the gospel of fear? Who was the primogenious being who, in a language unknown to us, for the first time uttered the cursed word "fear"? And was this first fright a real horror, or was it a ghastly mirage? But millenniums and cruel atavism embodied this first cry of horror into generations. The inexperienced youth and grey wiseacres in sinister unison began to sing the hymn of fear. There was created an entire cult of horror. But what has a striving, honest man to fear?

All the lightning and thunder of the Universe teach us that there is nothing to fear—one has but to know. The wise heart convinces the brain that fear is the most absurd invention. The highest ordainments proclaim that the human spirit is eternal and cannot be harmed. People read this Truth, and yet the habit of atavism, of fear rips them and crushes them to the earth. They do not listen to the voice of the heart. Science itself comes to aid the heart. All the latest strivings of science prove that knowledge frees man from fear. How many wonderful basic energies are unveiled by science! And human life can be absolutely transmuted.

But *terror antiquus*—the ancient terror still reigns. People still fear to know. For the majority of people, science is still sorcery. *Horribile dictu*, but humanity is not far from medieval superstitions, when for every desire to know, people were burned at the stake or beheaded. It makes no difference that the inquisition of today applies, instead of fire, still more cruel methods. Fire destroyed the body, but many other methods torture the spirit; and in their evil inventiveness, they subject the world to convulsions of horror. Under various pretexts, by various forms of scarecrows, someone tries to prohibit and deny. We all know these deniers. And what is at the bottom of this crass ignorance? Open the crude-colored feathers of the bloated ignoramus and you will discover the grey feather of fear—and as the hair stands on end, so does this feather rise, not from noble indignation but from ugly fear alone.

Every cognizance is already fearless. And liberated science is also fearless. Everyone ascending the summit, at the moment of having made this decision, already rejects fear. There is deep significance in the advice that one should apply medicinal help against fear. So much is said about suggestion. Research of psychic energy becomes a science, and should not all sciences be turned first of all toward the annihilation of fear?

Fear is an attribute of ignorance. Fear is poison. Fear is fossilization. Fear is paralysis. Fear is defeat. Fear is decay. Fear is destruction. Fear is annihilation.

In *The Ring of the Nibelung,* the sorcerer Mime tests Siegfried because a hero is needed who does not know fear. Mime tries to frighten young Siegfried with abominable horrors, but the hero simply does not know what fear means. Mime describes to him the terrible dragon, but Siegfried only asks where he can find the monster. The spirit of the hero does not know the shackles of fear.

Every hero, when seeking attainment, is free from fear. All ordainments preach fearlessness as the motive power of evolution.

From the East resounded the great ordainment: "*Ma bhayi*" "Fear not!"

In response to this mighty command, there thundered from the depths of ages: "Warriors, warriors, we call ourselves. We fight for noble virtue, for lofty effort, for sublime wisdom. For this reason we call ourselves warriors!"

SHANTI

ORION shines in full radiance. We remember how before the bow of our steamer this same constellation was shining. We remember in what mountains and from behind what peaks was shining Orion—the Magnificent. And now we know precisely to whom it is shining and who is looking at it. The same heavenly Signs!

*   *   *

In the Temple of Heaven, we also found the sign of the Banner of Peace. The tagma of Tamerlan has the same sign. The sign of the three treasures is widely known in many countries of the East. On the chest of a Tibetan woman, one can see the large fibula representing this sign, the same fibula we see in Caucasian archaeological finds and in Scandinavia. The Madonna of Strasbourg has this sign, just as have the Saints of Spain. Upon the icon of Saint Sergius and Saint Nicholas is the same sign. Upon the chest of Christ in the famous painting of Memling, the sign is immortalized as a large fibula clasp. When we look over the sacred images of Byzantine and Rome, the same signs unite the Holy Images throughout the world. India also knows this great triune sign.

The consciousness of people, in their multiform striving toward the Highest, was united upon the same steps. In the desire to express the Highest, precisely the multiformity of approaches is such a precious sign.

On mountain passes inviolably stands this sign. To convey the concept of speed, hurriedness, and necessity, the Sign is carried by a White Steed. And haven't you seen this same sign in the Roman catacombs?

Yet there are people who will not wish to think of the Highest but will try to attach to this sign some of their personal, bemeaning considerations. But then one could equally say about many other great signs that they were used for a different meaning and for seemingly different purposes. In such expressions, man will, all the sooner, manifest his own self.

When taking a stranger into your home, you can at once discern his nature by the degree of his attention shown toward surrounding objects. There are people who, standing before a beautiful picture, will pay attention to the gilded frame. Others, looking at the Venus de Milo, will find no better question to ask than, "But where are her arms?" Another approaching a miraculous icon will mention the unattractiveness of the image because of the austerity of its expression. There will be found people who, finding themselves amid beautiful objects, will pay attention to the most insignificant.

Ex ungue leonem—by the claws one knows the lion. Likewise one can say, "By the dirt, you will know the mice." It is sometimes even said to listen to people judging that which they do not know and to which they even do not give a thought. Besides, they judge only according to their desire to praise or condemn. Not knowing how to argue, such condemners will put forth simply their yes or no. They will not try, not even for their own sake, nor out of mere decency, to provide themselves with some arguments: for them, the only thing worthy of consideration would be either the place, the personality, or the time in relation to that which they affirm or deny. In their denials they are ready to pronounce any slander; they will never stop before blasphemy, if only to carry out their evil prejudice. The great seer, Gogol, expressed the same thought in these sad words:

"We have the remarkable gift of making everything insignificant."

Precisely, great creators have always acutely felt the entire horror, when under their very eyes something great was made insignificant. At the same time, the methods of such belittlement were the coarsest and most ignorant. If a mere constable would have ordered these ignoramuses to state the opposite, they would not have hesitated to do so for a minute because their judgment had no foundation whatever. They merely thought that their ruler—vulgarity—would be pleased with it. And this command, of course, fully corresponds to their own selves.

Anyhow, in all malicious violations, the great basis—goodwill—is first of all absent. What a beautiful word—goodwill! It is in the same rank where the other precious concept—compassion—stands.

The malicious ignoramuses know neither one nor the other. Moreover, goodwill and compassion will disturb the vile mind as something reminiscent of the great and rejected by them. The evil gift of making everything insignificant must be emphasized and brand marked as the most shameful. What is hidden behind this evil gift? Treason has already nested there. If an evildoer did not succeed in falsifying something, he will continue his treacherous actions in order to bring his offering, in one way or another, to the abyss of darkness. Even among the simplest commonplace objects, you can notice to what man pays his foremost attention. In the same way, you may judge people according to their attitude to the great Signs.

From behind the Si-Shan sparkles the magnificent Venus. We know that you in the Himalayas are also admiring it. We know from where, across what valley, and above what snowy peaks, you look in the evening hours at it. We look at the star, and we hear the murmur of the deodars and all the twilight voices and all the sounds of the mountains. How many calls and how much knowledge has been gathered around this one star? The heavenly Signs make attentive and unite hearts.

The same stars, the same heavenly Signs, fill hearts with goodwill beyond space and time. Where is true vision, there is peace!

VISION

PEACE to all beings! What can be more majestic than the march under the Banner of Peace? What can be more wonderful than the participation in this march under the banner of peaceful labor and creative constructiveness of the hosts of youth, singing hymns of beautiful achievements!

Verily, our times are difficult because of all the commotions of the spirit, all non-understanding, and all the attacks of darkness against Light. But perhaps this terrible tension is but the impulse in order to direct humanity through all storms and over all abysses to peaceful construction and mutual respect.

Just think what an unforgettable, epoch-making day is before us, when over all the centers of Spirit, Beauty, and Knowledge will be unfurled the one Banner. This banner will call everyone to revere the treasures of human spirit, to respect culture, and to have a new valuation of labor as the only measure of true values. From childhood, people will witness that there exists not only a flag of the Red Cross, so nobly established for the protection of the health of the human body, but that there also exists a sign of peace and culture for the health of the Spirit.

Above all the treasures of the creations of human genius will wave the Banner, which itself says: "Here are guarded the treasures of all mankind, here above all petty divisions, above illusory borders of enmity and hatred, as the Fiery Stronghold of Love, Labor and the all-moving Creation."

The human heart wants real peace. It strives to

labor—creatively and actively. It wants to love and expand in the realization of Sublime Beauty. In the highest perception of Beauty and Knowledge, all conventional divisions disappear. The heart speaks its own language; it wants to rejoice at that which is common for all, uplifts all, and leads to the radiant Future.

To the Temple of Peace all the best thoughts of humanity should be directed. Beautiful rays of hope illumine mutual understanding. In all languages, in various symbols, in exalted prayers, the same thought is manifested as the most sacred one, as the most opposing to evil. And evil—this fruit of ignorance— finally will wither before the great image of Peace.

We will cement space with our imperative calls for peace, and this penetrating call will span all precipices of old prejudices. While everything about war and hostility is pronounced with averted eyes, each word of peace is proclaimed with a straightforward glance and an uplifted countenance. In the sacred conception of peace, we are creating a high, constructive enthusiasm, and everything constructive and everything of enthusiasm is the basis of the coming evolution. From the all-unifying fields of art and knowledge, permit me to express my best wishes that the idea of peace should flower and will bloom as a beautiful tree, yielding its shade to all peaceful travelers and creative workers.

People talk especially about peace when they are afraid of war. But there are different kinds of wars: internal and external, visible and invisible. Which of them are more horrible remains to be seen . . .

Peace—in this one word is expressed the whole essence. "To live in peace means never to raise arms against each other"—this commandment was given in all languages, in all ages.

When one studies symbols and tablets, one will find in all images and hieroglyphics the same desire—the sacred prayer for peace. Thus, in all religions the first word is "peace."

"Blessed be those who have pity for everything living" because "all living things together suffer and wail up to now"—they suffer together with man, they perish with man, and they are saved with him.

With bloody food, there enters into man the spirit of killing, the spirit of war. But the spirit of peace enters only through bloodless food.

"To man Truth was given!" The Truth: "Do not kill!" For everybody it is always possible not to kill, not to make war. "If you will kill, you will die. Give life and you will live"—a child understands this, and yet this is the mystery of mysteries.

It is truly beautiful if amid the turmoil of life, in the waves of unsolved social problems, we still may hold up before us the eternal flambeaux of peace in all ages. It is beautiful, through the inexhaustible well of love and tolerance, to understand the great movements that have connected the highest knowledge with the highest aspirations. Thus in studying and admiring, we are becoming real cooperators with evolution, and out of the brilliant rays of supreme Light may emerge true knowledge. This refined knowledge is based on real comprehension and tolerance. From this source comes the great understanding. And from the great understanding rises the Supremely Beautiful, the enlightening and refining enthusiasm of Peace.

Contemporary life is changing rapidly; the signs of a new evolution are knocking at all doors. In real, unconventional science, we feel the splendid responsibility before the coming generations. We understand gradually the harm of everything negative. We begin to value enlightened positiveness and constructiveness, and in this measure, in merciful tolerance, we can prepare for our next generation a vital happiness, turning vague abstractions into beneficent realities.

It has been repeatedly inscribed on the scrolls of command that a spiritual garden is daily in need of the same watering as a garden of flowers. If we still consider physical flowers the true adornment of our life, then how much more must we remember and prescribe to the creative values of the spirit the leading place in the life that surrounds us? Let us, then, with untiring, eternal vigilance, benevolently mark the manifestations of the workers of culture, and let us strive in every possible way to ease this difficult path of heroic achievement.

Equally so, let us mark and find a place in our lives for the Great Ones, remembering that their name is no longer personal, with all the attributes of the limited ego, but has become the property of panhuman culture and must be safeguarded and firmly cared for in the most benevolent conditions.

Thus, we will continue their self-sacrificing labor, and we will cultivate their creative sowing, which, as we see, is so often covered with the dirt of non-understanding and overgrown with the weeds of ignorance.

As a caring gardener, the true culture-bearer will not forcefully crush those flowers that entered life not from the main road, not if they belong to the same precious kinds that he safeguards. The manifestations of culture are just as manifold as are the manifestations of the endless varieties of life itself. They ennoble Be-ness. They are the true branches of the one sacred Tree, whose roots sustain the Universe.

Should you be asked of what kind of country and of what future constitution you dream, you can answer in full dignity, "We visualize the country of great culture." The country of great culture will be your noble motto. You will know that in that country will be peace, where knowledge and beauty will be revered.

The great Gautama Buddha has manifoldly ordained the conception of peace and culture. Peace—signifies an unceasing construction. Culture—means an eternal cognizance and the betterment of life through foundations of glorious progress.

Impractical and perishable is everything created by hostility. The history of mankind gave us remarkable examples of just how necessary peaceful creativeness was for progress. The hand will tire from the sword, but the creating hand sustained by the might of the Spirit is untiring and unconquerable. So the sword can destroy the heritage of culture. The human mind may temporarily deviate from the primary courses but at the predestined hour will have to reoccur to them with the renovated powers of the spirit.

The foundations of peace and culture verily make man invincible, and realizing all spiritual conditions, he becomes tolerant and all-embracing. Each intolerance is but a sign of weakness. If we understand that every lie, every fallacy will be exposed, it means that, first of all, a lie is stupid and impractical. But what has he to hide who has consecrated himself to peace and culture? Studying the foundations of the Teachings, he can do nothing that would clash with the noble because knowledge is needed for evolution; helping those near, he helps the general welfare, which in all ages has been appreciated. Striving to peace, he becomes a pillar of a progressing state. Not slandering the near, we increase the productiveness of the common creativeness. Not quarrelling, we will prove that we possess the knowledge of the foundations. Not wasting time in idleness, we will prove that we are true coworkers in the plough-field of Culture. Finding joy in each day's labor, we show that the conception of Infinity is not alien to us. Not harming others, we do not harm ourselves; and eternally giving, we realize that in giving we receive. And this blessed receiving is not a hidden treasure of a miser. We understand how creative is affirmation and how destructive is negation. Amid basic conceptions, those of peace and culture are the conceptions that even a complete ignoramus will not dare to attack.

We are not astonished that we have received so many enthusiastic responses to our peace banner. Mankind's past is filled with deplorably sad and irreparable destructions. We see that not only in times of war but also during other periods of error, the creations of human genius are destroyed.

At the same time, the elect of humanity understand that no evolution is possible without the cumulations of culture. We understand how indescribably difficult are the ways of culture. Hence, the more carefully must we guard the paths that lead to it. It is our duty to create for the young generation traditions of culture.

There where is culture is peace. There where is the right solution for difficult social problems is achievement. Culture is the cumulation of highest Bliss, of highest Beauty, of highest Knowledge. In nowise can humanity pride itself on having done enough for the flowering of culture. For after ignorance, we reach civilization; then gradually we acquire education; then comes intelligence; then follows refinement; and the synthesis opens the gates to High Culture.

If our Banner of Peace is the impetus that will urge such an achievement on behalf of universal treasures, this alone will be the fulfillment of a colossal task. How much of the useful and beautiful could be easily attained!

Let us imagine a universal Day of Culture, when simultaneously in all schools of the world will be extolled the true treasures of nations and humanity. Verily, the protection of the treasures of culture belongs among those all-unifying foundations that permit us to gather in friendship without petty feelings of envy and malice.

We are tired of destruction and negation. Positive creativeness is the fundamental quality of the human spirit. In our life everything that uplifts and ennobles our Spirit must hold the dominant place. The milestones of the glorious path must from childhood impel our spirit to the beautiful future. Be assured, it is not a truism to speak about the undeferrable and urgent strivings of culture.

Let us realize how many highly useful projects can be easily introduced into life. I return to my long-cherished idea of a World Day of Culture. Cenotaphs recall the past. But everything connected with culture, with innumerable martyrdoms and magnificent attainments, impels our minds toward the future. Only think with what simple means, if acting in primary unity, humanity could establish traditions that would guide the young generations.

Let us welcome all those who, surmounting personal difficulties and casting aside petty selfishness, propel their spirits to the task of preserving culture, which above all, will insure a radiant future.

We must not fear enthusiasm. Only the ignorant and the spiritually impotent would scoff at this noble and unsullied feeling. Such scoffing is but the sign of inspiration for the true Legion of Honor. It would be outrageous if in touching on the great manifestations such attributes as "small" and 'little" were used. Thus, we should beware of committing that most hideous of all acts— disparagement. This would signify decay. Nothing can impede us from dedicating ourselves to the service of Culture, so long as we believe in it and give to it our most flaming thoughts.

Do not disparage! The great Agni singes the drooping wings. Only in harmony with evolution can we ascend! And nothing can extinguish the selfless and flaming wings of enthusiasm!

May the beneficial symbols, may the Banner of Goodwill be unfurled over everything by which the human spirit exists.

Peace to all Beings!

IV

FROM BEYOND

COMBATING IGNORANCE

THE extermination of ignorance should be carried out on a world scale. No nation can boast that it is sufficiently educated. Nobody has sufficient strength to conquer ignorance single-handedly. Knowledge should be universal and should be supported in full cooperation. Ways of communication know no limitations. Thus also the path of knowledge should flourish through exchange of opinion. One should not think that somewhere enough has already been done for education. Knowledge spreads to such an extent that a constant renewal of methods is required. It is horrible to witness fossilized brains, which do not admit new achievements. No denier can ever be a true scientist. Science is free, honest, and fearless. Science can change instantaneously and can enlighten upon world problems. Science is beautiful and, therefore, is infinite. Science does not tolerate prohibition, prejudice, and superstition. Science can find the great even in the quest of the small. Ask great scientists how often the most astonishing discoveries took place during ordinary research. The eye was open and the brain was not dusty. The path of those who know how to investigate without limitations is the Path of the Future. Verily the struggle against ignorance is undeferrable, as against decomposition and decay. Combating evil ignorance is not easy, for it has many henchmen. It lurks in many countries and is clothed in various garments. One has to apply courage and patience, for the battle with ignorance is the conquest of chaos.

Already five centuries before our era, there came from the East the blessed words: "Ignorance is the worst crime." Later on the great hermits of the first centuries of Christianity also ordained that "Ignorance is hell." Truly all fratricidal crimes have their origin in this dark abyss. The same evil source pollutes the world with lies and darkness, which create the most ugly, the most cruel, and abhorrent evildoings.

To swallow food does not yet mean to live. In the same way to be literate does not mean to be educated. Literacy is a natural food, but we see that as food it may be either useful or harmful because it can serve both good and bad. Education and culture are synonymous. In both is contained readiness for infinite cognizance. In the furnace of such a constant rejuvenation of consciousness, the very essence of man is being purified. Through the honest and unlimited labor of knowledge, people are ennobled and begin to understand the concept of service to humanity. The true scholar has an open eye and is moved by freedom of thought. But as everything in life, the eye and thought must also be educated. From the first steps of education an enlightened admission and broadening of the horizon should be laid at the foundation of primary schools. Knowledge should be freed from conventional limitations. Knowledge is the path to joy, but joy is a special wisdom.

The scientist and the artist know the meaning of the word inspiration. They know, what is realization, which opens to them new refined forms and reveals subtle energies previously unnoticed or perhaps forgotten. From antiquity there came the realization that thought is an energy, that thought is light-bearing. For ages certain people knew that thought can be transmitted. But even such an old axiom has only lately entered the scientific minds before the very eyes of our present generation. We all were witness, how quite recently the ignoramuses scoffed at so-called magnetism and hypnotism. It went so far that the same force under various names was accepted differently. Mesmerism was ridiculed and condemned, but the same force under the name of hypnotism received a certain right for existence. There are peculiar reasons why some pills have to be gilded and medicine phials have to be adorned with special attractive labels. And one can understand why some chemicals, which are now fully recognized, had to be veiled by the alchemists under the names of the eagle and the phoenix, and many other symbols.

We all remember how at the foundation by Prof. Bekhterev of the Neurological Institute, every sceptic ridiculed his experiments of thought transmission. The fact that the name of Bekhterev was widely revered and renowned did not save him from derision and not even from most formidable suspicions. Ignoramuses organized a whispering campaign, stating that a whole institution could not be devoted to the research of the nervous system and thought alone. They whispered of some political intrigues, about some love affairs, and even that Bekhterev had become insane. Such were the colossal allegations invented by ignorance. I remember how during this whispering campaign we painfully remembered the book by Gaston Tissandé *Martyrs of Science.* Verily, where are the limits when during our present generation a certain academy called the great Edison a charlatan for his invention of the phonograph, and certain universities did not admit women to higher education. I repeat that this happened not during the medieval ages but before our very eyes, and such shameful actions were committed not by illiterate savages but by people bearing the conventional official label of a scientist. Let us not enumerate the endless row of true martyrs of science in all countries; but since we quoted the persecution of education for women, let us also recall the case of the mathematician genius, Sophie Kovalevskaya, who was not admitted to any university and yet received world recognition for her work on higher mathematics. And there are not a few excellent scholars and physicians, who being persecuted by their colleagues were compelled to leave their own country.

The world is proud of the name of the great physiologist Pavlov; everywhere are being affirmed and admired his formulae of reflexes and other ingenious solutions of biological problems. But even this glorious international achievement crowned by the Nobel Prize, calls forth in certain circles a contemptuous shrugging of the shoulders. Amid the latter one, one will also discover ignorance. Verily no uniforms and robes, no dead scholastic labels can cover human hatred, envy, and bigotry. It is far easier to combat illiteracy than to annihilate the sinister hydra of hatred, with all of its many heads of jealousy, doubt, slander, and all hidden campaigns, which the forces of darkness so cunningly manipulate. The forces of darkness, the forces of ignorance—these shameful synonyms—are closely united. Of all feelings, love and hatred are the most powerful and unifying.

Of course, in spite of all ferocious attempts of ignorance, enlightened knowledge progresses in the whole world. Let us remember the recent achievements that made the world rejoice. Let us remember the remarkable discovery of the great biologist Sir Jagadis Bose concerning the life of plants. Professor A. H. Compton states that human thought is the most important factor of the world. Prof. S. Metalnikov of the Pasteur Institute makes most important research in the field of immunity and immortality of protozoa. Dr. Kotick investigates the transfer of sensitiveness. Dr. Walter Stempell of Müenster University proves the existence of invisible radiation of all living organisms. Dr. Paul Dobler of Heilbronn University affirms the existence of earthly radiation and its relation to the diving rod, which has till recently been ridiculed. Prof. Harry M. Johnson of Virginia University arrives at interesting conclusions regarding insanity. Dr. Otrian, in charge of a meteorological station in Germany investigates extraordinary cosmic influences. L'Abbe More, the French astronomer, makes the most interesting conclusions about sunspots. The American biologist Bernard Proctor investigates special life conditions on heights. The French scientist Dr. Levy Valency warns of possible epidemics of insanity. Dr. Riese experiments with the effect of rhythm. Dr. Bernard Reid, a British scientist, draws a parallel between ancient medicine and modern vitamin research. A Hungarian scientist discovers rays for invisibility. Everyone knows of the experiments of Professors Richet and Gilley and the research of Sir Oliver Lodge. Prof. V. van Haas of the Leiden University proves the impossibility of absolute zero. Dr. Kennon of Harvard speaks of the element of luck in scientific research. The chemist Mingley gives a bold prognosis of future discoveries. Prof. J. B. Rhine of Harvard and Prof. William McDougall have reached astonishing results at Duke University in the field of extrasensory perception and thought-transference. How many wonderful achievements! In every country there are enlightened scholars, who untiringly and fearlessly pioneer in the field of science. And still such great men remain solitary, and everyone in his field is subject to undeserved obstacles.

One can quote pages of research conducted lately that widen the frame of conventional thinking. Nature itself comes to aid every thinker. Sunspots, with all the deductions around them, of which the greatest authorities such as Sir James Jeans of Cambridge and Dr. C. G. Abbott of the Smithsonian Institute, remind us that the time is not far when ridiculed Astrology will turn out to be nothing less than a formula of Astrochemistry, and thus yet another branch of science will no longer be denied. People will understand that they are surrounded in life by powerful chemism and that they themselves represent the most refined and mighty chemical laboratory.

Everyone has read of the recently conducted experiments with the chemism of human secretions and radiation from the fingertips; some of these radiations are so powerful that they can kill harmful bacteria. Let us also remember the experiment of Prof. Yurevitch that proved that the energy radiated by man is a conductor and a connection that enables the combination of certain elements. And did not the famous experiments of Keely, which were so unjustly persecuted, prove the same? Thus the investigation of human radiation and psychic energy imperatively calls humanity toward an amazing transfiguration of life.

Ignoramuses like to scoff at the yogi of India. For them, walking on fire, sitting on water, the consumption of terrible poisons without effect, the stopping or acceleration of the pulse at will, the burial alive and return to life after several weeks—are but skillful tricks and charlatanism. But in the last issue of the *Modern Review*, there is an article, supported by photographs, on firewalking in Mysore. The journal quotes this in connection with the demonstration in London of the Kashmiri Khuda Bux, widely announced through the press of the whole world. Sitting on the water of the Ganges was regarded as charlatanism, and even people who had witnessed it whispered carefully: "Who knows, perhaps they were supported under the water." But quite recently, the British press reported the case of a woman, who lost weight to such an extent that this manifestation on the water was quite easy for her. The whole world was amazed to read about the striking phenomena of Theresa Neumann of Bavaria, and now the newspapers were filled with astounding accounts of Shanti Devi in Delhi, a girl of nine. This unforgettable case was verified by many reliable people.

From Latvia there comes news of the extraordinary ability of a girl of eight to read thoughts. There has also been registered a case of the reception of radio waves by a person without a receiver, and the astonishing faculty of two Italian boys to see through walls and other opaque objects. No doubt during the time of the Inquisition all these unfortunate persons, owing to their abilities, would have been burned at the stake. But even nowadays, the man who could catch radio waves mentally, had to go through a lunatic asylum! Let us also not forget the remarkable prevision and clairaudience of St. Joan of Arc, who saved France, but who for her abilities was burned on the pyre by the contemporary evil ignoramuses.

But not only the persons themselves who owned these extraordinary faculties but also those who conducted research in these fields have been subjected by ignoramuses up to now to endless persecution. Let us also remember the unjust scoffing to which the Society of Psychic Research was so often subjected, whereas the aims of the Society deserve full support. Every nucleus of a new unprejudiced scientific conquest is attacked. This creates an ugly sight. On one part, there are new educational institutions being opened, which by their very appearance seem to invite new research; yet on the other part, every unusual manifestation that did not enter into the elementary textbooks is not only ridiculed but also prosecuted. It means that the hydra of ignorance dwells not only in illiteracy but also in fossilized perception and in human hatred.

Every denial of Truth is ignorance and is harmful not only to the negator himself but to space as a whole. Opposition to Truth poisons space. But there exists a still more abhorrent action, when people who have also cognized Truth later turn away from it. Such shameful retreat into darkness is insane. One can find in the history of humanity that sometimes particles of Truth were realized, but afterward because of crass ignorance, certain pseudoteachers tried again to conceal from people these immutable facts. And actions resulted that in the future will be regarded as the most shameful pages of history. And without any proof of their inaccuracy, it was ordered to deny the obvious facts. As if a disbelief in the existence of the sun was commanded, because due to weak eyesight, somebody could not look at the sun. Thus owing to ignorance and egotism, someone forbade others to cognize reality. Let people remember how many apostates reveal themselves at various epochs. Perhaps such remembrances will lead humanity to honesty and justice.

Thus everyone, for whom Education and Culture are not empty words, should, in his field as far as he can, fight ignorance. Let no one say that he has no possibility to do so—this would be untrue. *Hélas*, open and hidden ignorance in all its cunningness exists everywhere. In every household a clear mind can discern where dust and rubbish have to be removed. And today when in the world there thunder guns and poisonous gases compete with each other, now the combating of ignorance is imperative. A defense of the best, most beautiful and most enlightened will be needed.

If anyone does succeed in his noble efforts, still it will be a heroic attempt and not an abstract intention. Besides, in every effort there is already a vital element of action. Therefore, every effort is already beneficial. No doubt some servitors of ignorance will whisper that precisely now words about culture and enlightenment are out of place. This is their typical trick—to find at every moment of life a reason why exactly at that hour a striving to culture and education are untimely. By this formula, the henchmen of ignorance betray themselves. "Mine" always reveals himself. But Good, Culture, and Education are needed at every hour.

There can be no such a state of consciousness in which it is untimely to be humane. And only human hatred could whisper denying this Truth; hatred—this horrible monster, in the darkness of its cave, always dreams of transforming mankind into beasts that should devour each other.

Verily, from small to great, everyone can, and it is the duty of everyone to bring his might to the cause of combating ignorance. Uniting in groups and by himself, everyone somewhere can stop the evil doings of the monster of ignorance. Every labor already contains the striving to perfection and enlightenment. Only ignorance can belittle labor as such and can shamelessly scoff at the quest of science. In just indignation against every grimace of ignorance, the worker for Culture will find a vital thought and thundering word and will record by beautiful deeds the victorious path of enlightenment.

Glory to the Knights of Culture! Glory to the heroes of labor! Glory to the Courageous!

FROM BEYOND

THERE is a particular kind of people who call themselves skeptics and who require "material proofs," and yet in this, for each proof they will find some disproof of their own. If a witness to something appears, they will say that it simply seemed so to him. If a great number of witnesses come forward, it will very likely be declared that mass psychosis took place. If they see the impression of something on a material film, they will probably suspect some cleverly fabricated falsification. In this they lose sight of the fact that a man who is too suspicious of others bears within himself the germs of that very thing which he is so ready to impute to others.

Among all the forms of evidence, the most striking ones for skeptics will be signs that have appeared on material objects. If something appears upon a film that was not in front of the camera at the moment of exposure, then even a sworn doubter will be shaken in his confirmed skepticism, that is to say, in his ignorance. So many times each one has had occasion to meet with people who have solemnly declared that if proofs should be manifested to them, they would proclaim far and wide that of which they had been convinced. But when these proofs that they were awaiting appeared before their very eyes, not only did none of them proclaim anything publicly, but they continued quite coolly to wear the same mantle of skeptical complacence. Does one need to cite examples of this?

Let us leave for a while the matter of personal observation and for the time being disregard the great number of witnesses, while we recall several episodes in the field of photography. A large amount of literature has grown up regarding the question of photographing forms "from beyond." In a book by Kautz can be found a whole series of prints that it is difficult to suspect of any falsification. Likewise it is just as impossible to regard as spurious those accidental prints that the photographers themselves consider due simply to defective films. I recall how, once in India, a photograph was taken of a deceased person, and on the print beside the body appeared a whole row of figures, which those intimate with the deceased conclusively recognized as relatives of his who had preceded him in death. Likewise we have had occasion to see simple passport photographs upon which in the most unusual places appeared faces which could not be accounted for. Photographers have been chagrined at deteriorated films, but such "deterioration" can take place far oftener than may be supposed.

Quite recently there was communicated to us the following "mysterious" episode, which took place during the filming of a motion picture:

This amazing story which occurred on the set in one of the Hollywood studios was related by the distinguished American cinema artist, Warner Baxter. During the making of the picture sequences, in the course of the action, he was to represent a man mourning over the death of his wife. The actor was in great form, and the director remarked that never before in his life had he played his role with such verisimilitude.

That evening the film taken was run off in the projection room at the studio in the presence of the director. After several minutes he rushed to the telephone and called Baxter.

"Come immediately," he said in a trembling voice, "something absolutely unbelievable has happened."

Baxter hastened to the studio in an automobile. The director led him into the projection room and told the operator to return the film taken that morning.

That which Baxter saw on the screen stunned him also.

He saw himself seated in an armchair in an attitude of despair. Suddenly behind his back appeared quite perceptible lineaments of a woman's figure. Neither Baxter nor the director could find any explanation for this astonishing manifestation. The possibility of the unobserved appearance of an outsider before the camera during the filming was absolutely excluded. Likewise there could be no question of a technical trick. The cameraman affirmed on oath that he had used an absolutely immaculate roll of film.

The next day the taking of this same scene was repeated, with all measures of precaution being taken. When this second film was run off, the amazed spectators again saw this mysterious apparition behind the actor's back.

In the words of Warner Baxter, to this day he has not succeeded in accounting for this astonishing manifestation. Some of the cinema artists who believe in the occult sciences affirm that in the case cited there took place a manifestation of some particular spirit. Others affirm that the thoughts of the actor, attaining a high degree of tension, took on a material form. The fact that the mysterious specter appeared in both the successive exposures excludes any possibility of fraud or trick.

Let us set aside for a while carrying out to conclusion arguments as to precisely how to explain the unexpected appearance of the figure on the film. On those themes it is possible to discuss at great length, and for skeptics such conjectures will still be unconvincing. But the very appearance of the figure on the film, which was testified to by the many who saw this registration, remains indisputable. It is especially characteristic that the episode occurred twice. It is entirely impossible to form conjectures and conclusions about precisely what attendant circumstances could contribute to such a manifestation. Obviously there exist such conditions, complicated as viewed by human thinking, which do not as yet yield to formulation.

We have had occasion to hear in what unexpected conditions the most remarkable prints have resulted. Yet at the same time, when according to human reasoning, the "best" conditions were arranged, no results were obtained. Precisely the unexpectedness of manifestations especially arrests the attention. In this very unexpectedness vanishes any suggestion of fraud. And again, what falsification could be looked for in those cases, when people not only do not rejoice at the manifestations but on the contrary consider them simply deterioration of the films?

It has been related to us, how a friend of ours obtained from a photographer's studio a so-called unsuccessful photograph, upon which in different positions there had come out some strange unaccounted for faces. The photographer was extremely apologetic for such strangely spoiled film and did not even want to give away a negative, which in his opinion as unsuccessful. In this it is characteristic that the apartment itself of the photographer was quite the usual type, in which there were made numerous exposures every day. And our friend himself was in a most ordinary and worldly frame of mind, being completely removed from thought about anything extraordinary. Many times we have happened to hear that surprising manifestations occur not when they are expected by the human reason but precisely in the most unexpected circumstances. We have happened to see the furniture of rooms where remarkable prints had been made, and it was amazing that in such a drab atmosphere, anything unusual could take place. Evidently there exist especially subtle conditions that for the present elude human thinking.

Likewise by their own premature conclusions, people frequently destroy the possibilities of significant manifestations. The grossest judgments during the subtlest manifestations can only be harmful. Before making any arbitrary conclusions, one should, without prejudice, collect all the available facts. In this matter, let people call you materialists—it is unimportant how they shall define your methods. But first of all it is important to display impartiality in relationships. The film is a material object. No one will suspect the film and the photographic apparatus of anything "supernatural." But if these material objects note down something most subtle, it is all the same by what path and what method, provided the new facts penetrate into the human consciousness. Everything that broadens and bestows new possibilities must be accepted with gratitude.

If a noteworthy fact comes out, not in a specially constructed laboratory but amid the most worldly surroundings, then certainly this detail in no way belittles its true significance. It is possible to call to mind so many of the most useful discoveries made not by specialists in the particular field but sometimes, as it were, by casual workers. From the domain of metallurgy, we have had occasion to hear how specialists have paid attention to the particular methods employed by certain experienced workmen. Precisely these "casual" methods subsequently proved especially useful in the hands of specialists, forming them into an integral and significant improvement.

Specialists divide themselves into two camps. Some, even those who are serious scholars, arrogantly pass by the most interesting facts if they are not arrayed in scientific garb. Whereas the others, amid the most ordinary surroundings, know how to observe and to work out the most important improvements. Of course it is well known that there has been inspected only the most insignificant portion of brain activity. Not without reason has attention frequently been turned to the fact that human natural relationships have been studied least of all. Call these domains psychology or, circumstantially, reflexology; give them any names that can assist your experiments, but guard these most precious fields against light-minded outrage.

It is highly indicative that such books as Alexis Carrel's *Man, the Unknown* have reached ten editions and are considered the most widely circulated in the international market. Man is still striving for cognition. Apart from epidemics of dances and newly devised games, people in all countries are striving for enlightenment. News has reached us that at present in Moscow upon suggestion of the late Maxim Gorky, a colossal block of buildings covering 450 hectares is being erected, dedicated to the study of man. The central place is occupied by the All-Union Institute of Experimental Medicine. Research with goodwill is the first factor in advancement.

SIGNS OF OUR ERA

THE Institute of Psychosynthesis in Rome, under the directorship of Dr. Roberto Assagioli; several institutes of parapsychology in Germany; metapsychical institutes in France; courses of psychology at Duke University in North Carolina conducted by Prof. Rhine; the Psychoneurological Institute in Russia; the Institute of Physiology, in the name of Pavlov; courses in psychology held by Professor Jung in Zurich; The Eranos Foundation in Ascona in Switzerland; The Yoga Institute in Bombay. The Institute for Research in Evolutionary Biology in London; interesting researches of the Lister Institute in England; experiments of the Icelandian Professor Kohlman in thought-photography; a special chair for Psychic Research at the University in Stockholm, and the innumerable Societies for Psychic Research spread throughout the world. One can quote endlessly such and similar hearths of living thought, which strive toward expansion of new limits in science. If even these wonderful achievements are as yet not united and are often under the pressure of hypocrisy and conventionality, still every unprejudiced observer can convince himself that lately, as true signs of our epoch, the paths of liberated science are victoriously widened.

In the ocean of printed matter, it is difficult to summarize qualitatively and quantitatively the entire scope of what takes place. Besides, not all ways of communication are accessible to the self-sacrificing worker, who in most cases does not possess wealth and riches. Usually means are subsidized only in the case of obviously utilitarian experiments. Similarly in the Middle Ages, it was easier to find means for experiments in transmutation of baser metals into gold; and now the great leading might of thought is hardly ever appreciated by the narrow utilitarian and mechanical consciousness.

Of course, all sorts of conventions, congresses, and correspondence serve the purpose; but in these casual contacts, there is much unsaid and misunderstood, and thus contemplated deductions are again delayed. Yet one thing is clear—that the so-called spiritualization of science is gradually introduced everywhere. The hysterical shoutings of ignoramuses and all those who harbor evil intentions remain isolated in their destructive hatefulness. It is true, these thundering attacks of ignorance are still deafening, but public opinion, however, expresses a persistent desire to combat ignorance. In encyclopedias one can find instructive examples of how recently severely criticized researches of daring pioneers are already now evaluated more cautiously. Thus all devotees of knowledge, being ready to combat ignorance, can compile encouraging records of what has been attained recently.

Yet to fight ignorance is imperative and undeferrable. No one should lull himself in the erroneous idea that there is already sufficient knowledge. In infinity, cognizance never suffices. The more efforts there will be toward realization of knowledge, the madder and uglier will be the convulsions of ignorance. Was not Paracelsus, so highly venerated today, killed by enviers, who hated his attainments? Even we witnessed how the great Mendeleyeff was not elected to the Academy of Science, and yet he established the periodic table of atoms. There are further numerous examples when achievements have been appreciated far away from the birthplace of the discoverer. One remembers the significant words of Rabindranath Tagore after the bestowal of the Nobel Prize. The great poet and thinker said to a delegation that had come to congratulate him: "Why do you congratulate me today and not before?"

In the saving box of life, one can find many examples that are quite out of place and which in the future should not be repeated. The organized combat of ignorance, the self-sacrificing crusade for Culture, the defense of science against all destructive attempts should become the significant seal of our age. The beautiful might of thought! The realization of psychic energy.

Let us cordially meet every scientific movement. Let us find strength to liberate ourselves from personal habits and superstitions. Let us not think that it is easy to conquer atavism, for the physical strata carry in themselves the prejudices of many ages. But if we shall firmly realize the burden of such sediments, then already one of the most difficult locks will be opened. Later we shall also unlock the next, when we shall understand why we have to apply in the earthly world full action. Only in this way shall we reach the third entrance, where we shall understand the treasure of the basic energy entrusted to mankind. He who will teach to acknowledge it will be the true teacher. Man does not reach the realization of his might without a teacher. There are various traps on the path of man. Every hidden or manifested asp hopes to conceal from man the most precious. He as a lost traveler does not know in what element to search for progress, but the treasure is within himself. The wisdom of all ages ordains "Know thyself." This advice turns the attention to the most sacred, which is predestined to manifest itself. The fiery might, temporarily called psychic energy, will give man the path to his future happiness. We cannot hope that humanity will easily cognize its own heritage; they will invent all convictions to defile every discovery of the energy. They will pass in silence over the predestined quality of their advance, but yet, the path is one.

We shall never deny that we watch with the greatest enthusiasm the attainments of science. Be this in the Society of Psychic Research, or in the cause of thought transference at Duke University, or in the matter of photography of the invisible world—absolutely to all scientific experiments every cultural person should be well-wishingly open. The diary leaves "Combating Ignorance" give, as it were, a reply to uncultural conspiracies. The aims of the Society of Psychic Research, its highest form, and also all experiments concerning psychic energy should be met with welcome open-mindedness and thorough scientific control.

Only ignoramuses are not aware of how many most useful institutions and university courses for investigation of psychic phenomena have been started lately in many countries. Only ignoramuses do not want to know how many scientific books have been published in this connection by such eminent scientists, as for example. Dr. Alexis Carrel's *Man, the Unknown,* and so forth. Thus, let every uncultural attack upon science meet with a definite well-founded resistance; may the silly, militant ignoramuses remain in their own hole, as they deserve.

We shall always remain well-wishers toward all sincere seekers and pioneers. The psychic researchers, physiologists to whatever camp they may belong, are true pioneers of the science of the future. Subtle manifestations, the power of thought, as the basis of human creativeness and progress will find a deserved place of honor amid the attainments of evolution. "Study all surroundings," "Cognise untiringly!" "The Heart is infinite," "Winged is thought."

From the depths of the ages come many encouraging calls. The human-cooperator receives support from all strongholds of the ancient and new knowledge. The study of the progression of collective energy can prove that unity is not only a moral concept but a mighty psychic moving power. When we reiterate about unity, we wish to suggest the cognizance of the great force that is at the disposal of every human being. It is impossible for an inexperienced research worker to imagine how collective energy increases. One should prepare the consciousness for such a manifestation. The success of the experiment depends on the striving of all participants. If even a single person does not wish to cooperate wholeheartedly then it is better not even to experiment. The power of united force was already known in antiquity. Solitary observers sometimes united for joint research with the result that a whole chain was obtained, and the observers placed their hands on the shoulder of the predecessors. One could witness the most extraordinary fluctuation of energy; when the striving was uniform the intensification of energy was enormous. Thus when I speak of unity, I have in view a real force. May all those who should know it, remember this.

Psychic energy in antiquity was sometimes called the "air of the heart." This was meant to indicate that the heart lives by psychic energy. Truly, as man cannot live long without air, so does the heart cease to live without psychic energy. Many ancient definitions should be benevolently reconsidered. People long ago understood a manifestation that now has been neglected.

The magnetization of water placed near a sleeping person is already proof of the emanation of his radiations and of the deposit of energy on objects. One should carefully study such deposits, for they can remind of the duty of man to saturate the surroundings with beautiful sediments. Every sleep is not only a study for the subtle body but also a nursery for psychic accumulations.

Experiments with the expansion of depository forces are also most instructive. One can notice that energy evaporates in different degrees. Some powerful radiations can last decidedly longer when they are sent by pure thinking. Hence pure thinking is not only also a moral concept but the real multiplication of power. The ability to conceive the true meaning of moral concepts pertains to the domain of science. One cannot light-mindedly divide science into materialistic and spiritual—there is no borderline.

One should conduct observations not only of concordant manifestations but also of disuniting ones. An experiment is valuable when manifold. One cannot at the beginning of an experiment preclude what irradients will be needed for the intensification of the reaction. One can enlist the cooperation of most unexpected objects, for the faculties of subtle energies cannot be limited. Such an infinity of possibilities does not interfere with the scientific methods of research. One can apply individual methods and accept such new manifestations courageously. No one can indicate where human power is at an end. And precisely not a superman but every healthy person can become winged by happy achievements. In every household psychic energy can be studied. No special expensive laboratories are needed to educate the consciousness. Every age brings its own message to humanity. Psychic energy has the aim to help humanity amid its unsolvable problems.

Knowing how to patiently study war conditions are most favorable for the experiment. There may be cosmic conditions or bright color schemes or experiments with minerals or observations of animal life. One can observe how the presence of a person in an adjoining room reacts upon the current of energy. Man does not realize in what mood he is at a given moment. One may see that man will affirm his best mood, but the apparatus will show irritation or other bad feelings. Man will not hide his inner feeling because of a desire to lie, but more often because he is incapable of defining his perceptions.

Besides the investigation of psychic energy with regard to color, tests are also on sound and fragrance. One can obtain the convincing effects of music; noting the distance and the musical harmonies themselves. Much is spoken about the influence of music upon people, but practical experiments are seldom conducted. One may study the influence of music upon the mood of a person, but this is commonplace. Of course, it is presumed that gay music imbues with joy and sad music with sorrow, but such conclusions are not sufficient. One should ascertain what harmonies are nearest to the psychic energy of man. What symphony can most powerfully induce rest or inspiration in man? One must try out various musical compositions. The very quality of harmonization will give the best indications about the path of sound in human life. Similarly one should investigate the influence of fragrances. One should keep close aromatic flowers and various ingredients that can excite or decrease psychic energy. And finally one can unite color, sound and fragrance and study the cooperation of these three moving forces.

People will, after all, understand what mighty influences surround them. They will understand that the entire routine of their life manifests a great influence upon their fate. People will learn to pay more attention to every object. They will surround themselves by true friends and will escape destructive influences. Thus the salutary energy will help in the reorganization of life.

Usually least attention is given to the most important. But we shall not be tired to reiterate what is most needed for humanity. Amid such seeming repetitions, we shall affirm the desire for knowledge. People have become accustomed to somebody else thinking for them and that it is the duty of the world to look after them. But everyone should bring his own cooperation. The ability to apply one's psychic energy will gradually educate the consciousness.

In the family, in schools, in public life, there will be affirmed the cognizance of subtle energies. The art of thinking in all its beauty will again become the beloved sport—the true wings of humanity.

SANTANA

MIRA's last issue contains remarkable stories. Let us recall them:

A Miracle Boy – The activities of a "miracle boy," who is only three years old, have created a great sensation in Copalgung. He is the second son of Babu Jogendra Nath Makaker, a telegraph clerk of a local post office. The boy's name is Ananta Kumar. He remembers his past life and has been giving amazing incidents regarding a previous life. One morning, the boy, without any rhyme or reason, burst into tears and suddenly cried aloud to his mother, "I will go home." Nobody could understand anything. Asked what he meant thereby, the boy said, "This is not my house. I am the inhabitant of the village Fajilpur (sometimes the boy mentions the village of Ulaijipur) in the district of Chittagon! In order to go to the village, one is required to go to Luxum by railway train. From Luxum a road leads to their village, which passes through a field. He gives the details of the home and family as follows: "I was the son of a Brahmi. I had a big house by the side of the village road, which consists of three bedrooms, one *biathakkhana*, and one kitchen. There were three tanks attached to the homestead. I left three sons and four daughters there." He occasionally mentions the name of "Meher Kalibari" and the name of "Sarbananda," whom he mentions as "Sarbananda Bhai." He gives some descriptions of a palm tree and a banian tree, at the foot of which an earthen pot is placed. He mentions the name of one Dakhinaranjan Thakur as the worshipper of Meher Kalibari. Almost every day, the boy cries and requests that his parents take him there. The movements of the boy are being keenly watched by some local gentlemen. The boy is always morose and thoughtful and does not like to play or mix with other boys of his age. One day while he was sitting silently, his mother asked him the reason for being so, to which he replied, "I am only thinking about how you will live if I go away." The other day when the boy was taking his meal, he stopped abruptly and remained so for some time. On being asked by his mother as to why he did so, the boy said, "You refused to give alms to the poor man who is still standing in the courtyard, so I do not want to take your food." The mother called the poor man and gave him alms, after which the boy took the food. In the morning he usually eats *muri* and distributes it to crows, dogs, and cats. He can recognize pictures of almost all the gods and goddesses.

A Five-Year-Old Hindu Lad's Spiritual Powers – A Hindu lad in the Dhanbad railway quarters is reported to be creating wonders and is believed to possess extraordinary spiritual powers. It is stated that he can at once say from the look of a person the particular disease he is suffering from; and he also prescribes herbs, barks, and other material as medicines. He spends most of his time indoors, worshipping in his own way, and can pronounce Sanskrit mantras very well, though he has never been taught any. He is about five years of age and is a nephew of an assistant station master attached to the E.I.R. at Dhanban. The quarters are being thronged daily by large numbers of men and women at all hours of the day to have a *darshan* of this lad.

It is praiseworthy that the magazine guided by the Venerable Vasvaniji records such striking facts. Quite recently, newspapers printed pages about the girl, Shanti, from Delhi. Every one of us could cite similar recollections, heard in various countries from witnesses. Thus, for example, our little niece in her childhood once assured her mother, when they went along the street passing a dilapidated old house, that they had lived in that house. When the mother reproved her, saying that they never lived in such poverty, the girl replied, "But, mother, it was not now, but when we were poor and you were sewing the whole day." This assertion of the girl was, of course, ascribed to a high temperature.

In Tibet we were told of a small boy who could not be kept at home, for he persistently tried to run away to what he called his own home. About the house of his father, he said that it was not his real home and that they had no right to keep him when he wished to return home. He repeatedly started out preparing for a journey and tying up on his back his sacred prayer book.

Similarly, in Mongolia we heard of a wonderful child, born on the bank of the river Iro, who uttered prophecies in his infancy and then again reverted to the ordinary child state, unable to speak. When he grew up later, he learned speaking as every common child but recalled nothing of his predictions.

Another child, when three years old, wanted to write his autobiography and began it with the words: "At last, I am born!"

Everyone can remember many instances when precisely amid children such extraordinary faculties manifested themselves. Especially in the earlier preschool period, children deserve attentive observation, without any prejudice and bigotry. Sir Oliver Lodge says, "With regard to reincarnation, I have always kept an open mind." And the Hon. Ralph Shirley, discussing the problem of rebirth, justly remarks, "The time has arrived when the theory of reincarnation should be examined from a scientific standpoint." Noted psychologists are studying this vital question. It is not for us to judge why the life that surrounds us often or rarely reminds us of these problems. Perhaps it is more correct to say that we ourselves do not sufficiently think and investigate them. Anyhow, everyone who will remember such episodes should not discard them light-mindedly but should carefully record them. Quite recently in a magazine, one could read that human radiations were classified as self-suggestions. It is difficult to understand what there can be in common between radiation and self-suggestion. Those who too often mention auto-influence, will they not themselves be guilty of self-suggestion? Every truth demands impartiality and scientific approach.

Unprejudiced aspirations form the pure stream of life—Santana.

"Urusvati", Himalayas
May 24, 1937

WAY SIGNS

HOW many milestones are there on every path and how little attention do we pay to them! To a friend of mine an acquaintance complained: "My whole life I have been awaiting a Sign. I send my best thoughts but I have no reply. Is this just?"

My friend asked her to tell him about her life. And she told him the following: "I was very rich, and this gave me the possibility to help people and to support a great many. Then, not of my fault, there came ruin. It is true, I do not starve. But, I no longer have the possibility to help as I did before. And this is my constant sorrow. I fail to understand why it was necessary to ruin me and thus place me under eternal complaints for not being able to help."

My friend explained to her: "Don't you see? Your expected answer had already been given, but you did not understand it. You mistook the good advice for a misfortune. For you unfortunately imagined that help should only be financial. Thus you destroyed the most precious realization that spiritual help achieves far greater results than a financial one. Admit it, you took pleasure in giving away from your surplus, not submitting yourself to any privation, nor to danger, nor to difficulties. And even now, not everything has been taken away from you. You do not starve, and it seems that you could help others all the more with your own worldly experience. How many new and useful advices you could give? From your own experience, you could prove to others the insignificance of material means, if they can be destroyed so easily. But if you will consider your present position as a misfortune, then what further reply can you expect? Only when you shall realize the usefulness of your present state, when you understand that the conception of money was perverted in your own mind, only then will you be ready for the next step."

The same friend has also narrated another case. He was told to show to a certain lady in Chicago a portrait. The lady was greatly moved upon seeing this portrait, and said: "How do you know the drama of my life? Once we were in Paris with some American friends and were sitting in a small cafe. Unexpectedly the same person entered whose portrait you have just shown me, and having seated himself not far from the door, began looking at me attentively. I understood within my heart that I should approach him and that in this would lie the future of my life. On the other hand, the conventionalities of behavior whispered to me that it would be inadmissible in the eyes of my friend to leave them and go to the stranger. A great struggle took place within me, and he continued looking at me, expecting me to choose my path. Some more time passed, the conventionalities, keeping me to my seat, and the stranger got up and went out. I understood that I failed to answer the call and had decided my fate according to conventionalities. In this lies the drama of my life."

On a later occasion, my friend told me of another remarkable way sign. He was told to open in a certain city an educational institution. After investigating many possibilities, he decided to talk over matters with a certain lady who had come to this city. She made an appointment to meet him in the morning at the local museum. Reaching there with expectations, my friend noticed a tall stranger, who passed him several times. Then the stranger stopped next to him and pointing to a tapestry hanging on the wall, he said: "They knew the style of living. We have lost it." My friend replied accordingly, and the stranger invited him to sit down on a nearby bench; and placing his finger upon my friend's forehead, he said: "You came here to talk about a certain matter known to you. Do not talk about it. For another three months, nothing can yet be done along this line. And then everything will come to you of itself." Whereupon the stranger, having given a few more important advices, quickly got up and waving his hand in a friendly manner, said "Good luck," and went out. My friend, of course, took the advice, never mentioned anything to the lady about what he expected, and in three months everything took place as predicted. My friend still cannot comprehend how it was that he never asked the name of this remarkable stranger, of whom he has never heard from since and never met him again. And this is precisely how things happen.

One more sign. A friend—an artist—was telling me that at the time his exhibition was held at a seaside city, he was in great need of a definite sum of money. But despite all the outer success of the exhibition, the sales were not progressing. It seemed that the more the friend was inwardly anxious the more difficult the situation became. The more so, since he did not want to make his need of money known in public. As if all kinds of unforeseen circumstances had come up against him, someone got sick, someone went away and had not as yet returned. The exhibition was coming to an end, and the friend was in a very sad mental state. A few days prior to the closing of the exhibition, in the morning, it was not yet eight o'clock when the telephone bell rang and the voice of a young lady said nervously and hurriedly: "I have only fifteen minutes before my boat leaves. I am at the door of your exhibition and I must have one of your paintings. Please come immediately to advise me which to select." Needless to say, my friend hurried to get there and found at the door a very nice young lady from Honolulu, who with a check in hand was waiting to decide about the picture. Having made her decision, she took the painting off the wall and, disregarding the protest of the man in charge of the exhibition, hurried to the automobile that was waiting for her. Of course, you will not doubt that the check was exactly the amount that my friend needed. Likewise, you will not doubt that the young lady did not know, nor could she know, the sum needed by my friend; but that is just how it happens.

I remember another very significant episode. My friends decided to visit a certain country, whereas another part of the world had been indicated to them. With good motives my friends yet persisted and had even bought tickets for the mentioned country. Yet the indication had to be fulfilled, and something unusual took place. All means prepared for that trip suddenly vanished in two or three days, and thus my friends had no other choice but to fulfill the indication. Such signs clearly point out what measures must be applied in order to safeguard the predestined.

And yet another sign. One of my friends had to see a man who was very dangerous for him. Of course, all thoughts were directed to avoiding this fateful meeting. By strange circumstances several times this meeting did not take place, some unexpected impediments suddenly arose. But in the end, apparently, it could no longer be avoided. Probably the power of the thoughts sent could not help any longer. And thus my friend, having come to the meeting place awaited the appointment. The time had arrived. But the dangerous man had not as yet appeared. And suddenly a great excitement arose, and it appeared that, in the end, this evil man could not turn up—for his heart had failed. Such measures also take place when there is no other alternative.

And here is another sign of long memories. The aunt of my wife with her husband and son went in a cold winter to visit a far-off estate. They lost their way. Night came. The storm increased. And they had to think of some kind of shelter. All of a sudden they noticed a manor unknown to them. They drove up to the gate. It appeared that the owners had not lived there for a long time, but the watchman agreed to open the house for shelter. As soon as their sleighs stopped at the door, the aunt of my wife, who had never been in this place before exclaimed in horror: "No, I shall never enter this place. Some terrible drama has taken place here." When her husband and her son began to persuade her, she said: "Go in and see for yourself." And then she described all the interior of the house and mentioned in detail a large painting of a lady in white. When the worried travelers entered the house, they were amazed to recognize that which was described to them; and when they reached the room with the portrait, they themselves were so upset that they immediately left this unhappy house. Many such signs can be met if we but find within ourselves enough attentiveness to discern them.

And one more sign of an answer. Our friends moved into a new house. The luggage had already been brought in. And among these was an old clock that was broken and could not be wound up any longer. The lady was thinking how long they would live in this new house. And all of a sudden, the old unwound clock struck loudly ten times. And this was the exact number of years that they stayed at this place. But many, perhaps, would not have paid attention to the mere striking of a clock.

Another sign. It had been indicated that a very valuable packet would be received. Time passed. Our friends had almost forgotten about it, having reached Paris on their travel, when all of a sudden a message was brought from the bank, Bankers Trust, to the effect that a packet had arrived. And it appeared that in this most usual way, the most unusual sending was delivered. As you see, it may also happen thus.

And how many letters from unknown places of origin have been received! How many necessary books were pointed out as if by chance, and how many remarkable dates may be heard by an attentive ear! How many benevolent signs are given in life! If these signs are given for the good, if their sole object is to help humanity, then verily they will be truly good signs. Some light-minded people fear whether they are good and do not know how to interpret them. But look heartily through the magnifying glass of the future and listen to the megaphone of coming events, and you shall see what is the purpose of these benevolent signs.

If a sign is given for the upliftment of the heart, for the purposes of healing, for the overcoming of difficulties, for faith and perfection, it means this sign is useful and one must know how to discern it. And let us again repeat, that one must not expect that those signs that would be dictated by our selfishness and limited egoism is already evil and limited. One must find within oneself sufficient benevolence, in order to accept the signs in that form, in that expression, that the Highest has ordained as the best.

When people pray for protection against nightmares and ghosts, this will be one of the very necessary prayers. Truly, one must protect oneself against all kinds of dark phantoms, from everything that tends to plunge us into the darkness, and first of all, one must guard against ignorance. The lack of desire to know and to accept—will this not already be a succumbing to the power of evil spirits? The man who leaves this earth and does not think about the future will be like the one who received a most valuable book but who did not open it beyond its binding.

Attentiveness in life will not be conventional and a morbid abstraction. On the contrary, the more attentive is man, the more beauty will open up for him. Every minute of concentration and silence, he will consider as one more merging into the beautiful height. He will think over and guard more carefully that which has been accumulated by him earlier. And the accumulated is not phantom-like, but of the spirit-eternal.

I remember a reliable story of the sea. A certain captain of a steamer fell ill and because of the incurable disease was taken to the hospital, thus having to leave forever his beloved ship. The new captain who was just as experienced, on passing a rocky island some distance away, decided to lie down to rest. At this moment, through his dream he heard a voice: "Take to the right." But he did not get up. Then the second time he heard the same command. And finally a thundering voice shouted for the third time: "Take to the right." Then the captain got up and ran up to the bridge, repeating the order, "Take to the right." And it was high time, for the ship was heading straight to the reefs. At the same time, in the faraway hospital, the former captain of the ship threw himself out of the window with the same command on his lips. Admiral T. will substantiate this true story.

Some people consider all such signs as Christmas fairy tales or as coincidences not worth of attention. The majority of these would-be skeptics are very timid themselves and, therefore, are even afraid to think that above their everyday life, besides their backyard weeds, there may be something that makes it worthwhile to think and pay more attention to life. The spasmodic attitude toward faith or the accidental reading of related books helps but little because everything is required in persistent, careful, and attentive striving. It is not yet sufficient if man now and then shows signs of attentiveness on his part. One must always be attentive. One must penetrate into the surrounding conditions as if it were a profound and beautiful book given for everyday application. Again, certain thoughtless people will call this way of thinking abstract philosophy. They understand high expressions in a narrow meaning. But is it not from love for sane pondering that the most solid and irrefutable facts are formed? The same thinking will safeguard from cruelty and coarseness. For why should not refinement and upliftment of our consciousness go hand in hand?

What a wonderful impression is made by a person of whom one may be certain that he will not admit cruelty nor coarseness; it is a guarantee against savagery. If you meet a person who has retrograded and relapsed into savagery, one may be sure that originally he did not try hard for the Common Good, nor try to improve himself.

Along the vast snowy plains, one may sometimes notice withered twigs, which have been placed there by someone to indicate a hidden road. Sometimes a traveler will attentively watch for them and will direct his steed along these signs. But there are also conceited travelers, who, surprised at the seemingly unreasonable windings of the road, continue their way without paying heed to these indications. How many unexpected difficulties and dangers they may call upon themselves amid the hidden hillocks and ravines! An experienced coachman when noticing the tracks of those deviating from the signs will regretfully wave his hand and exclaim: "Look how the devil lured them away!"

Precisely an evil force, precisely ignorance and conceit distract the attention of the unwise from the signs that had been so carefully safeguarded for them. The lessons in attentiveness will also be experiments in benevolence, and on these paths is already prepared a true protection. And along these way signs, travelers will proceed.

RAIN OF STONES

SOME radios report that in Ashkhabad, artificial rain was produced and that the latter, upon analysis, proved to contain 5 percent water and 95 percent other chemical substances. We may leave the responsibility for the truth of this statement to the radio agency, but even in itself, this communication, broadcasted the world over, underlines the trend of contemporary mechanical endeavors. After all, if the artificial rain contains 95 percent of some "chemical substances," then why not continue the same lines of overstraining higher energies, and why not produce a rain of stones?

When merging into mechanical conventionalities, it is not difficult to forget the elementary, guiding considerations. All the latest discoveries lead to a tension and perhaps even to an overstraining of unknown, powerful energies. We call forth to overstrained tension the uninvestigated forces and at the same time are astoundingly indifferent to the study of these cosmic reactions. Such indefinite denominations as electricity, radio waves, or X-rays are pronounced with extraordinary light-mindedness. We are also light-mindedly prepared to acknowledge all the casual aspects of these tremendous energies, not considering the distances along which, nor the consequences with which, these seemingly simple evocations may work.

You can easily observe how a teacher becomes annoyed, if one will persist asking him what electricity actually is. A multitude of conventional definitions calls forth in the student a light-minded attitude toward them and absolutely obscures his reasoning over the true causes and effects.

Every dentist who offers to examine you with X-rays will be equally irritated when you ask him about the benefit or harm caused by these rays. One often hears in reply that these rays are neutral and lead to no bad consequences. But if you remind him that these rays, penetrating the tissues, are very powerful and therefore cannot but produce some effect, then the physician, not having any definite argument to bring forward, will simply call you an obstinate patient. One should not, of course, blame only the physicians and teachers. The whole of humanity's reasoning is at present guilty of having deviated toward conventional mechanization without having conducted preliminary exhaustive research.

Formerly, it took centuries to build temples, and this spiritual burning was neither extinguished nor distorted. But nowadays, one often meets with an expression of horror at the mere mention of prolonged experiments, which are to last decades. A discovery had been made that by rays one may investigate the layers of paintings, thus distinguishing fakes and restoration. Overjoyed at such a possibility, people started testing by rays many and even the most valuable creations of art. At the same time, the investigators omitted the simple consideration as to whether such rays may not affect the colors of the paint in the future. It is just possible that such an action upon the paint may be beneficial, but it is more likely that the powerful ray will change and perhaps even decompose the substance. But the present times strive only to speed. People are remote from problems that will last many years and even ages, just as the present-day composer prefers to limit himself to a short song or dance instead of an extensive symphonic creation, or as the writer, even a very talented one, avoids the burdensome task of writing whole epopees.

Mechanical overcrowding raises the question as to whether mankind is worthy of the discoveries when the spiritual state of humanity is so far behind the "phys-mechanical strivings." Are people worthy to fly when these flights are connected either with murder or poisoning, or are but races for speed? Limitations go so far, where prizes are given for the length of hair or for the beauty of but one part of the body, such as hands or feet. And the thoughts about the integral whole and about that which moves the hands or feet is considered totally unnecessary. It is true, once upon a time, that the length of hair was useful for rope making (of that there are several historical legends), but of what importance is the length of hair in connection with the scope and depth of thought?

During all the races of mechanical speed, during all competitions and senseless inventions of one-day kings and beauty queens, the fundamental consideration of the art of thinking is absolutely rejected on to the second plane; and yet this art gave so many unsurpassed, remarkable schools in ancient times.

Precisely, the art of thought will help one to remember that the overburdening of space, and usurpations, and the conquest of basic energies must necessarily lead to a solicitous attitude to these cosmic problems. Electrification is a fashionable and technically easy occupation. Sometimes the intensity of electrification goes so far that people are afraid to shake hands, for they receive painful shocks. Some jester boasted that he would collect upon himself so much electricity that he would destroy his enemy. And let us also ask each other, "Does not such oversaturation give cause to new forms of diseases?"

We started with the jesting radio communication about chemical substances in an artificial rain. Perhaps someone will think that the golden shower of Danae was a similar product, and someone scratching his head will sigh, and say, "If only in a similar manner, we do not come to a rain of stones!" In many things humanity reverts to biblical times. Again, humanity contemplates the construction of a skyscraper of all nations—a tragical reminder of the Tower of Babel. Thus, mechanically are being produced from space "chemical substances"—the limits of which are not even weighed and discussed. Sometime ago, we mentioned the craze for robots, which at a time of increasing unemployment could act as a substitute for human beings in many mechanical contrivances. Again, mechanical hobbies without thought about cause and effect. Again, deviation from prolonged living experiences. Again, the evocation of those unrealized infinite energies for which humanity, so far, has not even corresponding definitions.

Humanity should both dare and succeed, but causes and effects come first of all! Some fool wasted his time in calculating how much dynamite would be required and how deep the hole to be drilled for it in order to explode the whole planet. He probably did not think at the time of the possibility of a rain of stones, which to a certain degree would have been helpful to his "philanthropic intentions."

We know as yet so little! The simplest manifestations perplex a specialist! Quite recently on various continents—in France, Mexico, India—the ocean gave us corpses of some unknown sea monsters. Their reality is obvious, for there exist photographs of them. What causes, what shiftings in the depths have thrown ashore these animals? Much takes place outside of mechanical formulas, and no prizes for speed, no conventional athletics, least of all a golf ball, can help in these realms.

"May we be spared from a rain of stones!"

THOUGHT

GOETHE once said to Eckermann, "Despite my name, I have not acquired the right to say what I really think: I must keep silent—not to disturb people. Yet I have a slight privilege. I know what people think, but they do not know what I think. . . ."

The science of thought at present especially occupies the minds of people. From ancient times, there resound commandments about this blessed energy. India is rich with such ordainments. Plato and Confucius and many wise men of various epochs persistently turned the attention of people to the great might that is accessible to all. But in the rush of materialism, this panacea was sometimes neglected. Hence it is significant that our age can inscribe upon its seal: "Thought is the law of the universe."

The names of Professor Bekhterev, Rhine, McDougall, and other eminent scholars who investigate the energy of thought will forever remain on the pages of honor in the history of culture.

Let us record the following remarkable research:

"Two Professors of the Cambridge University have succeeded in making cinema photographs of human thought. One of them is Dr. Adrian, Professor of Physiology and a distinguished Member of the Royal Society, the other is Prof. Mathews. Adrian, who has dedicated his whole life to the investigation of the mysteries of the nervous system, in 1932 received the Nobel Prize and only a few days back was awarded the Gold Medal of the Royal Society."

"When a person sits quietly in a chair with closed eyes and his thought is not occupied with anything serious, then his brain matter produces regular electrical discharges at the rate of about ten discharges per second. With the help of very complicated and ingenuous apparati and a photo-electric camera, Prof. Adrian succeeded in registering these discharges on a cinema-film. He likewise observed that as soon as his patient opens his eyes and begins to concentrate his attention on something, the frequency of discharges increases considerably and reaches usually about 2,000 per sec."

"The rhythmic impulses continue also during deep sleep and also when the person (or animal) is subjected to the influence of narcotics. The professor proved by experimental methods the similarity of vibrations in different persons of the sight of the same object or manifestation. Different thoughts, which arise as a consequence of the action of the visual nerves, give different impressions upon the film.

"Prof. Adrian confined his experiments mainly to that part of the human brain which controls vision. He proved that this region of the brain is extraordinarily small. And Prof. Adrian established the fact with the help of his apparati that the greater part of the human brain does not participate in any mental process.

"Prof. Adrian carried his experiments to such a degree of perfection that he can now easily change his photographic records of thought into sound and can broadcast it over the radio for the public. During a public demonstration the audience heard a great variety of sounds, varying with the visual impressions of the patient, who sat upon the stage and opened his eyes at the direction of the professor."

Thus something quite natural and perhaps long ago known is already being recorded already by crude mechanical apparati. Long before these mechanical records were achieved, the great Indian scholar Sir Jagadis Bose in similar experiments recorded the pulse of plants and demonstrated even for a casual observer, how plants react to pain and light and how the appearance of even a distant cloud reacts upon the pulse. Graphically he showed on a screen the agony of a plant's death, poisoned or transfixed. At the same time, he recorded the influence of human energy upon the life of the same plants, which not long ago were in the eyes of civilized people regarded to be but mere lower growths, devoid of any senses.

By the movement of the needle, which records the pulse of the plant, one can notice the influence of human energy of thought. A kind thought, a sympathetic thought could protect the plant from the action of poison. In the same degree, a hostile thought would increase the fatal action.

If only quicker, as quickly as possible, the realization of the importance and power of thought would penetrate into the minds of even the uneducated masses! It is ridiculous and humiliating to subject that lofty experiment upon human thought to the action of coarse mechanical apparatuses. But for a coarse consciousness, similar methods of investigation are necessary. The realization alone of the significance of thought would already considerably transform our earthly existence.

In the realm of television, important, purely mechanical improvements take place. It has just been reported that during the current year, this transmission of vision at a distance will receive new possibilities. This is quite possible since once the field has been entered, the results in this direction will no doubt accumulate shortly. Gradually the reflection of the quality of thought will also become apparent through television, when images of persons are transmitted.

Even some observant photographers point out that the difference of photographs depends not only on purely external conditions but also on the inner state of the subject. Thus also in this case we arrive at the concept of the reflection of thought.

Discussions about hypnotism and suggestion, that is to say about the trained methods of influence, have already become common. But the limited consciousness as yet but feebly admits that not only in cases of trained mental influences but absolutely cases of more or less clear thinking, powerful reactions upon the surroundings take place.

This consideration will once more remind us of the concept of responsibility, about which we recently had several evidences. What lofty beauty is contained in the idea of responsibility and service! And there is no such spot on earth where man would not be subject to these two great predestinations.

When we evoke from space words and sounds, are they not also followed by the ever-present properties of the energy of thought? Along tremendous distances the human voice, directed by thought, clearly resounds.

No doubt, across vast space together with the outer Sound are also stretched the inner strings of a mighty energy. Some will sense them quite clearly; another, though feeling them, will deny. And in such a negation there will be again present the element of fear. For the fearing consciousness shudders at the very hint that it is surrounded by influences and energies. Precisely that which should uplift people casts the weak-willed into fear. Precisely into fear, which is the consequence of something indefinite and chaotic. But fear will not save us from chaos. Fears are the very gates to chaos!

It is beautiful, being clad in valor, to realize the grandeur of thought and of all the energies that it sets into action. Though through mechanical means, nevertheless let people hurriedly approach the thoughts about thought in all its mighty significance. And instead of a chaotic fear, many seemingly complicated problems of life will become illumined by the realization of all the possibilities of thought. Not without reason was it said: "Act not only in body, but also in thought!"

What a beautiful concept: "Thought in Infinity."

MYSTERIES

ON the Karakorum Pass, at nineteen thousand five hundred feet, on this highway, the highest in the world, the groom Goorban began to question me:

"What is it that has been secreted in these heights? It must be that a great treasure has been hidden hereabouts, as the way to this place is surely arduous. Having traversed all the passes, one may chance upon a smooth vault. Something tinkles under the horses' hooves. It must be that here are great secrets, but we do not know the entryway to them. When will there be writings in books that reveal what has been hidden away, and where?"

All around this majestic Karakorum Pass, the white peaks glistened dazzlingly. All around us, without a break, rose a most brilliant scintillation. On the path itself, as if for a reminder, lay a great quantity of whitened bones. Were not some of these wayfarers going for treasures? Indeed, countless caravans have crossed the Karakorum for riches.

* * *

Here I am reminded of another tradition concerning a treasure. In Italy, at Orvieto, they related a remarkable legend to me about hidden artistic treasures. The story concerned either Duccio himself or one of his contemporaries. It was told in a lofty style that goes so well with the mellifluous Italian language.

"Just as it is nowadays, in olden times the best artists were not always understood. For the beclouded eye, it has been difficult to evaluate forms, especially lofty ones. People have demanded nothing but the observance of old rules, and beauty has not often been accessible to them. It thus happened with the great artist of whom we are speaking. His best pictures, instead of exaltingly touching the hearts of people, were subjected to condemnation and mockery. For a long time, the artist endured this unjust attitude toward himself.

"In divine ecstasy he continued to create many masterpieces. Once he depicted a marvelous Madonna, but the envious prevented the hanging of this image in its pre-destined place. And this happened not once or twice, but several times. When the viper begins to creep in, it invades both palace and hovel.

"But the artist, made wiser and knowing the madness of the crowd, was not distressed. He said, 'It has been given to the bird to sing, and to me has been given the power to glorify lofty forms. As long as the bird lives, it fills God's world with song. And so while I am alive, I will also glorify it. Since the envious and the ignorant put obstacles in the way of my works, I will not lead the evil ones into a worse bitterness of heart. I will collect the pictures rejected by them. I will store them securely in oaken chests, and availing myself of the goodwill of my friend the abbot, I will hide them in the deep cellars of the monastery. When the ordained day will come, future generations will discover them. If by the will of the Creator they must remain hidden, let it be so!'

"From this time on, people thought that the great artist had ceased painting. But hearing these suppositions, he only smiled because henceforth he was not laboring for the sake of the people's joy but for a higher beauty. And so, we do not know where this priceless treasure is preserved."

"No one knows in precisely what monastery, in what secret vaults, the artist concealed his creations. True, in certain cloisters old paintings have been found in crypts, but these have been found singly; they were not purpose-fully deposited there, and therefore could not be the trea-sure intentionally hidden by the great artist. Indeed, in the underground vaults they continue to sing *Gloria in Excelsis,* but searchers have not been fortunate enough to find what was indicated by the artist himself. Certainly, we have many monasteries and still more temples and castles that lie in ruins. Who knows, perhaps the tradition relates to one of these remains, already destroyed and razed by time.

"But have you been assured that this treasure is hidden within the boundaries of Italy?" asked one of the listeners.

"Of course, even in remote times people were going to other countries. May it not be that these treasures have likewise been unexpectedly dispersed or rather preserved in different countries?" Another person added, "It may be that this story does not at all refer to a single master. Of course, human practices are often repeated. Consequently, we find in history repetitions of human wanderings and ascents."

* * *

When we reached the middle of the Karakorum Pass, the groom Goorban said to me, "Give me a couple of rupees. I will bury them here. Let us too add to the great treasures."

I asked him, "Then do you think that treasures have been collected together there below? He looked surprised, even frightened. "But does the sahib not know? Even to us lowly people, it is known that there, deep down, are extensive underground vaults. In them have been gathered treasures from the beginning of the world. There are also great guardians. Some have been fortunate enough to see how, from the hidden entryways, come tall white men, who then again withdraw underground. Sometimes they appear with torches, and many caravaneers know these fires. These subterranean beings do no evil. They even help people.

"I know for a fact that one local boy was lost from his caravan in a snowstorm and covered his head in despair. Then it seemed to him that someone was moving around him. He looked around in the darkness, but there appeared no horse, no man—he saw nothing. Yet when he put his hand in his pocket, he found a handful of gold pieces. Thus do the great dwellers of the mountains help miserable people in misfortune.

* * *

And again the stories came to mind about the secret magnets established by the followers of the great philosopher and traveler, Apollonius of Tyana.

It is said that in definite places where it had been ordained that new states be built up or great cities erected, or that great discoveries and revelations should take place, there, on all such sites, were implanted portions of a giant meteor sent from the distant luminaries.

There has even been a custom of testifying to the truth of statements by reference to such ordained places. Deponents would say, "What I have said is as true as the fact that on a certain site has been placed such and such. . . ."

The groom Goorban again raised the question, "You foreigners who know so much, why have you not found the entryway into the underground kingdom?" You know how to do everything and boast of knowing everything, and yet you do not enter into the secrets that are guarded by the great fire!"

"Man lives in mysteries,
and these are numberless!"

ESSENCE

THE essential nature of people is fundamentally good. The first time this realization was fortified in me was during an experiment long ago with the extrusion of the subtle body.

My friend, a physician, had put to sleep a certain G.; and drawing out his subtle body, ordered him to send it into a house where he had never been before. By means of following his subtle body, the sleeper pointed out a series of characteristic details. Then he was directed to rise up to a certain floor of the house and to enter a certain door. The sleeping man outlined the details of the hallway, saying that there was before him a door. Again he was directed to go further and to tell what he saw. He described the room and said that a man was seated at a table reading. Then he was directed to "approach and frighten him."

Silence followed.

"I direct you to go near him and frighten him." Again silence, and then, in a timid voice:

"I cannot."

"Explain why you cannot."

"Impossible, he has a weak heart."

"Then do not frighten him, but as much as you can without harm, make your influence felt. What do you see?"

"He has turned and lit a second lamp."

"If it is not dangerous, increase your influence. What do you see?"

"He jumped up and went into the adjoining room where a woman is sitting."

At the conclusion of the experiment, we telephoned our

acquaintance, and without telling him about the matter, indirectly led him to relate his sensations. He said:

"Today I had a strange experience. A little while ago, I was seated with a book, and suddenly I felt some inexplicable presence. I am ashamed to tell you that this sensation was so sharp in its effect that I had a desire for more light. Nevertheless, the feeling became so strong that I went to tell my wife about it and to sit with her."

Apart from the experiment itself, which so clearly demonstrates the causes of many of our sensations, one detail had in it for me personally an unforgettable significance. In earthly circumstances the man would not take account of whether someone had a weak heart. He would frighten, abuse, cause him evil, without considering any such thing. But the subtle body, that about which the Apostle Paul speaks so clearly, in its essence is inclined toward good. As you see, before carrying out the order to frighten, there was manifested the consideration of sensing the condition of the heart. The essence of good whispered here that it would be dangerous to do harm to an already weak heart.

One such experiment, in the most ordinary everyday circumstances, already leads one beyond the boundaries of the bodily-limited. There resulted not only the extrusion of the subtle body, but a remarkable testing of the good of the essential nature. How much dark burden must weight down luminous subtle essence for people to reach such misanthropy as they do. Again, as St. Anthony has said: "Hell is ignorance." Of course, the whole dark burden is primarily from ignorance. In such a situation, how needful are good thoughts, which with their unseen wings touch the oppressed beclouded forehead.

When in their ignorance, people say: "Why these concentrations of thought, why these hermits withdrawing from the world? Why, they are egoists, and they think only of their own salvation." There is a great mistake in such a judgment. If even in the most ordinary experiment we could convince ourselves of the good and noble essence of the subtle body, if we saw that a thought of good transcended all commands, usually so unquestioned in such cases, then so needful are these thoughts of good. What simple yet touching solicitude is told in the simple reply about the weak heart. And right now there are not a few weak hearts, and who has the right to overburden them? Right now there are many mortally smitten hearts which could no longer hold up under a careless impact. And this will be murder just as precisely as killing with a dagger, bullet, or poison. Does not poison penetrate into the heart through an attack of malice? What an enormous number of murders—actual, intentional, malicious in their prolongation—takes place outside the reach of any courts or penalties! To poison a man is inadmissible; this is right. But then why is it possible to gnaw and tear the heart of a man? Surely if people would even sometimes, though briefly, reflect in the morning hours about something good, apart from their own selfish interests, this would be a great offering to the world.

Of course, ignorant cynics will probably sneer, considering that in any case this thought is nothing more than a blade of grass in the wind. Any cynicism about thought, about the spirit, about intangible possibilities will be a clear example of the grossest ignorance. When these ignorant ones, grinning maliciously, say: "Whither should we, of small culture, plunge into an ocean of thoughts"—this will be said not at all in humility or timidity but will be the expression of the ugliest arrogance.

* * *

Often people dream in secret of encountering something, as they say in popular language, supernatural. Precisely as if in the greatness of nature, there can be the natural and, as an antithesis, the supernatural. Of course, this ordinary expression, found in popular usage, does not lead to a true cognition. But the root of the matter is this, that as soon as people have chanced to come in contact with even the beginning of such an unusual manifestation, they have fallen into such unrestrained heart palpitation that the manifestation stopped short. It was suspended for the very same reason as in the case of the experiment related above. It has been clearly established that the uncultivated heart and the inexperienced consciousness cannot endure anything loftier than their trivial routine.

Very often certain inexplicable heart palpitations are spoken about. People attribute them to the category of sex, or to inordinate work, or to some other excesses. But among these manifestations not a few cases would be found, when some beautiful wings have already touched someone expectant or unexpectant, yet he at the first proximity to them would suffer a mortal trembling. This too will so often be from the incompatible distinction between earthly language and the Heavenly tongue.

So much good and compassion is contained in the simple consideration about the weak heart. If people, even in their everyday life would admit to themselves more often this humane thought about a neighbor's pain, about over-fatigue and weakness of his heart, then surely in this way, they would become in many cases more humane.

* * *

Manifestations of the dead have been recounted in all sorts of narratives. They are entirely beyond question. Among them it is undoubtedly true that many times, though with a highly needful goal in view, departed relatives and friend could not tell them their good news solely because of that same animal terror on the part of those to whom they appeared. Cases are known that when desiring to save a person from peril, departed ones have had to undertake a whole series of gradual approaches in order to free the person first of all from fear. Precisely fear so often prevents receiving the best news.

These manifestations, such good news and wishes to help, have been written about so much, that it is impossible to go into an enumeration of the individual episodes. Beginning with theological and on through many philosophical, historical, and poetic narratives, it is everywhere affirmed that there is no death as such, and that the proximity of the worlds can be sensed even amid everyday life. All this is past doubting. But malice and hatred, which have so taken possession of humanity in our time, make it imperative to recall once more that the essential nature of man is good, and that everything evil and hideously harmful will be first of all an additional effect of ignorance.

The very dark ones, those creatures that have fallen very low, exert their influence first of all on the ignorant. Their favorite expedient is intimidation in many ways. They try so hard to obscure and to lower the consciousness of their victim, that he feels himself isolated, alone; and finally, he can see his fortune in communion with the dark ones. And these, likewise, try to deprive the victim of all true joys, imposing upon him all the shameful surrogates of self-indulgence.

Man wishes to forget himself. Instead of wishing it possible to reflect more clearly and to take up arms in the spiritual battle, he is compelled to forget himself. In the delirious desire of forgetfulness, it is easier to take possession of him and make him an obedient instrument, cajoling him into ignorance. Whereas, only the thought of good, which lies in the foundation, can impel one to a thirst for knowledge. And then man does not lose a day or hour in order to learn, to make better, and to make beautiful everything possible. In this process, thought of good will also be a thought of beauty.

PROPHECIES

"WITHIN a hundred years, Mars and Venus will be inhabited." Such a "scientific" prophecy was reported not long ago by the newspapers. We copy this literally as we read it:

"A two-hour working day, the abolishment of old age, and in its place one's entire life spent as if in the interval from the twenty-second to the thirty-fifth year; the delivery of water to Mars and, likewise, the provision of oxygen to Venus will make them habitable. Such prophecies for the next century have been made by an American chemical society on the occasion of celebrating a particular anniversary in that country.

"Ten thousand scholars were present at this celebration.

"These forecasts were made by Dr. Thomas Midgley, a chemist and vice-president of the Ethyl Gasoline Corporation.

"Dr. Midgley says that within a hundred years, the causes of colds, influenza, tuberculosis, and probably also of cancer and many other diseases that are now regarded as dangerous will be eradicated.

"In the synthetic house of the future century, you will discard bedclothing as needless, heat your apartment instantly by merely pressing a button, and throw your soiled pajamas in the trash basket because cellulose products will be so cheap that it will not be worthwhile to launder them.

"With the discovery of certain hormones, indigestion will be unknown, and the taking of a single pill will give relief from all discomfort.

"Sleep will be undisturbed, and bad dreams will disappear. There will be sleeping tablets that produce only pleasant dreams, or tablets of another sort that will rid one of the need of sleep altogether.

"The engineering profession expects from chemistry a fuel that will relieve it of considerations that have hitherto handicapped it. The invention of such a fuel will make possible interplanetary communication.

"The use of gasoline, explosives, and other materials will undergo such a transformation that a new supply of energy will have to be found, perhaps in radioactivity.

"I do not wish to create the impression that interplanetary communication will immediately become accessible to everyone. Many preparations are necessary for this. Mars needs water, and Venus, a new atmosphere; all this requires the labor of future chemists and engineers.

"The world will be more healthful. The better health that will be found will make possible the development of such conditions of life and of intellectual occupations that presently insoluble scientific problems will be solved in a single day.

"Age will be under complete control; it will be possible for each one to arrange for an interminably long life by freeing oneself from casualties and maintaining life on nearly the same level. As an example, life could be prolonged at the same level as between the ages of twenty-three and thirty-five.

"Agriculture will become an exact science through the use of powerful fertilizers and synthetic hormones for producing the harvest. This will also signify a far larger and quicker meat supply. Chickens will grow to the size of pigs, pigs to the size of cows, and cows will attain the size of mastodons; yet in order to attain such growth, they will not have to be fed any more than at the present time."

Once again we point out that these forecasts are taken from a scientific report published in the newspapers. Many alluring prophecies lead to particular reflections. Thus, for example, a scientist who knows that more vitamins are contained in vegetables than in meat concludes his report with something presumably far more attractive to him, such as the growing of monstrous chickens as large as pigs. Likewise amusing is the fact that a scientist is concerned about bringing Mars and Venus into earthly conditions of habitability. For some reason he limits his thinking by desiring to subject the other planets to the conditions of Earth, perhaps the least of their sisters.

Very likely it has occurred to the scientist more than once that, while he dreams of subjecting the other planets to earthly conditions, the beings who dwell on the other planets are at the same time probably thinking about how to bestow their best conditions upon Earth. Would it not be conceit to assume that the inhabitants of the other planets must go about in earthly jackets and caps? Is it possible for the grandeur of the horizon to invoke thoughts full of earthly conceit?

Indeed, it would be beautiful if the prophecies of the learned chemist relative to the eradication of earthly diseases were fulfilled within a hundred years. Of course, what could be better? But unfortunately, it is not for chemistry, along with the engineering profession, to succeed in this direction. True prophylaxis will consist not in the swallowing of chemical tablets but, first of all, in the improvement of conditions of health in the mode of life. It is possible to swallow all sorts of tablets and still vegetate in extraordinarily filthy and slovenly conditions. One may think of discoveries in engineering and yet sully them with neglect, falsehood, and human hatred.

Surely, all Earth dwellers would welcome the forecasts of the learned chemist if in them a fitting place for spiritual development were allotted, if the great psychic energy, which in the last analysis is more powerful than any chemical tablets, were appreciated. One might ask, why longevity for people? Why remain outwardly at an age of no more than thirty-five years if, even since childhood, one is spiritually decrepit?

Why should people violate their great gift of

health-giving sleep, fastening upon themselves forced dreams, as do opium-eaters? Of course, all morphine and heroin addicts, and similar dope addicts, and drunkards likewise, instead of leading a healthy, thoughtful life, try to bring themselves by compulsion into an illusory state. At present, all the governments in the world are beginning to grapple with the evil of narcotism. Consequently, not by means of forcible tablets, but precisely by a healthy way of life is it possible to attain healthy, heartening sleep. Surely, people sleep, not for enforced dreams but for something far more essential.

To propagate life by force is just as monstrous as are chickens the size of pigs. In this forced attachment of one-self to the earthly shells, there is expressed an unwillingness to think more broadly, particularly within the confines of those countless planets and heavenly bodies to which the learned chemist would like to betake himself, probably clothed for such a triumphal journey not in an ordinary jacket but in formal evening dress.

One would think that the time had already passed when anyone could be dreaming merely about crude material solutions. True, there have been days when the severed head of a dog, under the influence of forced currents, began to bark, and the miscreants who contrived this announced that death had been conquered. Such conquerors of death show, first of all, that they themselves are much afraid of so-called death and that they limit their thinking to the earthly vehicles.

If people would glance more often at the boundless horizon and reflect about the relationship of Earth with Infinity, they would not be thinking about chemical tablets alone. The power of thought, the power of psychic energy would indicate to them entirely different paths on which they will not need artificial dreams and visions.

Tzagan Kure, June 21, 1935

THE FLAME OF THINGS

IT is mentioned in literature how by restriction of food and by other spiritual strivings, St. Isaac of Syria changed the entire form of his life. After a stay of five years as a bishop, he went back into the desert. There, in the great stillness of the desert, he perfected his precepts and admonitions in order to leave them in an expressive, brief, and unforgettable form:

"Those who are guided by benefaction always feel that some sort of thought-ray traverses the lines of a written work and distinguishes in their minds the external words from that which is spoken with great thought by the soul's knowledge. If a man reads verses of great significance without plunging deeply into them, his heart remains impoverished, and in him is extinguished the sacred force which, through actual soul cognition, imparts the sweetest savor to the heart. The spirit-bearing soul, when it hears a thought containing a hidden spiritual force, flamingly accepts the contents of this thought. Not every man is roused to wonder by what is told spiritually and has in itself great mysterious force. A word about heaven requires a heart not preoccupied with the earth."

"The Scripture has not interpreted for us the things of the future age, but it has simply taught us how, while yet here on earth, we can receive a sensation of delight with them, up to the point of our natural transmutation at departure from this world. Though the Scripture, in order to arouse in us a longing for future blessings, has portrayed them under the names of things always desirable and glorious, acceptable and precious to us, yet when it says that 'the eye has not beheld that, nor the ear heard,' it hereby announces that 'future blessings are inscrutable and bear no resemblance to the blessings of this place.'"

"Preciseness of naming is established for objects here, but for objects of the future age, there are no true authentic names; there is about them one simple cognition that is higher than any denomination and any component principle, form, color, outline, and all fabricated names."

"He is no lover of good works who has to struggle to do good, but he who takes upon himself with joy subsequent afflictions."

"The cross is a will that is ready for any sorrow."

"With the destruction of this age, immediately begins the future age."

"What is knowledge? Realization of immortal life."

"What is purity? Briefly put, the heart that forgives every living thing in nature." "What is such a forgiving heart? Incandescence of a man's heart about all creation, about people, about birds, about animals."

"The timorous man shows that he suffers two infirmities: love of his body and lack of faith."

"The thoughts that intimidate and horrify a man are usually engendered by the thoughts that he directs toward repose."

"The hope of rest at all times compels people to forget the great."

"Who does not know that birds fly into nets while having rest in view?"

"The first of all passions is self-love; the first of all good works is scorn of repose."

"Strive not to hold back the wind with your hand; that is faith without works."

"For every comfort, there follows suffering, and for every suffering, for the sake of God, there follows consolation."

"Fear habits more than enemies."

"He who is sick in feelings is in no condition to encounter and sustain the flame of things."

The very expression "the flame of things" shows an

extraordinary plunge into the subtlest world. Indeed, that is why what was enjoined by St. Isaac is so heartily conclusive because it is based on the discernment of the fiery essential nature. Many works of St. Isaac have vanished and not come down to us, but they did exist, and this is evident from repeated references in literature. No matter that to some the paths of St. Isaac are regarded as gnoseological. Except the definition "the flame of things," no other one will be right.

In all of his ordained precepts, first of all there resounds everything flamingly derived. That thought, that word that has been intertwined with the flame of the essence of things will have a special consequence. To write down and remember the fiery counsels will be a reinforcement on all paths, a steadfastness not from earth, but from the heavens. People have realized this fiery firmament and felt in themselves a cognizing sacred palpitation of the heart.

"Spiritual contemplation—it is not to be sought in mental labor, but it can be imbued only through Bliss. And so long as man does not cleanse himself, until that time he does not have enough forces within himself even to harken to it; no one can thus acquire it only through study."

"Just as it is impossible for one with his head under water to breathe the air, so is it impossible for one whose thought is plunged into mundane concerns to breathe sensations of the new world."

Thus, away from transitory earthly cares, St. Isaac strives toward sensations of the new world. Verily, he knows spiritual values when he says, "Irritate no one and hate no one"; "Be not inflamed with anger at him, lest he should see in thee the signs of enmity." These are counsels of the true builder who realizes that inflammation with anger is disastrous.

St. Isaac could speak noteworthily about the indispensable: "Agitated are the waters at the descent of angels." But this agitation is not wrath nor enmity, but only the flashings of sacred fire, which spiritualizes all that exists in the flame of things.

"The unburnable bush"—this icon full of fire reminds one about a beautiful and lofty miracle. The "Great Wisdom" of God rushes along on a fiery steed, and the "angel," benign silence, is also infallibly fiery. Those who first inscribed these symbols understood them not as abstract philosophizing but as inalienable truth, as reality. In this heart, in actuality, the flame of things is nearby and comprehensible and beautiful.

"The infirm in feelings is in no condition to encounter and to sustain the flame of things."

Thus, at the beginning of the eighth century, there enjoined St. Isaac the Syrian. From the Monastery of Maz-Matthew at Ninevah have been handed down to us these remarkable fiery counsels, which resound with invincible persuasiveness. Whether they were spoken yesterday or twelve centuries ago, they remain just as irrevocable.

THE UNTOLD

S CHOLARS say that absolute zero cannot possibly be attained. B. de Haas, professor at the University of Leyden, who in his laboratory experiments reached a point one five-thousandth of a degree above absolute zero, has declared that this ultimate extreme will never be attained.

Absolute zero is 459.6 degrees below zero Fahrenheit. At this temperature all gases become solid and all motion ceases.

Thus, still another absolute point has been recognized as impossible. Just as, precisely, a small difference exists between decompositions and, contrariwise, compositions. It turns out that that which is being synthesized loses something it formerly had and which could even be detected on the scales at the beginning of the experiment. A well-known experiment with the decomposition and mechanical composition of a potato shows that there remains something that eludes formulation.

Likewise, one can observe something untold in all manifestations. Moreover, precisely in this circumstance, which eludes formulation, will be contained something especially essential. Again, one is obliged to recall the fact that the weight of a man plunged into intensive thinking differs from his usual weight.

On the one hand, such a something is disappointing in its unattainability to the investigator. But on the other, precisely this something, even when detected by our crude physical apparatuses, always remains both inviting and inspiring. One should hardly be grieved or disappointed when such evident possibilities are already accessible to

"

earthly expressions. No doubt there will come into being in the investigations some new method, which in place of the imagined absolute will provide a new Infinity.

It is related that during their most critical battles, certain outstanding military leaders remained in their quarters as if absorbed in some customary, mechanical occupation. Those who do not know would admit all sorts of ironical considerations; some would even assume that in these moments the leader wished to absent himself mentally, under the influence of fear. But those who knew these great men intimately understood full well that, at this time, there was some process going on that could not be put into words.

The leader had done everything dependent upon his decision. At this time he could not rationally make changes where his orders were already being carried out. The leader wished to set aside the language of reason and allow something inexpressibly profound to create a new, influential process. Such a small mechanical occupation was not all simply time killing. On the contrary, this was one of the means of shifting his consciousness. It stands to reason that the consciousness can be shifted without any mechanical distractions, but for this, together with the art of thinking, one has to also be in full possession of the companion art of dismissing a thought.

Though the art of thought is not easy, yet the ability to leave off a thought can sometimes be even more difficult. Of course, for this it is needful that a given process of thought be entirely abandoned in order that the new formation in the consciousness may spring up without being burdened in any way. And this is very difficult, for here again the absolute is not reached in such an experiment.

Very often, people assume that they have ceased thinking about something, yet it still remains a mirage of theirs. They compel themselves forcibly to think about something else. But this very compulsion will leave behind some reflexes of the former thought. Yet in order to shift the consciousness, it is surely necessary to also attain some almost infinitesimal ciphers. And this, nevertheless, will be a relative matter.

Yet long ago from the heights, it was said, "If you wish to become a new man, breathe a sigh about the Untold. In a single sigh, people have been transported onto the verge of Infinity."

Thus, not by prolonged calculations but in a single sigh about the Untold is the consciousness renewed. And where a rocky cliff has appeared insurmountable, impassable, there are, unexpectedly, inviting avenues of procedure that have opened up.

But everything must be voluntary. In this concept is contained the greatest law. No coercion, no constraints enable the consciousness to be loftily transported. Voluntariness usually remains a not-very-well-interpreted concept. In the ordinary understanding, any freedom is often considered not concordant with good, with a heart concern for one's fellow.

Indeed, all testings and vital experiments demonstrate sufficiently how much a luminous voluntariness transforms all actions. Of course, this beautiful desire emanates from the depths of the chalice of consciousness. It results in both self-abnegation and a desire for continuous creativeness in all spiritualized labor.

Again, it is very difficult to differentiate where true voluntariness is and where some alien considerations have drifted together. In military organizations, there are volunteers. But among them, only certain ones will be true volunteers, while the volunteering of the others will be tinged with extraneous considerations. There are entire army units where the members are supposed to be volunteers, but in reality, they are trying to evade or to conceal this or that feature of the worldly drama.

In all thought processes, willingness plays the principal role. Without it there remains only a gross mirage that never renews the consciousness.

What luminous sigh about the Untold can produce that inexplicableness by relative formulas? What transference of consciousness helps to change matter into spirit, or rather, one degree of the status into another? Where the will terminates, where desire is extinct, where the command is wordless, there does a single sigh about the Untold renew everything.

The most refined *pranayama* is not to be compared with a sigh about the Untold being borne into the great expanses.

People read bookish words about the most great. These words are beautiful, but where there is the Word, there the best words require something still greater—the Untold.

It is asked, "Is it for me to think about the Untold?" Verily, precisely thou, precisely on all paths, earthly and heavenly."

ETERNAL LIFE

IN his book, *The Fear of the Dead in Primitive Religion*, George
Fraser brings in the wise words of the Omaha tribe
about death: "No one can avoid death, and no one must
fear death, since it is unavoidable." Likewise, the ancient
Mayans calmly said, "I go to rest." If we remember the
words of Socrates before his departure, before draining the
cup of poison; or the thoughts of Plato and even Epicurus
about death, not to speak of the lofty attitude toward this
act in the teachings of India, we see the same reasoned,
wise consciousness about death as about the alteration of
existence. We see the same consciousness of eternal life,
which is so cleanly enjoined by the sacred Covenants.

Meanwhile, in the confused minds of the West, particularly in the eighteenth and nineteenth centuries when
negation laid its dark path, we see a sort of animal terror in the face of the natural change of existence. Even
recently this could be written about, as the intellectual
de Sevigné expressed herself: "Death is so fearful, that I
hate life more for the reason that it leads to death, rather
than for "the thorns with which the path of life is sown."
The idea of death poisoned life for Alphonse Daudet, Zola,
Goncourt, Maupassant, and other apparently fearless and
broad thinkers.

At the same time among people living close to nature,
the word "death" is not generally employed. They say, "He
has departed," or "He has passed away," meaning that he
has terminated this cycle of existence. People in contact
with nature are in contact with the basic teachings of truth:
People, being made natural thinkers, likewise naturally

understand the significance of a change of being. Fear of death, it would seem, could only arise in malefactors who darken their consciousness with crimes and intentional wrongdoing. It is fully understood that each traitor fears such a striking change of existence. Indeed, within himself he entirely understands that he is being plunged not into non-existence but into some other form of existence. If in his present existence, he has overburdened his heart with quantities of dark purposes and actions, then, indeed, he does not know if it will be easy for him in some conditions unknown to him. Doing unworthy deeds yesterday, man tries to avoid responsibility for them. Such terror at the unavoidable passage into the unknown world is fully understood by people who have darkened their earthly existence with heinous deeds, either material or mental. Surely, it is not necessary to repeat again that thought will be even more potent than word or muscular movement.

Does it not seem strange that, along with criminal beings, certain apparently broad thinkers have also fallen into an animal-like terror before a change of existence? One would like to know if they easily changed their earthly homes. Perhaps, too, on the earth, some of them were not easily moved about. It is well-known that some people believe they can create and think only in their long-occupied domestic environment. Each unusual surrounding already hinders them in expressions of their creativeness. But surely it would seem that precisely diverse impressions and unforeseen experiences and dangers must sharpen thinking, resourcefulness, and boldness. According to courageousness, you can form an opinion about many other qualities of a man. But, of course, courage is tested not by sitting by the stove but there where conflict is encountered with the elements, with darkness, and with all ignorance.

Each one has had an occasion to see people who at a tranquil dinner table employed the boldest speech; but when found face to face with those dangers, about which they were just now speaking so bombastically, they showed themselves in a completely different light. Probably if one speaks with these people about death, they will generally say, "Why speak about such terrible subjects?" This means that they doubt in the goal-fitness of the Universe, with all the strikingly inspiring changes of existence. Apparently they have heard enough about the fact that everything is found to be in motion. It would seem that the newest discoveries would demonstrate sufficiently the fullness of space, and for all that, they are frightened at such a significant and solemn passage into a world new for them. Even for trivial earthly journeys, they will make their wills, not only because they are exceptionally solicitous of someone, but also because, for them, this act is thought of inseparably with the fear of death.

Non-religious people confronted with death hasten away after the completion of rituals. When, in their opinion, the danger has passed, they are the first to relate a blasphemous anecdote. In a recent issue of the magazine *Twentieth Century,* among some very interesting opinions about the ideas and realities of the twentieth century, Professor A. R. Badya, says, "The world is losing the sense of religious values. In its revolt against petrified beliefs and meaningless ceremonies, it falls into the danger of casting out the child along with the bath water. In its suspicion of religions, it is made blind to the meaning and significance of religion." Thus, the learned professor correctly judges and refers carefully to the higher values. In reality, to use the current saying, many children have already been poured out with the bath water. But, of course, among these lightminded outpourings, humanity has cast out precisely that which could strengthen it in creativeness both mental and material.

He who knows about eternal life, by this very fact knows also his joyous responsibility for each action, mental and muscular. In prayers is introduced this great significance of the words "eternal life." He who thinks upon this understands that life is always multiform, both in the horizontal and vertical sense! Even according to primary physical laws, he understands that each minute everything is altered and never arrives again at the former state. In this movement is contained the greatest creative generosity. And how joyful and beneficent the obligation to participate according to one's strength in this all-inclusive creativeness!

Rousseau observes: "He who affirms that he meets death calmly and without fear is simply a liar." Why the great writer Rousseau took it upon himself to speak for all humanity is that he himself must have been afraid of death. Indeed, this act goes beyond the limits of commonplaceness. Therefore, it must be met with a special tranquility of the heart. This consciousness will be far indeed from the so-called calmness before the taking of daily food or any everyday action. But, precisely, in a particular, inspired tranquility, when facing the great change of existence, one will discover a very real magnanimity, which always goes together with wisdom.

The Apostle said clearly and briefly, "We do not die, but are changed." Here, in a few words, is contained the attestation of eternal life. And you remember the words of the Bhagavad Gita about the invisibility, unchangeableness, and eternity of Being. In all ages, in all the ends of the world has eternal life been solemnly and triumphantly confirmed. It means there must have been some unnatural, violent shocks to lead humanity into such an ignorant understanding of the act of the change of existence. At the same time, people begin to speak about life on other planets about which, only recently, even notable astronomers merely shrugged their shoulders. We remember how, for such affirmations, Flammarion was threatened with a loss of scientific standing and with being placed in a class of amateurs. But as of now, the better scientific authorities refer far more cautiously to such recognitions of eternal life.

Indeed, such a basic concept may be perceived only in affirmation. Each ignorant doubt imposes on this clear affirmation well-nigh incurable cleavages. It is deplorable to see when intelligent thinkers fear death and, with that, infect the ignorant masses. Why are they not imbued with that luminous knowledge that belonged to the most ancient wisdom and was confirmed by the best thinkers of all ages? In accordance with the best, you, too, arrive at the best.

NEW LIMITS

THE question has been raised: When does life become extinct from the legal point of view? From London, one writes: "When the man is dead. When the remnants of heart action and breathing have ceased, it must be considered that life has abandoned the human body."

The strange episode of the fifty-year-old gardener from Harley, John Pickering, who is at present recovering from an operation during which his heart action and breathing stopped for five minutes, is bringing about an entire revolution in the medical world.

The case of John Pickering has upset the criteria of the medical reference books. All those present at his operation agreed with the statement of the physicians and verified his death.

Any physician, in fact, would certify death at a complete absence of pulse, breathing, and heart reflexes, as was done in Pickering's case.

In *The Principles and Practice of Medical Jurisprudence*, Taylor says:

"If no sign of a heartbeat is revealed in the course of five minutes, a period that is fifty times longer than is required for making an observation, then death must be regarded as unquestionable.

"There is every reason to assume that if the heart absolutely stops beating for a period longer than one minute, death is certain. The same observations also apply to breathing."

The contradictions that arise in the case of Pickering indicate that the manuals of principles must be revised.

They were written before the discovery of adrenalin, that life-giving stimulant that restores people to life from that state that, in the opinion of medical authorities, has been called death.

The consequences are very far-reaching, and it is difficult to foresee them. In the first place in cases of apparent death, relatives will require the most extreme measures of their physicians.

Questions also arise in the social and legal fields: For example, what about the last will and testament in such a case as that of Pickering? Will life insurance premiums continue to be demanded? Will marriage be terminated by such a death?

Indeed, besides these questions that spring up, there can be enumerated many others no less significant. In general, the moment of so-called death becomes an extremely conventional one and, in reality, is subject to revision.

Thus, for example, a case has been cited, when under hypnosis, a death that has been pronounced inevitable has been considerably deferred. Likewise it is explicitly related that a quasi-dead man has uttered words under the influence of suggestion. Most likely, some will say that this is impossible. And yet precisely the authors of the widely used reference books would assume that the above-cited case from London would have had to be recognized as a terminative death.

Let us not recur to all the erroneous or contemptible conclusions that in their time have led humanity into error. One can recall how, at one time, people defamed experiments with steam, with electricity, and with many manifestations that have now become matters of common knowledge, even in primary schools. It can only be regretted that now, the same as in days past, negation obviously predominates and much is made difficult by these destructive snarls and growls.

Many times, people have been advised to keep diaries or written records in which to list known, authentic facts. Just as meticulously as meteorological observations must be carried out generally and persistently, likewise many other facts must be noted down in all their unusualness.

One has occasion to read about the birth of quadruplets and even sextuplets. The fact in itself is extraordinary. But when all such facts are gathered together, observations based on them can be very instructive.

Generally speaking, without any negations, one must steadily go on learning to peer into actuality. When timid people exclaim, "This is impossible!" one should refer to such negative outcries more than cautiously. All those new limits that are seeking recognition in the everyday life of present-day humanity must be realized, primarily in good.

Even when we speak about new limits, can we affirm that they are new and that they are limits? Who assumes the presumption to insist that this very thing has not some time been known? Perhaps that language has been forgotten in which these same facts were enunciated, but no one can assert that in the essence of one's being they were unknown.

It is cause for rejoicing to note how recognition of the past and, together with it, the prognosis of possibilities is made broader and deeper. The authentic written record of the ordinary, inquisitive man can produce immeasurable usefulness by lessening superstition and ignorance, and by corroborating true experimental investigation.

Peking, March 14, 1935

COSMIC SIGNS

NEW Year's Eve. Three friends had gathered for a chat. One of them recalled the story of an eyewitness of the terrible, instantaneous destruction of Quetta. They are sitting on the veranda, having just returned from a theater in a most happy mood, when they suddenly heard some cosmic roaring. They ran into the garden, and there before their very eyes, in one moment, Quetta collapsed. In this instantaneous destruction of an entire city, burying over fifty thousand victims, was, as if revealed, a terrible cosmic Sign.

One of the listeners remembered ancient indications from various Puranas that predicted how entire cities will perish, how the earth will become dry, how whole nations will become extinguished, and others will revert to primitive worship. He mentioned the prophecies about the end of the *Kali Yuga* and continued:

"And don't we see all these signs before our very eyes today! Are not entire cities destroyed by cosmic forces or human hands! Is not the death rate in many countries higher than the birthrate despite all endeavors of governments? Have not some people returned to nature worship? Have not terrible droughts devastated huge areas? In magazines, daily we see pictures of destructions caused by ravaging gales, sandstorms, and tornadoes. Some governments already try to prevent the epidemic droughts. Forests disappear; rivers become barren. Grasses are strangled by sand dunes. Every one of us has witnessed such horrible sights of morbid deserts. Some people do not as yet pay attention to such obvious realities. But the farsighted are already on vigil. Seeing all this, how can anyone say that predictions are not true!"

The third interlocutor quoted from Biblical prophecies and added, "One can imagine how the masses who lived at the time of Amos, Ezekiel, and Isaiah scoffed at these seers. Also, nowadays we know of many discoveries and predictions that are ridiculed and insulted. Ignoramuses never heed anything that is beyond their narrow understanding or threatens their mercenary profits. But true scientists have already proved the transmission of thought, and the world has benefitted by their many beautiful discoveries. And how the ignoramuses laughed at these new possibilities, which they themselves now use daily! Remember how even Edison was declared a charlatan by the academy, how the energy of steam was denounced and railways were derided, and how it was declared by a scientist that the flight of heavier-than-air machines is an 'absolute impossibility,' thus stopping the development of aircraft for almost a century. The list of ignorant mockery and envy is endless. In history we can trace that such insults were not only a thorny crown for the inventors but a testimony of true achievement."

During this conversation another friend had silently joined the company. He exclaimed, "Stop this nonsense about fossilized prophecies. My prediction is the best. Yesterday I announced that there will be a boom on the exchange today. And so it is. Before all of your prophecies will become reality, mine is already in my pocket. What does it matter whether Quetta was destroyed? Perhaps this will contribute to the rise of my cement factory stocks. And cannot the drought, about which you wailed, bring me profit in some way? The more deserts, the better. Humanity will flock into cities. We will feed it with canned goods. My movie shares will rise. You all are not good to me. You may even try to revivify the deserts, and all the urbanists will run away to the country. Here you are drinking some mineral water—where is your whisky and soda, and where are your cigars? It is boring to sit with you miserable people! You don't even understand the advantage of deserts and shelled cities! The more craziness that is manifested in cities, the more it is profitable! Even if your predictions ever prove to be true—when will that be? I am young, but mother earth will last during my time. And remember, it was a king who said, "*Aprés nous le deluge.*" "After me, let there be a flood!" About whom do you worry—about your heirs? But maybe they don't deserve any better. And what does it matter if somewhere somebody worships a tree stump. We will manufacture these stumps for him by the thousands. If humanity is to be poisoned by narcotics, tobacco, and alcohol, we will make money on patented medicines. You hopeless people! There stands a gramophone, but I dare not use it. All your Bachs and Beethovens make me sick! You have no jazz, foxtrot, carioca—and yet you imagine you are up to date! To sit with you is simply to waste an evening!"

And he slammed the door from the outside. He was especially annoyed that the three not only did not lose their temper but, shrugging their shoulders, even looked at him as upon a certain zoological specimen.

The physical drought is menacing, but the spiritual emptiness is far greater. Besides caring for irrigation of the soil, let there also be remembered the need for the uplifting of the human spirit. Without such spiritual fertilization, all attempts at reforestation, grass sowing, and other good efforts will be in vain. All this brings results only when people actually realize why they live and when they will again pronounce the sacred word of Love. In Love, the quality of labor will improve.

In love, deserts will again flourish.

CALLS FROM AFAR

MANY people have known Lady Dean Paul, a talented composer and a very cordial and cultured person, but not many have known that all of her of life, she has been in closest contact with the world beyond. Through some turn of destiny, by means of some particular qualities, she has constantly viewed the Subtle World, invisible to others.

I will never forget how, when returning from the opening of my exhibition at Brighton, in the railway coach Lady Paul had a heated argument with P.N.M. P.N., an incorrigible materialist, who tried in every way to prove to her that all her visions were nothing else but hallucinations evoked by herself. To this, Lady Paul, smiling sadly, retorted that she had no wish whatever to see them, that they were things that she could in nowise imagine, but that to her regret, she continued to see many circumstances of events past in the subtlest reality.

Among her narratives we recall, for example, a characteristic episode in a newly rented villa. Lady Paul—knowing that especially in long-occupied places, there are greater possibilities for all sorts of materializations—always tried to select new residences, preferably just built and where no one had yet lived. And so it was in this case. The villa had just been constructed and, according to the owner, had never been occupied. The first night D.P. suddenly felt that next to her in bed lay a dead body. Then she saw that from the room she was occupying, there was being carried out a coffin, which passed with difficulty through the doors and left a deep scratch on them. Upon arising the next morning, after such an unpleasant night, D.P. examined the door first thing and, to her horror, found precisely that deeply incised scratch, the cause of which she had so realistically viewed in the night.

The owner was summoned, and he admitted that a woman had actually died in this room after living there only two days in all.

In another case, also when removing to a new lodging, D.P. was expecting a new servant who had been recommended to her. She awakened very early, and to her surprise she saw a neatly dressed, affable old woman moving through the apartment. Naturally, D.P. assumed that this was the new servant, and she merely wondered how she could have entered her bedroom so early. At this point the old woman went to the mantelpiece upon which were placed some old portraits and began to gaze at them intently. Then to D.P.'s amazement she actually leaped up, and gradually rising to the ceiling, she disappeared. Only then did it occur to D.P. that this was not the servant at all.

Another time, being awakened at night as if by a push, D.P. saw, seated near her on the bed, a man, as she said, with a most unpleasant marauder's face. The visitor gazed fixedly at her for some time and then gradually vanished.

There were a great number of such manifestations, both by night and by day; sometimes they had the direct effect of driving D.P. into despair. In all sincerity, she exclaimed, "Certainly I have no wish to see them! And why do all my other friends see nothing of the sort, and yet I have to encounter all these uninvited visitors?"

Moreover, it happened that her unbidden guests would move objects all about, and people calling upon her would see the movement of an object with the cause of it remaining invisible.

Especially have many similar accounts been disclosed in connection with the recent war. Thus, for example, the son of V. J. Karentsov, who was killed on the British front, appeared to his mother and communicated the place and circumstance of his death. The general staff denied the possibility of this, giving out the information that at the indicated place, there was an impassable swamp. But after several months, a friend of the deceased arrived and established the facts of the case. It appeared that in order to shorten the lines of communication, a brushwood trail had been laid through this marsh.

Likewise, one of our American friends related how at Verdun, in going to change the garrison, they encountered on the way the platoon that was to have been replaced. The whole command not only saw this platoon in detail but unsuccessfully tried to hail it. Proceeding to the post, they noticed a sentry standing silent, and when they touched him, they found him to be a corpse. The fact was later substantiated that the entire platoon had been annihilated by an unexpected raid by the Germans.

Entire books could be written about all such individual and mass manifestations. One hears about the same things in the Orient—in China, Mongolia, Afghanistan—where various traditions are connected with definite places. Concerning objects moving about without any visible cause, one can often hear about such from entirely trustworthy people.

We have before us some photographs of Mrs. F. with extraordinarily realistic images of the subtle world. Spirit photographs have been taken without any special wish for it. Rev. Solntsev, in Serdobol, has related several unusually clear visions that have appeared to him. Thus, for example, a gravely ill midshipman promised to appear to him and bring him news of his death. Several months passed. One evening, being occupied at his worktable, Solntsev heard behind him the sound of a door opening. Turning around, he saw his young friend in a lieutenant's uniform, at which he was surprised. His friend saluted him and then, as it were, went out through the door. Later on, Solntsev realized that actually at this time, his friend had departed this life, and that his promotion to lieutenant had come after his death and, therefore, he had been buried in an officer's uniform.

A similar instance was related by H.I.'s grandmother, when, according to an agreement with her, a student who was dying of tuberculosis appeared to her, and she even conversed with him. Others in the room at the time heard this conversation. Rev. George Spassky, a man who died in Paris last year, likewise experienced, more than once, the most extraordinary manifestations.

Especially valuable are the accounts of perfectly balanced people, who can calmly and consciously appraise the circumstances beheld by them. Indeed, it is possible to hear a great number of authentic narratives, but such communications will, of course, be of a completely different order. As in everything else, what is needed are simplicity, directness, and preciseness; in a word, everything that is included in the concept "honesty." It is especially valuable when those who have viewed something do not try first off to attribute this to some extraordinary peculiarities of their own, but simply determine and establish the fact in all its surrounding circumstances. If a crude photographic film can take impressions of subtle forms, so much the more, can the human consciousness, under known conditions, perceive them.

PAST AND FUTURE

WE were in Switzerland in 1906. A clairvoyant arrived at the hotel where we were staying, and there were many who wished to consult her.

"Would you like her to read from a book that has not been opened?" they asked us. E.I. had just received a book from Paris by parcel post and without opening the parcel, she quoted a page and a line; and the woman at once, with her eyes shut, read the sentence, which became evident to all so as soon as the book was opened.

"Where will we be next year?" we then enquired.

She then described our journey on a small steamboat, adding that the people around us were speaking some language that was not French, German, or Italian, and which she could not understand.

The next year we left quite unexpectedly for Finland.

After this she correctly described the fate of my pictures at the Greenwald exhibition. She also described the rivers of blood, which signified the Great War and revolution and the death of the Emperor, as well as the beginning of our institutions in America. She also saw an immense quantity of sheets of paper covered with writing, and here she seems to have foreseen the immense correspondence we were destined to have with all of our institutions in different countries.

We also consulted another clairvoyant in Switzerland. Those present thought of certain tasks, and taking each of them by the hand, she immediately executed what they had imagined. This she did for all she casually encountered—counting the money in pocketbooks, reading names on handkerchiefs and pronouncing them with a French accent so that "Boris" became "Bori." She predicted the delivery of certain letters and was able to describe people who were in the thoughts of those present.

We remember many cases of this sort in Europe, Russia, and in the East, yet people attach little importance to such phenomena, failing to see their significance, and so treat them as something merely incidental.

Afterward, when events have shown how well-founded such premonitions were, we regret that we did not give them more attention and commit them to writing.

Had this been done we should have had written proof of the value of the clairvoyant's art. Many people prefer to think of a clairvoyant as a charlatan or adventurer, in the business sense.

We also recollect the case of an old Hindu in Agra, who spread out a collection of human and animal figures on a many colored carpet. He then began to play a very beautiful melody on a reed instrument, and these figures of warriors, rajahs, *bayaderès*, tradesmen, elephants, and tigers began to move about and execute the most intricate dances.

The effect was very fantastic, but one of the onlookers wishing to have an explanation exclaimed, "I know how it is done now—under each figure runs a connecting thread." The old man was offended and, gathering up his figures, went off in silence. It was evident, of course, that the figures could only move on wires that were invisible against the mottled carpet; in fact, no one doubted it. But the enchantment was gone. It was a pity, because all such subtle energies require a subtle atmosphere if they are to live in natural harmony and not weigh on those through whom they are manifested.

Those who take part in such experiments are expected to give close attention and not disturb the atmosphere with exclamations. Some people, as if by autosuggestion, feel the need to cough, sneeze, or laugh, and do not realize that their departure can cause harm. They wonder what

sort of energies these can be that fear the sound of cough-
ing or disturbance, and in this way, they show their complete ignorance of the subtle realms.

Materially minded people often deplore the fact that
nothing exceptional ever happens to them, and then conclude that this is the same with everyone, and they usually
end a discussion on this subject with "Well, let's have a
drink."

Being grossly egotistical they will not admit that others
can experience what they themselves are unable to detect.
They conclude that because they are ignorant, everybody
else must be ignorant; and so, with much creaking and
squeaking, the gates are barred with the lock of ignorance.

And so, the extraordinary that occurs in everyday life
is obliterated by gluttony, ignorance, and superstition. If
we paid more attention to the past, for which we are all
responsible, then we should have more control over its
resultant, which is the future.

A rational and rapid advance would ensue, the slime of
stagnation would be removed, and a movement toward a
new and more beautiful condition of consciousness would
set in.

THE CHALICE

THE chalice is a well-known symbol and one which is to be found among all peoples. From sacred, tribal, and martial symbols to the image that represents the nervous centers, these figures have always attracted great attention.

Many researches have been made into the subject, and the image of a flaming chalice can be found on the most ancient monuments.

On many a stone sculpture of Central Asia, the guardians of the desert can be seen clasping to their hearts the chalice of the living fire.

The fire and the chalice are often combined; and when we remember that the ancients knew of the chalice as a nerve center and a depository of all perceptions, then such comparisons take on a deep meaning.

The chalice has never been overlooked as a center, although it may have had another name in ancient times.

The most primitive and inexperienced folk seemed to have been aware of this important center, for they mention a sort of formation in the chest. Some of them attributed this to a formation in the stomach or the heart, but more advanced races seemed to have been aware that such nervous tension is not caused in this way. Such phenomena often coincide with important psychic reconstruction. This is often the case with those who are able to make considerable psychological progress but voluntarily or involuntarily neglect to do so.

Many people will describe this state as one of anguish or grief, one which is often accompanied with pangs.

It is true that such tension often resembles anguish,

and there are many who consider that if their hearts ache, it is because of something they cannot perceive. This shows how careful we should be to note all signs transmitted by our organism.

Without superstition, prejudice, or ignorant fear, we ought to discover how we can best employ our efforts and take advantage of every circumstance.

Plenty of occasions are offered to us to acquire new faculties of apprehension. There are a number of signs, such as flashing appearances, aromas, and sounds, but coarseness generally prevents most people from taking advantage of these signs. We say "coarseness" because all such perception depends upon a refinement that has been previously or recently acquired. It is only coarseness that prevents us from recognizing these beautiful signs and the responsibility that goes along with them.

People often refer to distant possibilities when they are near to certain sources; they begin to dream of distant adventures and avoid all those possibilities that are near at hand.

But the heart and the chalice will grievously remind us of what is necessary. Such warnings may, by their very intensity, promote illness; but instead of listening to them, man tries to numb their action.

Someday these people will begin to realize that instead of petty everyday matters, they could contact what is great and irreplaceable.

If they try to justify themselves on the score of age or their intention to do better in the future, nevertheless, we should remember that opportunities never repeat themselves.

Future intentions can create all sorts of possibilities, but this will be another matter, and former tasks will remain unfulfilled.

Meanwhile, every defection, especially if it is of a spiritual order, will soon make itself felt since all such unfulfilled tasks are deposited in the chalice.

If we glance back through history, we will see that lost

spiritual possibilities are like so many holes in the road. Circumstances cannot be estimated according to popular standards because the smallest seed will outweigh lumps of gold.

In the end, people will have to return to the spiritual path. They cannot expect to go on indefinitely, hovering over flowers like so many butterflies sporting around the flower beds of life; but consciously or unconsciously, they will have to turn their attention to the foundations. And when this occurs, the heart will beat freely, no longer oppressed by what was perverted or unfulfilled.

Terror and degeneracy rise up through the substance of the chalice with results that are now beginning to make people wonder.

It is not, however, too late to repair matters, although the result when attained will not be so closely connected with Higher Thought.

It is always possible, however, to turn in the right direction.

The center of the chalice, which is the seat of memory, preserves all treasures and misfortunes.

In a life of storm and turbulence, these spiritual sediments are stirred up. Many wounds are, of course, healed, but the scars remain, within or without, and the chalice or heart will make itself felt. People should try to direct thought along the right channels so as not to lose what is lying at the threshold.

The heart and the chalice are like sentinels, which stand on guard to warn us that we should not put off until tomorrow what we can do today, nor should we darken our perceptions with petty considerations.

We should not spoil another's holiday, becloud a luminous perception, or allow dark thoughts to intrude themselves on solemn grandeur, which would be like a hammer falling on the strings in the midst of a fine symphony.

Nor should we consider a fine symphony as something that falls from heaven, while we ourselves are obliged to crawl here through a life of filth and refuse.

"As in heaven, so on earth," and here, in the midst of life resound the highest canticles. Let us not darken these torches; let us not extinguish the luminous flame in the chalice.

It is not by chance that the highest achievements of mankind together with our daily tasks are connected with the chalice.

Symbols live on from the most remote epochs, although people often play with such symbols out of sheer ignorance, repeating them in a lighthearted way, without caring whether their reference is justified or not.

Provided it is joyfully realized, such a responsible attitude has nothing narrow about it. Every failure of the spirit is deposited in the chalice, but spiritual joy shines out with the beauty of the diamond.

It is often said that we live in an epoch when all joy is being driven out of life, whereas the life of primitive people is still joyful.

Beautiful, however, remains the joy of the spirit, which cannot be broken even by the terrors of death. Spirit and Fire! The flame above the chalice!

The more luminous it is, the more beautiful are the treasures it preserves.

Even amid the deserts stand the guardians of the flaming chalice.

TARNHELMS

EVERYONE will remember the tarnhelm of Siegfried, which made him invisible, and this helmet of invisibility was always considered as one of the most precious treasures of the hero.

Many tarnhelms may be found in ancient folklore, so also nowadays.

Someone was puzzled as to why in a volume of letters, a certain thinker continuously reverted to one and the same subject. The reader did not realize that the letters were written at different dates and were addressed to different people in various parts of the world. For this reader, the invisible correspondents molded into one person. For him, they remained forever invisible. And the reader apparently imagined that the letters had only him personally in view, not taking into consideration any outside circumstances. Invisible friends, invisible listeners, invisible coworkers—they are all as if they belong to the domain of tarnhelms in fairy tales.

Even till recently, invisibility was either denied altogether, or it was considered charlatanism, or something nebulous, just as people considered telepathy. It is most difficult for the average man in the street to become accustomed to the fact that he is surrounded by anything invisible. When stories about Angel-Guardians were told, this also was left to old *ayahs*. Yet since antiquity, iron birds were foreseen, as well as words from space, audible across seas, and fiery iron serpents were predicted.

In the same manner, as in many folklore, there lived and lives the persistent idea of tarnhelms. In the best fairy tales and epical legends, the idea of invisibleness was continuously expressed in the most picturesque symbols. And in the lowest reality, during wars, was practiced a smoke screen for invisibility. That was the coarsest solution of all legends and fairy tales.

And now the newspapers report, without any sensational headlines, the following:

"Rays that make one invisible": A young Hungarian scientist has apparently succeeded in bringing to reality the fairy tale of the tarnhelm. The demonstration of such rays took place on a square in front of a statue. As soon as the apparatus was switched on, the statue suddenly disappeared from sight, and one could only prove that it was still there by touching it. After a few minutes, the statue again became visible, as if emerging from a fog."

Thus the predictions or recollections of folklore have again entered into life. In the same manner, iron birds cross the skies, iron serpents carry people, and the word thunders out from space, and the tarnhelm has again materialized. One can realize how everyday life will be transformed by these recent discoveries.

There is a story of a person who made fun of his lady acquaintance. Having moved to a new house, he saw from his window in an opposite flat, how his friend was just getting up from bed. In the same room was a telephone. The joker rang her up and during the conversation mentioned the success of television. His friend expressed doubt. But when he began describing her night gown and various other details, the lady, in horror, dropped the receiver.

A similar joke recently appeared in the papers, about certain residents of London, who having heard about the success of television, became seriously worried about the inviolability of their homes. The directors of the television company had to explain that no such danger existed. In other words, at the moment there is no such danger, but once having entered the field of invisibleness, one may expect many new developments. It is important to establish the principle.

Let us compare the primitive daguerreotype with the splendid results of modern photography. In some countries, up to now, people do not know about the application of photostats instead of the easily forged copies of documents. But in the courts of other countries, photostats are already accepted as documents. By the way, I cannot help remembering a curious episode of how a lady, pretending to be cultured, refused to permit the making of a photostat of a rare book from her library for fear that this procedure might destroy the book. Let us also remember the primitive railway, a prototype of which is exhibited at Grand Central in New York. It has nothing at all in common with modern railways. Thus, if the principle of invisibleness is discovered, then also from it may result the most tremendous surprises.

One cannot bar such mechanical achievements, for by one way or another, they will penetrate into life. Hence, one should study by what other natural means real equilibrium may be established. And let us again remember the blissful properties of the human spirit. If a dog senses non-physical things, ergo, how many times more can a vigilant human spirit conceive all these subtle matters? And how naturally can such knowledge be attained! At first, it will be an unconscious sense; then it will develop into straight-knowledge, which will lead to a fully conscious realization. At this stage, all mechanical tarnhelms will be conceived. And the whole of daily life will be transformed in a better, spiritual direction.

When one reads of the achievements of Rishis and other holy hermits, with what subtle fiery knowledge are they imbued! They generously gave out in their enlightened ordainments the fundamental principles of life. Ages pass, the methods of expression are changed, but the truth remains immutable. The great Rishis and hermits knew unfailingly what the heart represents and how to evoke it into blissful action.

What a beautiful word is Bliss!

In the face of these highly natural, beautiful ways, all

mechanical rays become poor and limited. Yet for those who do not want to grasp the higher, even these lesser paths will have already formed the elementary trail. In different languages, in varying expressions of thought, people yet strive for the basic signs of the epoch. This means that all who have heard of this resounding thought are obliged to create from it real harmony. It is instructive to witness how very important mental processes take place not only amid one nation, not only in one country, but often in the most unexpected combinations.

Thoughts strive along some universal outlines. There where, due to ignorance and mediocrity, people deny the higher spiritual paths, there still remain some lesser possibilities—the mechanical ways. And these ways, neverthe-less, lead in the direction of achievement. But the spiritual gates remain above all. The entire existence reminds us of these unavoidable paths. Even the most unusual diseases also remind us of new conditions of life. Many so-called heart and nervous diseases, unusual inflammations, cancer epidemics, poisonings by gasoline and narcotics, and other carelessly evoked energies—all this knocks upon the human consciousness, as Fate in Beethoven's Symphony No. 5.

We read:

"A hundred years ago, in June of 1835, Baron de Morog, a member of the Supreme Agricultural Council, read in the French Academy a report on unemployment and social sufferings that threatened France and the whole world owing to the introduction into industry of an influx of new machineries. The Paris papers have now extracted from the archives of the Academy this prophetical report and printed the following excerpts, which are truly significant:

"'Every machine!'—de Morog wrote in his paper—'re-places human labor and, therefore, every new mechanical invention makes in industry superfluous the work of a certain number of people. Taking into consideration that workmen are freely accustomed to earning their means of existence, and that they, in most cases, have no savings, it is easy to imagine the irritation that will gradually be caused amid the working masses through the mechanization of industry.'

"The member of the Academy foresaw that 'despite the improvement of technical output, the material conditions of laborers would become worse,' from which would arise 'moral, social, and political danger.' The report of de Morog made such a great impression upon the Academy that it sent to the King, in 1835, a special memorandum about the necessity to regulate the mechanization of production. This memorandum, however, received no further attention."

Thus, by other ways, people arrived at the consideration of regulating mechanical achievement. This is not a wailing against machines, nor an ignorant grumbling against improvements, but a call for proper co-measurement. During the centuries, so many tarnhelms have become visible, but on the other hand, many realized visions of the past have now been lost.

Whatever may be the calculations, without spiritual equilibrium no real progress can be achieved. A rough handling of invisible energies may lead to innumerable repercussions. How much true knowledge is needed in order that all the millions of unemployed may find a useful and joyful labor—as Life preordained.

If tarnhelms could conceal something, then the Spirit can reveal Truth in its full splendor.

PARAPSYCHOLOGY

NEW upward flights of thought bring to life new words. Not so long ago the concept of psychology won for itself the right of acceptance—we need not repeat the significance of this Greek word, for it is sufficiently well known to everyone. Psychology has gradually conquered new fields and penetrated into the depths of the human consciousness. It has been linked with neurology and dealt with in the "Institutes of the Brain"; it has touched upon the domain of the heart and concentrated upon the study of energy and thought.

Long ago, Plato asserted that Ideas rule the world, but only comparatively recently has a science of thought been constituted. It is quite natural that this broadest of provinces should require a new and refined designation. Thus there has resulted the significant superstructure upon the concept of psychology; there was born parapsychology. Radio waves, sensitive photographic films, and many new paths of science have become allied with the fields of parapsychology, and not by chance has man's attention been drawn to this higher domain, which must transform many of the basic features of life.

In the dark period of the Middle Ages, any investigations into the region of parapsychology would surely have been terminated by the inquisition with torture and the stake. And even now our contemporary "inquisitors" are not above accusing learned investigators of sorcery or insanity. We recall how our friend, the late Professor Bechterev, was not only subjected to official persecutions for his research into the study of thought, but in the devious turns of public opinion, there were more than once heard whispers about a nervous malady of the scholar himself. We likewise know that for their research in the domain of thought, serious scientists have been visited with all sorts of official annoyance, and sometimes have even been deprived of university appointments. This has happened both in Europe and in America. But evolution flows on over any human obstructions and calumnies. Evolution is unyieldingly resistant to dark ignorance, and life itself displays the brilliant advancement of that which even in the recent past would have aroused the scoffing of the ignorant. Surely we cannot forget that even in our own time one scientific Academy pronounced Edison's phonograph the trick of a charlatan. Not so long ago a certain physician asserted that since microorganisms required such great magnification for study of them, they could have absolutely no significance or application in medical practice! You may see statements of this kind being circulated right now by the printed word. But since stagnation has an ossifying effect, all the live portions of humanity will be irresistibly impelled to true broad cognition.

We know that in America alone some forty scholars are occupied with the study of thought energy. Before us lie copies of the journal *Parapsychology*, published under the editorship of Professor Rhine (Duke University, South Carolina) and his books *Extra-Sensory Perception* and *New Frontiers of the Mind*. Professors Rhine and McDougall have worked for many years upon thought transmission at a distance. We have already had occasion to make note of their brilliant results in this field. Now Professor Rhine has taken into collaboration an entire large group of intelligent students and together with them has carried out a series of most instructive experiments.

At first the transmission of thoughts was effected at the shortest intervals and in the simplest formulas; after this the experiments passed on to involve greater distances and were made complicated in the thought content. In the course of several years, it became established that thought can undoubtedly be transmitted at a distance, and that for this, people do not at all have to become some sort of devotees of the supernatural, but they can operate within the limits of the mind and the will. It is unquestionable that the domain of thought, the field of disclosure of the subtlest primary energy, has been ordained for the immediately forthcoming days of humanity. Thus, precisely science, call it material science or positive or as you please, but precisely scientific cognition will reveal to mankind those domains to which the most ancient symbols have alluded.

If world thought be directed along a definite path, a great number of unexpected auxiliaries can be discerned by the observant mind of the investigator. People have appeared, sometimes most ordinary ones, who can detect radio waves without a receiver or can see through dense objects, thus confirming the fact that the senses can act outside the limits of physical conditions.

There is a young girl in Latvia who reads thoughts, doing this under the surveillance of physicians and scholars. Medical supervision excludes any sort of charlatanism or self-interested exploitation. In the last analysis, such phenomenon ceases to be supernatural since through training, the students of the University in South Carolina can attain very significant results by perfectly natural means.

Likewise, extremely remarkable are experiments with a recently devised apparatus that records the most subtle pulsations of the heart, which have hitherto been undetected. Recently Dr. Anita Muhl described to us the most interesting experiments performed by her. These showed that lofty thought heightened tension enormously and refined the vibrations; whereas ordinary thought, not to mention that of a low order, immediately lowered the vibrations. Moreover, it was noticed that the unified thought of a group of people constituting a chain augmented tension extraordinarily. Doctor Muhl brought back observations made during her recent visit to Iceland and Denmark, and now India, where she is sojourning, will undoubtedly provide her with new impulses.

Of course, any such considerations, even though confirmed by mechanical apparatus, will continue to remain *terra incognita* for the majority of people. But fortunately evolution has never been brought about by the majority but has been realized by an unselfish minority who are ready to subject themselves to the thrusts of the ignorant. But the right judgment of history is inevitable. The names of ignorant opponents of knowledge become symbols of infamous retrogression. The name of Herostratus, who destroyed works of art, has remained in schoolbooks, but not at all in connection with the matters that this madman had in mind. The names of the ignoramuses who voted for the expulsion of the great Aristides from Athens have recently been discovered in the course of excavations upon the Acropolis and added to the dark roster of the ignorant and the deniers. Surely we cannot forget the man who could detect radio waves without apparatus and who, in our civilized days, was immured in an insane asylum because physicians of a certain type could not admit the existence of this faculty. In general many human capacities confound people of a sluggish, retrogressive nature, and they will have to pass through many shameful hours, when all the things which they have denied shall occupy a place in the precise sciences.

Even at present, certain obscurantists regard the transmission of thought at a distance as verging on witchcraft. We can cite examples when this field, already established by scores of scientists, provokes gross ridicule and mocking cries about the reception of news out "of the blue sky." Without speaking of the examples recorded in the literature of all ages and peoples, it is permissible to remind the ignorant that the radio waves, which have already become a part of their everyday life, are received precisely out of the blue sky. It is sad to reflect that people give no thought to many obvious manifestations and to the cosmic fundamentals or laws that lie behind them. Sometimes the ignorant are not averse to repeating parrot-like certain truisms without understanding their significance. Thus, those who jeer at news from the blue sky do not suspect that they are speaking about what has already been established by scientific investigations and recorded by machines.

So much has been said and written about the subtlest energies, which are so gradually being apprehended by humanity! The absurd prohibitions created by the inertia of stagnant deniers are beginning to fall away. Only yesterday we read about the establishment of a special governmental committee for the investigation of Hindu popular medicine. The ordinances of the Ayurveda, so recently ridiculed, are coming to life again under the hand of enlightened scholars. In Moscow has been founded an Institute for the Study of Tibetan Medicine; western scientists have found to be of vast significance the indications given in ancient Chinese annals, which are entirely conformable to the latest European scientific discoveries. And the ancient medicine man who brewed a potion from toads has found his justification in contemporary science, which has revealed the large quantity of adrenalin in these amphibians; moreover, there has been found in these creatures a new substance, buffonin, which is closely akin to digitalis. One might cite a multitude of similar examples among latest discoveries. The ass hide of Chinese medicine has also been justified in the matter of vitamin content by the latest researches of Doctor Reed.

Another scientist, Doctor Reele, has determined under the most ancient symbols the existence of indications, the significance of which has now been understood and thus advanced by science. In such manner, in different branches of science, the ancient elements of knowledge are making their appearance under a new and entirely modern aspect. If these parallels be collected, there results a voluminous treatise. But the crowning dome of all these quests will be that fundamental domain which now goes under the name of parapsychology because in its basis lies everywhere that same great primary or psychic energy. The visionary dream of thought has already been formulated in the science of thought. Human thought that anticipates all discoveries is borne into space and reaches the human consciousness precisely "out of the blue sky." The brain activity of man is comparable to electrical phenomena; recently the biologist G. Lakhovsky asserted that all ethical teachings have a definitely biological foundation. Thus in its turn Lakhovsky's work confirms the experiments of Doctor Muhl with electrical apparatus that records graphically the significance of qualities of thought. Even the myth about the cap of invisibility receives scientific confirmation in the discovery of rays that make objects invisible. Thus there arises everywhere new and boundless knowledge replacing recent negations and mockery. To all deniers can only be given the advice: "Know more, and stop not your ears with the wadding of criminal ignorance." In remote antiquity it was said that ignorance is the forefather of all crimes and offenses, of all miseries and calamities.

Call it parapsychology or science of thought, be it revealed as psychic or primary energy, it is alone clear that evolution imperatively directs mankind to the discovery of the subtlest energies. Unprejudiced science is striving in quests for new energies in space, that infinite source of all forces and all cognition. Our age is the epoch of a world outlook based on Energetics.